India-Pakistan Peace Process and J&K

India-Pakistan Peace Process and J&K

by

Dr. Sudhir S. Bloeria

Foreword by

Shri C D Sahay

Former Secretary (R)

Vij Books India Pvt Ltd
New Delhi (India)

India–Pakistan Peace Process and J&K

First Published in India in 2018

Published by

Vij Books India Pvt Ltd
(Publishers, Distributors & Importers)
2/19, Ansari Road
Delhi – 110 002
Phones: 91-11-43596460, 91-11-47340674
Fax: 91-11-47340674
e-mail: vijbooks@rediffmail.com
web : www.vijbooks.com

ISBN: 978-93-86457-97-4 (Hardback)

ISBN: 978-93-86457-98-1 (ebook)

Dedicated to all those, across the divide,

who are genuinely interested in the

India-Pakistan Peace Process.

Contents

Foreword

Being asked to write the foreword of any book is always a matter of great honour, more so when the book is authored by a very dear friend of decades; an acknowledged expert on J&K affairs and when the subject covered is India-Pakistan relations. But it is also a great challenge since the theme relates to the most complex aspect of India-Pakistan relationship - 'Peace Process and J&K'.

Yet, I decided to take up the challenge, not because I claim the required expertise on, or familiarity with, the entire gamut of issues involved. I did it simply because I didn't have the option to say no to Shri Bloeria; with whom my relationship goes back to 1993-95 when I was posted to J&K as Commissioner, Special Bureau, Govt. of India. I met him first time when he was Principal Secretary to the governor Gen. K.V. Krishna Rao. That marked the beginning of a relationship that has over the years, grown only stronger in content and depth.

Those were the worst days of militancy in J&K. When, why and how it started and progressed have been recorded in detail and analyzed in depth by the author, tracing the developments right since 1931 with the formation of the Moslem Conference headed by Sheikh Sahib, the birth of National Conference in 1938, developments during the especially turbulent years of Partition, the military action of 1948-49 etc. Attention has been given to the internal political manipulations and instability, absence of focused approach to developmental activities and failure to effectively deal with initial symptoms of militancy as these first surfaced. Having had the benefit of observing these issues through different phases, from a ring side seat, the narratives in this book should be taken as authentic; compulsory reading for anyone looking for in-depth and unbiased account of the extreme complexities surrounding the Kashmir story.

Since the topic of discussions is India-Pakistan Peace Process, considerable space and attention has also been devoted to the developments taking place in parallel, on the other side of the border. A reading of these, clearly explains the reasons for absence of formal, structured and substantive dialogue between the two countries for many years, till PM Vajpayee decided to undertake the famous 'Bus Yatra' to Lahore on February 22, 1999 and the signing of the Lahore Declaration with PM Nawaz Sharif. The great euphoria was however, short-lived as the Pak Army Chief Gen. Musharraf, in an act of utter 'betrayal' launched the Kargil War (May-July, 1999).

One would have thought that this act of madness would have conclusively derailed the peace process, particularly as the IC-814 hijacking quickly followed in December 1999. It was an ISI backed operation to secure the release of one of their favourite militant leaders, Masood Azhar of Harkat ul Ansar (subsequently renamed as Jaish e Muhammad after Azhar's release).

But Vajpayee was fully committed to the peace process, endorsing the short-lived Hizbul Mujahideen ceasefire in July 2000, subsequent Non-Initiation of Combat Operations (NICO) also known as the Ramzan Ceasefire (Nov. 2000) and extending an invitation to Gen. Musharraf for the Agra Summit that eventually took place in mid-July 2001. The author has incisively summarized the Summit by quoting the two leaders on page 195-196 in the book. But more significantly, all these initiatives failed as "Musharraf the commando could not fathom Vajpayee the Chanakya" (page 194).

The next set of initiatives had to pend for a while on account of successive acts of terror in all of which Pakistan's involvement was writ large. Notably, it began with the 9/11 attack on the World Trade Centre in New York, (Sept 2001), on J&K Assembly in Srinagar (Oct. 1, 2001), attack on Indian Parliament (Dec. 2001) and at Kaluchak (May 2002). With these, Kashmir watchers perhaps justifiably thought the proverbial 'last nail in the coffin' of the peace process had been driven in.

But once again the Chanakya in Vajpayee surprised everyone by 'extending a hand of friendship towards Pakistan,' at a public rally in Srinagar on April 18, 2003. Later, in an 'emotionally charged' speech in the parliament, he said, "…this would be my third and final effort at improving relations with Pakistan…Now, whatever happens, will be decisive." (Page 217).

Govt. of India followed up these with a slew of Confidence Building Measures (CBMs) announced on October 22, 2003 and Pakistan offered Eid Ceasefire in November. The author acknowledges (page 224) that "This was probably the most successful cessation of hostilities between the two countries". (I can personally claim some credit for these and other related developments that followed-CDS). In December that year Musharraf publicly announced that "Pakistan was conditionally prepared to give up its traditional stand of implementing UN Resolutions…" (Page 225). And then came the Vajpayee-Musharraf meeting in Islamabad and the famous joint statement of January 6, 2004 stating that Pakistan will not allow any territory under its control to be used to support terrorism in any manner and that India will resume dialogue "that will lead to peaceful settlement of all bilateral issues, including Jammu and Kashmir, to the satisfaction of both sides." (Page 227).

These developments marked the resumption of the bilateral 'Composite Dialogue' with Pakistan on the one hand and with the APHC leaders on the internal front. But, as usual there had to be a setback and that came in with the NDA government losing the Parliamentary election in 2004. However, contrary to the general perception, the peace process continued under the UPA government of Dr. Manmohan Singh (MMS). The new prime minister, in his characteristics quiet manner, started giving greater thrust to the CBMs initiated by the previous government through a number of new initiatives while strengthening some of the existing ones. Recounting these in Chapter VII, the author highlights the holding of FS level meeting in June 2004 followed by those between the two Foreign Ministers in September and MMS and Musharraf in New York on the sidelines of the UNGA session. For easy recall, the first six month's scorecard of the UPA has been summed up on page 241-2 and it looks pretty impressive. Of particular note were initiatives on the internal front, including a commitment to unconditional dialogue with anyone and everyone who abjures violence. In September 2005, the top APHC leaders met PM and in January 2006 there was interaction with non-APHC leads too. And then came the most notable one; the first Round Table Conference in New Delhi (Feb. 2006) followed by the second RTC (in Srinagar (May. 2006) and the third one in April 2007. Regrettably, under obvious advice from their mentors across, APHC leaders missed out on a great opportunity to contribute to the internal political process on the flimsy ground of inclusion of Pakistan in the deliberations.

That too was happening with the two FMs meeting in Islamabad in Feb. 2005 and again in Oct. 2005; Musharraf's visit to New Delhi in April 2005; the Havana meeting in Sept. 2006 on the sidelines of the NAM Summit and FS level meeting in New Delhi in Nov. 2006. That all these were taking place despite continuing terror strikes by the militants': 14 of these are listed on page 250/1, stands testimony to India's extreme patience and commitment to the process of engagement. But obviously, this could not go on endlessly. The peace process that had peaked in 2005, started losing shine and pace by 2007 largely due to internal problems faced by Musharraf. Speaking in the National Assembly, Pak FM Qureshi admitted that the two countries had held 83 meetings at various levels to attempt to resolve the Kashmir issue, 37 of these at the level of Heads of Govt/ State, 19 meetings between FMs and 27 involving FSs. And he asked, "If all these meetings at various levels for all these years have not been able to break the logjam, what is the guarantee that the parlays in future will be able to produce any result?" (p 264).

That very question is currently reverberating even today, louder in India than in Pakistan. The dialogue process got totally derailed following the Mumbai carnage (Nov. 2008). The NDA government under PM Modi tried to give a boost through various initiatives in partnership with PM Nawaz Sharif till the Deep State stuck again through Pathankot and Uri and the mounting level of militant activities in the Valley.

Today, we are once again facing serious uncertainties in the State in terms of understanding and countering a new phase of Pak sponsored terror in the Valley. One of the key elements in all the discussions relating to the developments in the Valley, has always centered on the question of India-Pakistan dialogue. Some elements in the local political establishments and most strategic and security experts conveniently advocate resumption of bilateral dialogue with Pakistan as the easy, indeed only way to break the current logjam. Is that really so? Have these dialogues, formally structured or otherwise, not happened in the past and with what results? Has Pakistan been really serious about resolution of outstanding issues with India through such dialogue?

Answers to these questions can be found in Shri Bloeria's present book, 'India-Pakistan Peace Process and J&K'. In my view, this book is a timely exercise to help us better understand all the arguments for and against the proposition. To make the task easier for the readers, the book's chapterisation has been beautifully sequenced, starting with an incisive narration of the background of the conflict leading to the Partition, the well planned attack by the 'Raiders' and the Pak military, India's military response, the British designs, J&K's accession and the UN intervention at India's initiative. The most significant conclusions of the author are succinctly summed up on page 33 wherein it is stated, "Pakistan learnt some very significant lessons for their first confrontation with India namely; (a) Belligerence pays, (b) A mix of covert and open aggression is cost-effective and gainful, (c) High pitched propaganda, manipulation of UN systems and influential friends is a very potent combination and (d) India would react to aggressive actions defensively and localize areas of conflict". Are these lessons still not valid and being pursued by Pakistan?

But then the counter questions are equally significant and relevant. Do we let the situation continue to drift, should we allow Pakistan "a free run with its new found weapons and instruments of Jihad and terrorism" (p 378), can India do something differently within Kashmir, should that wait till the current kinetic approach succeeds in restoring peace and order in the state, can these be done before India goes into election mode for 2019 etc. etc.? Equally significant and relevant questions for Pakistan are whether the elections due there within the next three days make any difference to the India-Pakistan relations, will the likely election/nomination/selection (chose as you will) of Imran Khan as the next PM make any difference in army loosening its control, will any eventual resolution of the Afghan imbroglio make any difference in relieving Pakistan of its perpetual sense of insecurity etc. etc.?

With my years of intimate involvement, while in service, with Kashmir and Indo-Pak relations, permit me to make a bold statement that it would need a massive 'leap of faith' on the part of Pakistan to move radically away from its anti-India policies. As one of my Pakistani interlocutors mentioned during a recent Track II meet, the best case scenario favours maintenance of 'strategic stalemate" in our relations. That's not very encouraging yet that's not why we should give up trying.

With these words, I once again compliment Shri Bloeria for authoring a real masterpiece, examining all aspects of India Pakistan relations. I commend this book to all those interested in understanding Kashmir and in evolving better India-Pakistan relations.

New Delhi

July, 22, 2018

C D Sahay

Former Secretary (R)

Introduction

I have had an inexplicable connection with J&K; with all the three regions of Jammu, Kashmir and Ladakh. I was born in Jammu city on September 3, 1945. After finishing my military training in the then Officers Training School, Madras in April 1966, I was commissioned in the Jammu and Kashmir Rifles (JAK RIF). Six years later, after taking part in the 1971 war with Pakistan – in the Fazilka sector on the western front - when I left the army to join the Indian Administrative Service; I was seconded to the J&K cadre. This was notwithstanding my strenuous efforts to go to Himachal Pradesh. My years in the army took me to a three winters tenure in Kupwara district of Kashmir and my first posting, on joining the civil administration was as SDM Kargil, in the then Ladakh district.

At the time of India's independence, I was almost two years old and thus have no memories of the tragedy of partition. My very first reminiscences of this unfortunate event relate to the fall of Kotli town, now part of the Pakistan Occupied Kashmir (PoK), as my eldest maternal uncle and his family were amongst the last to leave that ill-fated town in 1948. I heard stories of unspeakable miseries rained by the invading Sudan tribesmen and the Pak army there. One also learnt about the valiant defence of Kotli – literally till the very end – by a small contingent of the State Forces troops commanded by a gallant Major Bishamber Dass. We, the younger lot, heard stories from family elders and people around about ransacking, looting and burning of Mirpur and Bhimber towns; as also pushing out of the Hindu population from there. Poonch was not on my mental plain then and Kashmir was to enter the consciousness much later. To the growing child in me the horrors of 1947-48 were confined to the three towns of Kotli, Mirpur and Bhimber; all of them part of the PoK now.

I also faintly recall the Praja Parishad agitation of 1952-53 and resultant curfews in Jammu city; as well as tales of the exploits of underground political workers- often spoken in hushed tones. As a child, I was ignorant about and not aware of the arrest of Sheikh Mohammad Abdullah in August 1953, and consequent political upheavals in the state.

My father was an officer in the then J&K State Forces and we moved to Gwalior in December 1953, along with the unit he was then posted in – The J&K Body Guards Cavalry, *Risala* as it was commonly called. His orderly there was a soldier named Kamal Singh. I used to help him learn Hindi and Maths in order to pass the basic army tests and he would in return narrate me the details of his exploits in the 1947-48 war. He was a good storyteller and it was through him that I heard quite a bit about Pakistan army, its soldiers, the tribal raids and landing of the Indian army in Srinagar etc. For the first time, it was here that the broad contours of J&K issue and Indo-Pak conflict were formed in my mind. From him also I learnt few elementary things about trenches, bunkers, cavalry charges and the like; as also the fact that the Indian army generally looked down upon all the State Forces as inferior entities – which obviously hurt the professional pride of soldiers like him. I was to find out later that the J&K State Forces were the only erstwhile princely army which was merged in its entirety with the Indian Army and renamed first as the J&K Regiment and later – till now- as the Jammu and Kashmir Rifles (JAK RIF). This happened sometime in the mid and late fifties.

This was also the time one heard elders talking about the stout defense of Indian case by Krishna Menon in the United Nations. Still, not much entered my mind about the nuances of either the J&K issue or, in the broader perspective, the India - Pakistan tense relations. In the school library, in Gwalior those days, one read more about 'Panchsheel', the five principles of peaceful co-existence with China. We thought the ancient Indian wisdom had won over this newly emerging country.

It was after my return to Jammu- and the college there- in July 1962 that one reached the age and also had means of access to understand the heavily layered Indo-Pak relations and the central place the state of Jammu and Kashmir had come to occupy in that paradigm. Occasional visits to the Special Court, only a short distance away from our college, which was holding the Sheikh Abdullah trial; ignited my interest in gathering more and more information on this issue. During the period we were also equally – if not more – interested in getting a glimpse of Sheikh Abdullah and Mirza Afzal Beigh, his loyal and competent lieutenant during the former's turbulent years. Incidentally, a decade and a half later I would work as Deputy Commissioner Jammu under the supervision of the two gentlemen who respectively became the Chief Minister and Deputy Chief Minister of J&K State Government.

Back to my college days; from where I went to join the Officers Training School, Madras and passed out from there in April 1966 as an Officer of the Indian Army; allotted to the JAK RIF Regiment. It was a proud moment for me to have not only joined my father's regiment but also be an inheritor of around 150 years of its enviable legacy.

During the 1965 Indo-Pak war, I was a cadet in the OTS Madras. As young and keen soldiers in the making, we followed all the developments carefully as also professionally discussed some of the important battles of this war. Most of us were quite excited about the rumors of our training being cut short and all cadets sent to the allotted units to join the war. That eventuality never happened. But, by then we had gained enough professional knowledge to understand the import and meaning of terms like Op Gibralter; Op Grand Slam; Tank battles; Air combat and strafing etc.

My first posting on getting commission, was in a battalion located deep inside the then NEFA and present-day Arunachal Pradesh. A few months later, I was posted to a new unit being raised at Alwar in Rajasthan. Less than a year thereafter, this unit moved to Kupwara district of Kashmir valley. We were located in the general area of Karnah valley, with the headquarters based in Chowkibal village. I stayed there for almost three years from December 1967 to mid-1970. It was a tough period manning the high-altitude posts and also, simultaneously, gelling together of men and officers into a fine fighting outfit. That is where, in fact, I actually came to understand various aspects of the J&K situation and consistency of Pak interests and involvement from 1947 onwards. This was also the time I realized that both countries were, till then, busy in playing the roles for which the script had been written by the British Imperial interests – way back in the 1920s. This role was later, after the Second World War, taken over by the US heading the Cold War coalition of the Western Bloc.

As a young company commander, I operated along the live border against Pak troops positioned opposite us; and there learnt a few tricks of the trade which only such adversities can teach. Soldiering is a serious business and there is no scope for a lack of physical fitness; raw courage and a capacity to lead from the front. Happy memories of soldierly camaraderie and some reckless decisions are still with me; as also the lesson never to trust the other side. Always be alert and never lower your guards. This is what I learnt during the deployment of our troops against the posts manned by the Pakistan army. That caution has remained till date. I also acquired a lot of knowledge about Pak intentions, designs and ways of working during this tenure.

There were other two lessons one carried from those days and which proved useful during my civilian service in the state. One was about the significant goodwill that the army has in the border belt. In spite of all the vicissitudes and negative propaganda during the militancy years, this premise still holds good; and in fact it is the back-bone of the Civic Action programmes of the army at present. Providing of rations, medical and education facilities to the villages around has always remained an important function of all army units located in the Valley. The second was a realisation acquired over those years of interaction with the local population, that people in general living at the periphery of the Valley – effectively on or near the borders as also in the deep interiors, were much poorer and deprived than those staying in and around Srinagar and other urban centers. Both observations remain true even today.

My next stint was of over a year; spent in the Abhohar - Fazilka area of Punjab, where I was posted in an Independent Brigade headquarters as a Ground Liaison Officer, responsible for directing own aircrafts over the enemy targets in case of war. By the beginning of next year, 1971, the situation in the Eastern part of Pakistan started deteriorating and soon reached explosive proportions. The contours of the great human tragedy unfolding there are now well known to require any description; however, we were – as soldiers, preparing for the armed confrontation during later part of the year; including mobilisation of the forces. Sometime in the month of November that year, General Manekshaw, our Chief of Army Staff, visited our location and addressed the officers and men of the formation. He said that in his opinion the war with Pakistan was likely to start soon and would expect all his forces to fight the enemy across the border and on the other side. In this very inspiring talk, which was his trademark, he emphasized that he would never forgive two things in his force; one was an act of cowardice and the other anyone misbehaving with a woman. Both, he asserted, would be punished as an example for others and without any regard for the rank of the offender.

The war started, like in other sectors, during the evening of December 3, 1971. As the initiator, Pakistan had the advantage of location and timing and was thus able to breach the first line of defences in our sector and occupy a vital bridge over a ditch-cum-bund, along which our important positions were based. The task of re-occupying this bridge was given to a Jat battalion, which launched an attack during the night of 4/5 December. The valiant Jats fought hard, including a fierce hand to hand encounter and almost achieved their objective; but at a crucial moment of the combat lost their brave company commander who was leading them from the front. In spite of a number of causalities, they failed to capture the bridge. In a rare occurrence of this nature, commanders from both sides fought with grit and determination and ended up killing each other. The brave Indian Major was awarded a posthumous Vir Chakra; whereas his Pakistani counterpart – who was an elder brother of the erstwhile Pak Army Chief Raheel Sharif – got a posthumous award of Nishan-e-Haider – Pakistan's highest military gallantry award. Another incident, the memory of which I have always carried, occurred a few days after the war started. While visiting one of the forward posts, I was told that they had managed to capture few Pakistani soldiers, who were waiting to be shifted to the higher headquarters. My first impression of seeing these people was that they looked exactly like our boys – and the imagery has stayed with me.

In a nutshell, that thirteen-day war has been an unforgettable period and a very valuable learning experience in life; deeply and indelibly etched in one's mind. War is war; in which no quarters are asked for and no consideration shown; it is a serious business as also harsh and pitiless reality – only soldiers can realize the real import of the implications.

Soon thereafter, I joined the civil services – the Indian Administrative Service – in July 1972; and was allotted to the J&K cadre in spite of my efforts to go to Himachal Pradesh. That year four of us from the state, the largest number in a year till and since then, had qualified the competitive examination and the state government was keen to get each one back in the state cadre. For me, that was the beginning of a new profession and a new form of life; outside the uniform. The years spent in the army; the training and grounding in that job immensely helped me in the new profession; but also because of this profile, I did get to undertake difficult assignments over the years. One of my most memorable jobs was being the Deputy Commissioner of Jammu, my home district when the legendry Sheikh Abdullah was the Chief Minister of the state. Very soon I realized that he was really a tall man – in all respects. He would be bemused by the occasional transgressions of young people like me and very patiently, almost in a paternal manner, explain the right way to tackle a tricky issue. I genuinely came to regard him as an elder and showed him all the deference till his very end. During his lifetime one thought the Kashmir issue, and by implications, Pakistan's involvement in it was going to be a thing of the past. But, his death and subsequent political happenings changed the course of events in the state.

Dr. Farooq Abdullah taking over the reins of the state administration, after the death of his father – he being toppled over by his brother-in-law Ghulam Shah in July 1984 and the six months of Governor's rule thereafter in March 1986 were followed almost in quick succession. Then came the celebrated Rajiv Gandhi-Farooq accord leading to the March 1987 Assembly elections; which proved to be a water-shed development for the state and brought back Pakistan as an active player once again in the internal affairs. Pakistan took advantage of the emerging situation and adroitly exploited the openings; learning astutely from the experiences gained in Afghanistan and also out of the disturbed conditions it had created in the neighboring state of Punjab. Also encouraged by the success of its nefarious designs there; Pakistan tried to replicate the lessons learnt and resorted to sabotage and subversion of the established order in J&K. It launched massive and well-coordinated efforts to spread militancy, terrorism and trouble in this state and to create conditions in which it expected the Valley to fall into its hands. That, of course, was not to happen – but the intentions were certainly evil and designs depraved.

The sequences of events from Sheikh Sahib's death in September 1982 till the imposition of Governor Rule in January 1990, when the dark clouds literally burst, are certainly a tragic part of the down-hill slide of the state. History will not forgive the National Conference and Dr. Farooq Abdullah for shirking responsibilities and deserting the post when the nation and people of the state needed them most. The next over six years was a period of sorrow and deep gloom for the residents of J&K. Things did hit the rock bottom before the process of recovery started.

Good governance is an integral part of any effective government. However, in a conflict situation and disturbed environment, where lives and interests of ordinary people are under pressure, the issue of a functioning government becomes even more crucial. This is exactly where the governance system failed the people of the state when the trouble started. By the beginning of 1990, the administration in Srinagar and some other towns of the Valley had almost collapsed. Within months, the efficacy of the government hit the lowest levels. With considerable difficulty, a semblance of essential services and supplies was attempted by a beleaguered administrative structure and that too with unexpected disruptions for indeterminate periods. The first two years of the nineties was a most trying and difficult period. From the beginning of 1990, the terrorist activities spread beyond Srinagar city in a big way; leading to a virtual collapse of administrative machinery and destabilization of political structure. The proxy war unleashed by Pakistan had entered its most destructive stage. Large scale targeted kidnappings and killings took place, wanton destruction of government institutions and buildings was resorted to; the state police was demoralized and the judiciary threatened in a systematic manner. Sinister efforts were made to undermine and especially target Indian support structure. Central Government establishments like Accountant General's Office, BSNL, Post and Telegraph Department, and even some banks virtually became defunct under terrorist threats. Also, the ethnic cleansing initiated ruthlessly by the militants forced the migration of almost the entire Kashmiri Pandit community from the Valley. The terrorists also spread the arc of their activities south of Pir Panjal to the districts of Poonch, Rajouri and Doda as well as in the hilly tracts of Udhampur. This enabled the terrorists to increase the number of their hide outs and establish local training camps. Spilling over activities on the other side of Pir Panjal also provided these elements with the opportunities to slip across the ridge line whenever the pressure of security forces became intense on either side of the Pir Panjal.

However, it took the state administration and the security forces sustained and dedicated efforts of almost three years to get an upper hand over the situation and improve conditions in a gradual but determined and progressive manner. In 1993 two developments of far-reaching consequences took place in the state. In the month of May Unified Headquarters (UHQ) was established, resulting in a more focused and better coordinated conduct of operations against the terrorists by pooling the resources of different security agencies as well as intelligence organizations. The other event was the birth of All Party Hurriyat Conference (APHC); a loose grouping of thirty outfits, which was formally introduced to the public of the Valley on September 9, 1993.

By the end of 1994, the security forces had unmistakably gained an upper hand and the life of public in general, as well as, the functioning of the state government, had returned to almost normal levels. A year later, the situation was brought under enough control for the central and state governments to publicly speak about the prospects of holding elections and bringing back the elected representatives in power. The plans for electoral contests became clear soon thereafter; as the preparations for Assembly elections were initiated during 1995 - but due to certain reasons the electoral process could be carried out only in 1996. This remarkable endeavour began with the conduct of Parliamentary Elections, along with the rest of the country in May-June, and the Assembly Elections during September that year. These efforts, particularly for the Parliament Elections, were a noteworthy joint achievement by the agencies of the central and state governments acting in tandem. The end result was a successful massive administrative and logistic enterprise involving transportation of over five hundred companies of central para military forces as well as polling personnel exceeding ten thousand from outside the state; arranging their arrival and reception in the state and move them from one place to another under constant threat of terrorist attacks, without suffering even a single casualty, for almost a month of their stay in the state. These initiatives and actions also firmed up the ground for further consolidation of the democratic process; which has been carried on successfully since then.

The credible Assembly Elections in 1996 brought back to power the National Conference and Dr. Farooq Abdullah in the state for the next six years. However, it is debatable whether this government was able to achieve all that it had promised and embarked upon. At least the general public opinion did not appear to feel that way; as was evident in the next electoral contest six years later. Even though some development works picked up and restoration of the damaged infrastructure was also taken in hand, but this administration failed to give a decisive push to ending the militancy as also infuse a fresh blood into the important task of institution building in the state. Few opportunities were missed by this government; the unfortunate consequences of which began becoming clear later on.

During the last two decades, at least three times it appeared that the state was coming out of a thick fog of gloom and despair; as the end appeared in sight. The first time it happened was in the aftermath of the successfully held Assembly elections in 1996, in which the National Conference secured a huge and clear public mandate by becoming the single largest party, in terms of elected representatives, in all the three regions of J&K. It was, without doubt, a massive and clear mandate for the restoration of normalcy and return of peace. But the political and administrative classes failed to put their act together to deliver the desired results and a very favorable opportunity was lost. Another round of conducive circumstances prevailed after 2002 Assembly elections with the new coalition government giving thrust to inclusive politics – bringing the inter-regional temperatures considerably down – as also a visible forward thrust to development activities. This was coupled with a considerably enhanced capacity of the security forces to deal effectively with cross-border movement. The next propitious opportunity came around with the unexpectedly impressive participation of the people of the state, including the Valley, in the 2008 Assembly elections held in the aftermath of the wide spread disturbances in Jammu and Kashmir regions due to the land controversy related to Shri Amarnath Shrine Board. But each time the separatist elements and their mentors across the border proved more than a match for restorers of normalcy, peace and tranquility. These outwitted the policy makers and implementing agencies of the centre and state quite comprehensively; by shrewdly shepherding and preserving their resources and at the same time very skillfully taking advantage of every small opening that presented itself. It is quite clear that the ISI and its cohorts have been constantly changing and evolving their tactics according to the ground situation in the state and to ensure optimum utilization of the resources available. That this happened even during the period when relations between India and Pakistan were on the mend; is something quite troubling and needs to be thought over.

On a different plane, Pakistan was having an upper hand in many international forums, as compared to India, during the first five years of the 1990s. It did create difficulties for India, as an example, in the proceedings of the Human Rights Commission in Geneva; with a defensive India resolutely defending her actions in J&K. These troubles were further increased by the backing of Pak actions by US government, particularly the partisan and pro-Pak stand so publicly taken by Ms. Robin Raphel, the then Assistant Secretary of State in the Bill Clinton administration. During that period India was constantly pressed upon 'to do some more' to accommodate the Pakistani demands. This adverse situation, for India, slowly started changing from 1996 onwards. First, it was the conduct of credible Parliamentary as well as Assembly elections, in which people of all the three regions of J&K participated in good numbers. Then came the nuclear explosions, so publically conducted by both countries; making it all the more difficult for America to turn a blind eye to Pakistan's open nuclear status and ambitions. To further add to the growing American discomfort with Pakistan actions; was the Kargil war between the two countries during May-July 1999. No nation bought General Musharraf's theory of 'mountain shepherds' being villains of the piece during this crisis and the Americans tersely asked the Pakistanis to back off from the bleak heights of this Himalayan region. The Kargil conflict also decisively brought forth the superiority of the Indian conventional combat capabilities and hollowness of the Pakistani claims of operating under a nuclear over-hang. The world at large also appreciated the Indian restraint in this engagement.

The whole scenario was further and dramatically changed with the terrorist attacks on the World Trade Centre in New York and some other targets in America on September 11, 2001. For the entire world, the US included, Pakistan emerged as a leading focal point of international terrorism, and that perception has not changed – if anything it has deepened over the years. For tactical reasons and also dictated by the ground realities; the Americans and Pakistanis have collaborated, for their respective mutual interests, but the earlier element of trust and friendliness has always been missing. It has been a disturbing relationship at best and deeply distrustful at times. The pressure has been building on Pakistan, over the years, to 'do some more' and to that extent, the shoe now is on the other foot. Recently, Pakistan cozying up to China and enthusiastically welcoming various facets of CPEC has added another factor in the formers relationships with other countries of the world – particularly for America and India; and for all those desirous of seeing peace process flourish in this sub-continent.

The contours of this gamut have been aptly described by the *Times of India*, in an editorial dated September 20, 2017, as "…Having had its way for so long Islamabad now threatens to play its China card – it even fanaticizes about a new Cold War where it will square off with Russia and China against the West and India. But China has stakes in the global order as well and it too has a lot to lose from the jihadi militias Pakistan harbours. If, let us say, the US fails to bail out Pakistan during its next financial emergency, it would be interesting to see how quickly 'iron brother' China rushes to assume its liabilities. It's past time to call Islamabad's bluff and get it to end support to terror, which destabilizes the region and the world". But all this is also a game of intelligent speculation and in the realm of future – as of now the harsh realities of the present situation would matter more than anything else.

Jammu and Kashmir has been struggling with the scourge of terrorism for three decades now. This has caused untold miseries to the people of the state; with thousands losing life and many more getting hurt. The turmoil has also resulted in huge losses to public and private properties. Apart from the fact that the normal day to day life has been adversely affected, the entire social fabric has been under very severe strain. However astonishing it may seem, a closer scrutiny would reveal that while the outer surface may have appeared to be frayed, the core of the traditional secular frame work of the state has essentially not changed; and the locals have continued with their age-old practices unmindful of the violence and causalities. J&K has emerged as the crucible of social harmony and religious tolerance; providing shelter and solace to a large number of people belonging to different places, regions and faiths. This is where the hope for a better future lies and an improvement in the Indo-Pak relations would add another positive dimension to this optimistic speculation.

The whole process of peaceful co-existence between India and Pakistan is like a game of checkers, also at times swinging like a pendulum from one end to the other, mostly remaining on the dark square thereby indicating lack of mutual trust and also the absence of good neighbourly relations. Any effort to play the blame-game would further complicate an already difficult and tangled relationship. Right from August 1947, ties between the two countries have been strained, often bordering on hostility. For a short period after the birth of Bangladesh and signing of Simla Agreement, there was a hope of a positive relationship. But, that was not to be and future developments in the sub-continent took a different turn. In the decades that followed; mutual suspicion grew instead of lessening of tensions. The eighties and nineties proved even more unmanageable from this point of view; than any period before that. But for a short period of four years – between 2003 and 2007 – the two nations have continued to live uncomfortably as neighbours; till the very present.

What lies in store for the future? That is a million dollar question and one entity in the sub-continent that can presumably answer this query rightly is the Pakistan army; its high command and the all powerful collegium of Corps Commanders. The security and foreign policy related decisions there are the exclusive preserve of the army brass and not in the control of the political class. This fact is known to all and equally well established. One can also, at the same time, safely presume that the public at large in Pakistan – the civil society – is, and has been, in favour of improved relations and peace with India. A promising beginning was made towards the later years of General Musharraf's regime. Before those gains could be consolidated, the Mumbai attacks of November 2008 took place and the clock was firmly set back. There has been no positive breakthrough since then.

Where does one go from here? This is a moot point that begs for an assured answer. The scenario is both bleak as well as positive – depending on the way one looks at the current happenings in the region as also the world over. There are enough pessimists and prophets of doom, but in the ultimate analysis, the most reassuring aspect of the future of Indo-Pak relations is the latent feeling of friendship still existing between the two people. This collective sentiment is dormant; yet powerful enough for a perceptive observer to take notice of. One has yet to meet a visitor from either country, who has gone to the other side and not returned with a happy experience of the friendship and hospitality shown by the ordinary people.

If and when will this goodwill gather the 'critical mass'? That is where our collective hope lies.

This book attempts a panoramic overview of the peace process, in different stages and phases over the past seven decades, between India and Pakistan from 1947 onwards; with special reference to the state of Jammu and Kashmir.

CHAPTER - I

Background of the Conflict

The state of Jammu and Kashmir came into existence in March 1846 when Maharaja Gulab Singh got possession of Kashmir, in addition to the existing territories of Jammu and Ladakh already in his control. The inclusion of Kashmir into the realm of Gulab Singh took place with the Treaty of Amritsar on March 16, 1846 between him and the British Government represented by Frederick Currie and Henry Montogomery Lawrence, in the aftermath of the decisive victory of the British forces over the Sikh army in the battle of Sobraon and the entry of British into Lahore a month earlier. The British did not cede Kashmir purely for the consideration of money; they did not create an empire in India by selling real estate, but primarily due to the prevailing geo-political situation. This was explained by the then Governor General in his letter dated March 14, 1846 to his principals in London, as "It will be seen by the draft of Treaty now forwarded that, in consequence of the inability of the Lahore Government to pay the sum stipulated as indemnification for the expenses of the war, or give sufficient security for its eventual disbursement, the Hill territories, from the Beas River to the Indus, including the provinces Kashmir and Hazarah, have been ceded to the British Government. It is not my intention to take possession of the whole of this territory. Its occupation by us would be, on many accounts disadvantageous. It would bring us into collision with many powerful chiefs, for whose coercion a large military establishment at a great distance from our provinces and military resources would be necessary.... Now, distant and conflicting interests would be created and races of people, with whom we have hitherto had no intercourse, would be brought under our rule, while the territories, excepting Kashmir, are comparatively unproductive, and would scarcely pay the expenses of occupation and management...."[1]

In the next few years, certain adjustments were made between the parties with a view to rationalizing the respective possessions rather than transfer of any significant territory. Maharaja Gulab Singh's son and successor, Maharaja Ranbir Singh added more area to his kingdom with the conquest of Gilgit, Chitral, Hunza and Nagar in the Northern Region. With the boundary adjustment and the conquests, by the end of 19th century, Jammu and Kashmir comprised an area 2,22,870 Sq. Kms becoming the largest Indian princely state. This considerable land mass was administratively divided into three provinces of Jammu, Kashmir and Gilgit and frontier areas of Skardu, Ladakh and Kargil.

In the aftermath of the great uprising in 1857 the British government assumed direct responsibility of governing their Indian possessions and with that the conflicting interests of the British and the Russian empires, the moves and counter-moves of the Great Game, came into play bestowing considerable strategic importance to the northern areas of the J&K ruler, as these bordered Afghanistan and China, and thus became extremely important to the British strategic considerations. With this began British manipulations in Gilgit and further north and their virtual control of these parts of the J&K territories from the 1880s onwards. The British obsession of this area was significantly evident in their policies and calculations, in the context of the perceived southward expansion of the Russians, which the former was not prepared to be extended anywhere south of river Oxus in Afghanistan. This whole gamut has been elaborately described in a book titled, "Where Three Empires Meet" by E.F. Knight (Longmans, Green & Co, London, 1919). The British fixation with this area continued even after their departure from India in 1947. This has been one of the major factors the British diplomacy and maneuvers in the Indian sub-continent, during the first half of the twentieth century. In consonance with their geo-strategic perceptions, the Gilgit province continued to be of vital importance to them even after the lapse of British paramountcy in the sub-continent. If this area was not to remain under British control, which obviously it would not after August 15, 1947, then it should be part of a more pliant and friendly state. For this, the ideal situation would be, from

1   K.M. Panikkar, "GULAB SINGH", Martin Hopkinson Ltd, London- 1930, pp. 161-162.

the British point of view, for Jammu and Kashmir State to become part of Pakistan. If that too was somehow not accomplished, then Gilgit should be under the effective control of Pakistan with secured communications to the area. As the events unfolded during the critical months following Indian independence, the British complicity in affairs of the sub-continent achieved this objective successfully.

However, strategic manipulations of the political developments in India by the British rulers had started right from the beginning of the twentieth century and these grew in intensity and effectiveness in direct proportion to the growing struggle for independence. By the 1920s their tacit support to the growth of All India Muslim League, under the leadership of Mohammed Ali Jinnah, as a political entity against the Indian National Congress, was becoming evident. But the growth of the Muslim League did not become widespread amongst the Muslims of India and remained generally confined to the United Provinces and Bihar till almost the forties. Even during this period, there is ample evidence to show that in the Muslim majority provinces the people's support lay elsewhere. In Punjab, the ruling outfit was the Unionist Party, which had towering leaders like Sir Sikander Hayat Khan and Sir Chotu Ram. In Bengal the Krishak Party held sway and Khudai Khidmatgar Party or the Red Shirts were the prominent players in the North West Frontier Province. According to the acclaimed Pakistani writer Tariq Ali, "Ghaffar Khan and Dr. Khan Sahib, two brothers from a landed family in Charsada, decided to launch a political, nonviolent struggle against the British in 1930. The Redshirt movement, as it became known (because of the color of the shirts worn by its supporters rather than any other affinities; their inspiration was Gandhi, not Lenin), spread rapidly through the region. Ghaffar Khan and his volunteers visited every single village to organize the peasants against the empire and branches of the movement emerged even in the remotest village.... This area with a large Muslim majority preferred to remain aloof from the Muslim League and the idea of Pakistan, though the League would acquire a base in the Province with the help of the imperial bureaucracy and police force and a combination of chicanery and violence. The British, who had assiduously encouraged the division between the Hindu and Muslim communities, were confused and irritated by the Redshirts"[2].

---

2   Tariq Ali, "The Duel", Simon & Schuster UK Ltd, London- 2008, pp-20-21.

The 1937 elections, held after the passage of the Government of India Act 1935 giving autonomy to the provinces to form their elected governments, further reduced the political standing and importance of the Muslim League in the public perception. The onset of Second World War, which started in September 1939, brought in its wake compulsions of the hard-pressed British Empire. The unstinted support of the Muslim League to their war effort, coupled with the British policy of counterbalancing the Congress and its machinations of sowing seeds of discord between Hindu and Muslim communities; all these factors coalesced to hugely bolster the sagging fortunes of the Muslim League. It not only became a live and kicking organization, and a force to reckon with in the sub continent, but also confident enough to lay the ideological foundation of Pakistan on March 23, 1940, in Lahore. From this point onwards there was practically no looking back for the League and along the way, its rising fortunes were bolstered by a combination of factors. These included Imperial support, based on the British world view and safeguarding their interests, miscalculations of political opponents as also fortuitous circumstances. Undoubtedly, the foremost element amongst these was the solid government support so assiduously marshaled by the British.

Right from the beginning of the twentieth century, the British policy in India carried the unmistakable strains of being pro-Muslim. Adept in the art of statecraft and with a deep understanding of international developments, they must have foreseen the inevitability of granting independence to India sooner or later and, therefore, set about making the best possible bargain. During the three year period, from August 1942 – when most of the eminent Congress leaders were behind bars following the Quit India Movement – the British provided tacit support and a conducive environment to Muslim League to grow so much that they could drive a hard bargain with the Congress leadership. This was done on the assumption that Pakistan, more than India, would serve the strategic interests of Britain. As events unfolded later, their calculations were not off the mark. Once Pakistan came into being, the senior British functionaries in the sub-continent, especially those belonging to the military, were more favourably disposed towards Pakistan. Their actions were very carefully crafted to fit into the grand designs of the British imperialism. Britain had not yet come to terms with its diminished power status in the international power structure that was emerging after the Second World War.

The decision to partition British India into two sovereign States set the stage for the lapse of British Paramountcy in the Indian sub-continent; with the creation of Pakistan on August 14 and grant of independence to India on August 15, 1947. The whole process was set to be completed in less than two and half months, starting from the unveiling of the Mountbatten Plan, for the transfer of power to the two Dominions, on June 3, 1947. This division of the country brought about untold miseries on a very large number of people. An estimated fourteen million persons, both Hindus as well as Muslims moved from one part to another, leaving their homes and hearths of generations, if not centuries. Equally unfortunate were the tales of murder, loot and rape, leaving behind a trail of blood, helplessness and hopelessness. The partition was admittedly an unmitigated disaster, a great human tragedy of immense proportions and without going into the 'ifs' and 'buts' of history and trying to put institutions, governments and peoples in the dock; the stark fact is that people of both sides suffered immensely.

As in other princely states, the British paramountcy over J&K state was also to lapse on 15th August that year. But unlike most of the rulers of princely states in India, Maharaja Hari Singh of Jammu and Kashmir found it difficult to decide on the issue of accession before the cut-off date. This, in spite of almost clear British preference, and also advice to this effect by the Governor General Lord Mountbatten to Maharaja Hari Singh, for the J&K state to join Pakistan. Not only the ruler of the state, but also the most popular political leader, Sheikh Mohd Abdullah did not favour an accession with Pakistan. The persona of Sheikh Abdullah came into prominence with the founding of Muslim Conference by him in 1931, which led the struggle for the popular rule and against the feudal order. Towards the end of the decade, he converted this organization, which had by then acquired a very popular base in the Kashmir Valley, into a secular political entity called National Conference. A smaller group styled as Muslim Conference split from it. This outfit, having a support base amongst the Muslims of Poonch and Mirpur districts of J&K state, allied with the policies and plans of the Muslim League. The National Conference, on the other hand, had a lot of ideological affinity and considerable common interests with the Congress. Also due to shared political thought and identical human vision, both Nehru and Abdullah became close personal friends. Jinnah did make a visit to Srinagar in 1944 and made efforts to bring Sheikh Abdullah around to his thinking and the ideology of Muslim League, but he did not succeed.

As ruler of the state was not decisive about the accession of his state, he instead made an offer of a Standstill Agreement to both India and Pakistan on 12th August. Whereas no agreement was signed with India, the same was executed with Pakistan. The postal and telegraph services in the state were placed under the control of Pakistan Government. An eye witness recalled this event as, "I remember the Pakistani flags flying over central offices of departments like Post and Telegraph after the Maharaja of the state signed a Standstill Agreement with the new dominion of Pakistan on August 14, 1947. No such agreement was signed with the government of India".[3] The J&K state was also promised that existing arrangements for import of rice, wheat, cloth, kerosene oil, petrol and ammunition etc. from West Punjab would continue. However, soon after Pakistan came into existence, its rulers put into operation plans to force the Maharaja to accede to Pakistan. The strategy for achieving this end was a multi-pronged approach based on armed invasion, subversion of Muslim population – including the military personnel, particularly in the belt of Poonch-Mirpur-Bhimber on the western border – and economic blockade of the state.

The economic strangulation of the state was carried out effectively and in a planned manner. This adversely affected availability of essential items like rice, wheat, salt, kerosene oil and petrol. Restrictions were placed in the smooth operations of banking and postal services. Also, by mid-September railway services from Sialkot to Jammu, the only rail link the state had with outside world, were suspended. Repeated reminders and requests from state authorities brought no relief. Instead, the Pakistani response became offensive, accusing the state government of atrocities against Muslims of Poonch and threatening remedial measures. In addition to the economic and commercial blockade, Pakistan mounted a very effective propaganda campaign in the Poonch-Mirpur region. Soon, by the third week of August communal incidents were started in Rawlakot and Bagh areas of Poonch and the security situation in this sector deteriorated rapidly. The Pakistani attacks by well armed civilians, assisted by men of Pak army, spread over a wide arc succeeded in splitting the State Forces in penny-pockets. The worsening situation also necessitated committing

---

3   Balraj Puri in "The Tumultuous Years" in Epilogue, October 2007, p-4.

some reserves in the Poonch sector. The conditions now, from Pakistan's point of view, were quite conducive for the entry of raiders into the Valley and execution of final phase of their plan aimed at the capture of Srinagar.

The stage was set for J&K to become a flashpoint between India and Pakistan. Since then, for the past seven decades, the contentious issue has continued to sour relations between the two countries.

The invasion of Kashmir by the tribals was meticulously planned, carefully timed and well executed. By the middle of October, the economic blockade had choked economy of the state, created shortages of essential commodities and adversely affected the efficacy of administration. Civil strife was effectively engineered in the south-western parts of the state which also drew the crucial reserve forces away from the Valley. Also with the winter about to set in, access to Kashmir by road would be closed for the next six months, from the south and India, as the only motorable link to Valley from Jammu, the BC Road, remained snowbound at the Pir Panjal range over Banihal. During this period the only dependable road access to the Valley was the existing Jhelum Valley Road linking Peshawar in Pakistan with Srinagar via Abbottabad and Muzaffarabad. Thus Pakistan had very carefully chosen the timing, taking into consideration prevarication of the Maharaja regarding accession.

The main attack, code-named "Operation Gulmarg", was planned and launched by the Army Headquarters of Pakistan. The main force consisting of armed tribals from the North West Frontier, with stiffeners and a liberal supply of arms and equipment from the regular army, was organized into units of about one thousand each, called Lashkars. For effective command and control, each Lashkar was provided with the services of one army Major, a Captain and ten JCOs. The entire force was commanded by Maj. Gen. Akbar Khan, with the code name Tariq,[4] and the date for launching of operations was fixed as October 22, 1947. This plan envisaged six Lashkars to advance along the main road from Muzaffarabad to Srinagar via Domel, Uri and Baramulla. Two Lashkars each were to make subsidiary moves from Haji Pir Pass to Gulmarg and Tithwal to Handwara, Sopore and Bandipur, with the twin objectives of securing large chunks of territory, as also to protect the flanks of the main

---

4   Tariq is the name of a legendary military commander who led Arab forces into Spain
    in seventh century. On landing on the coast of Spain he had burnt his boats to spur his
    troops to fight for victory.

column. It was a sound plan indeed. The 7 Infantry Division of Pakistan Army which was to concentrate in Murree-Abbottabad by 21st October, was ordered to be ready to move into J&K territory to back up the Lashkars and consolidate their hold on the Valley.[5]

It is reasonable to believe that at least the C-in-C of Indian Army, Gen. Lockhart and Field Marshal Auchinleck, the Supreme Commander were kept informed of the invasion plans by the Pak Army C-in-C Gen. Messervy, who was in constant touch with both of them. The matter was too serious, having bearings on the British Foreign Policy, to have been kept close to his chest by Gen. Messervy. Neither of the two British Commanders made timely disclosure to Indian political leaders or military commanders.[6]

The main defences on the access to Srinagar were located at Domel, ahead of Muzaffarabad, where two approach roads from Murree and Abbottabad met before leading towards Srinagar along the Jhelum gorge. These defences were manned by 4 J&K Infantry, composed of Dogras and Muslims in equal proportions. A few days earlier, the Commanding Officer, Lt.Col. Narayan Singh had refused a suggestion for replacement of his Muslim troops there with Dogra soldiers, saying that all his boys were like sons to him. On the night of 21/22 October, when the main attack developed, the Muslim troops manning defences joined the raiders, forgetting their oath of loyalty and betraying the confidence of their commander. After Domel had been secured by the raiders, there was practically nothing between them and Srinagar city.

Realizing gravity of the situation and a very serious breach in defences of the state, which now directly threatened Srinagar city itself, Brig. Rajinder Singh, Chief of Staff of the State Forces rushed towards Uri, in the evening of 22nd October itself, to stem the raiders advance. Forgetting his rank and status he collected all available military personnel, arms and equipment in the Srinagar cantonment and personally headed a heterogeneous force comprising about 150 men, a section of Medium Machine Guns and a detachment of 3-inch Mortars. It was an initiative on his part which would find a rare parallel in the annals of military history.

5   S.N. Prasad and Dharam Pal, ed. "History of Operations in Jammu and Kashmir", Ministry of Defence, Government of India , New Delhi – 1987, pp 17-19.

6   Lt. Gen. L.P. Sen (Retd), "Slender was the Thread", Orient Longman, New Delhi- 1969, p.21.

What followed is the substance and essence of which legends are made. Leading his tiny force by determination and personal example, Brig. Rajinder Singh was able to delay the raiders advance by four very crucial days. The hostiles could enter Baramulla only on the night of 26th October. The town was put to sword, fire and plunder; worst kind of atrocities were committed and abominable criminal acts perpetrated on the hapless local population. Brig. Rajinder Singh's determined rearguard action and the hostiles lust for loot in Baramulla, gave a critical breathing space to the Indian forces which started landing in Srinagar from October 27, 1947, to fill the breach and stop the advance of raiders towards Srinagar.

In view of the grave developing situation, Maharaja Hari Singh made a formal request on 24th October for dispatch of Indian troops to save Kashmir from the invaders. In view of the serious conditions there, V.P. Menon, Secretary, Ministry of States was flown to Srinagar the next day to assess the situation. He returned on the morning of 26th October along with M.C. Mahajan the Prime Minister of the State and apprised the government of the critical situation in the Valley and that the raiders might reach Srinagar any day. The Defence Committee of the Cabinet – interestingly headed by not the Prime Minister of India but the Governor General Lord Mountbatten – decided that Indian troops would be sent to the state only after its formal accession to India. Menon flew to Jammu the same afternoon, where Maharaja Hari Singh had also arrived, and returned to New Delhi with the Maharaja's request for the troops as well as the Instrument of Accession, duly signed by him. With the acceptance of the request for accession by the Governor General, during the night of October 26, 1947, the State of Jammu and Kashmir became an integral part of India. The next morning onwards Indian Army troops started landing in Srinagar.

By 2nd November almost a brigade strength of troops had reached Srinagar by air, and Brig. L.P. Sen, D.S.O., arrived to assume command of 161 Infantry Brigade there. Over the ensuing week, two important battles took place. The very next day a heavy engagement occurred in the Badgam high ground, not far away from the airfield, between a company of 4 Kumaon and the hostiles. The Kumaonis fought valiantly against a much larger force and ensured the safety of the airfield. Amongst those killed there, was Major Som Nath Sharma, who was posthumously awarded Param Vir Chakra. He became first recipient of the highest gallantry award of independent India. Four days later on 7th November at Shaltang, about eight kilometers north of Srinagar, an important battle took place between raiders and the troops. That morning a large force consisting of thousands of raiders, with hundreds of lorries nearby, started attacking the army positions with the objective of entering the city. A pitched clashed ensued, which was well coordinated by the Indian side involving the infantry troops, armoured cars and fighter aircrafts. Within a short period, the hostiles were routed and forced to flee towards Baramulla leaving behind 500 dead, their lorries, dumps of ammunition and supplies.[7] This decisive battle of Shaltang shattered the dreams of the invaders of reaching Srinagar, forever. The fleeing raiders were chased by the army which occupied first Baramulla and then also Uri on 13th November. From this point the troops of Brig. Sen could have pursued the raiders further and reoccupied Domel, Muzaffarabad and Kohala. But for inexplicable reasons the direction of his advance was changed from east-west direction to north-south and the force under him directed to undertake the relief of Poonch by moving on the Uri-Poonch road over Haji Pir Pass.

By the end of 1947, the Valley was cleared of the raiders beyond Uri, even though some of these elements remained in the north Kashmir, including Gurez valley. In Jammu division, Chhamb was cleared of the hostiles and Poonch garrison continued to hold, ably helped by the air force support. Rajouri area as well as major parts of Poonch and Mirpur districts were under the enemy control, which had also occupied Jhangar, posing a threat to Nowshera. The force build up by the year end had reached three brigades in Jammu division, whereas in Kashmir only one brigade, 161 Infantry Brigade was located. It was probably not easy to maintain a larger force during the winter months by air those days. In the Northern Sector, Gilgit, along with a large chunk of land, had passed on to the hostile elements by virtue of a coup headed by a British officer Major Brown, on October 31, 1947. It was shortly handed over to Pakistan, virtually on a platter. Much more was to happen in this region during the next year in 1948.

Nothing much of military significance took place during the first two months of 1948, except for top level changes in the command structure of both armies. Lt. Gen. Sir. Roy Butcher took over as C-in-C of Indian Army and Lt. Gen. K.M. Cariappa, the senior most Indian officer, assumed

7   *Ibid* pp 90,98.

reins of D.E.P. Command which was directing all operations in J&K. In Pakistan Lt. Gen. Sir Douglas Gracey was made the new C-in-C of the army. Thus the top level command of the armed forces of both countries still remained with the British officers. Whereas this formulation helped the interests of Pakistan, it was certainly detrimental to Indian concerns. Two significant achievements were made in Jammu area in the first half of the year. On 18th March, Jhangar was recaptured, this time for good and Rajouri was liberated on 13th April. With these two tactically important objectives in hand, Indian efforts to link up with Poonch received fresh impetus – though this objective was realized more than six months later.

By the summer of 1948, almost eight brigades of Indian army were operating in J&K. Hence, the JAK Div under Maj. Gen. Kalwant Singh was bifurcated into two divisions, namely Jammu Div under Maj. Gen. Atma Singh and Sri Div with headquarters at Baramulla under the command of Maj. Gen. K.S. Thimayya, D.S.O. While the force level in Jammu region was about five brigades, the same in Kashmir amounted to three brigades strong. Indian Army's summer offensive in the valley opened on 18th May with push by 163 Infantry Brigade under Brig Harbaksh Singh, through Dragmula and Handwara. Chowkibal was retrieved on 20th May and three days later Tithwal, across Nastachun Pass, was recaptured. As compared to these successes, the efforts of 161 Infantry Brigade to capture Domel floundered after some initial gains. Gen. Thimayya's decision to launch 77 Para Brigade too in pursuit of his Domel objective did not improve matters. He then asked the commander of 163 Brigade to plan the thrust to Muzaffarabad from Tithwal. However, this operation could not be carried out due to the paucity of troops. Brig. Harbaksh Singh had asked for one additional infantry battalion and that too was denied to him on the pretext of the paucity of troops, by the Army Headquarters. Thus ended India's summer offensive without achieving its aim of capturing Domel. The only consolation, in addition to the gains made by Brig. Harbaksh Singh in Tithwal sector, was the clearing of Gurez valley of raiders, after armed clashes, and its occupation by Indian troops. Hence, with the hostiles driven out of Gurez valley, the threat to Srinagar from North was removed.

S.K. Sinha, an astute military analyst and who had participated in the planning of J&K operations as a staff officer, has opined, "We would perhaps have done better to undertake this offensive with a bigger force, despite difficulties of maintenance. A reserve brigade to exploit the success at Tithwal and turn that operation from a diversionary thrust into an outflanking manoeuvre may have got us to Domel before the enemy's reinforcements came to his rescue"[8]. The speed of advance of 163 Infantry Brigade to Tithwal had caught the Pakistanis very badly off the guard, and given sufficient troops and resources, an advance from there to Muzaffarabad was well within the realm of possibility. Lord Birdwood, in his assessment of these operations, has postulated even greater success. He maintained that after the loss of Tithwal, "Pakistan's situation was now grim, and had India only used air supply more aggressively to maintain the impetus of this outflanking success her forces would so severely have threatened Muzaffarabad as to force Pakistani withdrawal from the whole of northern sector. Luckily for Pakistan, they paused"[9]. Also according to Lt. Gen. L.P. Sen, "Army Headquarters handling of the operations in Kashmir in 1947-48 leaves more than a little room for speculation whether the formations deployed were really intended to score a decisive success which they could and would have achieved had reinforcements been moved in, or whether it was the intention that their capacity should be limited to a strength where only a stalemate could result. From the attitude adopted by the Army HQ, the second would appear the correct assessment"[10].

The situation prevailing in the Valley at this time was to continue with minor changes till the end of the conflict. In Jammu region also, except for the recapture of Mendhar and link up with Poonch in November 48, nothing else of much importance happened till the declaration of ceasefire on January 1, 1949. However, in the Northern Sector, significant developments took place during 1948, after Gilgit was occupied by the hostiles following a coup by Major Brown on 31st October the previous year. Since then, considerable area was lost to the Pakistanis and Indian troops were faced with heavy odds in that vast, desolate and strategically important region.

For the last over six decades, the defences and the general control and supervision of the Gilgit region and areas north of it, like Chitral and Hunza etc. was managed by the British directly, even though technically this

---

8   Maj. S.K. Sinha, "Operation Rescue", Vision Books, New Delhi – 1977, p. 77. (The author retired as a Lt. General; was also the Governor of Assam as well as J&K)

9   Lord Birdwood, "Two Nations and Kashmir", Robert hale Limited, London – 1956, p. 71.

10 L.P. Sen, n.6, p. 294.

entire region remained part of the territories of the J&K state. Therefore, traditionally not much force was stationed in this region. In conformity with the general pattern of force deployment in the state, only one unit was located in the entire vast Gilgit – Ladakh sector as under:

i.   Battalion less two companies   -   Bunji

ii.   Company less platoon   -   Leh

iii. Two platoons   -   Kargil

iv.   Company less platoon   -   Skardu

These troops belonged to the 6th Battalion of the State Forces, under command of Lt. Col. Majid Khan, and were composed of Sikhs and Muslims in equal numbers. The Muslim troops came from Poonch area whose loyalties had been subverted. Of the two companies at Bunji, one was a Muslim company and the other of Sikhs. The Muslim company sent to Gilgit before October 1947 on the requisition of the Governor, also joined rebels after the coup. The Sikh company in Bunji was attacked, while their route of withdrawal was blocked at Astor by Captain Matheison, another British officer working under Major Brown and commanding a contingent of Gilgit Scouts there. These Sikh troops were either killed or taken prisoners. Lt. Col. Majid Khan was also taken prisoner by the rebels.

After the fall of Gilgit and Bunji and confinement of the commanding officer, the second in command Major Sher Jung Thapa, based at Leh, took over reins of the 6th Battalion. On orders, Thapa moved to Skardu on December 3, 1947, taking along with him a platoon each from Leh and Kargil. He started organizing defences based on the fort of Skardu and finding the number of troops insufficient requested for reinforcements from the State Army Headquarters. After making all-out efforts a company plus of troops was organized and this column, with three officers, left Srinagar on January 13, 1948. By sheer grit, endurance and determination this body managed to cross Zojila Pass, in the middle of severe winter, on foot by marching in three separate groups. Finally, they all managed to reach Skardu, the last column reporting there just in time. The siege of Skardu began on the night of 14 / 15 February 1948. At that time Thapa's force was a total of 285 combatants, including the new arrivals. This was too small a force for the effective defence of the garrison. To make matters more difficult, he also had to take care of over 250 civilians who were also inside the fort. Two abortive attempts were made to reinforce Skardu, as also his request to withdraw to a more defendable position in Kargil was rejected. Thapa (He was promoted as Lt. Col. in May 1948) manned his defences valiantly, against all odds, for full six months, fighting till his ammunition and supplies were exhausted. Skardu capitulated on August 14, 1948, after a long and heroic struggle under his inspired leadership. The siege of Skardu, for which Sher Jung Thapa was awarded the prestigious Maha Vir Chakra, would always be remembered with due deference in the annals of military history of independent India. After the surrender, the troops and civilians suffered immensely at the hands of hostiles who let loose mayhem of murder, rape and torture. Thapa's own life was saved by Maj. Gen. Kalwant Singh who managed to secure the intervention of Indian Army's C-in-C Lt. Gen. Roy Butcher on his behalf.[11] Skardu fell as a result of lack of appropriate strategic appreciation by the Indian political leadership, "ham-handed relief operations"[12] and the inability of the Air Force to provide requisite support.

The valiant performance of the doughty defenders of Skardu notwithstanding, its loss was a major blunder for which the senior military commanders, as well as the decision makers at the top level, have to share the blame; more by the political leadership at the helm of affairs. The Defence Committee of the Cabinet in its meeting on December 5, 1947, had taken a decision to hold Poonch at any cost. The executive action and military responses accordingly flowed from this determination of political direction and priority. Unfortunately, no such importance was given to Skardu, and a significant area of great military value, which should, in fact, have been treated as a "vital ground" for the defence of the state, was lost. A success at Skardu could have been built upon to use it as a springboard for developing further operations in the north towards Gilgit. Similarly, the blame for the failure of the two relief columns to reach Skardu does primarily lie with their commanders, but a more competent handling of these by the senior military leaders, up the chain of command, could have given positive results. Another opportunity to keep Skardu firmly in Indian hands was lost when the success in capturing Gurez, at the end of June 1948, was not exploited further. While the raiders were on the run there, a rapid advance over the Burzil Pass towards Skardu was possible. Such a

11 Author's interview with Brig.(Retd) Sher Jung Thapa, MVC, in February 1991.

12 Lt. Gen. Vijay Madan, "Jammu and Kashmir Operations 1947-48; the Other Version", USI Journal, New Delhi, July-September 1992, p.314.

course did require an additional force of more than a battalion and its air maintenance for a week or ten days. This could, and should, have been arranged.

During this period the situation in and around Leh was becoming precarious. Practically denuded of military force and consequently bereft of defence of the town and people around, this Buddhist majority area was easy prey for an invader. Rumours were already afloat of the impending attack by the raiders. Realizing the delicate situation there, 161 Infantry Brigade managed to spare and dispatch a strong platoon[13] of Lahaul-Spiti soldiers, under the command of Major Prithi Chand and Capt. Khusal Chand. This small body of troops closely followed by two platoons of the State Force, left Srinagar on February 16, 1948, and after a hazardous crossing over the Zojila Pass, reached Leh on 12th March. The task given to Major Prithi Chand was to beef up the defences of Leh and to raise, organize and train local militias. The three platoons of the State Force, now available there, were also put under his command. The local people very happily and voluntarily came forward for the training and defence of their homes. In a month's time three hundred Ladakhi Home Guards had been trained and armed to form the 7th Battalion of Jammu and Kashmir Militia with Prithi Chand as its first Commanding Officer.[14]

While this small force was busy in training locals and organizing some semblance of defensive positions around Leh, the raiders tried hard to capture Skardu fort during March and April but failed due to strong resistance put up by the defenders. After leaving sufficient men there to continue the siege of Skardu, the hostiles regrouped rest of the force and struck simultaneously at Kargil and Drass on 10th May. While a week company of the State Force at Drass was able to beat back this attack, Kargil fell into the hands of hostiles. With this, the land access to Leh was cut off. Due to new enemy advances in the region, Leh was now in a greater difficult situation, being threatened from Nubra and Khaltsi-Saspul axis simultaneously. On the latter route, the raiders ingress at its peak went as far as Taru village, less than twenty kilometers from Leh town. The only

---

13 n.6, Lt. Gen. Sen, who was then commanding this Brigade has shown the composition of this group as 40 men, including a signal detachment.

14 Prithi Chand and Khushal Chand were in fact first cousins hailing from the Lahul-Spiti area and thus had a natural affinity with the Ladakhis. Both were later decorated with MVC each, for displaying conspicuous gallantry and outstanding qualities of military leadership.

way to avoid a disaster there was to establish an air-link with Leh. But this was a risky proposition as with unpressurised aircrafts, then available with the IAF, flying and landing at such heights was neither recommended nor attempted earlier. However, with the hostiles' pressure on Leh increasing, the gamble of landing unpressurised Dakota aircraft at recently prepared Leh airfield was taken in hand. This was courageously done by two senior force commanders, who had almost become legends by then. On 24th May, Air Commodore (Baba) Meher Singh, DSO, accompanied by Maj. Gen. Thimayya, GOC, Sri Div made the historic landing there. The visit of two senior commanders and the establishment of an air link raised the morale of troops as well as of the civilians of the area. Soon airlifting of more troops started and Leh was literally brought back from the brink. Within next couple of months, the troops concentration in this area, through build up by air and moving on foot from the Manali route, reached a strength of two Battalions plus. The main task was now to push back the enemy as far as possible.

With practically knocking at the doors of Leh in the east, the raiders had by June end, after occupying Drass on 6th June, reached very near Zojila Pass; which if it went in their hands, the enemy could threaten the Valley from east. Between the attacking men and the Pass was one company of the State Force, till they were reinforced by 1 Patiala at Zojila in June itself. The excellent performance by this unit ensured that Zojila area remained the western end of the Pakistani advance there.[15] With the fall of Skardu in the middle of August that year, the primary aim of the Indian army in this sector was now to achieve a breakthrough at Zojila and establish a land link with Leh, before the onset of winter. All planning and exertions were directed towards this end. For the success of any such venture, Zojila held the key.

Earlier attempts to take this Pass having failed, the successful assault was made on November 1, 1948, with the help of tanks. For the first time, anywhere in the world, tanks were operating at a height of 11,000 feet. This time the Indian forces broke through the enemy defences, and after consolidating their position there moved on towards Drass; which was occupied on 15th November. This success was followed by taking up Kargil

---

15 1 Patiala, now 15 Punjab, was a battle hardened unit of the Second World War in the Burma campaign. By virtue of its outstanding performance during five months at Zojila, the Battalion was awarded 6 MVCs and 12 VrCs, a feat difficult to achieve by any unit.

eight days later. In the meanwhile, fruitful operations were undertaken against the hostiles by troops in and around Leh and these were met with a string of victories, driving the enemy further to west and north. The two columns of Indian troops established link up in the evening of 24th November. With this, Leh had finally been saved, though literally by skin of the teeth.

Almost simultaneously, the year-long siege of Poonch had been successfully broken with the meeting of Poonch garrison troops with those advancing from Rajouri side on the night of 19th and 20th November. The link up with Poonch was a notable success and credit for this should go to the defending troops, who valiantly withstood enemy attacks for full one year, as well as to the local population which not only extended a helping hand to the forces, but also established a shining example of brotherhood and communal amity during the crisis period. Similarly, high praise is deserved by the people of Leh and areas around for fighting shoulder to shoulder with the soldiers, as also keeping their traditions of amity and strong bonds between different communities intact. An inspiring example of peoples' participation in the defence efforts was the award of MVC to a local boy from Nubra area, C. Rinchen.[16]

Nothing else of significance happened in J&K till the declaration of cease-fire on January 1, 1949. During the fourteen months of fighting in the state, Indian forces' performance was quite creditable, particularly considering the resource constraints and handicaps. They were able to clear the Valley of the hostiles starting from the very doorsteps of Srinagar at Shaltang. The troops also achieved good success in Gurez and Tithwal sectors. Zojila-Leh axis too was restored thereby ensuring that a large tract of the Ladakh area remains in Indian hands. In Jammu region as well, Chhamb, Nowshera-Jhangar and Rajouri were successfully taken back from the enemy. Lifting of the siege of Poonch was the most notable success in this sector. However, on the debit side, Bhimber, Mirpur and Kotli still remained in Pak hands in Jammu province. In Kashmir the very important objectives of Domel and Muzaffarabad eluded till the end. In the Himalayas, the entire Gilgit region of great strategic importance, right from the confluence of Suru and Indus rivers to the farthest north, could not be liberated. The ground situation at the time was heavily in favor of

---

16 A legendry soldier in his lifetime, he retired as Lt. Col. in Jammu and Kashmir Rifles. He was also awarded a Sena Medal in 1962 and second MVC in 1971.

the Indian army and had the operations continued, the possibility of further success was strong.

During these operations, the force levels on both sides were almost at par. The Indian army strength consisted of two Infantry divisions, with 12 brigades, having 50 battalions and units of the State forces, plus 12 battalions of J&K Militia. The force build up on the Pakistan side was also to the extent of 2 divisions, 40 "Azad Kashmir" battalions. In additions, there were 4,000 irregulars of Gilgit Scouts and Chitral Scouts as well as over 15,000 tribal raiders[17].

The British complicity and active interventions to safeguard their imperial and global interests during this conflict became quite obvious. For example, "independent India's first Governor General was a British, the C-in-C of the army was a British, and the Chief of the Indian Air Force (then RIAF) also was a British. It was, probably, not realized that, notwithstanding their extra-ordinary personal qualities, these eminent men were the nationals of another country which still retained considerable, if not crucial, interests in the sub-continent. In such a set up Indian leaders could not exercise undiluted sovereign authority entrusted in their hands by the nation"[18]. Two other examples will further underline this point.

The Pakistan Army's Commander-in-Chief, Lt. Gen. Gracey presented a military appreciation to the Pakistan government in April 1948. It was an impassioned plea which would have done proud to any Pakistani national. Part of it read as, "An easy victory of the Indian Army, particularly in the Muzaffarabad area, is almost certain to arouse the anger of tribesmen against Pakistan for its failure to render them more direct assistance and might well cause them to turn against Pakistan----. If Pakistan is not to face another problem of about 2,750,000 people uprooted from their homes; if India is not to be allowed to sit on the doorsteps of Pakistan to the rear and on the flank, at liberty to enter at her will and pleasure; if civilian and military morale is not to be affected to a dangerous extent; and if subversive political forces are not to be let loose within Pakistan itself, it is imperative that the Indian Army is not allowed to advance beyond the

17 S.N. Prasad, n.5, pp 373,378.

18 Sudhir S Bloeria, "The Battles of Zojila", Haranand Publications, New Delhi-1996, p.229.

general line Uri-Poonch-Nowshera"[19]. In the hindsight, it becomes amply clear that the Indian army was deliberately not allowed to go beyond this line. The impediments in the path of an Indian advance were not only the forces of Pakistan. They were effectively assisted by an influential section of the British-Indian establishment. Also, the measure of success that Lord Mountbatten achieved in India, from the British point of view, is reflected from the kind of reception that he received on his return to England on June 23, 1948. "Both the Duke of Edinburgh and Mr. Attelee were at the airport to invest this home coming with unique distinction, for I doubt whether a royal Duke and a Prime Minister of the day have been present together before to greet a Viceroy or a Governor-General on his return"[20].

The Government of India made a formal reference to the UN on January 1, 1948, that due to the operations carried out against the Indian State of Jammu and Kashmir, by the nationals and tribesmen of Pakistan, a situation had risen which might lead to an international conflict. The Security Council was urged to request the government of Pakistan to prevent all kinds of aid being given to the raiders. The tortuous course that the proceedings of the Security Council took in this case, and the attitude of Western Powers, shattered India's faith in the United Nations as the international body dedicated to and created for the maintenance of peace all over the world. The Security Council on January 17, 1948, asked both India and Pakistan to refrain from doing or permitting any act which might aggravate the situation. A key UN resolution, on April 13, 1948, outlined a truce agreement and mentioned, "The Government of India and the Government of Pakistan reaffirm their wish that the future status of Jammu and Kashmir shall be determined in accordance with the will of the people and to that end, upon acceptance of the truce agreement, both Governments agree to enter into consultation with the Commission to determine fair and equitable conditions whereby such free expression will be assured". It also, significantly, further stated, "The Government of Pakistan will use its best endeavors to secure the withdrawal from the State of Jammu and Kashmir of tribesmen and Pakistani nationals not normally residents therein who have entered the State for the purpose of fighting...

19 Madan, n.12, p. 315. A part of this appreciation has been reproduced by him, quoting from *Defence Journal- Volume 3-4, 1992(Karachi)*, as well as Maj. Gen. (Retd) Akbar Khan in his book, "Raiders in Kashmir".

20 Alan Campbell Johnson, "Mission with Mountbatten", Robert Hale Ltd, London-1951, p. 347.

when the Commission shall have notified the Government of India that the tribesmen and Pakistani nationals referred to... have withdrawn...and further, that the Pakistani forces are being withdrawn from the State of Jammu and Kashmir, the Government of India agrees to begin to withdraw the bulk of its forces from that State in stages to be agreed upon with the Commission."

In other words, Pakistan was required completely to demilitarize its part of J&K, followed by substantial demilitarization by India. The former never happened and, therefore, neither did the latter. The UN Security Council established its Commission for India and Pakistan (UNCIP) through its Resolution of April 21, 1948, outlining a plan for ceasefire, a truce agreement and the proposed plebiscite. The Commission arrived in the sub-continent in July 1948 and appealed to both governments to refrain from taking offensive actions which might aggravate the situation. The Government of India complied with its wishes and declared that her policy would henceforth be defensive. On August 13, 1948, the Commission adopted a Resolution calling for a cease-fire. India accepted this Resolution after getting certain assurances from the Commission. Pakistan did not accept it. The UNCIP made a supplementary Resolution on December 11, 1948, with a view to bringing about Pakistan's acceptance of its earlier Resolution of 13th August. This was, later, formalized by a Resolution of January 5, 1949. Its acceptance was conveyed by Government of India on December 23 and by Pakistan on December 25, 1948. The acceptance of this Resolution by the two countries led to the cessation of hostilities on January 1, 1949. The ground situation was demarcated as the Cease-Fire Line and it was almost exactly where General Gracey had said it should be. He signed it for Pakistan and General Roy Butcher did so for India.

It is a well-determined fact that Pakistan agreed to a cease-fire only when both military as well as domestic circumstances turned unfavorable. One year of conflict had put a heavy strain on her limited financial resources which were not capable of sustaining protracted operations. Also, Jinnah had died in September 1948, considerably shaking the political stability of Pakistan. In addition, a series of important victories by Indian troops had demoralized the Pakistani forces. On the other hand, there was a marked improvement in India's military position during that period. Shortly before that, the successful police action in Hyderabad had removed a major irritant in the Indian polity. More importantly, it had also released 19 battalions which had been stationed for the Hyderabad area. These were now available for deployment in J&K. It was from that relative position of strength that India agreed to accept the cease-fire, thus bailing Pakistan out of a difficult situation.

The decision of Government of India to take the issue of J&K to the UN has been roundly criticized in India for the last over six decades. The condemnation has generally ranged from Prime Minister Nehru's inadequate grasp of high international diplomacy and lack of understanding of the functioning of UN systems; to Lord Mountbatten's undue influence over the top Indian political leadership. In any case, notwithstanding the correctness or otherwise of such faultfinding, the entire discussion on this subject can at best be of academic interest only.

In addition to getting control of a very large and strategically important territory, Pakistan learnt some very significant lessons from their first confrontation with India. Some of the important ones being:-

- Belligerence pays.

- A mix of covert and open aggression is cost-effective and gainful.

- High pitched propaganda, manipulations of the UN systems and influential friends is a very potent combination.

- India would react to aggressive actions defensively and also localize areas of conflict.

Pakistan has over the last seven decades dealt with India keeping in mind these deductions and Indian response has always been predictable. Right from 1947, through 1965 to Kargil operations in 1999 as also during the militancy of the last over two decades both parties have dealt with each other on the expected lines[21].

The geographical area of the J&K state in August 1947 was 2,22,870 square kilometers and India lost thirty-seven percent of this territory to Pakistan, including the strategically important Northern Areas of Gilgit, Chitral, Hunza etc. That these events also had very strong and substantial Anglo – American finger prints have been very competently documented

---

21 Dr. Sudhir S Bloeria, "Conflict in Jammu and Kashmir: Impact on Polity, Society and Economy", Ed – V.R. Raghavan, Vij Books India Pvt Ltd, New Delhi- 2012, pp, 16-17.

by researchers and commentators after the mid-1990s when the official records of these countries pertaining to this period became public. Partition of India was an extension of the "Great Game", orchestrated by Great Britain since the latter half of the nineteenth century. Two recently published books, both by former Indian Foreign Service officers, give graphic details of behind the scene activities and manipulations that lead to the division of this country; as also adversely influencing India's military campaign in J&K through senior British commanders heading forces of India and Pakistan and later supporting Pakistan to the hilt in the United Nations Security Council. First book was published in 2002 by C. Dasgupta titled "The War and Diplomacy in Kashmir 1947-48". The second account has been authored by Narendra Singh Sarila under the caption, "The Shadow of the Great Game-The Untold Story of India's Partition", in 2005. Both these well researched publications are based on declassified documents in UK and the USA, and unfold the roles played by Lord Mountbatten and the British service chiefs in India and Pakistan during the 1947-48 war, working in tandem with the British Joint Chiefs of Staff, diplomats and the political establishment.

The efforts of the state government, during this period were mainly concentrated on meeting the Pakistani challenge and providing all help to the Indian troops. Maharaja Hari Singh had, after signing the Instrument of Accession, appointed Sheikh Abdullah as the head of the Emergency Administration who quickly moved in to take firm control of the administrative setup and establish his writ over the state machinery. Under his leadership the National Conference cadres and people in general fully supported efforts of various army formations, particularly those operating in the Valley, making their task so much easier. The senior military commanders, in the state, had established very cordial relations with the Sheikh as also his Home Minister Bakshi Ghulam Mohammad. Both of them also became members of the National Constituent Assembly, taking part in the drafting of the Indian Constitution. However, after the hostilities on the border had come to an end and peace and normalcy restored, the Sheikh was able to devote attention to building of the political systems commensurate with the devolution of power to the people. He also found that most of the leaders of Muslim Conference, the only organized political rival of his National Conference, along with their areas of influence – Muzaffarabad, Kotli, Mirpur and Bhimber – had gone under the occupation of Pakistan. In that sense, there was no political opponent left in the arena to oppose him or his party. Thus, the ground swell of public support and political monopoly, at least in the Valley, coupled with the fact that the Prime Minister of India Jawahar Lal Nehru was his personal friend, whetted his appetite to carve out a special status for himself. He, with the active connivance of a close set of advisors – headed by Mirza Afzal Beigh – started working towards giving an autonomous character to the State. But, for this, the immediate need was to have a separate constitution for J&K. In this pursuit, the first hurdle was crossed successfully when the leaders of National Conference and central government met in New Delhi in May 1949. After discussions, it was agreed that the provisions in the constitution of India with regard to governments in states would not apply to J&K and that a constitution of J&K shall be framed by the constituent assembly of the state.

The provisions of the constitution of India, which came into force on January 26, 1950, made the accession of the state to India final. Also, in accordance with the May 1949 agreement it contained a special stipulation in the form of Article 370, to define the relationship between Centre and J&K. Therefore, in line with general understanding a proclamation was issued by the *Sadar-i-Riyasat* Yuvraj Karan Singh, on May 1, 1951, regarding J&K Constituent Assembly; which included the following, "A Constituent Assembly consisting of representatives of the people, elected on the basis of adult franchise, shall be constituted forthwith for the purpose of framing a constitution for the State of Jammu and Kashmir." In October 1951 the J&K Constituent Assembly was elected. Out of 75 Members, 73 belonged to the National Conference and were declared elected as unopposed. The dictatorial tendencies of Sheikh Abdullah so displayed started alarm bells ringing in the centre. This situation was further complicated by the statements, made inside and outside the Constituent Assembly, by Sheikh and his associates questioning the finality of accession with India and also hinting at efforts towards enlarging autonomy of the state to a much greater extent. In order to work out the outstanding issues, if any, and unambiguously define the contours of the relationship between the Centre and J&K, the NC and national leadership discussed the entire gamut in details for a period of two months in Delhi. The outcome of these parleys, known as Delhi Agreement, was announced on August 24, 1952. This way most of Sheikh Abdullah's demands were met and hesitations removed to the extent possible. But relations between him and New Delhi went on deteriorating. Also, his main support base was in Kashmir valley and not in Jammu or Ladakh. In Jammu a substantial opposition developed against him and his ways of functioning, headed by a newly formed political entity named Praja Parishad, which launched agitation against Article 370 and the Delhi Agreement. By the end of 1952, the anti Abdullah movement and sentiments had become very strong in Jammu belt. This growing agitation made the Sheikh increasingly suspicious and hostile to New Delhi and his views became ever more strident and uncompromising. In practically a last ditch effort, Nehru met Abdullah in Srinagar in May 1953 but their differences could not be reconciled. The latter's defiance came out in the open and he started even more vociferously demanding virtually an independent status for the state. The matters had almost come to a head. Under the authority of *Sadar-i-Riyast* Karan Singh, Sheikh Abdullah was removed from the position of Prime Minister of J&K and arrested during the night of August 8-9, 1953. Bakshi Ghulam Mohammad was appointed the new Prime Minister in his place. Under his charge, apart from multifarious developmental activities, the J&K constitution - over five years in the making - also came into being on January 26, 1957.

The incarceration and deposition from power came so suddenly that it virtually paralyzed political responses from the Sheikh and his associates. Bakshi, on the other hand, moved swiftly as also decisively, to get a firm hold on the state administration and suppress dissent and disturbances. He ably checked any adverse fall out as a result of this change of guard. Sheikh's lieutenant Mirza Afzal Beigh formed the Plebiscite Front (PF) on August 9, 1955, to coincide with former's arrest two years earlier. Though he never formally joined the outfit, it was generally known that the PF had the blessings of Sheikh Abdullah. In addition to demanding unconditional and early release of the Sheikh, the PF outlined its policy as being based on the premise that the accession of the state by Maharaja was temporary and provisional and its finality was conditional on the determination of the will of the people through the plebiscite. The formation of the PF and its political stance had the advantages of keeping both Sheikh and Beigh relevant in the affairs of the state; as also to ensure that a segment of public opinion, howsoever small, remained interested in this political rhetoric.

But the main beneficiary of the PF launching was certainly Pakistan. During the period of 1947-53, there were no takers for the Pakistani cause or stand in Kashmir. This development virtually came as an answer to the prayers of Pakistani rulers for a breakthrough in the state, and they were quick to cash in on the opportunity. Pak under-cover operators began frequent secret visits across the cease-fire line to establish contacts with dissident leaders of the National Conference and some emotionally charged youth, who were followers of the deposed leaders and the new outfit. Though numerically insignificant, small groups were taken across for indoctrination and training. This way the very first batch of saboteurs was organized; in a way marking the beginning of cross-border militancy in J&K.

Objectionable activities of the PF resulted in the institution of the Kashmir Conspiracy case in 1958 against Sheikh Abdullah, Mirza Afzal Beigh and others. Their release from custody in 1964 gave a new impetus to the PF activities, even though G.M. Sadiq – then at the helm of affairs in the state – admirably contained these at the political level. The two also carried out anti-India propaganda abroad which resulted in their fresh detention in May 1965. However, with the release of Sheikh Abdullah in January 1968, the activities of the PF picked up once again, including almost open attacks against India besides challenging the finality of accession. The 1974 Indira-Sheikh accord put the lid on the PF firmly and finally, as the Sheikh confirmed Indian sovereignty over Kashmir and ended demand for a plebiscite. The PF was dissolved and merged into National Conference, when Sheikh Abdullah revived the old party after coming to power in February 1975. But Pakistan was not to let go of the toe-hold she had obtained in J&K; more so after the fall of its eastern wing four years ago.

The anti-Indian activities of PF and some important personalities close to the Sheikh have been recorded by few writers and columnists. These are also mentioned in good details by B.N. Malik in his two-volume book titled "My Years with Nehru". But as, for political reasons, the cases launched in the courts against the PF and its leaders were never taken towards logical conclusion, there has been no judicial determination on this count. Therefore, all charges and accusations in the matter have remained in the realm of conjectures and speculations only.

Reverting back to the early sixties, India had suffered a humiliating setback when its army clashed with the Chinese forces, over border disputes, on the Himalayan heights in the north and east during October and November 1962. The weaknesses of Indian Armed Forces and their state of unpreparedness were exposed to the outside world. Pakistan took due notice of this development and reached out to the Chinese, in the classical fashion of enemy of the enemy being a friend. This new found friendship and diplomatic hobnob led to the 1963 agreement with China by virtue of which Pakistan ceded two percent of the J&K territory, in the Northern Sector, under its illegal possession to the former. A year later, the whole of Kashmir valley was plunged into a deep crisis by the mysterious disappearance of the Holy Relic from Hazratbal Shrine in Srinagar during the last week of December 1963. Despite being in the throes of winter and major part of the valley covered under snow, large gatherings of people took to the streets in a spontaneous mass outpouring of grief and concern over this development. Even though the Holy Relic was found eight days later and respectfully restored in the proper location, the people's reaction was misinterpreted by Pakistani policy makers as ample indication of pro-Pak feelings in the Valley and other Muslim majority areas along the cease-fire line.

Pakistan's military dictator General Ayub Khan, egged on by his acerbic Foreign Minister Z.A. Bhutto, grossly underestimated Indian military strength and national resolve to meet a crisis situation. He was ready for a fresh misadventure against India, and from his point of view, there could be no better place for starting the trouble than Kashmir. A diversionary and testing strike was made by Pakistan much further south in the Rann of Kutch, in Gujarat state, during April 1965. It was a limited engagement in which Pakistani tanks were used in this desert like terrain. Very soon a stalemate occurred and the crisis was defused through British mediation, leading to arbitration by international tribunal. The verdict of this came later in 1968, according to which Pakistan was awarded 910 square kilometers of the Rann of Kutch, as against her claim of 9100 square kilometers. Though not known to others, Pakistani rulers had, by this ingression, probably tested the ground to their satisfaction and to the extent of their requirement. General Ayub Khan and his associates decided to go ahead with their plans and designs, based on the main premise that the Indian army would not be able to defend itself against a quick military campaign in J&K. This inference rested on the twin assumptions of poor performance of the Indian army in 1962 as also a belief that trained infiltrators could mobilize a mass uprising by the Kashmiris against India.

Thus, Pakistan undertook a major effort in sending armed infiltrators across the cease-fire line, particularly in the Valley, and this endeavor was code-named "Operation Gibraltar". According to the plan envisaged, a good number of trained and armed volunteers, some of them also army personnel in civilian clothes, (called Razakaars in their parlance) were sent into across the CFL. This action was carried out by the end of July and beginning of August. These Razakaars were supposed to converge at Srinagar and mix up with the local population on 9th August, the day of Sheikh Abdullah's arrest, and to enhance the usual protest demonstrations to a major armed strife. From Pakistan's point of view, this was to serve the twin purpose of attracting international attention to the "disenchantment of Kashmiris with India" and also to create conditions in which military intervention looked justified. However, Operation Gibraltar floundered and collapsed even before it could actually take off. The Razakaars could not reach Srinagar on the appointed date as most of them were caught and neutralized by the Indian army near the Gulmarg-Tangmarg area in north Kashmir; largely based on information provided by the local people. Proving both assumptions of Pakistan as wrong, apart from lack of support from local people, the Indian army – realizing the extent and mode of this significant infiltration - moved swiftly to plug the gaps on the borders as also crossed the CFL in some areas to consolidate its position. It was in this context that the Indian forces claimed a major success by capturing the famous Haji Pir Pass, on the Uri-Poonch axis eight kilometers inside the Pak held territory, on August 28, 1965. By end of this month a sort of stalemate ensued.

Piqued by the total failure of Operation Gibraltar, and with the intention to break the impasse as also regain initiative, Pakistan launched Operation Grand Slam, on 1st September. With this, the gloves were off and regular combat between two armies began, the initial advantage being with Pakistan the initiator. That afternoon the entire Chhamb area in Jammu sector came under heavy artillery shelling as the surprised Indian forces there were attacked with an overwhelming ratio of troops and tanks. The Pakistanis were aiming at making a breakthrough in this sector, capture the strategic town of Akhnoor and thus cut off the only land route to the entire Rajouri-Poonch area, threatening Indian army's flank and the sole supply route there. Notwithstanding almost desperate resistance by the surprised and outnumbered Indian troops, Pakistan made a breakthrough and rapid advance initially. India resorted to air strikes to blunt and stop the enemy advance. Pakistan responded by calling its air force also to join the combat and a full scale war ensued. For some inexplicable reasons and in spite of progress being made in this sector, the Pakistani high command replaced the GOC of its forces Maj. Gen Akhtar Hussain Malik with General Yahya Khan and this change over adversely affected the momentum and edge of the Pakistani attack. Coupled with this factor; effective employment of the IAF as also regrouping of Indian forces the Pakistani advance was effectively stymied.

To Pakistan's utter surprise and against all her calculations, India crossed the International Border on the Western Front on September 6 forcing Pakistan to switch resources from and reduce the pressure in Akhnoor area. With her inability to capture Akhnoor, Operation Grand Slam had practically failed. The initial Indian advance in the Western Sector took the troops across the well prepared defensive positions on the Icchogil canal to right up to the doorsteps of Lahore. To relieve pressure in this area Pakistan attacked at Khem Karan. Now the two countries were engaged in some very heavy fighting, in an all-out struggle involving all three wings of the armed forces. A very heavy tank battle took place around Khem Karan where Pakistani armor, based on the famous American Patton tanks, was badly mauled by the Indian defenders around 10th of September. Pakistanis lost about 97 tanks as against 32 Indian tanks. This effectively put a stop to the claims of superior tank force by the Pakistani side. The same story was repeated when the diminutive IAF Gnats worsted technically more sophisticated F-86 Sabres and F-104 Starfighters of the PAF.

By the time cease-fire, mandated by the UN and actively backed by the US and Soviet Union, became effective on September 23, 1965; the war had almost reached a stalemate with both forces holding the territory of each other. According to independent sources, Indian army suffered 3,000 deaths while the figure of Pakistani casualties was 3,800; as against over 1900 square kilometers of the enemy territory occupied by Indian forces, the Pak army controlled around 550 square kilometers of Indian soil. This armed conflict which beyond any doubt was started by Pakistan, was to have long-term impact on the polity, economy and in fact, the very future of Pakistan. Both Operation Gibraltar and Operation Grand Slam had miserably failed to achieve their respective goals and targets, and blame for this serious setback was squarely laid, at the doorsteps of the Pakistani dictator General Ayub Khan. He had in the first place conceived the plan and then gone on to flesh out the strategy and working details to put the whole concept on ground in operational terms.

Any objective assessment of the 1965 War should take into consideration the fact that there is no official history of this confrontation made public by either of the countries. On the Indian side, a draft historical perspective was prepared by the Historical Division of the Ministry of Defence, reportedly way back in 1992, but the same has not been officially released due to lack of the mandatory security clearance. Therefore, recourse has to be taken to unbiased international agency reports and credible reminiscences of senior commanders who took part in these operations. The force mobilization of both countries was almost of matching levels, with Pakistan having a slight edge in quantity as well as the quality of the tanks and guns it had been able to deploy and use against India. Most of the major battles were fought by the infantry and armored units in J&K and along the western borders, with air force and naval resources employed in supportive and subsidiary roles. Many details, though, for want of authentic records remain unclear. But one thing is certain that the seventeen-day war witnessed the largest tank battle since the Second World War. Also, despite the effective cease-fire rendering this confrontation inconclusive, both India and Pakistan claimed victory- though former with greater conviction. Most neutral assessments too have reached the conclusion that India had an upper hand when the cease-fire was declared. Also, generally this conflict is seen as the strategic and political defeat for Pakistan as it had neither succeeded in fomenting insurrection in Kashmir nor been able to garner meaningful support at international level.

The international powers saw this war more through the prism of contemporary Cold War paradigm, rather than the impact it had on either of the countries or the correctness of their respective stand. The end of hostilities also brought in its wake geo-political shifts in the sub-continent, with Pakistan leaning towards China more than ever before and India getting firmly closer to Soviet Russia.

In the ultimate analysis India had more reasons to celebrate and the Indian Prime Minister, Lal Bahadur Shastri, was hailed as a national hero in the country. Correspondingly, not only General Ayub Khan was blamed for the failure of the nation's plans, the war also resulted in wide-scale economic slowdown in Pakistan, virtually ending its impressive economic growth since the early 1960s. As per independent sources the war greatly cost Pakistan economically, militarily and politically. It also triggered a more intense arms race in the sub-continent, with India progressively gaining a greater edge over Pakistan in terms of conventional war fighting capabilities. In that sense 1965 war saw the last of Pak ambitions of arms parity with, as also self-acclaimed military superiority over, India.

As a sidelight, some details have recently come in print regarding the presence and activities of Pak trained and inducted armed guerrillas (Razakaars in Pakistani parlance) in the Rajouri-Poonch sector – south of Pir Panjal range – of J&K. The account which has been penned by a well known writer, and one with close knowledge of the ground realities, states in parts, "The ceasefire line, as drawn in 1948, was porous and hence not only crossing of the line but coming in, going out and staying on for longer times, getting married, settling property issues was nothing unusual.... The Razakaars were already in Rajouri and Poonch as early as June 1965.... As armed Razakaars spread out across the region, the minority Hindu population rushed towards the townships sensing imminent trouble. Razakaars with the support of locals had total control of the administration; at many places, they had their own tehsildars and thanedars (the Police Station House officers) 'appointed' and the government officials 'terminated'.... A number of living witnesses recall the hovering of Pakistani helicopters and airdropping of ammunition and ration at many places.... With this air prevailing across the region, the locals had no idea of how an India-Pakistan war was shaping up along the borders. As it happens in situations like this, not many locals knew the exact motive and plans of the Razakaars and not many Razakaars were in knowledge of the next step proposed by Pakistan. The eruption of war in the month of September, however, spoilt the party.... As people look at the history they try to connect some dots to understand that why somewhere in early September 1965 the whole lot of Razakaars pulled out leaving their local supporters in lurch and the 'new administration' directionless.... the fact that over 80,000 people from Rajouri and Poonch fled to Pakistan administered Kashmir during this operation explains a lot. Nearly half of them returned after the Tashkent agreement to tell the stories that Pakistan was less than kind to welcome the refugees instead of the desired territorial gains"[22].

---

22 Zafar Choudhary, "The Unwritten Story of 1965 War", in Rising Kashmir, Srinagar, dated August 14, 2015.

Following the Tashkent agreement almost four months after the ceasefire declaration on September 23, 1965, and thereby India agreeing to the *status quo*, including vacation of the important Haji Pir Pass, there was a wave of consternation in India. But, this sense of disillusionment turned into a national mourning when the Prime Minister Lal Bahadur Shastri died while still in Tashkent itself. His dead body arrived in India in the midst of a grieving people. In Pakistan it took a few months for the population to realize the true performance of Pakistan army; that she had lost more territory to India than gained in the conflict and that the military also failed to make even a single critical break-through in the war. The whole concept of invincibility, so assiduously built there, of Pak army lay in shambles. General Ayub Khan faced rising civilian discontent, headed by his erstwhile Foreign Minister Bhutto, who left the government to start his own political outfit named as the Pakistan People's Party (PPP). Ayub Khan, unable to meet the rising wave of disaffection, handed over the reins of power to his protégé, the Army Chief, General Yahya Khan in March 1969. That the latter would be even a greater disaster for his country was not yet known.

Yahya Khan, like his predecessor, began to rule with an iron hand but soon found that he could not control the rising tide of civil strife. What followed is best explained in the words of a leading Pakistani intellectual and writer, "The Yahya military regime, unable to quell the mass upheaval in both parts of the country, was forced to promise a general election on the basis of adult franchise. Its advisers evidently believed it could concede this as a diversionary tactic.... which were finally held in December 1970, the Awami League was given a free hand and won a tidal victory. Of the 169 seats allotted to East Pakistan in the National Assembly, the League won 167. Its bloc in the National Assembly (a House of 313 seats) gave it an overall majority throughout the country and entitled it to form the central government. Such a prospect traumatized the West Pakistan ruling oligarchy.... it was clear that the army would try to prevent a meeting of the National Assembly. In this, they were greatly helped, if not led, by Zulfiqar Ali Bhutto, who refused to countenance a Pakistani government led by the majority party. Bhutto's Pakistan People's Party had triumphed in the western portion of the country and should have negotiated a settlement with the victors. Instead, Bhutto sulked and told his party to boycott a meeting of the new parliament that had been called in Dhaka, the capital of East Pakistan, and thus provided the army with breathing space to prepare a military assault.... This made a split inevitable; Bengal now went into noncooperation mode.... Even before the formal invasion took place on March 25, 1971, hundreds of Bengali lives had been lost at the hands of what was seen as an oppressor army dispatched by West Pakistan.... Operation Searchlight was brutal but ineffective. Killing students and intellectuals did not lead to the quick and clear victory sought by the Pakistani generals.... All this was taking place while most pro-Yahya Western governments averted their eyes and hoped for the best. As the news of offensive spread, the predominantly Bengali East Pakistan Rifles mutinied"[23].

The events started moving fast from the beginning of March 1971, a kind of inexorable march of deteriorating situations ultimately leading to the break- up of Pakistan. The Pakistan army cracked down on Dhaka on the night of 25th March. The Awami League bore the major brunt and many of its prominent leaders fled to India and sought refuge there. Sheikh Mujib-ur-Rahman, the Bangla leader was arrested and taken to West Pakistan. The next day independence of Bangladesh was declared on behalf of Mujib. The army launched Operation Searchlight in an attempt to kill the intellectual elite of the eastern wing. In the mayhem let loose by the army it is estimated that around two million civilians were killed, wounded or maimed; many thousand women raped and eight to ten million people fled in panic to seek refuge in neighboring India; which opened its borders to allow refugees a safe shelter. The governments of Assam, Bihar, Meghalaya, Tripura and West Bengal established refugee camps along the border. This flood of refugees put a further intolerable weight on India's already strained economy. When repeated requests to international community failed to elicit a reasonable response, the Indian Prime Minister Indira Gandhi concluded that it may be economical, in the long run, and perhaps more sensible to go to war against Pakistan. By the end of April 1971, she asked the Indian army chief, General Manekshaw if he was ready to take on Pakistan. The latter refused to go to war immediately and asked for few months more time to plan and prepare; and also said he could guarantee success if she allowed him to prepare for and fight the war on his terms and at a time of his choosing. To these stipulations, she agreed and the Indian army started preparing for the impending armed conflict under the leadership of General Manekshaw. The main Indian objective in the eastern sector was to capture Dhaka as early in the war as possible and on the western front to prevent Pakistani ingress on the Indian side.

---

23 Tariq Ali, "The Duel", Simon & Shuster UK Ltd, London- 2008, pp. 77,78 and 83.

By November the war seemed inevitable. During one of his talks to the frontline troops in Fazilka, in the western sector, Manekshaw said in his typical style that he had only two messages for the 'boys' going to face an imminent war soon; one was to deny any ingress to the enemy and second direction was a very stern warning not to misbehave with any woman across the border. He said he would not forgive any misconduct on this count. These directions went down the line in clear and crisp terms. On 23rd November Yahya Khan declared a state of emergency in Pakistan and urged his people to be prepared for war. On the evening of 3rd December at about dusk time, the PAF launched pre-emptive strikes over eleven airfields in north-west India. The IAF responded by hitting Pakistani targets the same night. The India – Pakistan War of 1971 had started.

This war lasted for thirteen days, one of the shortest armed clashes between two countries. During this period, Indian and Pakistani military – all the three wings of army, navy and air force – fought on the eastern and western fronts. The Indian forces were able to achieve their primary objective of reaching Dhaka in a short time – by 15th December - by continuous fighting and manoeuvres which reflected dash, innovation and a capacity to break-through for greater success in a blitzkrieg manner. Nothing went wrong for it in the eastern sector. Over six months planning and preparations paid handsome dividends in successful and well-coordinated land, sea and air operations. The conflict ended after the Eastern Command of Pakistan army signed the Instrument of Surrender in Dhaka on December 16, 1971, confirming the birth of a new nation of Bangladesh. It was a momentous and historic occasion; and India was first to officially recognize the new country on December 6, 1971. The guns also fell silent on the western front at 8 p.m. on the 16th. In this conflict over ninety thousand Pakistani troops were taken as Prisoners of War (PoW) by the Indian army.

Calendar of important events leading to the birth of Bangladesh had been as follows:-

- March 7, 1971 – Sheikh Mujib-ur-Rahman declared in a massive public rally in Dhaka, "The current struggle is a struggle for independence".

- March 25, 1971 – Pakistani forces launched Operation Searchlight, a systematic plan aimed to eliminate all resistance.

- March 26, 1971 – Declaration of Independence announced, on behalf of Mujib, from Kalurghat Radio Station, Chittagong.

- April 17, 1971 – Exiled leaders of Awami League, located in India, announced the formation of a provisional government.

- December 3, 1971 – War between India and Pakistan officially began.

- December 6, 1971 – East Pakistan recognized as the independent nation of Bangladesh by India.

- December 16, 1971 – Lt. Gen. A.A.K. Niazi, supreme commander of the Pakistani army in East Pakistan, surrendered to the allied forces of India and Bangladesh in Dhaka. India and Bangladesh gained a historic victory.

- January 12, 1972 – Sheikh Mujib-ur-Rahman assumed power in Bangladesh as the first popular Prime Minister.

It would be useful to briefly look at the roles played by major world powers interested in the developments of this region. The Soviet Union had quite early, during the emerging of a crisis situation, realized that an independent Bangladesh would weaken in this region the traditional rivals of US and China. It, therefore, supported India as also the cause of Bangladesh and provided all help to the Indian forces and the Mukti Bahini during the war. In the Indo-Soviet Treaty of Friendship and Cooperation signed in August 1971, an assurance was held that the Soviet Union would undertake effective measures in case of armed threat to India by US or China. This clear stand was widely welcomed by the Indian people and also boosted the morale of her forces.

The US supported Pakistan politically and materially throughout 1971; even turning a blind eye to the atrocities committed by her formal ally in East Pakistan. Both President Nixon and his Secretary of State Kissinger steadfastly backed Pakistan right till the very end of the emerging critical situation. They needed Pakistan also for the good terms she had established with China, which Nixon wanted to visit in February 1972 as a part of his *rapprochement* policy. Nixon also, famously, sent an American Task Force led by the aircraft carrier USS *Enterprise* into the Bay of Bengal in the middle of the war. The strong and unyielding attitude of India, ably supported by the naval elements of USSR, effectively neutralized this move. As a strong ally of Pakistan and also due to an adversarial relationship with India; China kept a worried and wary eye on the developing situation in this region. However, despite American encouragements and proddings China did not mobilize forces along the Indian borders and only actively supported demands for an immediate ceasefire after the war broke out.

In this war, Pakistan literally painted herself into a corner diplomatically, politically as also militarily. With the loss of more than half of her population in the eastern wing to a new country and almost one-third of her army in captivity; it was a complete and humiliating defeat for Pakistan. Due to the state-controlled propaganda which had been painting a rosy picture, the defeat and setback came as a rude shock to the Pakistani public. Unable to control the erupting situation, General Yahya Khan surrendered power to Bhutto. The latter was sworn-in as President and the first civilian Chief Martial Law Administrator on December 20, 1971, of the new and smaller Pakistan. The loss of eastern wing also disproved the two-nation theory which was the very basis of the creation of Pakistan; as merely the Islamic bond had failed to keep the two wings together. It shattered the prestige of Pakistani military – which was partly redeemed by Bhutto deploying the army to manage Balochistan situation 2-3 years later – and according to international observers, it also lost a third of its army, half its navy and a quarter of the air force. With a view to investigating the political and military causes for defeat Pakistan government, under Bhutto, had constituted Hamoodur Rahman Commission, but as expected its report did not see the light of the day.

More than thirty years later, a leading Pakistani Daily prominently analyzed the causes for this breakup and it would be worthwhile to quote it in some detail. The write-up mentioned, "We routinely discuss the tragedy of the separation of East Pakistan in December 1971, but it is only this year that some of us have told the truth about what happened. Appearing on private TV channels, Mr. Mehmood Ali held the martial law of 1958 responsible for what later transpired.... General (Retd) Zaidi accused West Pakistan of evolving a military strategy that pretended to defend East Pakistan by building up the military defences of only West Pakistan. General (Retd) Farman Ali accepted as true the Bengali accusation that most of the foreign exchange earned in East Pakistan was spent in West Pakistan. Raja Tridev Roy stated that West Pakistan ignored the linguistic nature of Bengali nationalism in East Pakistan and tried to impose Urdu there.... However, the latest version, an even more significant one, has come to light with the publication of historian K.K. Aziz's book 'World Powers and 1971 Break-up of Pakistan'. The following facts extracted from the history of the Pakistan Movement raise the question whether or not East Bengal should have joined West Pakistan in the first place.... The Aligarh movement set up Urdu as the language of all Muslims of India, ignoring the fully developed Bengali language in which the Muslims of that part of India expressed themselves. Most northern Indian Muslims thought Bengali a Hindu language. But the real bias against the Bengalis came to the fore when the Muslims went to meet the viceroy in a delegation in 1906, later to be known as Simla Delegation. The delegation was 35 strong with only five members from Bengal. Out of the five, three were actually not from Bengal, and of the remaining, one was Urdu-speaking, which left only one Bengali to represent Muslim majority Bengal.... Finally, when in 1946 the Muslim League decided to join the Interim government in Delhi it sent five men to the Viceroy's Council. The Bengali member it chose was a Hindu from the non-scheduled castes! No wonder therefore that East Pakistan opted out in 1971 by calling in India and thus rejecting the two-nation theory"[24]. Also in a similar vein, Tariq Ali has opined, "The majority view in Punjab was that drunk and incompetent generals combined with an Indian military intervention had lost them Pakistan. As I have argued, this was a simplistic and chauvinist view that ignored the structural exploitation of East Bengal by a predominantly West Pakistan-based elite"[25].

While Zulfiqar Ali Bhutto, now firmly in power in Pakistan, was trying to come to terms with the new realities and manage the civil unrest, the Simla Agreement which Indian Prime Minister Indira Gandhi signed with him in Simla on July 2, 1972, came to his as also Pakistan's rescue. It stabilized the new and diminished Pakistan and established the credibility of Bhutto. Also by releasing all the PoWs, in batches by end of the year, the strength of Pak army was virtually restored, and it started rebuilding of the military capabilities once again. The army also gained some of the lost prestige when the new government deployed troops in Balochistan to contain upheavals there two years later. Realizing the potential of newly rich Arab countries, Bhutto reached out to them and firmly established stronger ties with these cash-rich nations in the West Asia, particularly

---

24 Editorial titled, Talking About 'Fall of Dhaka', in Daily Times dated, December 18, 2003.

25 Tariq Ali, n-23, p. 105.

with Saudi Arabia and Libya. King Faisal and Col. Gadaffi became almost household names in Pakistan. Shifting the moorings of Pakistan from the sub-continent to the West Asia, as also its long-term consequences, did not bother him. The rich cultural heritage of pre-Islamic era there coming in conflict with the projections of a theocratic state also did not seem to worry him. This alliance brought in its wake problematic issues like fundamentalism, sectarianism, religious exclusivism and then terrorism also. All these later day troubling matters had their roots to this period. However, liberal financial help from this region did stabilize the economy and also helped Bhutto to pursue his nuclear dreams more determinedly – this despite serious American misgivings. Bhutto was so enamored of acquiring the nuclear status for Pakistan that he famously spoke of "eating grass" for this purpose; and cleverly started calling this favorite project as the Islamic Bomb. This, he reckoned would also involve a number of other countries and, more importantly, provide Pakistan with much greater financial resources.

Bhutto also gave 1973 constitution to the country and thought all these measures had increased his popularity amongst the people of Pakistan. But, in fact, he was only becoming increasingly unpopular for various reasons; mostly due to his personal and arrogant conduct. He also failed to address the structural weaknesses of Pakistan's social and economic milieu. This was to cost him dearly. Bhutto called for general elections in early 1977 under the new constitution. Even though his PPP won these elections, the opposition parties which had formed a joint front against PPP; called Pakistan National Alliance (PNA), alleged that the elections were rigged and did not accept the results. The opposition group also boycotted the provincial elections and declared the central government headed by Bhutto as illegitimate; launching a nationwide agitation as also demanding the overthrow of his regime. This agitation soon gained momentum and became widespread by the month of April. In this rising civil disorder, the army stepped in, assumed power once again, and declared martial law on July 5, 1977, with the COAS General Zia-ul-Haq becoming the new ruler of Pakistan as the Chief Martial Law Administrator. Some political analysts believe that the army struck just as Bhutto had arrived at a compromise with the opposition parties and before the new formula could be announced.

When Bhutto made Zia the army chief on March 1, 1976, he least expected the latter to turn against him. He had so carefully chosen the person for this prestigious appointment that Zia superseded seven Lt. Generals senior to him. Bhutto surely must have rued this decision later. He was first incarcerated and later tried by Supreme Court on the charge of complicity in the murder of a political opponent. Both his trial and execution, less than two years later, became controversial matters. These did not seem to bother Zia, who became President of Pakistan in 1978 and ruled the country in that capacity for ten years, till his demise in August 1988.

Two developments on the borders of Pakistan helped Zia to firm up his regime with the American help. The first was communist backed *Saur revolution* in April 1978 in Afghanistan which in its wake brought the Soviet military in the country next year. Also in February 1979 the long time American ally, Shah of Iran – on western borders of Pakistan – was deposed by an *Islamic revolution* there. Both these occurrences greatly perturbed the Americans and by implications strengthened Zia's rule; as the US wanted a stable Pakistan at any cost. Pakistan had become a frontline state for American designs, particularly in relation to Afghanistan. Details of the subsequent years have been described very well by Steve Coll in his famous book *Ghost Wars*. General Zia understood his role well in these situations and made full use of almost unlimited, and also unaccounted, flow of funds and weapons from America. The latter, in turn, looked the other way regarding Pakistan's developing nuclear programme and steady rise of terrorism in the country. It also did not object to the export of terror culture, and infiltration of armed militants, by Pakistan to India – first in Punjab and later to J&K. The Americans always felt happy and grateful that Pakistan was fighting their proxy war in Afghanistan. In fact, Zia had exported his own brand of this proxy war to India. Pakistan's deep involvement in spreading terror across its eastern and western borders spawned a multi-national brand of armed militancy; also giving rise to suicide charges and assaults. Out of his own acute religious beliefs and also driven by the compulsion of continuing his hold over a volatile internal situation, Zia actively encouraged the creation and spread of fundamentalist and sectarian organizations within Pakistan and later outside the country also. The international terrorism was to singe the Americans, in their own country, over two decades later.

The ISI chiefs and officers, during this period, dutifully remembered Zia's famous dictum, "The water in Afghanistan must be made to boil at the right temperature". The ISI also learnt important lessons from its association with the American CIA; particularly about the concept of deniability and creating multiple organizations to fight for the same cause; as also the need to keep them on a tight leash and under effective control. The current militancy in J&K which began in September 1988 was an improved version of the Pakistani attempts in 1947 and 1965, refined with the experience gained and lessons learnt by the ISI from its involvement first in Afghanistan and later in Punjab. "A blueprint of activities was prepared and set into motion by the beginning of 1988. This aimed at creating and spawning disturbances in the state by misleading the youth, appealing to the Muslim sentiments of the population; further expanding magnitude of activities and enlarging the base of sympathizers which had been started well in advance and to begin insurgency by armed militants, trained and provided with arms and explosives by Pakistan. The third attempt to annex and appropriate the state of Jammu and Kashmir had commenced; by far the most sinister and cunning"[26].

General Zia was killed on August 17, 1988, in an air crash in Pakistan but before his death, this soft-spoken and apparently mild-mannered Pakistani dictator had created huge problems for India in the form of Siachen crisis, the insurgency in Punjab followed by the spread of militancy and fundamentalism in J&K. His massively bleak legacy in Pakistan – in the spread of fundamentalism, sectarianism and terrorism - has been no less dangerous. The shock effects are still being felt there even almost four decades after the man ceased to exist.

It is not that sincere efforts were not made to bring lasting peace between India and Pakistan by either country. Right thinking and well-meaning people on both sides of the border have been making efforts in this direction from 1949 onwards; in fact, soon after the guns fell silent on both sides in J&K after the first Indo-Pak war.

---

26 Sudhir S. Bloeria, "Pakistan's Insurgency Vs India's Security", Manas Publications, New Delhi-2000, p. 94.

CHAPTER - II

EARLY EFFORTS

Many scholars and observers of the Indian sub-continent feel that under the influence of Lord Mountbatten – who was also probably motivated by a desire to safeguard the British Imperial interests – the Government of India made a formal reference to the United Nations on January 1, 1948; in that it informed the world body about Pakistani aggression. A mention was made that due to the operations carried out against the Indian State of Jammu and Kashmir, by the nationals and tribesmen of Pakistan, a situation had arisen which might lead to an international conflict. The matter was referred under Article 35 of the UN Charter for taking measures which could resolve and end the dangerous situation; and the Security Council was urged to impress upon Pakistan to end all kind of support to the raiders and end the hostilities. It is another matter that India's faith in the United Nations as the international body dedicated to and created for the maintenance of peace all over the world, turned out to be misplaced.

The first act of importance by the UN was to call upon both countries to show restraint and work towards diffusing the situation and also to appoint a five-member United Nations Commission for India and Pakistan (UNCIP). It comprised representatives from Argentina, Belgium, Columbia, Czechoslovakia and the United States. The UNCIP was headed by the Czech delegate named Josef Korbel[1]. The Commission made a

---

1   Josef Korbel (1909-1977) was then serving as a diplomat in the government of Czechoslovakia. He later sought political asylum in the US and became well known as a teacher and author of Diplomacy and International Relations. His daughter Madeleine Albright became the first female Secretary of State of U.S.A. in 1997. Also, one of his students, Condoleezza Rice was the first woman to be made the US, National Security Advisor in 2001 and four years later as the Secretary of State there.

visit to Pakistan and India during July that year with a view to getting the first-hand feel of the situation in the sub-continent as well as the ground situation. Based on its impressions of the prevailing conditions, and also after holding discussions with both the countries, it adopted a three-part resolution unanimously on August 13, 1948. This is, essentially, what Pakistan has been referring to as the "UN Resolution" for over the past six decades.

Part I of this Resolution dealt with ceasefire and cessation of hostilities. It mentioned, in part, "The Governments of India and Pakistan agree that their respective High Commands will issue separately and simultaneously a cease-fire order to apply to all forces under their control and in the State of Jammu and Kashmir as of the earliest practicable date or dates to be mutually agreed upon within four days after these proposals have been accepted by both Governments". Part II asked for the complete withdrawal of Pakistani forces, following which India was expected to thin out the bulk of its forces and keep only those required for maintaining law and order. This portion, in parts, read "As the presence of troops of Pakistan in the territory of the State of Jammu and Kashmir constitutes a material change in the situation…., the Government of Pakistan agrees to withdraw its troops from that State…. The Government of Pakistan will use its best endeavour to secure the withdrawal from the State of Jammu and Kashmir of tribesmen and Pakistani nationals not normally resident therein who have entered the State for the purpose of fighting…. Pending a final solution, the territory evacuated by the Pakistani troops will be administered by the local authorities under the surveillance of the Commission…. Pending the acceptance of the conditions for a final settlement of the situation in the State of Jammu and Kashmir, the Indian Government will maintain within the lines existing at the moment of the cease-fire the minimum strength of its forces which in agreement with the Commission are considered necessary to assist local authorities in the observance of law and order….". Part III of the Resolution mentioned, "The Government of India and the Government of Pakistan reaffirm their wish that the future status of the State of Jammu and Kashmir shall be determined in accordance with the will of the people and to that end, upon acceptance of the truce agreement, both Governments agree to enter into consultations with the Commission to determine fair and equitable conditions whereby such free expression will be assured". The composition and structure of the Resolution is significant as it implicitly recognized the Pakistani aggression and also the word "plebiscite" is not mentioned anywhere.

India accepted this Resolution, after getting certain assurances from the Commission; but Pakistan did not do so and put forward a number qualifications and reservations which almost meant rejection of the proposals. Keeping in view Pakistani reservations, the Commission further discussed the contours of its proposals with the two Governments and made a supplementary Resolution on December 11, 1948. This was later formalized by a Resolution of January 5, 1949. India conveyed acceptance of this Resolution on December 23, 1948, with Pakistan following suit two days later on 25th December. The acceptance of this Resolution by both countries led to the secession of hostilities on January 1, 1949. The ground situation was demarcated as the Cease-Fire Line; which continued to exist until it was replaced by the Line of Control (LoC), after the Indo-Pak war of 1971. Felt encouraged by these developments, the Commission returned to the sub-continent in February 1949 to further implement the terms of the Resolution. But, it failed to make much headway, primarily because of Pakistan's refusal to vacate the territory under its control and to withdraw men and forces from there. Korbel, later mentioned in his reminiscences that the Commission faced "enormous difficulties". By December that year, the Commission declared its failure and submitted a final report to the Security Council. That was practically the end of effective UN efforts in J&K; even though lengthy, meaningless and desultory debates on this issue continued for many years thereafter in the UN.

It is interesting to note that Sir Owen Dixon of Australia - a name other than Josef Korbel which is generally associated with UN initiatives on J&K - who succeeded the Commission as the United Nation's Representative for India and Pakistan, had this to say about Pakistani aggression against India, "When the frontiers of the State of Jammu and Kashmir were crossed by the Hostile elements, it was contrary to the international law and when in May 1948 units of the regular Pakistani forces moved into the territory of the State, that too was inconsistent with the international law"[2].

A well known local political analyst and insightful observer of the developments in the State had expressed this opinion about the cease-fire line, "The cease-fire line in the Kashmir region follows a well- defined

---

2 *Kashmir and UN*, Government of India Publication, New Delhi 1957, p.6.

ethnic and cultural divide between Kashmiri and non-Kashmiri people. In the Pakistan-held part of the State, the people cannot be culturally identified as Kashmiris. So, Azad Kashmir and Pakistan Occupied Kashmir (PoK) as it is called by the Pakistanis and Indians respectively are both misnomers. If we bear in mind the fact that the major thrust of Indian policy was to build up sentiments of Kashmiri patriotism as the most viable bulwark against the appeal of Pakistan, the cease-fire line would seem to serve its purpose. It consolidated and crystallized Kashmiri identity, and put it in a dominant position in the State while protecting it from the influence or the challenge of a community which had close ethnic and cultural affinities with Punjabi Muslims and hence with Pakistan.... India has rarely made a serious claim or effort to liberate the Pakistani-held part of the State. The National Conference leadership was not greatly enthusiastic about getting back an area which had always been hostile to it in the past. In any case, the loss of PoK territory was the price India had to pay for the inordinate delay in settling the question of accession"[3].

The tortuous course that the proceedings of the Security Council took in this case; successful attempts by the Pakistanis to obfuscate the main issue of their having committed an aggression, and the attitude of the Western Powers utilizing this opportunity to their advantage in the overall strategy of cold war scenario is all well known and documented. In this context, a logical and valid question arises as to what was the necessity and compulsive circumstances which influenced the Government of India to knock at the doors of the United Nations in the first instance. Various academicians and analysts have attempted to provide an answer to this enigmatic puzzle; and the following two are part of a host of this category.

The official history of the war, from the Indian side, mentions this towards the end, "The enemy could not be beaten decisively by local action within the boundaries of J&K. For decisive victory it was necessary to bring Pakistan to battle on the broad plains of Punjab itself; the battle of J&K, in the last analysis, had to be fought and won at Lahore and Sialkot, as events brought home in 1965. So, if the whole of J&K had to be liberated from the enemy, a general war against Pakistan was necessary. There can be hardly any doubt that Pakistan could be decisively defeated in a general war in 1948-49, although both the Indian and the Pakistan armies were

---

3   Balraj Puri, *Kashmir Towards Insurgency*, Orient Longman Limited, New Delhi, 1993, p.17.

in the throes of partition and reorganization then. But that was a much wider question, and rightly or wrongly, the government did not decide to have a general war with Pakistan. Nehru, the apostle of peace, must have hoped that Pakistan's aggression on Kashmir would prove a temporary aberration; that all enemy forces would be peacefully withdrawn from the State under the impartial advice of the UN, and that India and Pakistan would live ever afterward as close and friendly neighbours. It was a vision worth pursuing, even though it finally proved a mere illusion"[4].

In somewhat similar vein, a former Indian diplomat has opined, "India too has been living in hope that somehow it will be able to get the bilateral relations on a consistent and peaceful track. In that pursuit, Nehru remained an incorrigible idealist till the very end. He was certainly conscious of the realities of Pakistan, but his public posture and his policies were rooted in the hope that aspiration might somehow triumph over experience. Unfortunately, that was not to be. His idealistic belief that there should be no reason for a long-lasting quarrel between two brothers led him to refer the Kashmir issue to the UN, a mistaken step that was both unnecessary and unwarranted; a step that succeeding generations of Indians are ruing and paying a price for every day, in terms of life and capital resources"[5].

In spite of the crisis in J&K and the huge communal migration and conflagration triggered by the partition, Nehru, as the Prime Minister of India, and his colleagues concentrated on the process of nation-building; drafting and adopting a constitution for the country, integration of princely states as well as deepening the roots of democracy. They all also wished well for the neighboring Pakistan, even though the latter had practically trashed the UN Resolution on the peaceful solution to the Kashmir issue. In this quest, Nehru reached out to the important political personalities in the U.K., the U.S. and even his Pakistani counterpart, Liaquat Ali Khan. With the last, he seemed to have struck a chord. One of the earliest acts of cooperation between the two countries was the understanding reached amongst these personalities on the issues relating to minorities; and this compact was mentioned as the Nehru- Liaquat Pact of 1950.

---

4   S.N. Prasad, Dharam Pal, *History of Operations in Jammu & Kashmir,* History Division- Ministry of Defence, Government of India, New Delhi, 1987, p. 375.

5   Ambassador Rajiv Dogra, *India and the World,* Wisdom Tree, New Delhi, 2015, p. 96.

The communal riots which had broken out in the two countries, at the time of independence, had a huge impact on the status of minorities left behind in both nations. Even after the partition and migration, almost half of the Muslims living in the sub-continent remained in India and not insubstantial number of Hindus stayed in the two parts of Pakistan. Both communities had initial problems of settling peacefully and looking forward to an assured and bright future in their respective regions; in addition to being apprehensive about showing their loyalties to the new nations. In fact during the course of 1949, when it became almost clear that the problem of J&K had become a causality to the ongoing cold war without any chance of peaceful settlement of this imbroglio; the simmering issue of the status and condition of minorities came to the forefront as another major point of contention between the two nations. Indo-Pak ties were already strained and for some time it appeared that this matter may also reach a flash point, sooner than later. It was at such a delicate juncture that Liaquat Ali Khan issued a statement in Pakistan emphasizing the need for communal harmony and proposed a meeting with his Indian counterpart to work out ways and means to avoid flare-ups and the fear of war; as also ensure harmony amongst all communities in the respective countries. India responded positively and the two leaders met in New Delhi on 2nd April. The parleys were held in a cordial environment and lasted for six long days, mainly concentrating on allowing the refugees to return to dispose of their property, returning of abducted women and looted property, not recognizing forced conversions and giving legal cover to minority rights. On April 8, 1950, the two Prime Ministers signed an agreement, generally known as the Nehru – Liaquat pact of 1950. It was almost like a proclamation of rights for the minorities in India and Pakistan which primarily aimed at alleviating the fears of religious minorities and undertaking effective measures to promote communal harmony. Both countries also agreed to ensure equality of citizenship to the minorities as well as security in respect of life, property and personal honour. To effectively put all these measures into practice, it was also agreed to set up Minority Commissions in the respective countries. In addition to the fact that this pact was generally recognized as a good beginning to better relations between India and Pakistan; it was also speculated that during the course of their six-day long confabulations, issues other than those affecting the minorities' interests were also discussed. It would be more than mere conjecture to presume that other thorny matters were also put on the table and deliberated upon in a congenial and friendly atmosphere.

Nehru, of course, was a recognized phenomenon in India; and Liaquat too carried a lot of weight in Pakistan, more so after the demise of Jinnah in September 1948. But, this good beginning based on mutual respect and understanding was tragically cut short by the assassination of Liaquat Ali Khan in Rawalpindi next year.

Liaquat Ali Khan, as the Prime Minister of Pakistan and a very capable successor to M.A. Jinnah, was probably placed in a unique and significantly high position in Pakistan to grapple with the tangled Indo-Pak situation. Also, he was the one the Indian Prime Minister Nehru approached sincerely for this purpose. Reportedly there were differences in approach between him and Jinnah on the matter of diffusing the conflagration in J&K; and the former was careful in not getting into any controversy with the Qaid-e-Azam – as Jinnah was fondly called in Pakistan. As long as Jinnah was alive, Liaqat Ali did feel circumscribed by the authority and public hold of the former. Many contemporary political observers did believe that the two statesmen, Nehru and Liaqat, were genuinely interested in finding a middle path and workable solution. But with Liaqat Ali Khan's assassination in Rawalpindi on October 16, 1951, this hope too vanished. The situation was back to square one. Till then the British, more than the Americans, were working behind the scene to put pressure on Indian leaders, particularly Nehru, for agreeing to a negotiated settlement of the J&K problem. The difficulty obviously, from Indian stand point, was that all such proposals were made to safeguard British interests in this region rather than keeping the Indian concerns and benefits in mind. A whole lot of archival material, now available publically in UK and the USA, amply proves this point.

After the demise of Liaquat, there was no one in Pakistan with that kind of authority, status, empathy and vision whom a person like Nehru could comfortably relate with. General Ayub Khan, who took over the reins of Pakistan and effectively managed the systems there, was still few years – seven to be precise – away. In the meanwhile, Pakistan was to firmly entrench itself in the Western camp by becoming a member of CENTO and SEATO groupings. Nehru, expectedly, reacted indignantly to the US-Pakistan military pact of 1954 and wrote to his Pakistani counterpart as, "…. This produces a qualitative change in the existing situation and therefore, it affects Indo-Pakistan relations and more especially, Kashmir…. It made all talks between the two countries about demilitarization absurd when the object was militarization of Pakistan"[6].

Thus, considerably and in a way deeply disappointed by the death of Liaquat Ali Khan, Nehru diverted his attention for the next few years towards the internal situation in the country, particularly the constitution making process in the State of Jammu and Kashmir; more so since the Constitution of India had already been adopted and promulgated on January 26, 1950. As it had been agreed upon earlier that there would be a separate constitution for J&K, the State Constituent Assembly had started working on it earnestly. However, Sheikh Abdullah felt that on certain important and ticklish issues more clarification was required and greater coordination between State and the Center would be necessary. Therefore, a series of discussions took place amongst the representatives of State and the Centre; and an arrangement was arrived at in the month of July, later known as the "Delhi Agreement – 1952".

Some of the main points on which both sides agreed included that while the residuary powers of legislature vested in the Centre in respect of all other states; for Jammu and Kashmir they remained in the State itself. The Union Government also agreed that the State should have its own flag in addition to the Union flag, but it was accepted by the State Government that the State flag would not be a rival of the Union flag; it was also recognized that the Union flag should have the same status and position in Jammu and Kashmir as in the rest of India. There was also consensus with regard to the position of Sadar-i-Riyasat – Head of the State – and though he was to be elected by the State Legislature, he had to be recognized by the President of India before his installation. Further, "… it was accepted that the people of the State were to have fundamental rights, but in view of the peculiar position in which the State was placed, the whole chapter relating to 'Fundamental Rights' of the Indian Constitution could not be made applicable to the State, the question which remained to be determined was whether the chapter on fundamental rights should form a part of the State Constitution or the Constitution of India as applicable to the State". In addition, there was a great deal of discussion regarding "Emergency Powers" of the Government of India and in order to meet the State's view point, the Government of India agreed to the modification of Article 352 in its application to J&K by the addition of the following words: "but in

6   Balraj Puri, n-3, p.19.

regard to internal disturbance at the request or with the concurrence of the Government of the State" at the end of clause (1).

The whole mutually settled constitutional arrangement which envisaged a special position for Jammu and Kashmir was "an unwritten understanding between Jawaharlal Nehru and Sheikh Abdullah. An announcement that Jawaharlal Nehru had made in Parliament on July 24, 1952, is called the 'Delhi Agreement'.... Nehru had done this following his talks with the Sheikh who had afterwards returned to Srinagar from New Delhi in a triumphant mood and announced in the city's Lal Chowk on July 28, 1952: "Kashmir is part and parcel of India"[7]. However, it appears that these considerable concessions to Sheikh Abdullah whetted his appetite to want even more and aspire for greater freedom of action as the head of the State Government. From this point onwards the relations with New Delhi took a downward slide. Sheikh's seemingly defiant public statements as also his controversial contacts with some foreign dignitaries complicated the matters further, till the things came to a head by the middle of next year. New Delhi could find no way to rein him in; other than to stop him in the track. It was reportedly a reluctant Nehru who gave in to the mounting pressure of his colleagues and advisors and agreed to the dismissal and detention of Sheikh Abdullah on August 9, 1953. This step not only plunged the J&K State in a deep internal convulsions but it also had significant external dimensions in India's relationship with Pakistan.

On a different plane, though, it can be said to the credit of Nehru and Sheikh Abdullah that even this major step against the latter and his long incarceration did not diminish their mutual respect and admiration.

Nehru then made another effort to mutually settle the Kashmir issue and held talks, during May 14-18, 1955, with Pakistan's Prime Minister Chaudhury Mohammad Ali and Defence Minister Iskander Mirza. Nehru had preferred and proposed a 'final settlement' based on agreed and mutually acceptable variations in the cease-fire line; including ceding of territory to Pakistan. His visitors, on the other hand, wanted to discuss the possibility of division of the State on communal basis; and that was something not acceptable in principle to the host. These parleys also failed to produce any tangible outcome. Thereafter, the events in Pakistan

---

7   Pushp Saraf in the editorial of *Border Affairs*, New Delhi, July-Sep 2000, p. 3.

moved rather rapidly, in the backdrop of political instability and prolonged unceasing machinations by various political personalities – big and small.

In this general scenario of considerable instability and political mercurialness, seemingly desperate measures were undertaken to make a beginning of some visible authority and stability in Pakistan. "At 10:30 p.m. on 7 October (1958) Pakistan became a dictatorship under President (Iskander) Mirza. Ayub was named Chief Martial Law Administrator (CMLA). At 11 p.m. corps commanders received their orders and the diplomatic corps were summoned at 11.30 p.m. Ayub sat beside Mirza when the latter briefed the ambassadors. Troops moved into key positions in Karachi, Lahore and Dacca (now Dhaka)"[8]. Twenty days later Ayub took over as the President of Pakistan, sending Iskander Mirza into exile. Thus General (later Field Marshal) Ayub Khan became the first military ruler of Pakistan on October 27, 1958. This was no sudden development and there is enough material available, printed as well as archival, to surmise that "As the domestic political edifice crumbled and headed for a fall, the army was already working towards a future in which it would control the direction of the country, at first from the sidelines and later directly"[9].

Nehru and Ayub met for the first time at the Palam airport in New Delhi on September 1, 1959. A joint statement issued at the conclusion of this meeting mentioned the need to improve ties and the requirement for a more 'realistic, rational and sensible' relationship with each other. This signified a good beginning and cordial association between the two leaders. Another positive factor in this scenario was the presence of Rajeshwar Dayal as India's High Commissioner to Pakistan. He shared a particularly personal and warm relationship with Ayub going back to almost two decades. That was the time when the current generation of Indians and Pakistanis, across the divide, still fondly recalled the good times spent together before 1947. Rajeshwar Dayal was posted as the District Magistrate in Mathura in 1940 and established a very warm relationship with Ayub, who was also stationed there. He has stated about this in his memoirs, "The sole Indian officer, in charge of a small unit of the Service Corps, was a young Indian Captain, Mohammad Ayub Khan.... Almost every evening he would be at our house"[10]. The Indian High Commissioner made good use of his

---

8   Shuja Nawaz, *Crossed Swords*, Oxford University Press, Karachi- 2008, p.156

9   *Ibid* , p. 89.

10 Rajeshwar Dayal, *A Life of Our Times,* Orient Longman, p. 57.

contacts and reach to the Pakistani President and this hugely helped, as also eased, the process of finalizing the Indus Water Treaty, with the World Bank acting as a facilitator. This treaty was signed on September 19, 1960, at Karachi, for which Nehru travelled to that city. There is an interesting photograph of Nehru and Ayub standing side by side in a car, waiving at and acknowledging greetings of the public in a street in Karachi.

The Indus Water Treaty (IWT) has been, unarguably, the most enduring and working bilateral instrument between the two sparring neighbors. This treaty has survived three regular wars, and a number of military stand offs between them. Some analysts feel that the main reason for its success is the fact that being the upper riparian state only India could have violated this treaty, which it has chosen not to do and that is the singular factor for continuing relevance of this accord. However, the truth remains that, notwithstanding occasional pin-pricks and road blocks put in the way of India's development projects, Pakistan should also share a part of the credit for this success story.

As a part of the British legacy of the irrigation system developed by them in the pre-1947 united Punjab, this issue became hugely problematic in the post-partition era. The plains of Punjab not only stood divided but also the extensive Indus irrigation network too was adversely affected with the headworks falling in India while most of the canal system ran through Pakistan. With the aim of satisfactory utilization of the existing infrastructure and to determine and delineate rights and obligations of each country, both India and Pakistan entered into serious negotiations spread over many years in the 1950s. This effort was effectively led by the World Bank and the IWT was signed in 1960. It must be accepted that over six decades ago then, a different political, economic, ecological and energy environment prevailed in the region, with across the board more favorable centre - state as well as intra state relationships in the sub-continent. These factors coupled with the genuine desire of the leaders of two countries for a peaceful co-existence, made the signing of this almost path-breaking initiative a reality.

Since then there has been almost a constant clamor in both countries against the Treaty, with increasingly strident voices for its re-negotiation or, worse, unilateral abrogation. In India, the most vocal criticism comes from J&K, as all the three western rivers Indus, Jhelum and Chenab, whose waters are allocated for unrestricted use by Pakistan flow through this state.

Thus J&K is denied to tap the potential of these three rivers basins for agriculture, transport and energy purposes. A simple and glaring example is the fact that all Hydro-electric projects in this state are perforce based on "run of the river" schemes and none of them works on the water storage principle which is so much more economical and beneficial. There is also a feeling in some segments in India that the IWT gave undue concessions to Pakistan which probably the then Prime Minister Nehru agreed in the fond hope, now completely belied, that this would buy peace. Since it did not help in bringing peace to Kashmir, they want to revisit the concessions then given to Pakistan under the Treaty. Similarly, across the border, there are tensions and misgivings in the Northern Areas and PoK on this issue. The controversies and problems in relation to Diamer-Basha and Mangla dams respectively are pointers in this regard. Also, the four provinces in Pakistan are deeply divided in terms of sharing the Indus water benefits. In particular, the Sindh agriculturist class is always accusing their Punjab counterparts of stealing their legitimate share of irrigation waters, whereas the Punjab farmer is perennially complaining of being given a short shrift in this matter.

Despite the considerable growth in both countries during the last over sixty years, agriculture still remains a very significant activity in the rural life and economy and hence so much more emphasis on the irrigation facilities and the availability of water; something the resource base of which is consistently declining due to natural and ecological factors. This has put further pressure on both countries to strive for meeting the ever-increasing demands of water and also given a handle to the extremist elements, across the border, to raise the bar and press for precipitative measures. The saner elements on both sides, however, are shy of tampering with something that has ostensibly worked smoothly so far.

All things considered, the IWT has been a major success in the otherwise troubled bilateral relationship; it has indeed been a landmark and lasting achievement in the process of affecting peace between India and Pakistan.

After signing the IWT in Karachi on 19th September, Nehru had a summit meeting with General Ayub, two days later, in Murree. The meeting took place in the cool environs of this hill station and plush settings of the President's lodge. It was a one to one exchange of thoughts and ideas amongst the two leaders without any *aides* or advisers; which lasted for more than an hour. Ostensibly, Ayub had pinned high hopes from this get-together and expected some perceptible movement forward on the vexed issue of Kashmir, from Pakistan's point of view; whereas it seems that his Indian guest was not prepared to go beyond making practical variations in the existing cease-fire line and converting the same into international borders. As it happens in all failed negotiations, both sides ended up blaming each other. The Indian version appeared in the third volume of S. Gopal's biography of Nehru in 1984; whereas the Pakistani account is contained in Ayub Khan's memoirs published much earlier in 1967. But these details were only of historical and academic interest and did not have much value beyond that.

Thus, the second and last meeting between the two men ended without achieving anything substantive, which appears rather unfortunate, and this can be said, with the advantage of hind sight. The mutual cordiality, trust and relations have never been so good, between the two heads and people of the sub-continent; either before or after that time. In addition, in democratic India the popularity of Nehru was almost at all time high; whereas in Pakistan Ayub was effectively in control of things. So, any concession made by either of them would, in all probability, be acceptable to the public across the divide. However, that was not to be and a rare opportunity to improve the strained Indo-Pak relations thus slipped out. Some political analysts do believe that the prime mover behind this summit was the Indian High Commissioner to Pakistan, Rajeshwar Dayal, who had good reach and very cordial connections with both Ayub and Nehru; and that just before this meeting Dayal had been moved out of this assignment and sent to Congo as the head of the UN Mission there. Had he been present in Pakistan during the crucial summit, they believe, the outcome would have been much more positive. But, these are at best conjectures and wishful thinking which become 'ifs' and 'buts' of certain historical happenings. One thing, though, is certain that India and Pakistan did miss a ripe opportunity in September 1960 in Murree.

During the very next year, the Chinese made substantive moves in the sub-continent by which, on the one hand it concluded a border agreement with Pakistan in the Northern Areas – something null and void from Indian perspective as also not acceptable to India- and on the other it provoked and pressed India hard on the border disputes in the North East Frontier Agency (NEFA) and Ladakh. This conflict environment in the Himalayas had been in the making ever since China had annexed and occupied Tibet in the early fifties; and this flared up a decade later. The Indo-China border clashes in NEFA and Ladakh took place during October and November 1962, with Chinese declaring a unilateral cease-fire on 21st November. For a variety of reasons, including lack of preparedness and bad generalship, the Indian army suffered reverses in both sectors. This created a new strategic imbalance in the sub-continent, with hitherto absent China emerging as a relevant factor in the Indo-Pak ties. It also shifted the focus of Western Powers, from their confirmed ally Pakistan to India. These nations were still in the throes of the Cold War and now, in addition, haunted by the threat of a communist ingress into India; a thought particularly disturbing to the USA.

This Indo-China conflict created three side effects in the region. The American military aid to India increased significantly and visibly, to the consternation of Pakistan. The fighting capabilities of the Indian forces came under cloud and doubts appeared in the capabilities of the Indian army. This, in turn, emboldened Pakistan to adopt a more aggressive posture against India to settle outstanding issues. In fact, looking at the developments in a holistic manner one can arrive at the conclusion that seeds of the 1965 Indo-Pak war were effectively sown at this time only. Additionally, Pakistan had also to contend with a more India friendly John F. Kennedy Presidency in the White House.

The contemporary scenario in Pakistan has been very comprehensively described as, ".... political shifts abroad,.... as well as changes in the region.... were to shift the political balance in the subcontinent. Ayub found himself fighting a rearguard action to preserve his special relationship with the United States on the one hand while opening up the doors to China on the other. At home, rising expectations of the rapidly expanding population were to test the stability of a system built on shaky political foundations and an economic development strategy that ignored basic needs while allowing a select few to amass seemingly unbridled wealth"[11].

It is also widely believed that the United States effectively nudged India to accept and sign the IWT. However, after November 1962, the pendulum further swung to India's disadvantage. The Western military hardware made available to India did on the face of it appear to be credible

---

11 Shuja Nawaz, n-8, p. 189.

enough, in terms of quality as well as quantity, to face the Chinese threat effectively. Also, even though India was required to pay for whatever arms and equipment it was getting; but mere payment was not enough for US and UK. Could India please do something more to accommodate Pakistani interests and aspirations; particularly in the context of Kashmir – the Western powers pressed on India. Indian political leadership already demoralized by the recent military setbacks in a confrontation with the Chinese forces; was also under considerable stress at home. It, therefore, gave in to the pressure and agreed to the US – UK brokered ministerial-level talks on Kashmir. This initiative resulted in the communiqué of November 29, 1962, which mentioned about fresh efforts and attempts to "resolve outstanding differences on Kashmir and other related matters through talks to be conducted initially at the ministerial level". It was left unsaid that successful negotiations at this level would be followed by a summit between Nehru and Ayub.

What took place during the next six months is generally referred to as the Swaran Singh – Bhutto Parleys; as the delegation level talks between the two countries were led by these two Foreign Ministers. Indian foreign secretary, Y.D. Gundevia who took part in these discussions as a member of the Indian delegation, has given a detailed account about it in his memoirs titled, "Outside the Archives". There were a total of six rounds of talks held at Rawalpindi, Karachi, Calcutta (now Kolkata) and New Delhi. It was also during the course of these discussions that an announcement was made simultaneously from Peking and Karachi about the signing of an agreement between China and Pakistan which gave away a large chunk of territory in the Northern Areas of J&K under illegal occupation of Pakistan, to China. In spite of this provocation an enfeebled India chose to continue with the ongoing talks with Pakistan. It is reported that during the course of discussions Sardar Swarn Singh, the Indian Foreign Minister, offered even the entire Kashmir valley to Pakistan, but Bhutto – then puffed up with false confidence generated by the Indian setbacks and perceived military superiority of Pakistan – did not accept this bargain and wanted much more concessions. The talks eventually failed after the sixth round in New Delhi in the month of May 1963. Thus another item was added to the list of failed peace efforts to bring the two countries together.

Nehru's failing health, his slipping grip over the Indian political scene as well as reduced international stature; all these factors combined to make any substantive new measure towards the peace process so much more difficult. But, manfully and undaunted, he did not stop making efforts. Jaswant Singh, India's Foreign and Finance Minister over three decades later, had this to record about the unfolding contemporary scenario, "In a touching account Y.D. Gundevia, India's Foreign Secretary in Nehru's final years has shared with posterity the efforts that a 'fading, saddened and spent' Nehru made. There was a poignant heroism in those last efforts by Nehru.... In this milieu, against his own inclinations, Prime Minister Nehru began by accepting the advice of others and wrote to President Ayub Khan. Ayub's reply only rubbed salt into India's wounds.... If it was accord with Pakistan that was sought, then this Nehru initiative did not even take off"[12]. Practically as a last-ditch effort, Nehru sent Sheikh Abdullah, who had been released from detention earlier, to Pakistan as a messenger of goodwill. On May 26, 1964, the Sheikh persuaded Ayub to meet Nehru for the third time; but these efforts did not materialize as Nehru breathed his last the next day. With his death, an entire chapter in the history of independent India, as also of peace efforts towards Pakistan, came to a close.

About this period of 1964 and the beginning of the next year, Shuja Nawaz gives a Pakistani perspective of the prevailing situation as, "The Pakistan Army was now twice its size at partition and sucking up a larger share of national resources than before.... However, the young Foreign Minister Bhutto was beginning to assert his views with Ayub, particularly in matters dealing with the US and China. Bhutto also had developed close relationships with a number of younger generals, who saw an opening to resolve the Kashmir issue through military means and a window of opportunity that was narrowing with India's growing military strength.... By 1964, Bhutto, along with his like-minded colleagues at the Foreign Ministry and friendly generals, had started concentrating on renewing pressure on India to resolve the Kashmir issue.... In brief, Pakistan was running out of time if it was to effect a military-induced solution to the Kashmir imbroglio"[13]. Inspired by such presumptions and thoughts of military superiority, Bhutto wrote a letter to Ayub on May 12, 1965; which in part read as, "India is at present in no position to risk a general war of

---

12 Jaswant Singh, *In the Service of Emergent India: A Call to Honour*, Indiana University Press, U.S.A., 2007, p. 300.

13 Shuja Nawaz, n-8, pp. 200-201.

unlimited duration. India's capacity increases with the passage of every single day...."[14]

Thus, an overconfident Pakistan set in motion the first phase of its military adventure by sending hundreds of armed guerrillas across the cease-fire line and launching "Operation Gibraltar" around July 24, 1965. When this effort failed to achieve its purpose of stimulating the local populace to rise against the State Government and the Indian forces reacted swiftly and decisively; Pakistan embarked upon a full-scale military invasion plan on the 1st September, code-named "Operation Grand Slam". With this, the 1965 Indo-Pak war had begun, which officially ended with a cease-fire on September 23, 1965. When the fighting came to a halt, with both sides claiming victory but in fact, a sort of stalemate had ensued; the pressure on two countries started building up to reach a long-term arrangement of peace with each other. Pakistan, disappointed with what it perceived as the lack of American support, started counting on the Soviet Russia to bring about a face-saving accord with India. That is how the Tashkent Agreement – 1966 came into being; though seemingly brokered by the Russians, but with complete tacit support of the Americans also.

Though the delegations of India and Pakistan, headed by Shastri and Ayub arrived in Tashkent on January 3, 1966; the actual negotiations began only the next day and carried on for the ensuing five days. The Soviet hosts represented at the apex by Prime Minister Alexei Kosygin and Foreign Minister Andrei Gromyko, separately and jointly began with a series of parleys with the two parties, to bring down the issues of discord and concentrate on the common acceptable points; before embarking upon direct negotiations between the two countries. Notwithstanding many differences, the talks were conducted in a polite and friendly environment. It is also a matter of record that both Shastri and Ayub generally conversed with each other in Urdu accompanied by considerable civility and graciousness. The bi-lateral and tri-lateral discussions continued back and forth without achieving much during the first few days, till things began to crystallize. Most areas of discord were narrowed down and the nitty-gritty worked out during a series of lengthy parleys and negotiations on 9th January and the final shape to the Tashkent Agreement was given late in the evening. This accord was signed ceremoniously the next day, January 10, 1966. The Tashkent Declaration, heralding peace between India and

---

14 As quoted by A.G. Noorani in FRONTLINE of July 2, 2010, p. 88.

Pakistan had come into being. This was certainly a positive development in the overall prevailing situation in the sub-continent; particularly in the wake of the abortive Swaran Singh – Bhutto rounds of talks and later the Indo-Pak armed conflict. According to the agreed framework, Indian and Pakistani forces were to pull back to their pre-conflict positions; practically bringing back the 1949 Cease- Fire Line position. It was also accepted that the two nations would not interfere in each other's internal affairs; restore economic and diplomatic ties as also strive to improve bilateral relations.

In a tragic aftermath, Lal Bahadur Shastri died in his bed, the same midnight. Reportedly, he was upset, saddened and concerned about the negative reaction of people back home as conveyed to him by his aides in Tashkent[15]. A dispassionate evaluation of these parleys would indicate that the Tashkent Agreement contained the seeds of reconciliation and elements of long-term friendly relations between India and Pakistan. After all the top two architects of this declaration, Shastri and Ayub were both men of substance and high caliber and they must have reached this agreement only after satisfying themselves that details contained in the document were in the best interest of their respective nations. The cordial exchange between them after the signing ceremony also bears testimony towards this fact.

However, public reaction to this agreement in India and Pakistan was skeptical and antagonistic, if not downright hostile. The hype created about successes of the armed forces during the war was so high and not fully based on the ground situation – particularly in Pakistan – that the Tashkent Declaration was taken as a sort of major climb down and concession to the other party. In India, the return of Haji Pir Pass itself, connecting Poonch and Uri in J&K, became a major source of public anger; whereas in Pakistan the whole treaty was seen as a significant retreat by, what the people and media perceived as, a "victorious nation".

Shastri's death in Tashkent was certainly a major tragedy and significant jolt to the Indian polity. In the ensuing spontaneous outpourings of national grief, the Tashkent Agreement was taken as a sort of the last testament of a great departed leader; and hence the public opinion swallowed it without much noise and adverse reaction. But, the picture

---

15 As imputed by Rajeshwar Prasad, Director of the National Academy of Administration, Mussoorie; in his talk to the IAS Probationers in May 1974. He was Principal Secretary to the Indian Prime Minister during the Tashkent Declaration.

in Pakistan was different. "Ayub returned to Pakistan but did not make a statement upon getting home. Bhutto began distancing himself from Ayub. Meanwhile, public agitation began against the Tashkent accord, fuelled by the public's sense of having been let down after having been fed positive news about the war effort.... Once the euphoria produced by the official propaganda during the war had died down in Pakistan, people realized that Ayub Khan and the military leadership had failed the nation militarily"[16]. By the summer that year, Bhutto had been dropped from Ayub's cabinet. He floated his own political outfit; the Pakistan People's Party (PPP), from Lahore on November 11, 1967, and projected himself as the main torch bearer of Pakistani interests and anti-India crusade.

In fact, the ill-conceived adventure of 1965 proved to be the beginning of Ayub's downfall. The situation kept on deteriorating; with street demonstrations against the government on the rise progressively and the national economy on the down swing. The scenario ultimately came to such a pass that the then Pak army chief General Yahya Khan, a onetime protégé of Ayub, demanded and obtained resignation of the latter. Ayub relented, stepped down and handed over reins of power to Yahya Khan, who became President of Pakistan on March 26, 1969. Pakistan passed from one military ruler to another. This time, the army chief was not only less capable and lesser far-sighted; but also had a reputation of excessive drinking. The military regime was to prove disastrous for the country. A series of wrong decisions by Yahya Khan, combined with single-minded political ambitions of Bhutto ultimately led to the breakup of Pakistan and separation of its Eastern wing. The events leading to the 1971 Indo-Pak war also created a new country of Bangladesh on December 6, 1971. That is the day on which India recognized Bangladesh as an independent country; even though Sheikh Mujib-ur-Rahman declared independent Bangladesh at a massive public rally in Dacca (now Dhaka) on March 21, 1971.

The rest is history.

Indian victory in the 1971 Indo-Pak war and about ninety thousand Pakistani troops taken as the Prisoners of War (PoW), are well-known facts of the time and also recorded in considerable details by contemporary and later authors and research scholars. Also, by the beginning of 1972

---

16 Shuja Nawaz, n-8, pp. 239,240.

international pressure and domestic compulsions had started building up on both countries to open negotiations, for finding ways to unravel the current impasse and exhibit desire for peaceful co-existence in future. The Simla Agreement (now called Shimla) signed between India and Pakistan in Simla, the capital city of Indian state of Himachal Pradesh, on July 2, 1972, was thus an outcome of months of preparations of both sides. Bhutto, as President of Pakistan, reached Simla with his delegation four days in advance on 28th June. His strong and negative views on Indo-Pak relations were well known across the border; and this time he came fully briefed by the Pakistan army top brass as also armed with the private and public views of opinion makers in his country. But, all the same, he was also pragmatic enough to understand that it was hardly a meeting of equals. He had, apart from asking for other concessions, to secure the release of Pakistani PoWs from the Indian Prime Minister who had successfully broken up his country. Though from India's point of view, this was an ideal opportunity to insist on the final resolution of Kashmir issue and firmly demand the conversion of the existing cease-fire line into an international border; Bhutto was able to persuade Mrs. Gandhi that such a step would certainly destabilize his fragile civilian government and, worse, open the way for another military takeover in Pakistan.

Both sides seemed to have stuck to their respective stands quite rigidly, and even after four days discussions no breakthrough appeared plausible and the talks headed towards a failure. "Finally, on 2 July, Bhutto decided that Mrs. Gandhi would not come to an agreement and got ready to pack up and leave Simla. But he chose to use his farewell call on Mrs. Gandhi to make a final plea on behalf of the people of both countries.... offering her a way out of their impasse. She did not disagree and said she would give her answer at dinner that evening. After dinner, the exchanges continued...."[17] Later that night both sides hammered out a mutually acceptable accord and the Simla Agreement of July 2, 1972, was duly signed by Indira Gandhi as Prime Minister of India and by Zulfiqar Ali Bhutto as President of Pakistan.

The most important ingredient of this treaty was the assertion that both countries will "settle their differences by peaceful means through bilateral negotiations". By virtue of this stipulation any third party intervention, even that of United Nations, in any outstanding matter is precluded. Other

17   Shuja Nawaz, n-8, p. 331.

significant components of the Simla Agreement were the conversion of the cease-fire line of December 17, 1971 into the Line of Control (LoC), and the return of both armies to their earlier locations across the international border. It also facilitated the diplomatic recognition of Bangladesh by Pakistan. It was claimed later by some Indian officials that of the things left unsaid in the Simla Agreement included a private understanding between the two leaders that at an appropriate time Bhutto would work towards converting the LoC into an international border. But that was never to happen, and with both the protagonists' now long dead, this issue is at best a matter of conjectures only. It is also well known that Indira Gandhi was consistently in favor of suitable adjustments in the LoC. "On July 11, 1972, she told Shahid Kamal Pasha of *Morning News* of Karachi: 'If you look at the map, it does not appear rational and it has not proved so…' She would not like to force its rationalization on Pakistan. It would be done only through mutual understanding and consent (PTI: *The Times of India*, July 13, 1972)"[18]. This is the nearest one can come on the issue. Also, though not a part of the accord itself, India started releasing the Pakistani PoWs a year later.

Independent observers generally, and Indian analysts unanimously, believe that even though negotiating from a weak position, Bhutto was able to manage a favourable deal for his country and also did not compromise, beyond the semantics, on the basic position of Pakistan on Kashmir. He returned home to claim that he had saved Pakistan from the humiliation of giving up on Kashmir. Also, as some parts of the Simla Agreement were open to interpretations, these gave free operating space to Pakistan and were cleverly used to serve the requisite ends. All the same, a comprehensive and dispassionate analysis would indicate that in a number of ways the Simla Agreement was a more potent and effective instrument of peace between India and Pakistan than the earlier declaration at Tashkent. It provided for a robust structure and effective parameters for cooperation and reduction of tensions at the borders. Also, the respective positions of the two negotiating parties were decidedly different than six years ago; these were no more barely concealed belligerent opponents. In the present case, India was indisputably and demonstrably in a dominating situation and negotiating from a position of strength. Therefore, realistically speaking and also keeping in mind the large-heartedness of India displayed

---

18 As quoted by A.G. Noorani in Frontline dated March 10, 2006.

on earlier occasions in 1947-48 and 1965; a mutually acceptable outcome had been predicted. And that is what happened also.

Significantly, the two countries agreed to treat J&K as a bilateral issue; which itself was a major departure from the past. Also, the agreement to treat the cease-fire line as the LoC indicated a more secure and peaceful future across the borders. It also gave some advantage to both countries as each kept what it had occupied across the cease-fire line during the short armed conflict in December 1971; though India had an edge in this respect. For example, the constant threat to Kargil town was removed with the adjoining hill feature – commonly known as 13620, a reference to its height in feet – now in Indian hands. Acceptance of this principle also augured well for India, decidedly a greater military power since then.

It has to be accepted, at the same time, that due to internal developments in both countries over the next few years; the progress towards a more lasting peace which had been so wishfully hoped for during and immediately after the Simla Agreement, did not come to materialize. On the Indian side, an increasingly strident opposition to Mrs. Gandhi started manifesting itself, affecting the political climate in the country. India also had to deal with managing the international fallout of the peaceful nuclear implosion in 1974. A year after that came the Emergency rule in India; which badly shook the democratic foundations of the country and tarnished its reputation as a healthy and functional democracy.

The developments across the border, in Pakistan, were not only worse but also grew darker with the passage of every month practically. After the debacle of 1971, which pitch forked him into power in Pakistan, Bhutto had to struggle to consolidate his influence base and contend with a rising tide of expectations, democratic urges and opposition. He also launched Pakistan on the economically ruinous course of becoming a nuclear-armed nation. This ambition in the midst of a shaky economic situation put his country in a close embrace with the West Asian cash-rich nations; in particular Saudi Arabia and Libya. Pakistan's rich cultural and historical traditions were now subservient to the Salafi – Wahabi exclucism of this region. The Balochistan uprising in 1973 and Iran's discomfiture over this development also troubled him considerably. Bhutto responded by sending army to Balochistan which further alienated the Baloch people on the one hand; and gave a much needed toe-hold to the Pak army to resurrect its lost image in the country, after the disastrous performance in 1971. The army has never looked back since then.

By 1975, Bhutto was struggling shakily; badly hemmed by rising political opponents, under pressure from an increasingly assertive army, and also challenged by the expanding street lung-power of the fundamentalist outfits emboldened by the flow of petro-dollars from West Asia. In desperation, Bhutto sought to buy peace with right wing elements on one hand and the established traditional centers of power- the big rural landlords- on the other. He ended up literally falling between stools. Even cosmetics like declaring Ahmadiyas as non Muslims and a strident call for making an "Islamic Bomb" did not help his sagging position. By July 1977 Pakistan was once again under military rule and Bhutto was put behind bars; ending Pakistan's short flirtation with democracy. Later, General Zia-ul-Haq hanged him following a controversial judicial decision.

An objective assessment of Bhutto's contributions to his nation would indicate that he was an unmitigated disaster for Pakistan. He was one of the prime movers behind the Indo-Pak war of 1965 and also events leading to this ill-conceived venture. When the time came for standing up and getting counted for the calamity, he craftily sidestepped and blamed Ayub solely for the debacle. He bounced back to create a greater havoc for Pakistan in 1971. At the head of his newly formed political party – the PPP – he won in the Western Wing of Pakistan with large margin - in the elections conducted by the Yahya regime in 1970 – but fell short of the half-way mark at the national level; in which Shiekh Mujib-ur-Rahman of East Pakistan had a clear advantage. Bhutto did not relent or compromise in the larger national interest. His unbridled and positively unprincipled personal ambition pushed Pakistan over the edge, leading to the 1971 Indo-Pak war and the subsequent national disaster. Bhutto ultimately paid with his life.

Of many people who have attempted to portray Bhutto in words, the nearest description of the man is penned by Sir Morrice James, the UK high commissioner to Pakistan in the early sixties, who has recounted in his memoirs as, "Bhutto certainly had the right qualities for reaching the heights – drive, charm, imagination, a quick and penetrating mind, zest for life, eloquence, energy, a strong constitution, a sense of humour, and a thick skin. Such a blend is rare anywhere, and Bhutto deserved his swift rise to power.... I believe that at heart he lacked a sense of the dignity and value of other people; his own self was what counted. I sensed in him a ruthlessness and capacity for ill-doing which went far beyond what is natural.... Despite his gifts I judged that one day Bhutto would destroy himself – when I could not tell. In 1965, I so reported in one of my last despatches from Pakistan as British High Commissioner. I wrote by way of clinching the point that Bhutto was born to be hanged. I did not intend this comment as precise prophecy of what was going to happen to him, but fourteen years later that was what it turned out to be"[19].

In the otherwise bleak scenario in the wake of 1972 Simla Agreement, the Indira – Sheikh Accord of 1974 was undoubtedly a very bright spot in the Indian political scene of the seventies. During the years following Simla Agreement, Mrs. Gandhi had come to realize that Bhutto had no intentions of either deviating from Pakistan's traditional obdurate stance on Kashmir; nor had he shown any inclination to accord a status of finality to the LoC. She was therefore keen to affect a rapprochement with Sheikh Abdullah, who was a symbol of stability and solidarity in Kashmir; and through him to achieve strengthening of internal dimensions of this vexing issue to such an extent that it ceased to remain a thorny matter between the two countries. It can be safely presumed that the events leading to the 1971 conflagration and emergence of Bangladesh had created a considerable impact on the Sheikh and marked a positive shift in his attitude. The Simla Agreement also added to this changed stance as the two countries had agreed to resolve their outstanding issues peacefully through bilateral discussions. Further, this Agreement effectively made the issues in Jammu and Kashmir an internal matter for India.

On March 10, 1972, the election results of the State Assembly were declared, returning the Congress Party to power with a tally of 57 seats out of 74; which constituted a massive electoral mandate. Sheikh Abdullah's reaction to this development was seemingly positive and conciliatory seen in the backdrop of the statement issued by him; which in part mentioned, "My differences with the Government of India are not on the issue of accession but on the quantum of autonomy". From this and certain other public utterances by him and his trusted lieutenants, an inference could be drawn that he was not averse to entering into negotiations with Mrs. Gandhi on the issue of the future of J&K; and wanted the return to the status this state enjoyed in 1953 as also guarantees against the erosion of

---

19 As quoted by Shuja Nawaz, n-8, pp. 215-216.

Article 370 in future. On the other hand, the leadership in India was also aware of the ground realities to surmise that domestic problems of the state could not be effectively tackled without the active cooperation of the Sheikh, and that his return to the centre stage would have a very positive impact on the politics of Jammu and Kashmir. Thus the central and the state leaderships on one hand and Sheikh Abdullah and his aides on the other; began to explore and find common grounds of understanding and reconciliation within the constitutional framework of India. G. Parthasarthy was made the representative of Indira Gandhi and Sheikh nominated Mirza Afzal Beigh for further negotiations. The Beigh – Parthasarthy talks were initiated at Srinagar on June 16, 1972; and this dialogue continued for almost two and half years. Both sides covered a lot of ground during these parleys. In the initial stages Sheikh Abdullah insisted on the restoration of pre-1953 constitutional status of the state; but did not put this demand as a pre-condition for the talks as he soon realized that such a stance may end up breaking the dialogue; since the Government of India could not possibly concede beyond a point. Thus, the agreed compromise – as finally determined - was arrived at in a spirit of flexibility and cooperation; in that the Sheikh was assured that the Government of India did not either intend to abrogate Article 370 or ask for doing away with the separate constitution of the state.

After protracted discussions, Parthasarthy and Beigh signed a six point agreement on November 13, 1974 at New Delhi on behalf of the Indian Prime Minister and Sheikh Abdullah respectively. "The new accord accepted the State of Jammu and Kashmir as a part of the Union of India which was to continue to be governed by Article 370 of the Constitution of India, and have residuary powers of legislation. The Government of India agreed to 'sympathetically consider amendment or repeal of some category of central laws extended to the State after 1953 as the state legislature decides"[20]. Interestingly item 6 of the document mentioned, "No agreement was possible on the question of nomenclature of the Governor and the Chief Minister and the matter is therefore remitted to the Principals". This Indira – Sheikh Accord created a feeling of mutual trust and faith and bridged the long continuing gulf between the two sides. It also strengthened the forces of secularism and democracy as well as served the cause of national unity. This step was not only in the right direction and long overdue but also underlined the sagacity and farsightedness of

---

20 Balraj Puri, n-3, p.33.

both parties; and their capacity to rise above personal considerations in the interest of larger and national perspective. The two other important issues also agreed upon by the parties included the dissolution of Plebiscite Front and that even though Congress party was in majority in the state legislature, it will surrender power in favour of Sheikh Abdullah. After signing of the Accord in November 1974, the two sides got busy with working out the details of the change of power in the State to Sheikh Abdullah.

On February 25, 1975, Sheikh Abdullah assumed the office of the Chief Minister of Jammu and Kashmir at the winter capital of the state in Jammu. The wheel had turned full circle after a gap of almost twenty-two years. He was very happy with the agreement as also the turn of events and declared that he had returned to power as the country wanted him at this critical juncture to strengthen the ideals of secularism, socialism and democracy. His cabinet was very compact and also effectively efficient; having a member each from three regions of the state. Mirza Afzal Beigh- a towering political stalwart- from Kashmir, Devi Dass Thakur- a Judge of the High Court of J&K- belonging to Jammu and Sonam Narboo- a retired Chief Engineer representing the Ladakh region. After assuming power, the Sheikh travelled to Kashmir by road and all along in the Valley he was accorded a tumultuous welcome by celebrating and joyous crowds; indicating that he still maintained a very firm grip over the minds and psyche of the Kashmiri people. The Sheikh, with his small and well-knit team, quickly settled down to provide a visibly more efficient administration to the state.

However, this arrangement did not last for long. Soon Sheikh Abdullah announced the revival of his old political party National Conference, stating that it would help in giving an early concrete shape to the economic programme outlined in the historic document of 'Naya Kashmir'. It was also a clever ploy to connect well with the Kashmiri sentiments. Obviously, this step was not liked by the central and state congress leaderships and, after a series of negative developments; the state congress party withdrew its support to the State Government in March 1977. Sheikh Abdullah recommended dissolution of the State Assembly to the Governor and holding of the fresh Assembly elections. In the ensuing electoral contest, his National Conference returned to power, with a very comfortable majority in July 1977. Sheikh Abdullah now headed the State

Government on his own; as also lead his old political organization till his death, after a prolonged illness in September 1982.

Indira Gandhi had spent most part of Jawahar Lal Nehru's Premiership, as his daughter, in the Prime Minister's House. During that period she had observed, acquired and absorbed nuances of important national and international happenings; and later put these perceptions and practical knowledge to good use during her tenures at the helm of affairs. The J&K matters and multi-dimensional issues related to it were areas in which she had deep and abiding interest; and also acquired expertise over the years. She could look at these from various angles; local, domestic, national and international perspectives. The Indira – Sheikh Accord of 1974 was a manifestation of her comprehensive understanding of this vexatious issue and a desire to see its satisfactory resolution. The circumstances were favourable, the timing was right and major connected players in the requisite frame of mind. A good beginning was made towards the close of 1974 and early next year; but the political developments affecting her and the Congress Party at the national level soon overtook her initiative in Kashmir and she could not see the things through to the logical conclusion. The resultant drift worked to the advantage of Sheikh Abdullah and to the detriment of the state unit of her party. By the time she returned to power again in January 1980 and tried to pick up threads in J&K, the inexorable march of events there amply indicated that the initiative had slipped out of her hands. She was since then, till her death on October 31, 1984, operating in a reactive mode; at times adding complications in an already complex situation. Thus, in the middle of seventies a significant opportunity was lost to settle the Kashmir issue, with the active cooperation and willing participation of Sheikh Abdullah, his colleagues and followers. A positive movement in this direction would have changed the course of relations between India and Pakistan.

Across the borders in Pakistan General Zia-ul-Haq, having taken over the reins of power as the military ruler in July 1977, had consolidated his position and grip over the domestic scene. This was particularly so after 1979 when, from his point of view, two important developments took place in the neighborhood; the Islamic Revolution in Iran headed by Ayatollah Khomeini and the Russian military intervention in Afghanistan. Both these events, pitch-forked Pakistan as the front line ally of American interests in the region. While helping the Americans in Afghanistan, particularly,

Zia realized the mischief potential of Pakistan in waging undeclared proxy war in the adjoining countries. His confidants and close coterie of generals proved to be astute learners of the well-honed under-cover techniques of the American CIA. Details of this have been graphically mentioned by Steve Coll in his celebrated book titled, "The Ghost Wars". The stratagems learnt from them, he applied first in Punjab, with devastating effect; and later in Kashmir. The Indian state was under effective siege from 1980.

Notwithstanding the mischief potential of Pakistan and considerable problems it has been creating for India; it is almost a mystery that the country has all along struggled to firmly plant its feet on ground. The identity crisis and efforts to find its roots has been a constant and continuing endeavor. This existential dilemma and ideological complexity has been competently portrayed by Farzana Shaikh as, "More than six decades after being carved out of British India, Pakistan remains an enigma. Born in 1947 as the first self-professed Muslim state, it rejected theocracy; vulnerable to the appeal of political Islam, it aspired to Western constitutionalism; prone to military dictatorships, it hankered after democracy; unsure of what it stood for, Pakistan has been left clutching at an identity beset by an ambiguous relation to Islam.... Pakistan's key problems: its failure to withstand military dictatorships; its uneven social and economic development; its severe ethnic divisions, and even the pursuit of questionable foreign policies.... Most of Pakistan's politicians, especially in the early years, lacked a political base in the regions and were unsure of democracy, thus leaving them open to the appeal of authoritarian rule. However, their doubts over the fundamental question of Pakistan's national identity and of the place of Islam in defining that identity were no more acute than those of their military counterparts"[21].

It would be worthwhile to have a panoramic view of Pakistan since its inception.

It is an irony of history that the demand for Pakistan did not receive as much support in the Muslim- majority provinces of undivided India as it did in the Hindu- majority provinces where Muslims showed more loyalty to Jinnah and commitment to the idea of Pakistan. Punjab was under the Unionist influence, rejecting both Congress and Muslim League, till the end of 1945. Sind did not take enthusiastically to Muslim League until

21 Farzana Shaikh *Making Sense of Pakistan*, Foundation Books, Hurst & Company, London, 2009, pp. 1,9,12.

as late as 1946. In Balochistan, the Khan of Kalat wanted no connection with Pakistan pointing to his direct dealings with the Crown, like Nepal and insisting that after the lapse of paramountcy of the Crown, it would devolve on him and not on any of the successor states of British India. The Frontier province, under the inspiring leadership of Khan Abdul Gaffar Khan, maintained its *Red Shirts* and *Khudai Khidmatgars* in power right till Independence Day of Pakistan; or more realistically its date of birth on August 14, 1947.

The founding- father of Pakistan, Mohd. Ali Jinnah, after having fought for and got a separate country for Muslims of the sub-continent, had hoped that it would become a secular democratic republic. But that did not happen and the country is still struggling to find its roots and come to terms with its existence. "The uncertainty over who qualifies as Pakistani owes much to the nation's emergence in 1947 as something of a migrant state…. With independence these communities faced not only the uncertainties of defining themselves as Pakistanis in a land to which they had hitherto belonged simply as Punjabis, Sindhis, Balochis or Pashtuns, but also the challenge of positioning themselves in relation to more than 7 million Muslim refugees from India who arrived claiming an equal right to be Pakistani. At issue was a conflict that resonates to the present day"[22].

As already mentioned, Muslim League, the party which headed the Pakistan movement did not have a mass base in the country. There were other contradictions also. Both of its top leaders, Jinnah the Governor General, and Liaqat Ali Khan the Prime Minister, were immigrants from Bombay and UP respectively. Neither of them was familiar with the problems of Bengalis, Punjabis, Sindhis, Pathans or Baloch; nor could they speak the languages of any of the country's provinces. Dominant leadership in the party belonged to feudal landlords, rich professionals and merchants, with a liberal sprinkling of immigrants from India. Also, leaders of the new nation showed more preference to the concentration of power rather than the development of the normal political process. No attempt was made to free the people from age-old forms of repression by bringing about institutional changes. The first step in the wrong direction was taken by none other than the Qaid-e-Azam, Jinnah, when he chose to become the Governor General of Pakistan himself, thereby downgrading the office of Prime Minister; the constitutional repository of

---

22   Farzana Shaikh, *Ibid*, p. 47.

political power with accountability through Parliament to the electorate. He should have understood this better than anyone else in the country; as the foremost expert on the constitutional law, that as a successor state to the British India nothing would suite the country better than the time tested British model of Westminster democracy. Whatever chances were there for democracy to take roots in Pakistan received a serious setback with Jinnah's death in 1948; as Liaquat Ali Khan did not enjoy adequate status and he neither had the capacity nor the will to cultivate a mass base for the party. However, he also died in the early years of nation's formation, as an assassin's victim in 1951. The only leader having a mass following among his people was H.S. Suhrawardy, a Bengali from East Pakistan. The ruling class of Pakistan would not accept a Bengali as their leader, and hence Suhrawardy could never play the role his personality deserved in the formative years of Pakistan. Under the circumstances it is not surprising that the leadership embarked upon, with the willing cooperation from Civil Service, safeguarding its narrow and personal interests. People lost faith in the political establishment and hollowness of the party which got Pakistan created; was laid bare in the very first elections in 1954. Muslim League practically ceased to exist since then.

For the next two years Pakistan went through a series of crisis involving top level changes, sectarian disturbances, public unrest and deep American interest in the country. It became an Islamic Republic on March 23, 1956, when the Constituent Assembly adopted new constitution. This constitution had three main features. The central government became all too powerful at the cost of provincial autonomy; the majority community of Bengalis was denied their rightful share of political power and office of the President became the pivotal figure. Iskander Mirza became the first President of Pakistan. The next over two years saw a series of central governments, the most notable being under the premiership of Bengali leader H.S. Suhrawardy. Political squabbling increased; there was large scale discontentment among the people which the ruling elite feared would manifest itself in the general elections in 1959. On October 8, 1958, the army took over power in a coup d'état; aided and abetted by President Mirza who retained his office, with General Ayub Khan – the Army Chief - as the Chief Martial Law Administrator. However, within a fortnight Iskander Mirza was dismissed and Ayub became ruler of the country, the first military man to do so; a trend that was to be repeated in the coming decades.

After four years of military rule wherein power was shared by the bureaucracy, 1962 constitution was adopted by Ayub and "Basic Democracy" was born in Pakistan. Ayub became President under this constitution after defeating Fatima Jinnah, sister of Mohd. Ali Jinnah, in a farcical election. This second phase of Ayub from 1962 to 1969 saw the bureaucracy reassert itself and it was the senior civil servants and not the generals who determined policy. The 1965 war with India, an adventure of Ayub Khan, cost dearly to Pakistan and was beginning of the end of his regime. It dealt a serious blow to the already stagnant economy. A wave of unrest engulfed Balochistan which then spread to other parts also. The last straw to this regime came in the form of popular resentment organized and sustained by students, workers, lawyers and teachers; and this lasted for five months from November of 1968. Ayub's final efforts to cling to power by opening a dialogue with political parties failed and he stepped down on March 26, 1969. His parting gift to the country was handing over power to another General, Yahya Khan the Army Chief and the nation's destiny passed from the hands of one dictator to another. During the next over two and half years, Yahya Khan's misrule, general elections where peoples popular mandate was not implemented, war with India during December 1971 and creation of Bangladesh are events too well known to need any repetition. According to a well known political analyst, "The 'Two-Nation' theory, founded in the genteel living rooms of Uttar Pradesh, was finally laid to rest in the paddy fields of Bangladesh".[23]

The prestige of Pakistan army following 1971 war was shattered. A new military leader was considered inappropriate and under pressure, the top army brass decided to invite Z.A. Bhutto to take over the reins of power in the (West) Pakistan. He came to power on December 20, 1971; was ousted by a military coup on July 1977 and executed thereafter on the charges of complicity in a political murder on April 5, 1979. Bhutto's failure to establish a strong democratic base in Pakistan and the factors which led to his growing unpopularity and downfall are well known and have been widely written about by political commentators.

Bhutto also had certain positive contributions to his credit and his greatest gift to Pakistan was the 1973 constitution. For the first time a definite political structure was given to the country's polity and executive power, instead of being concentrated in the hands of one person - the

23 Tariq Ali : A General Paralysis – Sunday (Calcutta) Vol 11, Issue 4, 14-20 August 1983.

Governor-General or the President - the concept of executive accountability to the elected Parliament was established. Many other features of this constitution were laudable and it still remains a rallying point for all those parties and individuals in Pakistan who are interested in the full restoration of real democracy in the country.

Among the faults and mistakes attributed to his regime; the most glaring one was to take the historically tolerant and accommodating Muslim society of the country, which was steeped in the pluralistic ethos of the sub-continent, firmly into the fold of Muslim countries, particularly the wealthy states of the Arab world. Pakistan was able to get large sums as aid from the Shah of Iran, the King of Saudi Arabia and Col Gadaffi of Libya; to shore up its economy and also send considerable manpower to the Middle East countries, which in turn sent substantial remittances back home. Another advantage was the uninterrupted flow of critical oil supplies. But for all these benefits, the mid and long term damage to the Pakistani society and polity was considerable and long lasting. The Madarssah culture, which has seeped into the country's systems, rise of fundamentalism, sectarianism and terrorism can all be termed as bye products of this Pakistani shift.

His sharpened nuclear ambitions also turned out to be a mistake and liability for the regime. It is now well established that Bhutto took the decision to go nuclear in 1972, and the intention had always been to make an atomic bomb and not to use nuclear energy for peaceful purposes. He convened a secret meeting of top scientists in Multan in 1972 and asked them if they could produce a bomb. On getting an affirmative reply, he got seriously busy with arranging necessary resources for the project. The main financier for this effort was Col Gadaffi of Libya, whom Bhutto wooed no end and to boost his ego, called the proposed project as "Islamic Bomb". Bhutto publically boasted of making this bomb at all costs even if, he famously said once, Pakistanis had to eat grass. It also required a team of highly resourceful scientists and agents to scout all over Europe and collect the required material from a number of establishments and ship these clandestinely to Pakistan. In a major industrial espionage, a leading Pakistani nuclear scientist, Dr. A.Q. Khan stole critical secrets from a European nuclear consortium based in Holland. The Chinese and North Korean help in this regard, later, is also well known and documented.

"His biggest failure, however, was his own inability to emerge as a democrat. He did not encourage democratic practices within his own party. The party elections were never held. Bhutto nominated all important functionaries and ran the party as a one-man show. With the result that when the time came for a show-down with the military; he found that the party had lost much of its base amongst the masses. His high handed dealing in Balochistan to quell a popular uprising and the use of the army for this purpose, helped a discredited and enfeebled high command of the army to recoup its prestige and standing which it had lost with the debacle in East Bengal and re-enter the political stage…"[24] During the country's general elections held in March 1977, the opposition parties got united under the banner of Pakistan National Alliance (PNA) with the single policy plank of being anti-Bhutto. The PNA very vocally rejected the election results which showed land slide victory for Bhutto's PPP and a nationwide stir followed. This ended in the army seizing power once again, on July 5, 1977. General Zia-ul-Haq, the Army Chief, appointed himself as the Chief Martial Law Administrator. The populist tide in Pakistan had come to an end and Z.A. Bhutto was to share a major part of the blame for it.

The military junta when it usurped power projected the front of being a savior of democracy and promised to hold elections within three months, by October 1977. These were postponed again and again on one pretext or the other. General Zia's rule had seen the worst type of censorship, political repression, curtailment of citizens' rights and fanatic efforts to resort to religious fundamentalism. As the General tightened his control; he offered more and stronger doses of Islamisation to Pakistan. The Martial Law regime proclaimed "Nizam-e-Mustafa" (Islamic Law) to be the law of the land on July 10, 1979. Zia declared that the primary aim of his government was to see the establishment of pure Islamic State in Pakistan and he vowed to work for that end. Pakistan was thus firmly set on the path of religious fundamentalism and sectarianism. Terrorism was soon to be added; as the country became a breeding ground for spawning such elements to foment trouble on the Eastern side – first in Punjab and then in J&K in India – and to fight against the Russians on the Western side, in Afghanistan. America was to be the mainstay of the Zia and subsequent regimes in Pakistan for over next two decades.

---

24 Tariq Ali : Can Pakistan Survive – Penguin Books, London-1983, p- 123.

CHAPTER - III

THE BREAKDOWN

The last chapter provides a fairly well contoured panorama of the efforts made by India to address and come to terms with the external dimensions of the Kashmir issue. However, the establishments in New Delhi failed to make similar assiduous exertions to anticipate and tackle the internal dimensions which, to any perceptive observer or well informed political analyst, would appear to have an equal if not greater significance. It is almost like boosting the immune system of the body aimed at keeping the deceases at bay. If the internal situation is managed effectively and the malcontent elements kept within check; then the impact of outside interference, even when it takes place, gets reduced to very considerable extent. The first default occurred with the failure to channel and contain the political aspirations and ambitions of Sheikh Abdullah. This in spite of the near similarity of political ideologies of the National Conference and the Congress, as also a deep personal bond of friendship and admiration between the Sheikh and Jawahar Lal Nehru. This lack of understanding and inability to judge the mental makeup of the Kashmiri leadership and collective psyche of the people of the state, particularly of those belonging to the Valley, has been a significant lapse and continuous refrain during the past seven decades. The malady is evident from the way the Centre dealt with the first popular leader of the state and thereafter continued the same pattern.

Instead of consolidating the institutions of state building and firming up the nascent democracy in J&K; Sheikh Abdullah was allowed to run affairs of the state in a dictatorial manner. Consequently when he became difficult to handle; practically unanswerable to anybody or system in the state or at the centre, his government was dismissed on August 9, 1953, and he was placed under detention, with his deputy Bakshi Ghulam Mohammad sworn in as the new Prime Minister. For the next ten years, Bakshi ruled the state with benign inclusiveness, forging strong links with the centre and building institutions of development in the state. Some of his major contributions included adoption of the State Constitution on January 26, 1957, abolition of the permit system for entry into the state, establishing Medical and Engineering colleges, construction of the Jawahar Tunnel near Banihal to ensure year-round linking of the Valley with rest of India as also building of new Civil Secretariat both at Jammu and Srinagar. It was also during his time that the State Public Service Commission and J&K Academy of Art, Culture and Languages were set up and jurisdiction of the Election Commission of India extended to the state. It can briefly be summed up that while as Sheikh Abdullah, through providing proprietary rights of land to the tillers and other measures politically empowered the people; Bakshi Ghulam Mohammad put the state firmly on to the development path. Bakshi's administration spawned the emergence of a new middle class in the state, assertive, empowered and endowed with material and intellectual resources which, like a middle class anywhere else, impacted hugely on the economic, social and political development of the state.

Bakshi resigned, perhaps made to resign would be a more truthful statement, in October 1963 under the famous Kamraj plan of the Congress Party. His successor Shamas-ud-Din, a virtual political non entity and lacking in administrative acumen could last only little over four months. His exit was hastened by the missing of the Holy Relic from Hazratbal Shrine on December 27 and its recovery eight days later. The next incumbent to head the state government was G.M. Sadiq; a political stalwart in his own right and a man with considerable political sagacity, sound judgment and administrative astuteness. He became Prime Minister in February 1964 and continued to head the government till his demise in December 1971. Sadiq conducted the administrative affairs of the state very competently and effectively managed his flock of legislators. It was during his tenure that the National Conference was converted into J&K Pradesh Congress Committee with Syed Mir Qasim as its first President, application of Articles 356 and 357 of the Constitution of India extended to the state and the J&K Constitution amended to redesignate the Sadar-i-Riyasat as Governor and the Prime Minister as Chief Minister.

Though Sadiq was a veteran National Conference leader even before independence; his later efforts to steer his own political path had considerably reduced his hold over the party apparatus. Thus, even while he held a firm grip over the administrative and also legislative matters, his control over the party cadres generally remained tenuous. He was also perceived in the state as a nominee of the Centre rather than a transparently elected leader of the ruling party; which further diluted his hold over the political set up. Towards the end of his tenure and life, Syed Mir Qasim as the state party chief started posing a credible challenge to the leadership of Sadiq. The latter's death in December 1971 paved the way for Mir Qasim becoming the next Chief Minister of Jammu and Kashmir. Three years of his stewardship of the state were not marked with any significant achievements and he was generally seen as an ineffective helmsman. Unlike Sadiq who could manfully stand up to the Sheikh, release him from jail and deal with his public standing politically as well as administratively, Mir Qasim's image in the public perception was of a person subservient to and in the awe of Sheikh Abdullah.

The Indo-Pak war of December 1971 culminating in the Indian victory and creation of Bangladesh considerably weakened the anti-Indian elements in the Valley as also dented the political standing and bargaining power of Sheikh Abdullah. Flushed with new confidence and vigour, New Delhi sought to wrap up the notes of discordance in the state by opening a dialogue with him aimed at achieving a viable long-term dispensation acceptable to all concerned. The fact that in the Assembly elections held in March 1972 the Congress won 57 out of 74 seats gave further impetus to this resolve of stabilizing conditions in J&K by bringing around a perceptibly weakened Abdullah. These efforts culminated in the six-point agreement on November 13, 1974, between the G. Parthasarthy, representing the Prime Minister and Mirza Afzal Beigh negotiating on behalf of the Sheikh; paving the way for his return to power a few months later. On February 24, 1975, Syed Mir Qasim resigned as Chief Minister. Next day Sheikh Mohammad Abdullah was sworn in as the new Chief Minister of the state, supported by the Congress Legislature Party in the Assembly, once again holding reins of the state twenty-two years after he was deposed.

Sheikh Abdullah quickly moved to consolidate his position. A person of his political standing, long experience of public life and astuteness could not have been expected to be constantly fettered by a legislative support which was not under his sway. It is also probable that the timing of his decision was influenced by the declaration of Emergency in the country by Indira Gandhi on June 29, 1975. A shrewd judge of the public mood, he may have correctly assessed the impending steep decline in the electoral fortunes of the Congress. Be that as it may; barely a week after this development, he revived the National Conference after winding up the Plebiscite Front and becoming its elected President a few months later. His political consolidation, particularly in the Valley, was swift and thorough. The Congress pulled the rug from under his feet by withdrawing legislative support, after losing the Parliamentary elections in March 1977. Four months later; in the ensuing Assembly elections, generally regarded by political observers as the most fair since independence, the National Conference formed government on its own by winning 46 out 76 seats with congress getting a severe drubbing with only 12 seats; not even getting the second position which was claimed by the newly formed Janata Party on the basis of winning in 14 constituencies. Of the rest, three seats were bagged by Independent candidates and one by Jamat-e-Islami. With 40 MLAs from his party in Kashmir - out of total 42 seats - the Sheikh's sway over the Valley was once again complete and uncontested.

It is generally agreed by political analysts that while as his government provided excellent administration during the first two years; after the 1977 elections the Sheikh's attention was more focused on the worldly, domestic and filial contemplations. To be fair to him, his health was fast deteriorating and during the last two years of his life there were increasingly prolonged periods of confinements when, it almost became a public knowledge, a coterie of political personalities and senior officers close to the family were taking decisions on his behalf. The Lion of Kashmir had become barely confined to his lair. As it happens in such scenarios, the struggle for political succession to the patriarch intensified with his failing health. The first in the reckoning was Mirza Afzal Beigh his longtime political associate from the pre-independence period and the Deputy Chief Minister. On the charges of disloyalty his resignation was sought and obtained; following which he was disgraced and expelled from the party. Beigh died a broken man in June 1982.

As a logical consequence Sheikh Abdullah's eldest son, Dr. Farooq Abdullah, a medical doctor and a political novice, was anointed his political successor by getting him elected as the President of National Conference on March 1, 1981. Seven months later with his father becoming critically ill Dr. Farooq was inducted into the state cabinet as the Health Minister. The question of political succession to Sheikh Mohammad Abdullah appeared to have been neatly stitched and settled. But apparently, it was not so. Another serious contender from within the family emerged in the form of redoubtable Ghulam Mohammad Shah; elder son-in-law of Sheikh Abdullah, a man of considerable administrative capabilities also having a good hold over party legislators and the cadre. His tantrums and posturing kept the political pot simmering but he refrained from indulging in open defiance of the wishes of the ailing patriarch.

Succumbing to his illness, Sher-i-Kashmir Sheikh Mohammad Abdullah expired on September 8, 1982. Unprecedented scenes of mourning were witnessed in the Valley with estimated over a million of people joining his funeral procession. Dr. Farooq Abdullah, with the obvious consent of Prime Minister Indira Gandhi and in some haste, was sworn in as the new Chief Minister the same day. With the demise of Sheikh Abdullah, an era came to close in the Valley, and perhaps in the state itself. He was undoubtedly the most popular, influential and charismatic leader of modern Kashmir; who strode its political landscape like a colossus for over five decades. He was a towering personality, literally, endowed with lofty political thoughts, great vision and passionate commitment to alleviate the miseries of his people and work for their upliftment. His greatest gift to the people of Kashmir was a collective sense of self-respect coupled with political empowerment and economic betterment. The obverse side of his personality also reflected political ambivalence, which at times appeared deliberately crafted, and a burning personal ambition for unbridled power; manifestations of both of which have caused immense problems and difficulties to the very people for whose benefit he strove most of his adult life.

In the realm of political activity if there was one person who could have brought lasting peace to Jammu and Kashmir it was Sheikh Abdullah. For his inability to do so his apologists may blame the circumstances beyond his control, exertions of his detractors and machinations of the government of India. This crucially important issue has been and could be, argued endlessly. But the fact remains that when the time came to choose his successor to lead the National Conference, and the political conditions in the state were far from settled, he preferred his son, a virtual greenhorn in the rough and tumble of politics, over a more seasoned and capable leader from his flock of undoubtedly talented frontline cadre. The right choice at that moment could have made a substantively positive difference in the future developments of the state and the failure to do so was entirely his own.

This could also be the right point of time to take a stock of the handling of the internal situation in the state by the government of India. A glance at the first thirty-five years after independence does not give a very flattering account of New Delhi in this regard. While the leaders at the national level, most of them persons of great eminence and endowed with visions of political sagacity seeped in high democratic traditions, were engaged in laying down solid foundations of democracy and the rule of law in rest of the country; in J&K all administrative powers and political initiatives were left in the hands of one person. Just a few days after signing the Instrument of Accession, the ruler of the state was made to appoint Sheikh Abdullah as the Head of Emergency Administration on October 30, 1947; making him the virtual ruler of the state. The first sprouts of democracy came to sight after four years in the form of elections to the Constituent Assembly, for which on October 15, 1951, the National Conference won all the 75 seats; of this number 73 were declared elected as uncontested. This is something extremely hard to digest in any democratic setup, howsoever nascent it may be. Whereas it could be presumed, by stretching the logic, that huge popularity of the party and its leader could have made it possible to sweep the polls in the Valley, no such conditions existed in Jammu and Ladakh regions of the state. In fact, the National conference did not have a very strong base in the Jammu division and it was virtually unknown in Ladakh. With the Constituent Assembly packed to the last man by his nominees, Sheikh Abdullah had absolutely a free hand to not only run the state administration according to his whims but also be in a position to draft the Constitution of Jammu and Kashmir as well as fashion the contours of the state's relations with the centre as per his desires. And New Delhi cannot but share the blame of being a party to these developments.

India had a very sound moral and legal position on J&K. Not withstanding that and also in spite of a very favourable military situation on the ground in the last quarter of 1948, the country accepted the cease-fire with effect from January 1, 1949. This, coupled with the almost open hostility shown by the Anglo-American combine in the deliberations at the United Nations against Indian stand and interests, made it abundantly clear that India's external policy in respect of J&K had lain in tatters. These factors should have been sufficient enough for the rulers and policymakers at the centre to keep much-focused attention on and constantly monitor the internal policy as well as developments relating to the state. Instead, one individual and a single party were virtually handed over the mandate to be the arbiter of the future of the people of Jammu and Kashmir. When, by the middle of 1953, it became evident that the Sheikh was harbouring personal designs of his own and had gone too far down the road, the manner of his dismissal, arrest and assumption of the mantle of the Prime Minister by Bakshi Ghulam Mohammad appeared contrived and lacking in finesse. To trace roots of these developments to the uncontested election of the seventy-three members of the Constituent Assembly may not be a far fetched proposition.

It is a common knowledge in J&K that Bakshi was a very able administrator and that he initiated a lot of developmental works as well as built institutions of higher learning and technical education. In addition, he was also an astute political manager and kept his flock together. But in spite of all his good work, he was always more perceived in popular esteem as a nominee of New Delhi rather than a democratically elected popular leader. Also, what does one say about nurturing the roots of democracy and creating structures that would reflect the will of the people? The system of checks and balances, so essential a part of any democratic structure, was hardly put in place and invoked in the state commonly referred to as the crown of India. As long as he was in power he did not feel answerable to any person, group or institution in the state. The Constitution of Jammu and Kashmir came into force on January 26, 1957. Elections were held the same year for the Assembly in which the number of seats which the National Conference won uncontested was a staggering 43 out of 75. Almost similar feat was repeated during the next election, under Bakshi's regime, in 1962 when the number of uncontested seats was incredible 34. While as all over the country the roots of democracy and the efficacy of the will of the people had taken deep roots, the corresponding conditions in J&K can well be imagined on the basis of just one set of figures mentioned here-in-before. The policy makers and rulers in New Delhi; as also leaders of national stature across the political spectrum, all men and women of great eminence endowed with liberal political thought cannot escape the collective blame for the lack of democratic culture and traditions in the state.

Bakshi Ghulam Mohammad was undoubtedly a courageous man with a lot of political foresight, earthy commonsense and enormous administrative capabilities. But unbridled power coupled with the absence of credible systemic and institutional checks and balances began tarnishing his image of fair play and sense of proportion after a time. The voices against his arbitrariness and misuse of power, including by some members of his family, kept rising steadily till it became, by early sixties, difficult for the centre to ignore them. Like few other state Chief Ministers a via media was found to effect a change of leadership in J&K under the famous Kamraj Plan of the Congress Party, which mandated senior and proven leaders of the states to work for strengthening the party apparatus. Bakshi tendered his resignation as the Prime Minister of the state on October 4, 1963, and eight days later his successor Shamas-ud-Din was sworn in. Since the state Assembly and the legislature party were packed with the nominees of Bakshi, it was but natural that his successor was a person of his choice. In fact, it was widely believed that Bakshi would continue to rule by proxy and wait for a more fortuitous time to get back into the saddle. But the disappearance of the Holy Relic from Hazratbal Shrine towards the end of December, its recovery a week later and the huge crisis generated in the Valley during the intervening period, restricted duration of the ineffectual government of Shamas-ud-Din to little over four months. A change became necessary to restore normalcy and confidence of the people in the functioning of the government. Consequently, G.M. Sadiq was sworn in as the Prime Minister of J&K on February 29, 1964. Even though political analysts agree that under the circumstances he was perhaps the best choice available, but since majority of the state Assembly still consisted of Bakshi loyalists, it took deft political maneuvering and behind the scene arm twisting by New Delhi's representative, Lal Bahadur Shastri, to ensure smooth implementation of the intended change over. Strictly speaking, proper democratic norms were not followed for the change of guard at the helm of affairs once again. The end could not justify the means. Yet one more time political expediency had gained ascendency over democratic norms and a right thing was not done in the right manner.

Sadiq had a long career of political activism with the reputation of being a leading ideologue with Marxist thoughts within the National

Conference; even before independence. He was considered the leader of a brilliant group of young leftist intellectuals within the party and his views were always heard with respect by almost everyone across the political spectrum of the state. At the personal level, he was a suave, cultured and educated person who was always well dressed in all public appearances. He also enjoyed an unsullied reputation for honesty; the image of which did not even once get tarnished during his over seven years of stewardship of the state government. Sadiq made considerable efforts in bringing the state to the national mainstream. The National Conference was transformed into J&K Pradesh Congress Committee with Syed Mir Qasim as its first President and also the State Constitution amended to rename the Sadar-i-Riyasat and Prime Minister as Governor and Chief Minister respectively; to bring these at par with other states of the Union. As a successful political executive, he strove hard to provide an efficient administrative system and keep politics away from the administration. He also competently handled the release of Sheikh Abdullah at the political level and considerably reduced his charisma and political appeal in the Valley. However, with 22 out of 75 candidates declared successful uncontested in 1967, the Assembly Elections held during his time were also not without blemish.

Sadiq died on December 12, 1971, and Mir Qasim was sworn as the new Chief Minister. His was almost a natural succession brought about, for the first time in J&K, by following democratic practices and conventions. Though he had tried hard to dislodge Sadiq in his lifetime but could succeed only after the latter's demise. Like his predecessor, Qasim also had leftist leanings but did not display any such proclivities while at the helm of affairs; either in his political initiatives or in administrative matters. In fact he is remembered not only as an ineffective Chief Minister but also as being in awe of Sheikh Abdullah, which has been perceived in partially being responsible for the latter's return to power in 1975. Qasim also successfully lead the Congress back to power in February 1972 Assembly Elections; this time with only five uncontested seats. The emphatic Indian win over Pakistan in the 1971 war probably also played some part in this. His tenure of over three years, before power was handed over to Sheikh Abdullah in February 1975, could be fairly assessed as notable for three events. One was the unusual manner of this change of guards, the second related to the conduct of seemingly credible Assembly elections. It was also during his regime that the Jamat-e-Islami surfaced on the electoral scene notably for the first time winning five Assembly seats and garnering

7.18 per cent of the votes polled. This was to have a considerable impact on the future political developments in the state.

Returning to September 8, 1982, when young Dr. Farooq Abdullah was sworn in as the Chief Minister on the demise of his father. He was elected leader of the National Conference Legislature Party three days later. A few months afterwards he recommended dissolution of the Assembly and elections were held in June 1983 in which National Conference was returned to power with an impressive tally of 47 seats out of 76 while the Congress won in 26 constituencies, not an insignificant number. Though the National Conference secured most of its seats from the Valley whereas Congress success was largely confined to the Hindu belt of Jammu; a regional and communal political orientation was distinctly discernible. Also, the electoral contest between the two parties was quite bitterly carried out with even the top leaders of both sides often slugging out at each other. Prime Minister Indira Gandhi never forgot or forgave the invectives hurled at her during the acrid campaign. She not only did not show any magnanimity towards the young and debutant Chief Minister, who in quite some measure had come to power with her support but also continued to put all possible pressure to make him fall in line. Dr. Farooq first resisted the attempted transgressions and then openly defied her by hosting a three days Opposition Conclave on October 5, 6 and 7, 1983. It was a significant gathering of political stalwarts from across the country representing 17 political parties. The participants included important names like Jyoti Basu, N.T. Rama Rao, Sharad Pawar, Babu Jagjivan Ram, Chandra Shekhar, H.N. Bahuguna, Prakash Singh Badal, I.K. Gujral. At the Conclave, primarily Centre-State relations were deliberated upon and an agreed statement, which came to be known as Srinagar Declaration, was adopted and issued at its end. It made a total of 31 recommendations touching virtually all aspects of the subject under consideration. Item 10 (h) of the recommendations referred to Article 370 and *inter alia* included, "The special constitutional status of the State of Jammu and Kashmir under Article 370 should be preserved and protected in letter and spirit".

Such an open challenge was too much to digest for Mrs. Gandhi and plans were afoot in New Delhi to assert itself even more effectively. Notwithstanding the internal and external sensitivities of a state like J&K and the fact that neighboring Punjab was already struggling with a dangerous insurgency and hence this state required a very tactful handling;

personal considerations overrode caution and circumspection. It was decided to remove Dr. Farooq and replace him with another member of the family, his brother-in-law, G.M. Shah who had earlier on the death of Sheikh Abdullah been denied the opportunity to contest his succession claim in a fair and democratic manner. However, Governor B.K. Nehru not only refused to effect any such change in a manner not strictly covered by the constitutional provisions but also cautioned, in the larger interests pointing towards its political fallout, against any such undertaking. Nehru who was appointed the Governor in February 1981 was pre-maturely shifted to Gujarat and replaced by Jagmohan on April 26, 1984.

On July 2, Governor Jagmohan advised Dr. Farooq to submit his resignation as he had lost majority support in the Assembly. With the latter insisting on proving his strength on the floor of the House, he was dismissed by the Governor and G.M. Shah sworn in as the new Chief Minister. The Shah government was supported in the legislature by the thirteen MLAs who had defected from National Conference in addition to those belonging to the Congress. It was to be a coalition government.

The dismissal of Farooq government created widespread resentment amongst the NC cadres, particularly in the Valley and the new dispensation was perceived as one imposed on them by the fiat of New Delhi. It also further sharpened negative perceptions in the minds of neutral political elements, encouraged the separatists as also created large spaces of distrust and disaffection which were filled by religious and extremist forces. On the international scene also the reactionary forces were on the rise, perceptibly so since 1979. It was during this year that two cataclysmic events had taken place in the Muslim world. One was Ayatollah Khomeini led Islamic revolution in Iran and the other Soviet armed intervention in Afghanistan. Both events created a profound effect on the collective Muslim psyche all over the world spawning different groups and organizations with continuing long-term impact. Also in the neighborhood, General Zia-ul-Haq had been in power for the last seven years and had consolidated his grip on Pakistan by putting it firmly on the path of Islamisation, including that of the armed forces. Such developments, especially those in Pakistan, did have a corresponding influence in Kashmir. It is surprising that a perceptive person like Indira Gandhi could ignore so obvious implications of the existing and developing internal and external situations and instead divert her energies to the ousting of Chief Minister of a small state heading a state level party.

G.M. Shah came to power with the reputation of being an acerbic personality, short on patience and niceties but an efficient administrator and a competent political executive. Fate had probably been unfair to him. Here was a right person catapulted to the top at a wrong time and through questionable means. A good number of analysts believe that had he been the Chief Minister after Sheikh Abdullah, the turn of events in J&K would have been much better for the state and also for the nation. But in July 1984, apart from streamlining the administration, his major problem was to keep his flock of MLAs together; the mercurial Congress representatives and the fickle minded NC defectors. Hemmed by the limitations of the lack of public and political support he did manage to tone up the bureaucracy and instill fear in the minds of incompetent and erring employees. It must also be said to his credit that he dealt with the anti-national and subversive elements more decisively and firmly than any other government before him. He was particularly successful in choking the links between pro-Khalistan and pro-Pakistan leaders; in addition to disrupting the supplies of arms and ammunition as well as distribution of subversive literature to the anti-national elements. The leaders and activities of Jamat-i-Islami were put under rigorous scrutiny and intense pressure. Also, some government employees were dismissed from service for taking part in subversive and secessionist activities. A prominent name amongst terminated government servants was Abdul Gani Bhatt, who later became chairman of the All Party Hurriyat Conference (APHC). But time and events were running against him. Political equations between New Delhi and Kashmir had yet again changed.

In February 1986 the first ever anti-Hindu riots, in the living memory, took place in the Valley in Anantnag district. The Congress, as if on a cue, withdrew support from G.M. Shah on the grounds of communal violence, reducing his government to a minority in the Legislature. The Shah ministry was dismissed on March 7, 1986, and Governor's rule imposed under Section 92 of the Jammu and Kashmir Constitution. It continued for the statutory limitation of six months after which the state was brought under President's rule as per Article 356 of the Constitution of India. In the two years following the dismissal of Dr. Farooq's government in July 1984, momentous changes had taken place on the Indian political scene. Indira

Gandhi's assassination on October 31, 1984, by one of her bodyguards; was followed by her son Rajiv Gandhi taking over as the Prime Minister of India. In the Parliamentary Elections that were held in December, the same year, the Congress won an unprecedented landslide victory and returned to power in the centre. With the change in leadership at the centre as also in political perceptions on the part of Dr. Farooq Abdullah, the relations between Congress and National Conference improved considerably. The two leaders also established a warm and cordial rapport at the personal and political levels, including sharing a common public platform in Jammu. The Congress – NC accord enabled Dr. Farooq to return to power on November 7, 1986, on the revocation of President's rule in the state. Although elections to the State Assembly were due in 1989, Dr. Farooq Abdullah decided to go in for the polls in March 1987; which were contested by the two parties with electoral understanding.

The main reason advanced by both parties for forging an alliance was to accelerate developmental and economic activities in the state with the help of enhanced allocations from the centre. However, this logic did not appear to appeal much to the people of the Valley. Public sympathy which was with Dr. Farooq following his unjustified dismissal in 1984 had now evaporated as he was perceived to be a person who would deeply compromise for getting back into power. His personal standing and that of his party took a considerable setback. Many observers have noted that this accord proved an important turning point in the fast deteriorating political environment in Kashmir. Earlier agitations and political dissent against the state or the central governments were channelized through the medium of one of these parties. Henceforth this alternative to giving vent to secular protests was blocked. This was a major and very unfortunate miscalculation on the part of senior leaders of both parties. Most of the disaffected political elements in the Valley started gravitating towards the separatist and fundamentalist outfits and the hitherto hidden pro-Pakistan elements started coming to the fore. Alienation amongst the general public, already disappointed and distraught with the fast-moving developments in the state, often bewildering and beyond logical comprehensions, was rapidly increasing. The popular discontent struggling to find a legitimate and viable outlet was getting suffocatingly bottled up, giving rise to its own vicious cycle. In fact, after the demise of Sheikh Abdullah, there was hardly ever a leader of status, substance and means in the state with whom the masses could relate and feel comfortable. In this scenario of general disenchantment with mainstream political parties, the fundamentalist and secessionist groupings - Jamat-Islami being the most prominent and well organized amongst them- came together to form a loosely held political entity named Muslim United Front (MUF). It contested most of the 42 Assembly seats in the Valley in the 1987 elections.

The Congress-NC alliance entered the electoral fray with the self-assurance of returning to power with a comfortable margin and this confidence was not misplaced. There was hardly any opposition grouping in Jammu or Ladakh regions and in the Valley only MUF was expected to do well in some of the constituencies. Of the 76 constituencies, elections for which were conducted in March 1987, the alliance swept the polls with National Conference winning 40 and Congress gaining victory in 26 seats. Remaining ten seats were shared by MUF and Independents, four each and BJP registering win in two constituencies. While in Jammu and Ladakh the losing candidates and parties registered usual murmurs of unhappiness; the script went substantially wrong in Kashmir. The MUF made vociferous allegations of widespread rigging and malpractices during the polling and counting process. Being the primary beneficiary in this region main protests and ire were directed against the NC and Dr. Farooq Abdullah. Later revelations and developments did confirm that unfair means had been used in some of the constituencies, and at few places quite openly, by the ruling party; even though these took place on a much reduced level than what was being alleged. The subsequent behavior of some influential winning candidates made the matters even worse. A number of MUF candidates and their supporters were detained and manhandled, further fuelling the disenchantment and public anger and giving rise to disillusionment with electoral politics. It is also true that in the initial stage of militancy some of the front rank militant commanders and separatist leaders had been the MUF candidates or their election or counting agents.

It is generally believed that if free and fair electoral process was followed the total tally of the MUF would have been in the range of around ten; still giving the alliance a very wide and comfortable margin to form a stable government. But the charges of widespread rigging of elections in the Valley persisted, buttressed by public knowledge of wrong and high handedness at some places, putting a question mark on the efficacy of the entire electoral process. The refrain of protestors was picked up and enhanced at sustained pace by the media. The National Conference instead of meeting this rising tide of discontent politically, which the party apparatus could have been capable of, treated the matter as an issue of public order and used the state machinery to deal with it. This was another serious miscalculation. As it is the rank and file of the NC and general public in Valley were not enthused with its alliance with Congress. Allegations and charges of manipulations in the elections also adversely affected the credibility of the National Conference leadership. With the advantage of hindsight, it would be reasonable to consider the NC-Congress accord and electoral manipulations in some seats in the Valley as serious political miscalculations on the part of Dr. Farooq Abdullah; which became important factors in the rise of militancy in the state. Soon both NC and Congress became irrelevant in the emerging scenario of Kashmir.

How did the two most important political parties in the state come to this sorry pass? A probable answer may lie in the fact that right from 1947 onwards the handling of Jammu and Kashmir situation by the central government showed a lack of continuity and absence of an institutional framework. All through, till the militancy gained momentum, affairs of the state were influenced from New Delhi by the personality of the Prime Minister and his or her relationship with the head of the government in the state. The events and developments in J&K were greatly impacted by Jawaharlal Nehru, followed by Indira Gandhi and then Rajiv Gandhi; notwithstanding the short tenures of Lal Bahadur Shastri and Morarji Desai. These three personally oversaw the framing and conduct of the central government's policies as well as determined the political contours of relationship with Jammu and Kashmir. They were all influenced by their likes and dislikes of the major players in the state politics. This did help the state to garner more than a fair share of the centre's resources for its development on the basis of favourable personal equations but there was also an obverse side to this phenomenon. Handing over of unbridled powers to Sheikh Abdullah immediately after the state acceded to the Indian Union, dismissal of the Farooq Abdullah government in July 1984 and the NC-Congress alliance in November 1987 are just three examples of personal proclivities determining major political happenings which in turn had crucial and far-reaching consequences, not only for the state but also for the whole country. Instead, a political strategy fashioned collectively at the national level by tapping the vast pool of talent and experience available at the dawn of Independence and implementation of such policy framework through the institutional mechanisms, so well tried and tested in the central government systems, would have made a lot of difference in the fortunes of the state. Some of the defining negative developments that took place in the state could have been avoided.

At the dawn of Independence India had everything going in its favor in J&K. The people of Kashmir, only Muslim majority region of the state, had rejected the overtures of Muslim League and Mohammad Ali Jinnah himself. The political ideology of the National Conference was so much akin to the principles and policies of the Indian National Congress. Personal relations between Jawaharlal Nehru and Sheikh Abdullah were always cordial and pleasant; based on mutual respect and admiration. In fact, Sheikh Abdullah had also been the President of the All India State Peoples Congress in the early forties. When the Pakistani tribal raids of the Valley started in the second fortnight of October 1947, the local population resisted their advance and depredations all along up to the very doors of Srinagar city till the Indian Army came to their rescue; having been airlifted after the accession of the state. In fact, strong opposition offered by the inhabitants of Baramulla town to the tribal raiders from Pakistan, and the latter's acts of loot, arson and rapes, became all too familiar. After induction of the Indian Army in the state, the troops received whole hearted cooperation from the locals throughout Kashmir in the form of total and unwavering support in logistics, information and guides. In the 1947-48 Operations in Jammu and Kashmir, two civilians were decorated with gallantry awards. Mohammad Ismail received Maha Vir Chakra in the Zojila area and Jumma Mohammad got Vir Chakra in the Uri sector. It was a rare feat indeed. From that point to the scenario in 1987, forty years later, there was a huge change in the local conceptions and sentiments about India. The anti-Indian feelings had become palpably evident, particularly in Srinagar and other major urban centers of the Valley. How did this reversal of perceptions take place?

One major factor responsible for the turn around has been mentioned earlier. Another significant reason was the dealings of India with Pakistan, as also her handling of the Anglo- American block diplomatically; but most crucially the stopping of military operations and agreeing to the cease-fire at a time when the ground situation was extremely favourable to India on all fronts in the state towards the later part of 1948. India practically bailed out Pakistan from a serious predicament and a precarious military position which was wholly the latter's creation.

It has been a serious failure of the Indian political system that while in rest of the country people were enjoying benefits of complete freedom and unfettered power of the ballot, democracy could not strike deep roots in J&K. Except for the 1977 Assembly elections, nearly all elections held in the state in the first four decades after 1947 could not be termed free and fair. The people felt that who would rule them was not decided by them through the choice of their franchise but by someone else ruling in New Delhi at the time, and they can't be blamed for this comprehension. Even the 1977 Assembly elections were only a welcome change, a much-awaited whiff of fresh air so to speak, and not a turning point. It was twenty-five years later in 2002 that full empowerment of democracy was realized by the people of the state when, through the use of electoral franchise, they were demonstrably able to replace the existing government with the one of their choice. And then again repeat the same performance in the next Assembly elections in 2008. There is presently a happy and general perception that this electoral empowerment is not only irreversible but also at par with the rest of the country.

Along with democracy; the Indian political class also failed to effectively spread the essential message of secularism and other core values which the nation stood for. It is an irony that in J&K where people of all religions and communities had traditionally lived in harmony and healthy regard for mutual religious and cultural sensitivities; these customary feelings of tolerance, accommodation and lack of fundamentalist thoughts were vitiated over a period of time. The virus of intolerance and fundamentalism did not spread all of a sudden. It seeped in and gathered momentum slowly and could have been successfully addressed and eradicated if there was a resolute political will and solid public support to the governments in power and enlightened leadership in the principal political parties. Even the fast spread of education did not have a desired impact on this growing menace. On the contrary, on certain occasions, for immediate political benefits the rise of fundamentalist elements was not only ignored but positively encouraged also.

The centre too did not make sufficient efforts to assimilate and bring people of the state in the national mainstream. Historically and also due to the location and geography; they did not have much intercourse with the Indian mainland. The inhabitants of the Valley, particularly, remained isolated and insular. The central government failed to initiate special efforts to remove this sense of seclusion and remoteness. The traders were not encouraged or assisted to find markets for their goods in majors trading centers and places of tourist attractions in the rest of India. With the result, most of the famous Kashmir handicrafts items were sold locally to the tourists visiting the Valley; thus not only depriving the artisans and the traders the benefits of a huge national market but also limiting the opportunities of interaction and understanding more about each other. Similarly, if avenues were provided for higher and technical education to the youth of the state in other parts of India as also increased employment opportunities in government, public and private sectors in various locations outside the state; linkages would have developed more extensively and in an enduring manner. This did not happen and the state, especially the Valley, continued to remain secluded and self-centered. It took the Railways, for example, twenty-five years to connect the short distance of one hundred kilometers between Pathankot and Jammu and the state could emerge on the railway map only in 1972.

It is important to realize that even the people of Jammu, who have never harbored any anti-India feeling, would feel that national capital of New Delhi was very far distance away as the train was available only from Pathankot and up to that point one had to travel by road; another tedious journey of a couple of hours. It would not be an exaggeration to mention that the Jammu population really felt connected with the rest of the nation only after 1972 with railway connectivity becoming a reality. That the emotional integration and mainstreaming measures for the state were a very low priority for the national policymakers, can further be realized from the fact that it took another 33 years before the railway line was laid and made functional between Jammu and Udhampur; a distance of mere 60 kilometers.

However, after much persuasion and constant lobbying by the state government the centre ultimately realized the importance of rail connectivity to the Valley in its proper perspective. Today the most significant infrastructural project in the state is the extension of the railway line from Udhampur to Baramulla. Construction on this 285 Kilometers section was started earnestly in 2003 and, after suspension of work for 3-4 years in between is now proceeding with reasonable speed. At the current level of activity, the running of train services between Udhampur and Baramulla during 2020 is quite likely. Apart from the usual advantages of such schemes like economic development, environmental benefits and population satisfaction; the train connectivity of the Valley with the rest of the nation will pay huge dividends in terms of mainstreaming the local population and strengthening the psychological linkages. The people will feel not only connected but also wanted.

Strenuous effort for mainstreaming of the population and joining with the rest of the country, particularly the rail connection, should have been a very high priority with the national leadership. This inability has been one of the more glaring policy failures contributing to the fraying and weakening of bonds between state and the union. It becomes quite evident that in the first four decades after independence, lack of proper appreciation of some important issues and inadequate comprehension of political developments failed to mainstream the people of Kashmir and forge stronger links of the state with rest of the country. By the time 1987 Assembly elections ended, with strong arms methods used by the National Conference in some of the constituencies; the allegations of large-scale electoral rigging in the Valley were flying thick. It is now well known that though these charges were not entirely correct and the extent highly exaggerated, it is equally true that the elections were not without any blemish. Considering the rising wave of discontent against the party and people in power and the fact that by this time it had become pretty much clear that separatist elements and anti-India feelings were on the rise; the political outfit that mattered in Kashmir should have boldly faced and tackled the deteriorating situation.

With the Congress having a limited presence in Kashmir; the National Conference was the only major political party there on ground. Till that time it had a very effective organizational structure in place and a strong grass root presence. Most of the seats that the party had won in the Valley were on its own steam and it certainly had the capability and the clout to meet the challenge headlong. But in the most crucial period of its five-decade long existence, when it was time to show the guts of steel and unflinching faith in its basic creed; and when its legitimacy was being questioned and very survival threatened, the NC leadership blinked. It did not display enough fire in the belly to go to the field at the organizational level, muster its rank and file, galvanize the party apparatus and launch a political counteroffensive. The armed militancy had not yet become manifest and the political opponents of the party were neither organized nor united. It was very much possible for the NC to recover the lost ground and redeem its tainted image through meaningful mass contact and political exertions. This required considerable hard work, physical discomfort and may be risk of injury. It was certainly not a task without hazards, but to the perceptive mind, the consequences of inactivity were also significantly grave. However, its leadership individually and collectively chose the softer option, withdrew in the security shell and contented itself by occupying various high offices commensurate with the electoral gains registered by the party in the Assembly elections. The National Conference had missed an opportunity to refurbish its image and temper its strength by opting out of the option to undertake a trial by fire. It managed numbers in the legislature but compromised on the quantum of respect in public perception. It retained power in the state government but lost on the moral authority. From this point onwards it was almost a constant downward slide in the political fortunes of the National Conference with none of the influential and old-time leaders making any visible effort to arrest this trend. The party got a final chance, before the onslaught of militancy engulfed it; to show the flag and reassert itself when, on August 21, 1989, Mohammad Yusuf *alias* Yusuf Halwai, one of its Block Presidents was shot dead by militants in broad daylight in downtown Srinagar.

Yusuf was killed for no fault of his, except that he was an office bearer of the National Conference. His cold-blooded murder was widely condemned and sent a wave of indignation in the masses, particularly amongst people of Srinagar city. A Kashmiri can be highly expressive and vindictive when aroused. Here was probably the last opportunity for the party to consolidate and channelize the public anger and resentment against the militants and their separatist supporters and effectively roll back their increasing influence. It could have meant some vicious street fight, and maybe spilling of blood; this political outfit was quite capable of handling given its past experience of agitational politics. It had a strong cadre, the requisite muscle power, ample state resources at disposal; its survival had been constantly challenged and now it had a popular cause behind it to justifiably retaliate and settle scores. It was provided a perfect scenario for an effective and defining riposte. But the party flinched yet again. It was the most direct challenge thrown at the party by the emerging militancy. The NC did not pick up the gauntlet and instead of going after the militants and their overground support structure in a resolute manner; the leadership displayed impotent rage and indulged in breast-beating. The National Conference had effectively reduced itself to being a mere spectator in the fast deteriorating internal situation in Kashmir.

Barely a fortnight before the assassination of Mohammad Yusuf, the Jammu and Kashmir Liberation Front (JKLF), the main militant outfit at that time, had issued an ultimatum to the National Conference workers to quit the party. This was followed by targeted killings, abductions, extortions and threats to the NC cadre. A good number of party workers and office bearers started leaving the party and issued public statements of this intent. In the second half of 1989, the NC leadership not only lost its control over the party apparatus but became increasingly ineffective in providing meaningful governance in the state. Its political ally and the coalition partner the Congress, not having much base in the Valley and undergoing its own existential crisis in the centre, could do nothing more than merely being a fellow traveller. The situation spiralled further downwards in the month of December when militants kidnapped Rubiya Sayeed – the daughter of the then Union Home Minister Mufti Mohd Sayeed – followed by subsequent developments. The final scene of this politically charged drama got enacted on January 19, 1990. On that day Jagmohan was appointed the new Governor of the state replacing General K.V. Krishana Rao (Retired) and Dr. Farooq Abdullah and his party ministers resigned in protest. Governor's Rule was imposed under Section 91/92 of the State Constitution and the Assembly kept in suspended animation. The NC had gone into deep hibernation, if not in political coma, only to be resuscitated by favourable developments over six years later.

National Conference, the premier political party of the state which had a pioneering role in ushering in the democratic rule and political empowerment of the people for over five decades had become irrelevant, almost completely, to the prevailing situation. Apart from other contributing factors, the main reasons for this decline in fortunes were various acts of commission and omission by the party leadership during the last one decade; particularly after the death of Sheikh Abdullah. After the patriarch had passed into history, the senior and seasoned party stalwarts were systematically ignored and made to feel unwanted. The defection by a group MLAs and G.M. Shah run government for two years created a further schism in the rank and file. But, by far the damage to the efficacy and strength of the party was caused by opportunistic policies adopted by its leadership; discarding ideology and principles in favor of power and electoral gains.

Policies of the central government since independence and handling of the state by the Indian political class lay in shambles. Gandhi had seen a "ray of hope" in the fabled valley of Kashmir when large swaths of the subcontinent were engulfed in the fire of communalism and senseless violence. The same was now getting seriously singed in the heat and passion generated by religious fundamentalism and militant violence. In five decades the visible articulations of a peace-loving and essentially secular people had undergone an unexpected transformation. The changeover did not happen overnight. There were homegrown factors as also external influences which any sensitive national polity and sovereign government should have anticipated and responded appropriately in time. In a federal structure like India, it is the bounden duty of the central government to safeguard not only the national borders but also ensure internal peace and tranquility in each and every constituent unit. That it failed to carry out mandated functions is clear from the developments that were taking place at that point of time in the Valley and the whole state of Jammu and Kashmir. Kashmir has been a crucible for the great Indian experiment of democracy, secularism, plurality and inclusive growth. By the closing of the eighties, it had become obvious that appropriate political and governance attention was not paid to the adverse developing situation in the state. If nothing else, the prevailing conditions in neighboring Punjab, in the late seventies and early eighties should have given enough warning signals of the impending crisis in J&K.

With Punjab on the boil; due to Pakistan inspired and aided militancy, common prudence should have dictated the national policymakers to at least adopt the fire brigade approach and take all requisite measures to keep the political temperatures down in J&K. But that did not happen; instead, a series of ill-timed and potentially disastrous initiatives further vitiated an already deteriorating political situation. Prime Minister Indira Gandhi allowed her personal proclivities to get better of her sound political judgment, deep understanding of the complexities of Kashmir situation and comprehensive knowledge of the important leaders and opinion makers in the state. Was she working to a plan in posting Jagmohan as the Governor in April 1984 and then manipulating G.M. Shah taking over as the Chief Minister three months later? If indeed there was a method in what she was doing then she probably did not disclose the details to even her close advisors. But, with her sudden and bloody death in October the same year, the plot, if there was any, lost its script. The successor Prime Minister Rajiv Gandhi, her son, did not possess personal expertise on the state. He probably did not have time or patience to comprehend and grasp nuances of the multi-layered complexities of the historical perspective, important turning points and the fast-changing contemporary scene in J&K. He addressed the Kashmir situation in his youthful exuberance and with certain innocence, bordering on political naiveté; born out of essential goodness of his personality and desire to undo a perceived wrong. But having struck a political alliance, he did not even bother to oversee or counsel the conduct of his partner. And when things started going horribly wrong in the second half of 1989, he was not even the Prime minister. By January 1990, with the resignation of the democratic government in the state, the ball was back in the court of New Delhi; squarely this time.

In 1947-48 the sequence of events in the state and handling of the situation by the national leaders had resulted in internationalizing the Kashmir issue. The openly blatant Anglo-American support to the aggressor Pakistan in and outside the United Nations and the UN interventions in this behalf are matters of historical records. This was the external dimension of the Kashmir issue. However, over the next forty years, the internal situation in the state was not firmed up. From a princely state, its natural and logical transformation into a functioning and vibrant democracy; self-reliant economy and natural socio-political intercourse with rest of the country, like other states of the Union, was not taken seriously. Within parameters of the special constitutional status granted to the state, lot more could and should have been done. Not only the mainstreaming of J&K with rest of the country was neglected, the centrifugal forces so inherent in a hugely diverse region like this were also completely ignored. With the result that state-center linkages did not become strong enough and also within the state itself inter and intra-regional fault lines, between the three regions of Jammu, Kashmir and Ladakh, became increasingly manifest with the passage of time.

Most of all, the worsening situation in the Valley should have caused alarm bells to ring in New Delhi because of the mischief potential it held for Pakistan. Across the border, General Zia-ul-Haq the military ruler of Pakistan duly fortified by the unstinted support of America, for his help to the CIA in Afghanistan, took full advantage of the events unfolding in J&K. For the first time, Pakistan started making noises about the internal happenings in the state not only in the UN systems but also in other multilateral international fora. He succeeded considerably in drawing international attention to external as well as internal developments in J&K. The government of India was once again put on the back foot.

CHAPTER – IV

The Militancy

A question which often belies exact answer is the point of time when the seeds of exclusivity, obscurantism, religious fundamentalism and secessionism were sown in the state; more specifically in the Valley. One thing, however, is certain that these traits became manifest not in 1987 or 1989 as is generally believed to be coinciding with the beginning of militancy. In fact, the seeds of secession and pro-Pak feelings may have been sown even before India gained Independence and the very idea of Pakistan became a reality. The roots of these can be traced to the oldest political party in the state, Muslim Conference, which started its activities in 1931. This organization was headed by Sheikh Mohammad Abdullah for seven years. Although it demanded popular government from the ruler, the primary focus remained welfare of Muslims in the state. In 1938 a vast majority of this party- having supporters in almost the entire Valley- converted itself to the secular, with leftist leanings, National Conference; which was again headed by Sheikh Abdullah. The remainder minority group, mainly concentrated in the areas now forming part of PoK and some segments of Srinagar city, decided to continue as the Moslem Conference under the leadership of Chaudhury Ghulam Abbas and aligned itself to the All India Muslim League. The followers of this party and its basic tenets were to form the core of anti-India and pro-Pak outfits in the years and decades to come. After the tribal raids followed by the 1974-48 military operations in J&K and due to the overwhelming public support to the nationalist administration of National Conference headed by Sheikh Abdullah, the pro-Pak elements became dormant. Bulk of these people migrated to Pakistan and PoK; the rest went underground.

During the next six years, the political climate in Kashmir had undergone unexpected change with the relations between National Conference and New Delhi becoming increasingly bitter. This development, which gave some courage to the local remnants of the Muslim Conference, coupled with sustained Pakistani efforts to keep the trouble going in J&K resulted in the formation of the Kashmir Political Conference in Srinagar on June 19, 1953. The pro-Pak and anti-India elements got rolled into one. Almost simultaneously the gulf between National conference and the central government was widening due to mutual suspicion and serious apprehensions about each other's intentions. The breach became a gaping chasm with the dismissal and arrest of Sheikh Abdullah on August 9, 1953. This development sent a wave of anger and anguish through the collective Kashmiri mind. The almost dormant Pro-Pak elements surfaced in the garb of supporters of the detained leader and made an endeavor to strike a common cause between the two. So was born the first anti-India organization, though not necessarily in favor of Pakistan, named the J&K Plebiscite Front on August 5, 1955. It was headed by the former Revenue Minister and Sheikh's right-hand man Mirza Afzal Beigh with Ghulam Mohammad Shah, son-in-law of Sheikh Abdullah, as the General Secretary. As expected, it overshadowed the Kashmir Political Conference and for some time became almost the sole vent for the anti-India tirade. Not accepting the finality of the accession of Jammu and Kashmir to India, the Plebiscite Front demanded 'holding of plebiscite according to the UN Resolutions of 1948'. Even though the law enforcement agencies suspected this organization to be receiving funds from Pakistan and being involved in subversive activities; the same could not be substantiated in the court of law sufficiently to secure conviction of any of the front-ranking leaders on these counts.

The activities of Plebiscite Front and utterances of its leaders were certainly unpalatable for the Union Government but these did not serve the purpose of Pakistan. Sheikh Abdullah and his followers may have had their grievances against New Delhi and the way they were being treated and were making considerable noise about it, but their whole intent was to get what they wanted from the existing scheme of things. Maximum autonomy, bordering on virtual independence if possible, within the Indian Union appeared to be the purpose of their exertions. Stretching to the extreme; the Plebiscite Front could have been termed anti-India, but by no flight of imagination could it be deemed to be pro-Pakistan. This is where the rub lay for Pakistan. The establishment there - the politicians, the civil services and the army - knew very well that the Sheikh had not only rejected the two-nation theory but had also spurned advances of the Muslim League, epitomized by Jinnah himself, earlier and was not going to fall for it again. This bottom line did not suit Pakistan. Having lost the gambit of securing merger of J&K by force of arms in 1947-48; Pakistan wanted to achieve the same purpose by fomenting internal discord and strife so that the bond between state and the centre becomes untenably weak. For this purpose, only a subservient and client organization was required which would be totally in favor of joining Pakistan. This bill the Plebiscite Front did not fit in and hence its utility for Pakistan was not very significant other than being a source of inconvenience or embarrassment to India.

By the mid-fifties Pakistan had joined the western military alliance, and become a minor player in the Cold War scenario, in addition to and - this was far more important to that country - receiving liberal financial and military support shoring the economy and buttressing its military capability. The new found economic stability and military strength further whetted that nation's appetite to try and aim for reaching out and grabbing the forbidden fruit of Kashmir once again. But this time it decided to wait for, or create, local support base and collaborators. For that to happen, the internal situation in J&K was not yet ripe. The pro-Pak elements had still not gathered enough mass and were mostly underground. For them, an opportunity came later when the Holy Relic disappeared from the Hazratbal Shrine on December 27, 1963. As a large segment of Valley population spilled on to the lanes and streets of their respective villages, towns and cities with inconsolable grief and indignation demanding recovery of the Holy Relic; the State Government headed by a weak Prime Minister, Shamas-ud-Din, found itself unequal to the task. As would have been expected; the Pakistani agents and supporters tried to provoke the crowds towards anti-India and pro-Pak direction. For the next one week, till the Holy Relic was found and restored to its original place, efforts were intensified to unhinge Kashmir from India. But it did not work; as with the Holy Relic restored and satisfactorily identified, the people heaved a sigh of relief and went about their vocations with complete normalcy restored.

The sudden mass upsurge of the people of Kashmir on the disappearance of the Holy Relic was perhaps interpreted by Pakistan to be a most emphatic demonstration of their Muslim identity, but it did not take into consideration their concurrent Kashmiri and national characteristics. This misconception coupled with a false sense of military superiority over India made Pakistan to first launch guerrillas in Kashmir in August 1965 under "Operation Gibraltar" and when that failed due to no help coming from the local Kashmiris; it unleashed all-out war with India – almost pompously - naming the attempt as "Operation Grand Slam". Both initiatives were failed adventures as the Indian response and attitude of Kashmiris was contrary to Pakistani expectations. Pakistan received a further setback in 1971 after comprehensively losing another war with India and its culmination in the creation of Bangladesh as an independent nation.

However, up to this point even though nothing substantial had been achieved by Pakistan in its nefarious designs about J&K, but the underground activities of its supporters in Kashmir, coupled with various acts of commission and omission by the state and the central governments, had gained in strength and spread. The Jamat-e-Islami and Jammu and Kashmir Liberation Front (JKLF) - both off shoots of Pakistan's assiduous efforts to create a constituency for itself in the state - came into being in the sixties. These two organizations have been responsible for most of the anti-India and pro-Pak activities during the last over four decades. Most of the indigenous militant organizations and leaders who operated in J&K during this period were either spawned by them or owe their origin to them some way or the other. The story of their growth and spread needs to be told in some details.

Jamat-e-Islami

The Jamat-e-Islami Kashmir (JEI), although not a part of Jamat-e-Islami Hind, has received inspiration from the latter at least in the initial years of existence. In fact, both of these owe their founding allegiance to Maulana Sayid Abdul al Maudodi, a Muslim cleric and scholar who gained prominence in the nineteen thirties. The Jamat-e-Islami Kashmir was born in Shopian in 1942. It formally broke off all links with the parent Indian body in 1953. However, in the first couple of decades of its activities it did not find many adherents for the religious fundamentalism that is its creed, due to the essentially liberal Sufi Islamic tenets traditionally followed in Kashmir; as also because of the overwhelming political influence of Sheikh Abdullah in the Valley. But, it always possessed a band of highly committed and dedicated workers and almost right from the inception it has been regarded as the most fundamental and highly disciplined cadre based organization in Kashmir. It has an organizational structure percolating from the apex body to the Tehsil units. The central body consisting of 31 members is called Majlis-e-Shoora. It's most prominent head, Ameer-i-Jamaat; so far has been Syed Ali Shah Geelani.

After delinking it from the parent Indian body, the JEI has always looked up to the JEI Pakistan for ideological inspiration and support. It strives for the establishment of Nizam-e-Mustafa and for that Islamisation of Kashmiri society, according to the tenets of the religion as interpreted by it, is a pre-requisite. Therefore it is against the concepts of individual liberty, socialism and secularism which are the basic pillars of the Indian democracy. Instead, it subscribes to the concept of Ummah, a Pan-Islamic identity, which does not recognize any national boundaries. It considers J&K a disputed territory and questions the state's accession to India. While technically demanding the right of self-determination for the people of the state, there is no doubt that the JEI works for Kashmir becoming a part of Pakistan. In this backdrop, it was only inevitable that personalities and organizations which stood for secularism and against collaborating with Pakistan would be opposed by it. Its dislike and opposition to the National Conference and Sheikh Abdullah can be understood in this context. Their respective ideologies, allegiances and political thoughts have been divergent and also poles apart.

Conceptually, the JEI was not expected to dabble in politics but to confine its activities to the theocratic domain. But the ideological deviation was prompted and political discourse channelized by the strong links it had forged with its Pakistani counterpart and also, to an extent, by the political developments in the state nudging it in that direction. This group was weighed down by lack of following and resources in the initial years. The fledgling organization was not able to strike deep enough roots to feel comfortable and therefore welcomed any help that came its way. The first such opportunity came in 1953 when Bakshi Ghulam Mohammad came to power. To counter the influence of Sheikh Abdullah he needed support from whichever quarter it was forthcoming. The JEI took full advantage of this opportunity, for the material benefit as also because of its intense dislike for the Sheikh. For the latter reason itself, it was only too happy to make a common cause with Bakshi to run down the image of Sheikh Abdullah and reduce his influence and following. This support was obviously not based on principles, but had a significant material component also.

Close proximity to the power structure not only brought handsome financial gains for the JEI but also opened avenues for government jobs. To enhance his popularity and to shore up the credibility of his regime, Bakshi had embarked upon a number of populist and public-oriented schemes. One of the important measures was accelerated implementation of the policy of free education. Under this scheme, a lot of new schools were opened and also new teachers recruited. The JEI very shrewdly concentrated on the education sector with long-term benefits in mind. It got a good number of its cadres and sympathizers recruited in the government service as teachers. These people got a stable source of earning, contributed regularly to the organization and, even more importantly, in their own time and in their own way influenced the students with the JEI ideology. With the money that it had got, the JEI considerably expanded the network of its own educational institutions in the first few years; and then never looked back. At its peak, there were up to three hundred schools of different levels across Kashmir and Doda district of Jammu division, where it had made considerable inroads. In these schools not only slanted religious education was provided, based on its own interpretation of religion, the boys were also taught a distorted and colored vision of the history, with anti-Hindu and anti-India stance.

It was during the Bakshi regime that the JEI was able to really strike its roots deep - although it had not become so evident at that point of time - and also secured its financial position. It was now better prepared to weather storms. When G.M. Sadiq came to power in February 1964, he began to exercise the state authority without any political encumbrances. He was a man seeped in secular traditions and much influenced by the Marxist thought. It was only natural for him to put curbs on the activities and spreading the influence of the JEI. He effectively pursued this policy till halfway through his tenure of over six years; when he got hemmed in by the difficulties emanating from the centre as also the internal challenge posed by Mir Qasim to his leadership. With his grip loosening over the state administration, the JEI could feel a sigh of relief. After the demise of Sadiq when Mir Qasim became the Chief Minister in December 1971; it brought a host of new opportunities for the JEI. From purely being a religious organization; it got a favourable chance to spread its tentacles in the political field also.

Mir Qasim was a weak political executive; he did not have a mass base and, unlike Sadiq, lacked confidence to restrict the influence of Sheikh Abdullah and contain his following. Sensing a very favorable opening the JEI moved close to Qasim and put its followers and supporters at his disposal. Many of these joined the Congress while continuing to be members of the parent body. Some of them held important positions in the party and government. It was yet another opportune time to make inroads into the state services. This time around, the JEI cadres infiltrated into the higher educational institutions, judiciary and police also; in addition to getting jobs as teachers in the government schools. To cut the Plebiscite Front to size, Mir Qasim banned it and simultaneously encouraged JEI to take part in the 1972 Assembly elections. Which it did and with five of its candidates winning their seats, the JEI had transformed itself into a political entity of substance. Next to the Congress, which had won 57 seats, JEI was the second largest party in the Assembly with the BJP at third position with only three seats. For his immediate political, and also personal, gains Mir Qasim had created a monster which he did live to regret a couple of decades later.

With Sheikh Abdullah coming back to power in February 1975 the days of JEI's free run were over and it had to contend with the coercive power of the state against its designs, plans and activities. Sheikh Abdullah not only disliked the Jamat at the political level, but was of the firm belief that its activities were detrimental to the people of the state and was a negation of all the good that he and his followers stood for. He sincerely felt that the JEI preached opposite to the essential goodness of Kashmiriyat, which included religious tolerance, inclusive social intercourse, Sufi traditions of Islam; in addition to being against the two basic pillars of the state policy of secularism and socialism. His government did all that it could within the bounds of law to put restrictions and curbs on the JEI and the overground schools run by it. But by this time the Jamat had gathered enough clout, resources and organizational strength to bear the onslaught and keep itself afloat, though just barely, with much-reduced enterprise and far less visible public profile. Simultaneously, it kept its political presence in focus and contested the 1977 Assembly elections in spite of political odds and against the grain of the current public mood. Of the nineteen candidates it fielded, only one could get elected and it garnered 3.59 percent of the votes polled. Six years later in the electoral contest in 1983, it could not win even one seat, though the percentage of votes gathered by it was slightly higher than 1977 at 3.88 percent. The last participation of the JEI in the electoral process was during the 1987 Assembly elections, which it contested as a major constituent of the right wing, and anti-India, alliance named Muslim United Front (MUF). The MUF fielded 42 candidates of which four won garnering 18.20 percent of the votes. Different facets of this significant election have already been discussed.

While in the sixties and seventies the JEI was strengthening the organization, consolidating finances and venturing into the field of education; it simultaneously started taking effective control of religious institutions too. It made strenuous efforts to influence the Imams and Khateebs of the existing mosques to its professed ideology; also tried hard to ensure that new vacancies were filled by own cadre or supporters. During this period a large number of mosques were constructed in Kashmir and to man these, many clerics were brought from UP and Bihar. All of them were specially picked up die-hard practitioners of the fundamental tenets of the JEI. As a group, these Imams did more than anyone else to spread the virus of fundamentalism and obscurantism in the otherwise liberal Kashmiri society. The activities of this organization received a considerable impetus in 1980 with the visit of a delegation from Saudi Arabia. The office bearers of the JEI were able to convince the visitors; with deep pockets and equally deep right-wing religious beliefs, of its hard and sincere efforts to influence the local Muslims with the Wahabi doctrine of Islam. Resultantly, liberal funding from the Saudis further strengthened the resource base of the JEI, which it harnessed carefully to attract adherents in greater number, spread its activities and expand influence base in the government by seeking employment for the cadre and sympathizers on one hand and trying to influence the existing employees, on the other.

By the early eighties, the grip of the government over the administrative machinery had been considerably weakened, emboldening the JEI leaders to come out of the religious cloaks and openly embark on an anti-India diatribe and pro-Pak propaganda; even to the extent of insinuating that Islam was not safe in India. With a larger number of organizations joining the same chorus towards the later part of the decade, the JEI monopoly in this field began to get diluted. It could not but be a silent witness to first the rise of JKLF as the premier militant outfit in Kashmir, followed by its virtual eclipse and replacement by the Hizb-ul-Mujahidin. Unable to become a leading player and an arbiter in the developing situation during the late eighties and early nineties, the JEI quietly acquiesced to a marginal role; with only the ISI calling shots in the anti-India and pro-Pak groups. When in 1993 the APHC was formed, the JEI became one of its constituents.

With the JEI becoming increasingly involved in the separatist politics; it went through a lengthy existentialist crisis of its own. When S.A.S. Geelani declared on July 17, 1989, that his organization had sympathies with and also agreed with the principles aims and objectives of the terrorists; the Jamat got firmly identified with militancy network and all that it stood for. This was not liked by a section of the old and devoted cadre who was committed to the basic aims and objectives of the group which primarily related to and revolved around religious endeavors. However, with the terrorists' actions on the increase and the security forces on the back foot, in the initial years of militancy, the dissenting voice of this segment did not carry much weight. As the tide started turning against the militants, the critics of the pro-terrorist lobby gained an upper hand. It took almost eight years for the conservative adherents to assert, get the like-minded people in important organizational positions and marginalize Geelani and his supporters. In the Majlis-e-Shoora, the highest policy-making body, a meeting convened after a gap of eight years on December 11, 1997, JEI declared that it stood for "peaceful resolution of the Kashmir problem…" After that, the Jamat has continued to steadily distance itself from the terrorist violence and use of armed means for settling any issue, carrying on with its earlier activities, stated positions and theocratic stance.

Geelani, though one of the oldest and most influential leaders of JEI, has not come to terms with the official position of the organization on terrorism and violence and continues with his anti-India and pro-Pak fulminations. Considering his long-standing rigid political posturing, no one expects him to change his spots. He has gone too far down the line to now make a u-turn. It is also well known in the informed circles that his efforts, ardently backed by his followers, to take a high moral position will not stand the test of time and scrutiny of factual details. His acquisition of assets, financial transactions and benefits that his close relations have gained from government and other sources, would one day get revealed and then the true verdict about his morals and personal integrity would acquire finality in the public domain.

Also, mere dissociation from the militancy does in no way reduce the hazards that the JEI, its philosophy and activities pose to the fundamental pillars of democracy, secularism and socialism on which rest our state as well as national polity. It is for all the organs and segments of the governments and the civil society to tackle this challenge singly and collectively.

JKLF

The parent body from which the JKLF originated was formed by a group of anti-India Kashmiris in Pakistan in a meeting held in Peshawar on August 12 and 13, 1965. In this gathering, it was decided to form National Liberation Front for Jammu and Kashmir (JKNLF) with the objective of seeking the right of self-determination for people of the state, through various means including the armed struggle. At the apex level the organization comprised four wings; two of these headed by persons who were to become well known in separatist circles. The Armed Wing was led by Major Amanullah, reportedly then a regular officer in the "Azad Kashmir Forces", the Political Wing was headed by Amanullah Khan, Chief of Finance Wing being Mir Abdul Qayoom and Maqbool Butt in-charge of Coordination Wing. Two groups, including Major Amanullah and Maqbool Butt, clandestinely crossed over the Ceasefire Line on June 10, 1966. While the Amanullah group busied itself in imparting arms training to some youth in the jungles of Kupwara; Maqbool Butt spent two months going around the Valley, contacting known sympathizers and establishing secret cells in major urban centers. While this group was heading towards Kupwara to sneak back into PoK, it was involved in a gunfight with a police party leading to the death of a Police Inspector. This alerted the state police and in the massive search operations launched one militant was killed, one injured and Maqbool Butt along with another associate was captured. Subsequently, in search operations, a good number of JKNLF members were arrested by the police.

Maqbool Butt and his associate were tried for the murder of police officer and sentenced to death by a court in August 1968. Four months later both of them, along with one more person, managed to escape from the jail and slip across to PoK. Back in Pakistan, Butt continued with his activities and in 1969 came in contact with a visiting Kashmiri in Peshawar, named Hashim Quereshi. He indoctrinated and trained the new found recruit in the technique of hijacking an aircraft. Hashim Quereshi, with the help of one accomplice, undertook the famous hijacking of the Fokker Friendship aircraft of Indian Airlines on January 1971 while it was on a regular Srinagar-Delhi flight. However, Maqbool Butt's direct involvement with Kashmir was not yet over and once again he crossed over to the Valley in May 1976 along with two associates. There, he planned and executed a raid to loot one of the J&K Bank branches in Kupwara. In the ensuing sequence of events, the Bank Manager got killed and Maqbool Butt was arrested. He was tried in the Sessions Court at Srinagar and sentenced to death by the judge Nilkanth Ganjoo. In view of his earlier escape from the local jail in Srinagar, this time the government decided to lodge him in the Tihar Jail of Delhi. Maqbool Butt was subsequently hanged in Tihar Jail on February 11, 1984. Being the first well known militant name that had lost his life, Maqbool Butt became some kind of a cult figure among the local militants and underground anti-India and pro-Pak elements. An offshoot of this matter was also the cold-blooded murder of the Sessions Judge Nilkanth Ganjoo by the militants in Maharaja Bazaar Srinagar, on November 4, 1989. The Maqbool Butt episode in 1976 was the last known event credited to the JKNLF and it seems to have been given a quiet burial after that.

Almost a year later, the Jammu and Kashmir Liberation Front (JKLF) was born in United Kingdom on May 12, 1977, during a convention of the Kashmir Plebiscite Front. Apart from others, some former members of the JKNLF joined the new group. It is interesting to note that the actual Plebiscite Front which was born in Kashmir in 1955 and was dissolved by Sheikh Abdullah in 1975, had no presence in J&K after that; but far away in England the separatists not only met at a regular convention but also spawned a similar and more focused outfit to serve the ends of those individuals and countries inimical to the Indian interest. Not many guesses are required to figure out the source of inspiration, instigation and funding for activities like these. The handlers and organizers of the JKLF had learnt their lessons from the experience they had gathered in running the JKNLF and set about to consolidate the structure and organizational framework of the new unit by picking up committed and known faces; and also strengthening the overseas network before embarking on any adventure in the state. In February 1978, Amanullah Khan became its

General Secretary and within two years the JKLF branches had sprung up in PoK, Pakistan, UK, Denmark, France, Germany, Saudi Arabia, UAE and USA. Outside the subcontinent, the branches of JKLF have mostly restricted their activities to providing material and logistic support for the simple reason of not wanting to be on the wrong side of the law in the host country. Only on one occasion it carried out an operational task and paid a heavy price for it. On February 3, 1984, the JKLF abducted an Indian diplomat Ravindra Mahtre at Birmingham, UK, demanding the release of Maqbool Butt then in Tihar Jail. In the ensuing sequence of events, Mahtre was killed the next day and the death sentence of Butt was executed a week later on February 11. In UK the police arrested six persons, all members of the JKLF, on the charge of murdering Mahtre. They were all convicted by the court of law with two of the accused getting life imprisonment, the third sentenced to 20 years rigorous imprisonment and the other three sent to jail for lesser periods. Though the court acquitted Amanullah Khan from any direct involvement in this case; because of his objectionable activities, he was extradited from the UK in December 1986. That was the first and last overseas terrorist action by this organization which was to become well known in India and Pakistan in the late eighties and early nineties because of its active participation in the militant activities. In fact, it was the most prominent of the early militant outfits and is generally regarded as the one which lit the first fire.

Till the end of 1987, the JKLF had no formal presence in the state. The nucleus of this organization came from the core group of the Islamic Students League (ISL) which was created in Kashmir in 1986 by Shakeel Ahmad Bakshi, Abdul Hamid Sheikh, Ashfaq Majid Wani, Javed Ahmad Mir and Mohammad Yasin Malik, all important future militants. Many like-minded young men joined this group in a short time. During the 1987 Assembly elections the ISL members all actively worked for the candidates fielded by the MUF. When most of the MUF candidates lost the elections and prominent ISL activists finding their future prospects not bright in the developing situation; a state of mental frustration enveloped them. It was at this point of time that the local JKLF underground workers and sympathizers offered them help and support and thus a nucleus of this organization was born in the Valley.

The ISI had been waiting for the right opportunity of this kind for a long time. Right from 1972 when the Jamat-e-Islami acquired political prominence, except for the first couple of years of Sheikh Abdullah's second tenure as head of the state government, the internal situation was gradually and consistently deteriorating to the advantage of Islamic fundamentalists and Pakistan. In the midst of administrative and political mismanagement the anti-India sentiment was on the increase; which was duly exploited by the separatist elements, as well as the growing influence of the Jamat run Madarsas. The youth of the Valley was already politically confused and economically frustrated. Adding to this volatile situation the indoctrination of a contorted version of the religion made a very potent mix. The tinder was almost ready by the time the 1987 Legislative polls got over.

During 1988, all important members of the newly formed JKLF and many more crossed over to PoK and Pakistan where they were given training in handling arms and explosives; indoctrinated and met by prominent leaders like Amanullah Khan and Dr. Farooq Haider. Some out of this group were also able to meet the President of Pakistan, General Zia-ul-Haq. The Valley wing of the JKLF, the ISI thought, was now ready to launch an armed struggle for the "liberation of Kashmir". A practical manifestation of this occurred on July 31, 1988, with two explosions in different parts of Srinagar, one outside the Central Telegraph Office and the other near the Srinagar Club. The JKLF had thus announced its arrival on the scene. This was followed by a bomb blast in a passenger bus in Anantnag killing two people on September 1; and on September 18 (the night of September 17-18) the militants made an audacious attack on the residence of the DIG of Police Kashmir Range, with grenade throwing and firing. Although the attempt was foiled with losses to the militants, a statement of intent had been made and the arc of fear amongst the general population enlarged.

While the ground situation in the Valley was fast deteriorating and heading towards the boil, the rulers of Pakistan and the people at the helm of affairs there were closely watching the developing situation and waiting for the appropriate opportunity to arise and present itself for exploitation; from their point of view. The institutional memory was quite contemporary and wounds too raw for Pakistan to realize that unless it treaded carefully and caught India on the wrong foot, any new adventure may not only backfire but also prove costly. In this background, it would be necessary to attempt a peak into the frame of mind of Pakistani top echelon represented by Gen. Zia and his close advisors.

Steve Coll in his well-known book "Ghost Wars"; has described in graphic details, the American proxy-war efforts in Afghanistan against the Russians; spearheaded by the CIA and using the assets of Pakistan as well as *jihadis* of Afghan, Pakistan and few other nationalities. As a part of this narrative, and having a profound impact on the contemporary as well as future Indo-Pak ties, he has succinctly narrated the prevailing situation; Zia's thought process and the existing state of Pak ISI as, "America's primary actor in this subterranean narrative was the CIA, which shaped the anti-Soviet jihad in Afghanistan during the 1980s ….the agency struggled to control its mutually mistrustful and at times toxic alliances with the intelligence services of Saudi Arabia and Pakistan…. Yet Zia strongly encouraged personal religious piety within the Pakistan army's officer corps, a major change from the past…. He encouraged the financing and construction of hundreds of *madrassas* …. The border *madrassas* formed a kind of Islamic ideological picket fence between communist Afghanistan and Pakistan. Gradually Zia embraced jihad as a strategy…. To make his complex liaison with the CIA work, Zia relied on his chief spy and most trusted lieutenant, a gray-eyed and patrician general, Akhtar Abdur Rahman, director general of ISI…. Again and again, Zia told Akhtar: "The water in Afghanistan must boil at the right temperature." Zia did not want the Afghan pot to boil over…. When Akhtar had taken over ISI almost a decade earlier, it was a small and demoralized unit within the Pakistan military, focused mainly on regime security and never-ending espionage games with India. Now ISI was an army within the army; boasting multiple deep-pocketed patrons…. The service had welcomed to Pakistan legions of volunteers from across the Islamic world; fighters who were willing to pursue Pakistan's foreign policy agenda not only in Afghanistan but, increasingly across its eastern borders in Kashmir where jihadists trained in Afghanistan were just starting to bleed Indian troops…. ISI had been transformed by the CIA and Saudi subsidies into Pakistan's most powerful institution."[1]

In a way, Afghanistan was a sort of discovery trail and learning ground for Pakistan in its active involvement later in J&K. However, the deteriorating situation in the Indian state of Punjab, which fast developed

---

1   Steve Coll, *Ghost Wars,* Penguin Books, New York, 2004, pp. 16, 61, 63 and 180.

into an insurgency in the early eighties; unexpectedly came in Pakistan's way and it exploited the problems there as an "opportunity target", to the hilt. The militancy in Punjab was largely funded and supported by a section of Sikhs living abroad and it lasted for almost a decade and a half; creating huge problems and seriously disrupting the upward growth curve of the state. Some Sikh militant groups aimed to create an independent state of Khalistan by acts of violence directed at the central and state governments as well as the security forces posted in the state. Pakistan effectively plunged Punjab into a state of hopelessness and despair.

Its army and ISI were deeply involved in training, arming and guiding the Sikh militants; providing large amount of arms, ammunition and cash to them. The ISI operators regularly escorted Sikh militants for trans-border movement and provided safe havens for their shelter and dumps for weapons and explosives. The Pak state extended regular and sufficient help to various militant groups like Babbar Khalsa International (BKI), International Sikh Youth Federation (ISYF), Khalistan Commando Force (KCF), Dal Khalsa International (DKI), and Khalistan Zindabad Force (KZF) etc. "Pakistan's direct intervention in terrorism on Indian soil – specifically in Punjab – in the mid-eighties brought about an irreversible change in the situation. For the first time, agencies of a nation-state with their enormous resources and legitimate access to high military technologies, guaranteed supplies to non-state terrorist groupings."[2]

A former Director General of Punjab Police, who led the successful campaign against terrorism in that state, recalled, "The movement for the creation of Khalistan was one of the most virulent terrorist campaigns in the world. Launched in the early 1980s by a group of bigots who discovered their justification in a perversion of the Sikh religious identity, and supported by a gaggle of political opportunists both within the country and abroad, this movement had consumed 21,469 lives before it was comprehensively defeated in 1993. Thousands of others were injured and maimed; hundreds of thousands were permanently scarred by their experience of dislocation, the gratuitous loss of loved ones, and an unremitting terror that they endured for more than a decade…. 5058 civilians and 1003 policemen were killed in 1990 and 1991, and the state was brought to the verge of disintegration. A total of 1566 civilians and

---

2   K.P.S. Gill, *Faultlines Volume 3,* The Institute for Conflict Management, New Delhi, November 1999, p. 11.

277 policemen fell to the terrorist bullet through 1992 and 1993, and peace had been completely restored, political parties – including the now revived 'traditional' factions of the Akali Dal – had participated in Municipal and Panchayat elections that had secured unprecedented voter turn-outs, and a Constitutional government was squarely in charge."[3]

Punjab was of course not the primary area of interest for Zia and his senior advisors; as their main focus always remained on creating problems in Kashmir. This has been so, right from the very beginning irrespective of the periodical changes at the helm. It is necessary to recall the pattern of behavior of Pakistan right from 1947, when in October that year it had sent raiders into J&K. The design was to be repeated in 1965 and the same simulation continues since 1988, for almost three decades now. Sending in the trained manpower in a covert manner, including its own army personnel and denying its involvement has become the standard *modus operandi* of successive Pakistani Governments. K. Subrahmanyam, the indisputable doyen of Indian strategic thought, wrote a lengthy – 87 pages – article in May 1990 discussing in details the various aspects of Kashmir issue. It is an excellent source material on the subject. True to his style and moral standards, he has appended a note in the end; which needs to be quoted in some details. It reads as,

"Author's Post Script

It has been brought to my notice that the 'Op Topac' document referred to in the text and annexures is not a genuine official document but a piece of scenario writing by a team of researchers who have put together over a period of months, as a result of their painstaking research, their assessment of likely course of action that Pakistan intended to adopt in Kashmir Valley. The assessment published in July 1989, has been thoroughly vindicated by the subsequent events and hence the references do not, in any case, vitiate the analysis...."[4]

In the course of his very timely, significant and detailed examination of the subject he goes on to mention, "Unfortunately the political instability in Pakistan is not a transient but a perennial problem and Kashmir is one

3   K.P.S. Gill, *Faultlines Volume 1*, The Institute for Conflict Management, New Delhi, May 1999, pp. 1and 68.

4   K. Subrahmanyam, *Strategic Analysis,* Institute of Defence Studies and Analyses, New Delhi, May 1990, p. 198.

of the issues on which each party is attempting one-upmanship vis-à-vis its rivals. More dangerous is the involvement of the Army – especially the Inter-Service Intelligence which has a notorious record for wrong and risky assessments leading Pakistan to disaster.... 'Let there be no mistake, however, that our aim remains quite clear and firm – the liberation of Kashmir Valley.... We do not have much time. Maximum pressure must be exerted before the general elections in India and before Indian Army reserves which are still bogged down in Sri Lanka become available.... But the situation in Kashmir will be somewhat different; more like the "Infetada" of Palestinians in towns, and on the pattern of the Mujahideen in the countryside to attack hard targets. A period of chaos in the State is essential in the circumstances.... Finally, I wish to caution you once more that it will be disastrous to believe that we can take on India in a straight contest. We must, therefore, be careful and maintain a low military profile so that the Indians do not find an excuse to pre-empt us, by attacking at a time and at a point of their own choosing....'...."[5]. Last part of this quote is about Gen Zia, imaginatively, talking to his commanders and subordinate officers.

As so comprehensively articulated by Subrahmanyam, the strategy of Pak involvement in Kashmir was fashioned by Gen. Zia. Succeeding heads of governments in Pakistan – civilians and military – the army chiefs and ISI heads, either wholly followed it or made cosmetic changes. A number of external and internal factors together impacted on the law and order situation in the state, which started deteriorating from the beginning of 1988 with pro-Pakistani elements becoming increasingly active, accompanied by stray incidents of triggering of explosive devices, particularly, in the city of Srinagar. The disturbances, *bandhs* and acts of violence continued during 1989 with increased regularity and intensity.

The first incident of terror activities took place in Srinagar in July 1988, as already mentioned, in the form of two bomb blasts; the intended targets were the Central Telegraph Office and the TV station (near the Srinagar Club). Another high profile action followed two months later when an abortive attempt was made on the life of DIG Kashmir Range at his residence. Thereafter it was a stream of steady increase in subversive activities and anti-establishment demonstrations on one hand and progressive loosening of administrative hold on the other. An acidic

5   K. Subrahmanyam, *Ibid*, pp. 137, 181 and 183.

comment by a political analyst on the prevailing situation aptly mentioned that far from launching a counter moral and political offensive against the militants, the state government acted as a virtual witness to the declining law and order situation. The failure of National Conference to deal effectively with the growing disaffection at the political level aggravated the problem. Pakistan's efforts to create and stir up trouble in the state were facilitated by these developments and groups of youth continued to be taken across; trained and indoctrinated by the ISI to provoke and generate problems in Kashmir. The incidents of disturbances, *bandhs* and acts of violence increased in regularity and intensity during 1988 and 1989. However, even in this worsening situation the J&K Police under some competent leaders was still standing its ground, in and around Srinagar, amidst the increasing chaos and soldiered on with the task of managing the growing law and order problem. By the end of 1989, it had been successful in apprehending over half a dozen of top militants, including Yasin Malik, Javed Nalka, Mushtaq Latram.

In order to break the sustained pressure of police and secure release of their leaders in custody, the militants resorted to the kidnapping of Rubiya Sayeed, the daughter of the then Union Home Minister Mufti Sayeed in the beginning of December 1989. A weak and vacillating centre in New Delhi literally forced the state government to agree to the militant demands and to secure her release five militants leaders were set free. This led to a sudden spurt in the morale and activities of the militants. Soon thereafter the situation deteriorated fast and killings, arson and abduction became a menacing feature of daily life. This incident was certainly a watershed in the course of militancy in the state; which soon spiraled out of hand. The last straw, literally, in this fast nose-diving scenario was the appointment of Jagmohan as Governor of the State for the second time on January 19, 1990. As was widely expected, the popular government headed by Farooq Abdullah resigned – some political analysts believe that the wily politician in him found this as the easy way out. The straight offshoot of this turn of events was that New Delhi came in direct contact with people of the Valley without the advantage of the buffer of an elected government. The next five months represented a very bloody and chaotic; to some extent bewilderingly wild face of militancy violence in Kashmir. Some of the more notable incidents during this period included eight people killed in firing by security forces in Srinagar on 22nd January followed by Srinagar Doordarshan Director, Lassa Koul being shot dead on 13th February. Three days later the State assembly was dissolved on the orders of the Governor. On 1st March thirty people were killed in firing incidents at Zakura and Barzala by-pass in Srinagar. The Kashmiri Pandit mass exodus from the Valley also started at the beginning of this month. Later, on 24th March Independent ex-MLA Mir Mustafa – a highly respected person – was kidnapped by Hizbul Mujahideen and killed four days later. This was followed by the kidnapping of Kashmir University Vice-Chancellor Mushir-ul-Haq, along with his private secretary, and HMT General Manager H.L. Khera on 6th April. Khera was killed by his captors on 10th April; whereas the Vice Chancellor and his private secretary were murdered the next day. These four killings spread a wave of anger and consternation through the Valley; but the mayhem continued. On 21st May Mirwaiz Maulvi Farooq was also shot dead by militants. The public outpouring of hurt and rage could have been channelized by the administration against the militants; but – on the contrary - fifty people were killed when panicky security forces detachments opened fire on the mourning procession. Three days later Governor Jagmohan resigned and G.C. Saxena took over as the new Governor on May 26, 1990. With Saxena at the helm of affairs, began an agonizingly slow process of the revival of intelligence network in the Valley and putting back in place as also rejuvenating the state administrative structure block by block. But the initiative was still with the other side and lots of negative things were still happening. It would take a few more years of sustained hard work, at all levels, for the situation to turn around. Through that year, the militancy related and separatist inspired incidents were on the increase.

From the beginning of 1990, the terrorist activities spread beyond Srinagar city in a big way, leading to the virtual collapse of administrative machinery and destabilization of political structure. "In a symbolic gesture, signs bearing the name 'India' were removed from establishments such as the State Bank of India, Air India, Indian Oil, Bharat Petroleum, and Indian insurance companies. People were ordered to transfer money from Indian banks to the Jammu and Kashmir Bank. The militants' writ ran large: even public offices tacitly followed their order to observe Friday instead of Sunday as a holiday, and almost everyone, including the state-owned Srinagar Corporation, complied with its curfews and blackouts"[6]. The proxy war unleashed by Pakistan had entered its most

---

6 Navnita Chadha Behera, *Demystifying Kashmir*, Brookings Institution Press, Washington, D.C, 2006, pp. 146-147.

destructive stage. Large-scale targeted kidnappings and killings took place, wanton destruction of government institutions and buildings was resorted to, efforts made to undermine Indian support structure, especially targeting J&K Police and the Intelligence Bureau. All these activities were accompanied by a very effective and high profile media blitz.

The state government had, in a bold administrative initiative towards the end of January 1990, decided to reorganize the supervisory structure of the Kashmir division, which had eight districts under the charge of one Divisional Commissioner based in Srinagar. The new plan was to divide the Valley into three zones, with two districts each – Srinagar and Badgam remaining under the supervision of the then Divisional Commissioner Kashmir along with two districts of Ladakh region; two new posts of Special Commissioner were created, one each for Baramulla – Kupwara and Anantnag – Pulwama districts. The aim was to ensure more intensive supervision of the district administrations as also speedy redressal of grievances of local population along with better coordination and more cohesive operations of the security forces. Two months later similar administrative re-organization of Jammu division followed; with one Special Commissioner each posted at Rajouri and Doda looking after two districts, of Rajouri - Poonch and Doda - Udhampur respectively.

When the incumbent Special Commissioner joined his new station of duty at Baramulla, on January 30, 1990, the overall conditions there were chaotic and scary. The situation prevailing on the ground can be comprehensively summed up in his own words as, "The administration at all levels was clueless and at a loss to understand how to react to the obtaining situation. Even routine administrative actions would attract disproportionately strong retaliation from the public backed by separatist elements. Massive public demonstrations, involving tens of thousands of people, were being held. In few cases, thousands were seen to challenge the law and order administration and defy with impunity proclaimed prohibitory orders. Thousands of rabble rousers were crisscrossing the Valley in trucks and buses shouting anti-India and pro-azadi slogans. It was as if the common people were mesmerized by the gravity of the situation and responding to the prompting of separatist elements like robots without question. Handfuls of Pak-trained militants were deciding the day to day agenda for anti-national demonstrations..... The magistracy and police, even with the help of central paramilitary forces and army, were incapable of handling the extraordinary situation. In some cases, the forces had overreacted to situations in a panic with heavy collateral damage to life and property."[7]

To make matters worse, Radio Pakistan and "Azad Kashmir Radio" were at their loudest trying to whip up popular emotions in Kashmir. Particularly the broadcasts from Muzzafrabad were pointedly malicious, playing many times over the propaganda songs of the 60s and 70s exhorting the people of the Valley to rise against the state government. Prime Minister of Pakistan, Benazir Bhutto, was announcing in hysterical tone the moral and material support to the so-called independence movement in Kashmir. Forgetting all forms of restraint and decency expected from someone in her high position, she would try to ridicule even the person like J&K Governor, Jagmohan, by using the expression *Jago Mohan – Bhago Mohan*. She had instituted a special fund to finance the militant movement in Kashmir. This fund was apparently used to train and arm Kashmiri youth and to carry out subversive activities in the Valley. Pakistan was openly and brazenly instigating conditions of instability in Kashmir without even a fig of concealment or subterfuge. Given the mayhem and chaotic situation they had managed to create in the past few months, and the success achieved from their point of view, the Pakistani establishment thought it only prudent to push this advantage to the very hilt. For them, the scenario appeared to be like it was now or never.

As an interesting sidelight, it may be mentioned that few officers from Jammu, working in the state government departments and corporations and posted in Srinagar stayed there in spite of the turbulence around them during the entire 1989 and also most of 1990. Their personal security was assured by few militant commanders who had been lower-level employees and their erstwhile subordinates. It was during September 1990 that Majid Sheikh, by then an established and much-feared name in the ranks of the local militant cadres, contacted one of these officers and advised him to return to Jammu as he could no longer guarantee his security. He said things had changed for worse and with the arrival of some people from across the border, he and his associate commanders were no longer in control of things. This triggered the move of these officers also to Jammu.

---

7 Dr. Sudhir S Bloeria, *The Men Who Served Jammu & Kashmir*, Vij Books India Pvt Ltd, New Delhi, 2016, p. 48.

Within months of the start of militancy, the Pakistan ISI, which had trained JKLF cadres and supplied them with weapons and money, started raising some more militant organizations. This was done primarily for two reasons; one was based on the experience gained by the ISI during the Afghan operations which had taught this outfit the advantages of keeping afloat multiple groups, and the second reason – perhaps even more important – was that the JKLF clamored for Kashmiri independence – which was not a Pakistani strategic objective - and not for merger with Pakistan, and the former formulation was not acceptable to ISI. So after the JKLF had served their purpose by triggering off the first phase of militancy; the ISI cut off aid to JKLF and turned its attention to the Hizbul Mujahideen (HUM), which was armed to teeth and also encouraged to neutralize the JKLF cadres. Smaller outfits like Al-Badr, Allah Tigers, Tehrik-e-Jehad-Islami etc., were either disbanded or merged with HUM; which also fully supported accession to Pakistan and dominated militancy during the next three years. A noted commentator of J&K affairs, Balraj Puri, observed about the prevailing situation as "… must have persuaded Pakistan policymakers to conclude that the JKLF, which had pioneered the militant movement with the slogan of *kashmiriat*, had become redundant in the situation. The Front Chief Amanullah regretted that Pakistan which had earlier helped his militant outfit had 'now put a squeeze on the flow of arms to the JKLF. They have been creating difficulties in transporting the material'… The JKLF circles also accused the pro-Pakistan elements of providing clues to the Indian security forces regarding JKLF whereabouts, which made them further vulnerable to the attacks of the security forces… The cold war between the JKLF and Pakistan, ever since the latter withdrew its support to the former, culminated in Amanullah's two bids to lead a march from Pakistan Occupied Kashmir (PoK) across the line of actual control. Pakistan prevented the march by using force and killing twelve marchers on 11 February (1992), and by arresting Amanullah and 500 of his colleagues before the second threatened march on 30 March (1992)…"[8]

The two years of 1993-94 marked a phase in the violence-ridden state which effectively heralded the regaining of initiative by the government. During this period successful efforts were made to revive the whole state structure and restore various organizations, control systems and

---

8   Balraj Puri, *Kashmir Towards Insurgency*, Orient Longman Limited, New Delhi, 1993, p. 67.

developmental activities. The intelligence setup, particularly of the I.B. and the state police, was painstakingly brought to an effective functional level and the flow of intelligence became continuous, credible, reliable and actionable. Along with; an increasingly effective counterinsurgency (C.I.) grid, comprising different forces, was placed on ground. In the month of May 1993 the institution of Unified Headquarters (UHQ) was established to more effectively coordinate the efforts of different forces and organizations as also to ensure optimum utilization of the resources available. The creation of the UHQ was an innovative and a major step forward. On the administrative side, writ of the state administration was re-established and visible impetus given to the developmental activities. In the month of October; the militants laid a siege on the famous Hazratbal Shrine. The ability of the state government to get the siege lifted successfully, a month later, was a very major jolt to the terrorist groups, their overground supporters and mentors across the border. Few days after that, during the closing week of November, the security forces successfully took control of the entire Sopore town - thus far a stronghold of the insurgents - and effectively cleared it of the militant presence. These two developments had a demoralizing effect on the anti-Indian forces and also affected the recruitment of Kashmiri cadres in the Hizb-ul-Mujahideen. The ISI perceived it as a sign of fatigue amongst the Kashmiri militants. This assumption coupled with its desire to give further impetus to the flagging militancy in the state; prompted the ISI to impel more Afghan veterans, Pakistani nationals and foreign mercenaries into J&K. The new emphasis on non-local militants also adversely affected the fortunes of Hizb-ul-Mujahideen, which lost its primacy on the ground. The groups whose leadership as well as rank and file were based in Pakistan, started gaining ground as well as importance; and over time a pan-Islamic agenda also became part of the ongoing militancy in the state.

The ISI completed the process of taking over the terrorist movement by foreign mercenaries during 1994; and it also coincided with the emergence of two pernicious and fundamentalist outfits of Lashkar-e-Toiba and Harkat-ul-Ansar. By the end of that year, there were an estimated twelve hundred foreign terrorists operating in the state. This shift also enabled ISI to more effectively oversee the terrorist organizations and their command and control structure; and with these new levers of direction, it managed to create high- profile incidents in 1995 like the destruction of Charar-e-Shrief Shrine and abduction of foreign tourists. These not only created internal problems for India but also attracted the world attention thereby highlighting the Kashmir issue internationally. According to Indian estimates, by the middle of 1996 four hundred and thirty foreign mercenaries had been killed by the security forces and one hundred and eight were arrested. This induction of foreign mercenaries in such numbers in Kashmir not only impacted the ground operations but also displayed ideological undertones. It heralded a new turn in the ISI strategy and also coincided with the efforts of the State and Central Governments to conduct elections in the state.

It would be useful to take a look at the two important developments that have considerably impacted the situation in the state; that is, the Kashmiri Pandit migration from the Valley during the beginning of 1990 and the formation of All Party Hurriyat Conference (APHC) in 1993. First, the displacement of Kashmiri Pandits.

The ethnic cleansing initiated ruthlessly by the terrorists forced migration of almost entire Kashmiri Pandit community from the Valley. The rise of new militant groups, some warnings in anonymous posters pasted on the walls in the interiors of old Srinagar and few killings of innocent members of the community contributed to an atmosphere of insecurity for the Kashmiri Pandits. Prominent members of the community killed by the militants included Tikka Lal Taploo - a political activist, P.N. Handoo - Assistant Director of Information Department and N.K. Ganjoo-retired Sessions Judge. Many others fell to the bullets of the terrorists and panic spread through the community leading to an exodus from the Valley during February and March 1990. The first to leave were the urban Pandits. Terrorist outfits started identifying and denouncing intellectuals of the community followed by intimidation and violence. Places of worship and houses of Kashmiri Pandits also became targets of militants. The cumulative effect of all this was mass exodus of the community from the Valley to seek shelter in Jammu and other parts of the country. Still, an appreciable number stayed back hopeful of a let-up in the violence and also on reassurances of their friends and neighbors of the majority community. However, continued threats and apprehensions about life and property as well as warnings by the militants forced them to leave. At the culmination of this tragedy, it was almost a total ethnic cleansing.

During 1990-93 about 126 temples, 2050 houses and 183 shops of Kashmiri Pandits were set ablaze and the number of Pandits killed reached a figure of 116. Till the middle of 1990 about thirty thousand families of this community left the Valley and by 1992, this number rose to over fifty thousand. The first few years of militancy also saw the use of the migrant houses by terrorists and their wanton destruction. An astute observer of the Kashmir scene stated in 1993, "Whatever be the precise share of responsibility of government and the different political groups in vitiating the communal relations, it did seem at one stage, that the Kashmiri personality was so split that one part was swayed by the Hindutva wave while another was submerged by the Muslim fundamentalism."[9]

One of the important components of the central and the state governments' priorities has been the return of Kashmiri migrants to the Valley. These migrants have since been staying outside the Valley under difficult conditions. Almost fifty thousand families have left the Valley and have been largely concentrated in Jammu (twenty-seven thousand families) and Delhi (nineteen thousand families), the rest sprinkled all over the country. Their early return would not only end the traumatic experience of being uprooted from their abode of centuries, but would also close a tragic chapter in the lives of each individual, every affected family and the entire community. Seen in a wider perspective, the Kashmiri Pandit community is an integral part of the composite and pluralistic society of the Valley. Without their return, no claim of normalcy can ever be considered legitimate. Therefore, rightly one of the important components of the central and the state governments' priorities has been the return of Kashmiri migrants to the Valley.

It is a well known fact that most of these migrants belong to the category of government servants. A very limited number would be purely agriculturists or dependent on trading activities. Therefore, any strategy for their return should take into accounts the apprehensions and expectations of this particular segment. They are not likely to move back unless the conditions for their return are very safe and perceptibly conducive. The representative sections of the community, especially leaders of various migrant organizations, are very vocal, with extensive media contacts. This segment is not particularly keen for the return of migrants till they are able to extract maximum concessions and the most favorable package from the state and the central governments. Some of their demands, including that of a separate homeland, are so implausible that no government would

---

9   Balraj Puri, *Ibid,* p.67.

be able to meet them. At the other end of the spectrum; there are also a number of migrant families, mostly belonging to the agriculturist class, who are keen to return to their roots as early as possible. Between these two segments lies the majority of the migrant population that would follow either of the two groups depending upon which one would appear to be showing them the correct approach.

In this backdrop, it would considerably help if a policy framework of judicious mix of pressure and incentives is evolved to inspire, persuade and nudge a significant section of the employees, as also some agriculturist families, to return to their homes. Return of the Kashmiri Pandits to the Valley is absolutely essential for Kashmir to regain the glory of centuries old traditions of religious tolerance and harmonious living as well as being a great seat of learning for ancient scriptures; particularly *Shaivism.*

Right from the beginning, the coordinators of the current turmoil have been making efforts to forge some kind of front which could be presented to the outside world as the civilian face of the militancy; to provide a fig leaf cover to the violence perpetrated by the armed groups and if possible, a modicum of respectability as also acceptability to the constituents and individual members. The first effort in this direction was made in March 1990 to bring together under the banner of Tehreek-i-Hurriyat-i-Kashmir, an alliance of thirteen separatist groups. It collapsed quickly due to internecine struggle for the leadership of the group. The next step was creation of 'J K Liberation Council' in September 1991 with Maulana Abbas Ansari of Itihad-ul-Muslimeen as its patron-in-chief. After issuing occasional press releases, it became redundant very soon.

Against this backdrop yet another effort was made to form a body to "agitate for the goal of self-determination". An attempt was made to bring together many diverse organizations having separatist leanings, including Kashmir Bar Association, few workers and employees associations. This came to be known as 'All Party Meet' which held its first session in December 1992 in which various constituents participated and decided to form a common political platform under the banner of All Party Hurriyat Conference (APHC). It held first meeting on March 7, 1993, and formed a sixteen member executive body. The APHC was formally launched on September 9, 1993. The emergence of this outfit was also a culmination of six months effort started by Moulvi Omar Farooq, President of Awami Action Committee. It was announced that thirty religious and political parties had joined it and would be headed by Omar Farooq; though reportedly there were serious differences within as to who should lead the Conference. For record, the Jamat-e-Islami leader Syed Ali Shah Geelani staking his claim had said that they had accepted the choice "in the larger interest of unity". The first meeting of the Executive Committee was held on September 22, 1993. After the meeting, Moulvi Farooq said that the major task before APHC was to work for securing the right of self-determination and leave people to decide about their political future. To start with, the militant groups were hesitant in lending it their support. So the APHC leadership persuaded some of these outfits to extend backing; and consequently seven militant organizations issued a joint statement on 7th November asking people to support and extend all possible cooperation to the Hurriyat Conference. These groups were: JKLF, HUM, Al Jehad, Al Omar Mujahideen, Ikhwan-ul-Musalmeen, Al Burq and Operation Balakote.

By the middle of October 1993, a favorable opportunity came its way in the form of a siege of Hazratbal Shrine by the militants. But, by lack of imagination, factional rivalry and incorrect appreciation of the developing situation, the APHC failed to capitalize on the groundswell of public support. This, of course, is not to deny a competent handling of the crisis by the state administration; as a month later on 16th November authorities were able to clear the Shrine of all militants. Peaceful resolution of Hazratbal problem also resulted in considerable public humiliation for the APHC. Two months later, on January 13, 1994, after the Executive Committee meeting, its Chairman told the press that APHC would not enter into dialogue with New Delhi without the participation of Pakistan as the latter was a "necessary party" for a lasting and peaceful solution of the Kashmir issue. On 7th April the same year, it sent a four-member delegation to New Delhi on a "goodwill mission". This group was led by Prof. Abdul Ghani and had three other persons namely Moulvi Abbas Ansari, Ghulam Mohammad Bhat and Mufti Baha-ud-Din Farooqi. These people could not meet the American officials of State Department then on a visit to India – including the high profile Robin Raphael – which was ostensibly their main purpose; and had to content itself with only an interaction with few American think tank scholars and Dr. Karan Singh. Back in the Valley some constituents of this outfit raised objections on the constitution and mandate of this team. Such dichotomies and fissures have again and again manifested in the working and programmes of the

Hurriyat. However, to remain in the limelight its leadership has seized every opportunity of meeting visiting diplomats to Srinagar or flying to New Delhi to meet any visiting foreign dignitary.

During the first couple of years of its existence, the Hurriyat Conference was considered quite pro-American as stated outlook of both had somewhere an element of convergence in matters related to Kashmir. But later this attitude grew cold as the US State Department was no longer saying things that suited the APHC. This turn around came during the four-day visit of Frank Wisener, the US Ambassador to India, during June 1995. He said the US supported holding of elections in Kashmir at the earliest; and a possible solution to the Kashmir issue should be sought by peaceful negotiations between India and Pakistan as provided in Simla Agreement. Both of his observations were not to the liking of Hurriyat.

The lack of influence of this conglomeration over the long sequel of violence in the state and inherent contradictions of its stance have been aptly commented upon by a scholar as, "Hurriyat exercises no leverage over militants, either, as is evident from the United Jihad Council's public refusal to even meet Hurriyat leaders during their visit to Azad Kashmir and Hizb-ul-Mujahideen's outright dismissal of a Hurriyat plea to stop the violence and give peace a chance... If Hurriyat were to abandon its separatist agenda, it would not only run the risk of being eclipsed as a political force but might also invite the wrath of Kashmiris for having misled a generation of young men and women and for sacrificing thousands of lives. Hurriyat's most important challenge, as Mirwaiz Umar Farooq rightly states, is to redefine its goals, which in turn would shape the role it might play in the peace process."[10]

The APHC has, all along since its inception, been a loose group of disparate individuals and organizations pursuing their own agenda and activities. The only common denominator has been their pro-Pak leanings and anti-Indian stance. It has been affected more by the inherent contradictions rather than any palpable cohesion. Always keen to accept an invitation from the Pakistan High Commissioner in India; its interaction with the Government of India has been persistently negative, with very few exceptions. Right from the Hazaratbal crisis which started barely a month after its birth, the APHC has repeatedly displayed an utter lack of

10 Navnita Chadha Behera, *Demystifying Kashmir*, Brookings Institution Press, Washington, D.C, 2006, p. 245

influence over the militant organizations and their activities. However, it has never missed any opportunity to pitchfork itself on the centre stage taking a piggy-back ride on the subversive groupings and their actions. The frequent calls it has given for shut-downs and *hartals*, particularly in Srinagar, has immensely disrupted day to day activities of the people and put them to huge inconvenience.

The APHC initially appeared to be an impressive broad-based platform; made even more important by the decision of some terrorist outfits that henceforth all the calls for *hartals* and bandhs would be given by it only. But the notices for strikes and the like continued to be given by individuals and groups unabated. Also, the dissensions within the ranks of APHC have constantly come to fore as each constituent, over the years, has tried to establish its hegemony. Syed Ali Shah Geelani has caused maximum problems to the cohesion of this outfit; although practically all front rank leaders of the constituent groups have time and again displayed hardly ill-concealed ambition and clout to lead it.

Even while few others have led the APHC, the most visible face of it has been Mirwaiz Umar Farooq. Since inception, APHC has been through a number of ups and downs and there has never been an occasion when its claim of representing the people of the Valley has been tested. Paradoxically other than Pakistan government and the ISI; it has been kept afloat by the out of all proportion importance given by the government of India and the Indian media. The top echelon has been invited to meet the Indian Deputy Prime Minister and the Prime Minister more than once, further boosting their inflated ego and sense of self-importance.

The internal problems of APHC and appreciable reduction in the fear of the militant guns are, however, not the only major difficulties that it has to face. The political space within which it has to operate is also encroached by the two mainstream regional parties, namely the Peoples Democratic Party and the National Conference. The former with its slogan of Self Rule and strident stand against the security forces and alleged human rights violations has effectively taken a slice of the APHC propaganda plank. Similarly, the National Conference has been consistently demanding greater autonomy based on the Assembly resolution of July 2000 and, what it calls, the Delhi Agreement of 1952 between Jawaharlal Nehru and Sheikh Abdullah. This also considerably eats into the space of maneuverability of the Hurriyat.

It is generally believed in J&K that if APHC contests assembly elections it would not be able to win double-digit number of seats in the house of 87. Though the top leadership has not been able to present a united front, the group has consistently opposed any form of elections. Also over the years there have been serious allegations that top APHC leadership has misappropriated funds received from different sources. The posh premises and prime properties owned by various front-ranking leaders of this group is a common knowledge in Srinagar. The effective implementation of all calls for strikes and shut down by it is not so much due to its popularity or standing amongst the masses but because of the strong backing of the militant groups with gun in their hands and the inability of the state government to deal with the hooligan elements in its cadres and payrolls. It is also no secret that their leadership is mortally scared of the armed militants and, while being protected by the state police, would not take even a single step without nod from the ISI. Over the last two decades the central government has given so much importance to it that presently APHC has acquired the image of being one of the parties with whom parleys will have to be held for resolution of the Kashmir tangle. Unless these people are called to explain and pay for their acts of omission and commission against the laws of the land and the militants' threat to their lives considerably reduced, the APHC leaders will, in all probability, not behave and respond in any reasonable, positive and constructive manner.

On the other hand, while the state government was engaged in improving functional efficiency of all organs of administration; serious differences of opinion had come to the surface between New Delhi and Srinagar by the beginning of 1993. Consequently, there was a change of incumbent in the Raj Bhawan in March that year; when G.C. Saxena resigned and Gen (Retd) K.V. Krishna Rao was appointed as new Governor of the state. He achieved quite a bit during the first few months of his arrival. In the month of April an agitation by policemen of two Battalions, based in Srinagar, was effectively handled by him. This was followed by the establishment of Unified Headquarters, in the first week of May. The UHQ concept proved highly useful in optimizing the efforts of security forces and intelligence agencies in the counter-militancy operations. Six months later, in November the satisfactory handling Hazratbal crisis was followed by successful domination of Sopore town by security forces. Thus by the end of 1993, the ground situation had started turning in favor of the State. During the next one year, by the end of 1994, the security forces had unmistakably gained an upper hand over the terrorists and the life of public as well as the functioning of the administrative set up returned to almost normal levels. Setting up of a three-tier security grid, further proved a strong and potent measure in meeting the terrorist problem effectively. The creation of two sectors of Rashtriya Rifles; one each in Valley and Jammu division considerably enhanced the efforts of the security forces. An analysis of the existing situation would indicate that the terrorist apparatus so carefully and laboriously planned, raised and sustained by the Pakistani rulers and ISI with the aim of annexing control of the state had nowhere reached the intended objective. The entire effort had almost petered out and administrative structures in the state were back in control of the situation.

The next important phase in this militancy-affected state was that of Turnaround; and it lasted for almost two-years of 1995 and 96. During this period, the security forces gained upper hand over the militants by relentlessly pursuing intelligence backed security operations and the general public was also provided relief by a more efficacious and focused administration. This twin strategy to meet the militant threat proved successful; in the urban as well as rural areas of the state – particularly that of the Valley.

CHAPTER – V

The Transition

A n analysis of important parameters of terrorist related activities and success of the security forces during 1994 indicates that in spite of the appreciable level of continuing violence; the number of militants killed that year was a record high 1596. This figure during the previous four years, starting from 1990 was 550, 844, 819 and 1310 respectively. By the beginning of 1995, the security situation in J&K had been brought well under control and the State Government felt so much confident that some responsible circles started hinting about the conduct of elections to the State Legislative Assembly; leading to the installation of the popular government. In the next few months, plans for elections became unmistakably evident. Since a smooth conduct of elections required further blunting of the terrorists' capabilities, the counterinsurgency efforts were intensified with the augmentation of forces in certain identified areas and greater concerted efforts were launched in this direction all over the state – especially in the Valley.

The Election Commission of India (ECI) had already ordered the summary revision of the electoral roles in September 1994 after a gap of many years; and to make its intentions more clear, the Commission also appointed a very senior and competent officer of the State as the new Chief Electoral Officer. With this began the gigantic and hugely challenging process of restoration of democracy in the state, in right earnest. Two other administrative difficulties had also to be surmounted in this endeavour. One related to finalizing legal and administrative arrangements for enabling a large number of Kashmiri Pandit electors to cast their vote; as they had migrated from their homes located in various constituencies of the Valley and started living in and around Jammu city, in Delhi and many other places scattered all over the country. Then there was also a need to cater for the exigency of providing polling personnel in case the local employees were prevented from performing polling duties in some pockets. The level of participation by various political parties in the elections was also a very relevant factor. All this was in addition to the basic requirement of providing safe and conducive conditions on the ground from the security point of view for any such exercise to be feasible and credible.

The election process was given a decisive push with five high-level meetings taking place within a short span of three weeks; with the last one being held in the Ministry of Home Affairs, New Delhi on May 1, 1995. In this conference, the plans so far drawn were further fine-tuned and final arrangements regarding the availability of additional forces, the requirement for funds and various issues regarding coordination amongst different agencies were tied up. It was expected to be an unprecedented exercise and also a valuable learning experience for all concerned for any future venture of this kind. Therefore, after a series of deliberations and brain storming sessions; a blueprint of the electoral process started emerging. While working out the finer details, the agencies and officers entrusted with this task kept in view certain factors like the availability of resources and taking into consideration the imperatives of the ground situation as also recognizing the fact that the terrorist activities, though in control, were not fully eliminated. The requirement of substantial additional forces was a pre-requisite, as the adequate security of the prospective candidates in particular and political workers in general, were an important issue at hand and needed to be addressed effectively for smooth conduct of elections. This deployment pattern was worked out separately for pre-poll, during the actual conduct of elections and also for the post-election phases. The number of polling stations for the entire state came to 6500 covering all fourteen districts. Of course, the force deployment in each polling station depended on its determined classification as a normal, sensitive or hyper sensitive location from the security point of view. No one was prepared to take chances with any of such issues. The likelihood of the State Government employees, particularly in the Valley, not performing the election duty due to terrorist threats was also taken into consideration and contingency plans were worked out accordingly. This required planning and making arrangements for getting the entire polling staff from outside the state, including over a thousand Urdu knowing Presiding Officers; their training, boarding-lodging, transportation and security arrangements.

The thoroughness of plans and preparations coupled with the fact that by the beginning of May some units of additional forces started arriving in the Valley; must have given indications to the Pakistani handlers of militants and the ISI that authorities were serious about the intent of conducting elections in the J&K. Meanwhile, the seat of the government shifted, for six months, to the summer capital Srinagar on 8th of May. In spite of the separatists' call for a general strike on that day, a good number of government employees reporting for duty further rattled the operators across the border. Pakistan's machinations to sabotage the election process became quite evident when it created reprehensible mischief at the holy Shrine of Charar-e-Sharief; a symbol of communal amity and syncretic religious beliefs of the people of Kashmir. Some militants headed by Mast Gul – a Pakistan origin terrorist who had gained experience in Afghanistan – had entered this shrine a few weeks ago. Even though the security forces had cordoned off the whole area effectively; no precipitative action was launched for the fear of collateral damage to the revered structure and in the highly populated area around the shrine. On 9th May the terrorists put few houses on fire in the town, to put pressure on the forces and make a bid to escape. Over six hundred houses and one hundred shops were destroyed and damaged in this inferno. During the next night, these miscreants put the shrine itself on fire in a desperate attempt to break through the security cordon. In the ensuing fierce encounter around twenty terrorists were killed and a top ranking militant of Harkat-ul-Ansar, Abu Jindal, was captured. However, the leader of this nefarious group Mast Gul succeeded in escaping.

As expected, the burning of Charar-e-Shrief Shrine sent a wave of anger and consternation amongst people of the Valley. It was also a major setback to the general law and order situation and election preparations. Soon though it became apparent that in spite of Pakistan's propaganda machine working overtime; the people of Valley had realized in their collective consciousness that this act of sacrilege was a deliberate mischief on the part of foreign terrorists headed by Mast Gul, under instructions from Pakistan and that the security forces were in no way involved. This was further confirmed when Mast Gul surfaced in Pakistan sometime later and was accorded a hero's welcome there. Even though the election preparations in J&K went ahead notwithstanding this setback; the Election Commission of India announced towards the end of May that the elections were postponed indefinitely. However, even after this speculation in some quarters continued that the elections could be held during October – November the same year.

As the graph of militant violence did not register any significant decline; the efforts of security forces were further stepped up to keep the head of trouble creators low. The militants added another chapter in their nefarious designs by abducting four foreign tourists on 4th July from the Pahalgam area of Kashmir. Three days later two more such visitors were waylaid in the same region. A hitherto unknown terrorist outfit, Al-Faran, claimed responsibility for these kidnappings. This was typical of the ISI way of functioning. A day after his abduction, one of the tourists escaped and was rescued by the security forces that were searching for the foreigners in the area and he was airlifted to safety. The demand of Al-Faran for the release of some hardcore terrorists was not accepted by the government and on 13th August, the dead body of one of the abducted persons was found in Panzmulla village in Anantnag district. In spite of continued efforts to secure their release, none of the other persons could be brought back safely. These have since been believed killed by the terrorists, thus bringing the curtain down on another bloody chapter by the ISI backed outfits.

Immediately after the conclusion of the annual Amarnath pilgrimage – which kept the state administration occupied – towards the end of August; preparations for the conduct of Assembly Elections were resumed with renewed vigor. These included arrangements for additional forces, their accommodation and clothing for the winter months if required; arrangements for getting sufficient election material as well as electoral personnel from within or outside the state; stocking of essential commodities etc; as also political management to ensure adequate participation in the electoral process. A lot of effort was devoted to the planning and handling of administrative and logistic arrangements. By the beginning of October; the State Government was confident enough to recommend the holding of a four-phase election, spread over seventeen days, in the month of November. However, at the political level the situation had not yet firmed up sufficiently to ensure a credible participation; and this was an important consideration for all those planning for the return of the elected government in the state, particularly the ECI.

The contemporary scene has been described in one account as, "At the political level, during the month of October, increased political activity was witnessed both in Srinagar as well as in Delhi. The focal point of these efforts was to bring around Dr. Farooq Abdullah and his National Conference to participate in the elections.... Prime Minister P.V. Narasimha Rao took the matter directly in his hands... He issued a much-awaited statement from his foreign visit to Burkina Faso in the beginning of November 1995. This statement was expected to yield positive results in the political circles as it was hoped that the Prime Minister would indicate the contours of greater devolution of power to the State as was being demanded by the National Conference. However, he only indicated the willingness of the Central Government to consider cosmetic changes... and said that further course of action would be decided by the coordination committee in consultation with the elected representatives of the State. This generated considerable discontentment amongst the political circles in the State, particularly the National Conference leadership"[1]. The full Election Commission visited the state reaching Srinagar on 8th November. It went to Leh and Jammu also during the two days tour and held extensive consultations with the political parties, state administration, central security and intelligence agencies as also some other groups. The National Conference working committee decided on 9th November not to participate in the elections on the ground that its demand on autonomy had not been agreed to by the centre. The Election Commission on reaching Delhi the next day announced in a press conference that they were not recommending the holding of elections to the State Assembly as "the ground conditions were not conducive for the exercise". This postponement did not have much to do with the level of preparedness of the administrative machinery but more with the desire of the EC in holding a credible election. With yet another deferment; the needful could now be done only during the next summer. In the meanwhile, the general elections to the Parliament slated for early summer of 1996 were approaching fast.

In March 1996, the schedule for Parliamentary Elections in the country was announced by the Election Commission. Significantly it also mentioned the intention to simultaneously hold elections to the Parliamentary seats in J&K. For the six Parliamentary constituencies of the state, votes were to be polled in three phases, covering two seats each, on 7th, 23rd and 30th May 1996. As anticipated, and as it had happened on the earlier occasions of polling announcements, ISI prompted its

1   Jalil Ahmed Khan and Sudhir S. Bloeria, *The Dying Terrorism*, Manas Publications, New Delhi, 2003, p. 92.

terrorist organizations to engineer another nefarious incident with a view to forestall this third attempt of the government to enable the people to exercise their franchise in the State after a gap of seven years. As if on a cue; on March 24, 1996, a group of terrorists tried to force their entry into the Hazratbal Shrine. On being challenged by the JK Police guard posted there, the intruders fired at them and in the ensuing encounter, nine terrorists were killed. One sub-Inspector of the Police died and four persons on duty received injuries. In the melee which followed some armed terrorists managed to enter the shrine premises, giving rise to the apprehensions of a repeat crisis which occurred there during October-November 1993. This time though the security forces had a much better and effective grip on the situation and when they laid a cordon around the shrine and asked the militants holed inside to surrender; they vacated the shrine but instead of laying arms, moved to a nearby building. Thus, even though the threat to the shrine came to an end on 26th March; the presence of terrorists in the vicinity made the security forces to further tighten the cordon and progressively increase the pressure. Four days later the JK Police effectively surrounded the building in the occupation of the terrorists and gave the last opportunity to them to surrender, which was heeded by only three persons. In the fire-fight and action that followed 24 militants inside the building were killed; six personnel of the J&K Police also received injuries. The firm and effective action sent a meaningful warning to other trouble makers and this incident almost became a turning point in the Valley. This also heralded the coming of age for the Special Task Force (STF) of the J&K Police as its boys came out with flying colors in their maiden and important encounter which was a moment of glory for the STF. It was also a defining moment in the work culture, level of confidence and collective self- esteem in the J&K Police. This force has never looked back since then and only forged ahead constantly. From then on the STF, renamed in the later years as the Special Operations Group (SOG), remained in the forefront of anti-militancy strikes in the state. This fine body of specially trained and highly motivated men scripted many more successful operations in the years to come. However, for now, the ISI venture did not succeed in derailing the electoral juggernaut and with the induction of additional forces in the state; the head of the terrorists was kept low enough and area domination was achieved for many more months to effectively go through the elections. It was not that the militant organizations or their Pakistani mentors had a sudden change of heart; but the effectiveness and coordinated efforts of the administration, in all its aspects, which bore the fruits of success.

Since a major part of the Valley, practically two third – comprising Anantnag and Baramulla districts - was going for election in the second phase on 23rd May, there was a lot of media attention focused on the poll process. The print and visual media persons from all over the country - as also from abroad - representing all major newspapers, magazines and TV channels had descended on the Valley a few days before the polling. The administration had made special arrangements to facilitate regular briefing of the media and extensive as well as constant coverage of the events deemed important by the concerned persons and agencies. This policy of openness to the media proved beneficial for the State Government and helped it to get a positive press and TV coverage during the entire election period.

The effective management of the whole electoral process required a lot of planning, preparations and coordination since the State Government employees had decided not to participate in this exercise due to militant threats. Therefore, in addition to the security forces; all polling staff, medical personnel, and requisite transport had to be arranged from outside. Also, their reception, boarding, lodging and movement within the state needed to be planned and carried out in a foolproof manner. This was a massive exercise and all Deputy Commissioners – who were also District Election Officers of their respective districts – got fully involved in the process to work out and put in place the necessary arrangements. The crowning glory of this collective effort was evident on May 24, 1996, when almost 50,000 central paramilitary forces and 10,000 polling personnel were moving in over 5,000 vehicles in six different directions, practically all over the Valley, performing series of tasks from depositing polling material to striking camps, moving to various locations, returning some polling parties to airfields and taking the rest of them to new locations- carrying out the entire gamut of poll activity successfully without any mishap and in a professional manner. This kind of collective effort resulted in keeping the security situation well under control; in spite of exertions to the contrary by Pakistan backed terrorist groups, including the foreign militants inducted from across the border by ISI. The management of Parliament elections was a great example of teamwork and seamless synergy. The polling was completed in all six constituencies on May 30, 1996. It was a day of great satisfaction to all those, whose individual and collective efforts had made this singular achievement possible.

During these elections, "Notwithstanding all doubts and suspicions, the response of filing nomination papers was quite encouraging, as many as 183 nomination papers were filed by 164 candidates in the six Parliamentary constituencies. They included 113 independents. The remaining candidates belonged to eight political parties. After the last date of withdrawal, 110 candidates remained in the fray. In comparison, figures for the number of candidates who contested elections to the Parliamentary elections in 1989, 1984, 1980 and 1971 were 90, 85, 59 and 52 respectively.... INC won four seats, BJP and JD won one each. The voters turn out for the State was 49.02 percent.... The percentages in respect of the three constituencies of Kashmir Valley were quite respectable. Baramulla, Srinagar and Anantnag constituencies recorded 46.62, 41.00 and 50.13 percent of polling respectively. These figures compared well with 48.28 percent polling recorded in respect of Jammu constituency which witnessed near normal political activity. Udhampur constituency which included the disturbed Doda district recorded 53.54 percent polling"[2].

In many ways, the conduct of Parliamentary elections were a full dress rehearsal for the State Assembly elections which were to follow four months later; as a natural corollary. In some manner, these were anticipated to be considerably easier because of two main reasons. The State Government employees were expected to join in this electoral exercise and the National Conference, which had not taken part in the Parliamentary polls, was widely perceived to be keen to participate this time. The actual process for the conduct of Assembly elections was set rolling on August 7, 1996, with the issuance of notification of the polling schedule by the Election Commission of India. According to this, the polls were to be held in four phases with voting taking place on 7, 16, 21 and 30 September. As per the notification, the completion of polling process for all four phases was to be completed, on the same day, on October 8, 1996. "With the polling taking place in the six constituencies in Doda district with repoll in 23 polling stations of the Valley on 30th September, massive exercise of conducting Assembly Elections almost came to a close with only counting and installation of popular government left to take place. On the actual days of polling, the terrorists were not able to indulge in any

---

2   *Ibid*, p. 148.

significant acts of violence across the State except for one major incident in Srinagar district.... The overall voter turnout in the State was around 54 % and the percentage of invalid votes was nearly three percent. Both these figures compared very favourably with the normal national voting pattern.... The National conference had bagged forty out of forty-six seats in the Valley with two going to the Congress and one each to Janata Dal, CPI (M), Awami League and Independent candidates. In Ladakh region, National Conference had taken three out of four seats with Congress winning in the fourth constituency. The picture in Jammu region was more mixed. There National Conference once again emerged as the single largest party by winning fourteen out of thirty-seven seats followed by eight of BJP, four each of Congress, Janata Dal and BSP. One seat was won by Congress (Tiwari), one by Panthers Party and one by Independent candidate.... The National Conference had returned to power with a very impressive mandate from the people of the State across the board"[3].

The conduct of these two elections was the completion of a stupendous task; so successfully achieved by the combined efforts of various organs of the central and the state governments; which any system could legitimately be proud of. Here was a conspicuously notable example of teamwork and seamless energy of various individuals and organizations working together to achieve an objective. A few years later, a senior officer of the State Government – then posted as a Deputy Commissioner in one of the Valley districts – while talking about this unique experience told a friend, "I don't remember what I did, but I remember what we did".

Following the landslide victory of the National Conference, the public mood, particularly in the Valley, became jubilant and people were looking forward to installation of the new government with keen expectation. On 9th October, the President issued a proclamation revoking President's rule in the State and on the same day National Conference government headed by Dr. Farooq Abdullah was sworn in with a Cabinet of 27 ministers, including thirteen Cabinet Ministers, twelve Ministers of State and two Deputy Ministers. The swearing-in ceremony took place in an impressive function held in the Sher-e Kashmir International Convention Centre on the banks of the famous Dal Lake. This event became all the more memorable with the participation of leaders of national stature from almost all the major political parties in the country. The people of the state as well as

---

3   *Ibid*, pp. 192-194.

the rest of the country had great expectations from the newly installed democratic government and had hoped that this would herald complete return of normalcy and peace in the state.

The year 1996 will always have the position of a special reference point in the history of J&K state; as it was a turnaround period for the restoration of popular rule. This year began with the continuation of affairs of the state being run by the Governor's administration – as was happening since January 1990 (Even though technically the state had been placed under the President's rule after the first six months in accordance with the provisions of the State and Indian Constitutions). The intentions of the State Government had been made clear by pronouncements of the Governor at different times showing keenness for the return a democratic government. Working on such stated parameters; the state administration had assiduously made efforts to contain the terrorists' violence within manageable limits. The gaining of an upper hand by the security forces and firm handling of the Hazaratbal incident in the last week of March further demonstrated the resolve of the government to crush terrorism in all its forms. In this backdrop, the announcement of Parliamentary – and later the Assembly – elections were initially received with some degree of skepticism and apprehension by a section of the people. But, in both cases a stage reached where electoral process gained support from a major part of the public; and this proved to be a decisive element towards the restoration of the democratic process in the state. Pakistan tried its best to thwart and disrupt this collective change of perceptions by sustained efforts to disrupt the onset of the democratic process in J&K; by intimidating the people of the state – particularly in Kashmir valley and Doda district – by engineering various acts of terrorism aimed at creating a fear psychosis among the people. The ISI especially focused efforts to increase the level of infiltration and the proportion of foreign mercenaries; as also communalize the situation in important population centers of Jammu region and cause damage to the government buildings and communication infrastructure. These efforts were further intensified as the elections approached. All such nefarious designs were demonstrably neutralized due to the effective security operations undertaken by the forces on the borders and deeper inside. The cooperation of the local people also helped considerably in achieving a conducive environment for the elections.

The successful conduct of these elections were also major confidence building and morale-boosting events; for the public, in general, had perceived these developments as their capacity and ability to defy the diktats of the terrorists and as a manifestation of their collective desire to have peace and tranquility. This led to visible improvement in the overall environment with signs of growing normalcy in the lives of people and perceptible greater activation of the political forces in the state; particularly in the Valley. There the general streak of optimism and buoyancy in the mood of the people was almost infective; and particularly so after the Assembly elections which were widely seen as even the greater reflection of the people's correct mood – with the Valley-centric National Conference also taking an active part in this electoral contest. Of course, this whole gamut of activities leading to defining positive changes in the collective mood of the people and in the overall situation as well as the security matrix; also came with an attendant cost. The terrorism profile for 1996 indicated a very high level of violence with 5023 incidents taking place during the year; which resulted in an unusually large number of 189 security forces persons losing their lives. Also in the same year, greater pressure by the forces and targeted operations resulted in neutralizing a very large number of 1209 terrorists. But the highest cost for the return of democracy was paid by common people; and this fact is duly reflected in the civilian casualties during the year which, with a figure of 1424, has been the highest number of civilian lives lost during a single year, right from 1990 onwards.

After these Assembly elections, the National Conference emerged as the single largest party not only in the State Assembly where it had a strength of 57 MLAs out of a total strength of 87 – almost a two-third majority – but also as the leading entity in all three regions of the state separately. It now had the difficult task of consolidating its position in the Valley, while simultaneously making efforts to broaden base in Jammu and Ladakh; a task easier said than done as what was attractive in one part of the state was most probably not likely to go well in the other. However, there were common denominators of democratic and human values cutting across geographical barriers; but working effectively on such principles required leaders of substance, charisma and vision. The ruling party having lost its patriarch, Sheikh Mohd. Abdullah in 1983 was so much poorer – thirteen years later - and not fully up to this mark. The challenges before it could broadly be divided in three categories; political, administrative and security. The last of course was peculiar to J&K.

The leader of the National Conference, Dr. Farooq Abdullah appeared to have been unable to forget his unjustified dismissal as the Chief Minister in July 1984 and also not a celebrated exit from power, though under entirely different circumstances, in January 1990. Ironically, his return to the political centre stage during November 1986, on the basis of a new found alliance with Rajiv Gandhi, rested on almost complete confidence in the central leadership; and the Central Government, as also demonstrated a lack of sustained ambition for autonomy in the run-up to regaining driving seat of power in the state. This was almost exactly on the pattern of what his more charismatic father had done towards the end of 1974, for coming to power second time in J&K. So, back in 1996, there was ostensibly no reason for Farooq Abdullah to harbor any bitter feeling towards New Delhi; if anything he had a lot to be grateful to the centre for the liberal material support and executive exertion to ensure the return of popular government in the state. But the lure for ever greater freedom of action, as once demanded by Sheikh Abdullah; had both become an important political plank as well as a mill-stone around the neck of Farooq Abdullah and his National Conference. This desire to be close to the central government and also, at the same time, strive for the greater independent course of action was too much of a contradiction to be successfully reconciled and satisfactorily resolved. This inconsistency was nowhere more apparent than the NC being an ally of the NDA government in the centre – in fact Omar Abdullah, Farooq's son, was a Minister of State in New Delhi in the Vajpayee cabinet – and on the other hand the J&K Assembly passing the Autonomy Resolution; adopting the State Autonomy Committee Report, on June 26, 2000, on the strength of NC numbers in the House. Although, this resolution did not have any significant constitutional implications but it did open a Pandora's Box in the political landscape of the state. Whereas this move failed to create any ripples in Kashmir, there were loud voices of opposition in Jammu and Ladakh regions. It was also a development which Vajpayee Government in New Delhi could not afford to ignore beyond a point and hence soured the comfortable and congenial relationship enjoyed by the two parties and also the respective administrative entities. The almost immediate response of the Central Government was a decision of the Union Cabinet, taken on July 4, 2000, rejecting this resolution of the J&K Legislature. This Cabinet decision also made a reference to the discussions in detail by Sheikh Mohammad Abdullah with Prime Minister Indira Gandhi in 1974-75. It read in parts, "....In the above context, the Cabinet finds the resolution passed by the State Assembly of Jammu and Kashmir endorsing the report of the State Autonomy Committee unacceptable. The Cabinet feels that the acceptance of this resolution would set the clock back and reverse the natural process of harmonizing the aspiration of the people of Jammu and Kashmir with the integrity of the nation.... The Cabinet urges the people and the Government of Jammu and Kashmir to join hands in the endeavour to address the real problems facing the State: to root out insurgency and cross-border terrorism and to ensure accelerated development. The Centre would continue to provide all possible assistance for attaining these objectives.... The Cabinet, therefore, decides not to accept the resolution passed by the Jammu and Kashmir Assembly on the report of the State Autonomy Committee. The Government is of the firm conviction that national integration and devolution of powers to States must go together."

The handling of the political situation in the state by this government has been aptly commented on by a perceptive observer as, ".... despite having been in power for the last three years, the National Conference has not yet regained its old position. It is certainly yet not in a position to get the better of its political opponents in terms of popular support. On the contrary, its base has shrunk. It is absolutely naïve to think that the National Conference can recover its lost base by keeping the Hurriyat leaders out of the political scene.... Only his family's own history should have convinced Dr. Abdullah that political battles should be fought politically. He must gear up the National Conference to accept the Hurriyat challenge and counter it. For this, it is necessary that he intensely interacts with the people and recovers his ground as the self-appointed heir of the tallest-ever leader of the State. His inability to do so and his dependence on the police and state machinery to silence his political opponents may further reduce his own influence and that of the National Conference, much to chagrin of all those, including this writer, who had lent whole hearted support to him in 1996 Assembly elections in the hope that a popular regime would be better placed to redeem the State from its misery"[4]. Even though these remarks were made at the beginning of 2000, the deductions remained valid for the entire six years tenure of the NC government.

---

4   Puasp Saraf, *Bordrer Affairs*, January – March 2000, New Delhi, p.8

A degree of disappointment had set in, amongst people of the state, from the very first day of the oath-taking ceremony. With a cabinet sworn in of 27 members; almost one-third of the total strength of 87 MLAs and half the numbers of 57 ruling party assembly members; it was perceived more as an exercise in political accommodation rather than the expected emphasis on administrative performance and improved delivery systems. Many political observers felt that Dr. Farroq Abdullah should have smartly learnt from a similar experience of his father whose very compact cabinet formed in February 1975 had provided a model of efficient administration to the state for over two years. Sheikh Sahib's jumbo-sized council of ministers put in place after the July 1977 elections was far less effective in comparison. In fact, it became beginning of the public disenchantment with the regime at that time. The very size of the new cabinet in October 1996 sort of worked as a dampener amongst the general public.

As the events folded out and over the years this impression proved right; even though his official set up was headed by a very competent and seasoned officer of 1963 batch of the IAS with considerable experience of handling various issues both at the state as well as in the central governments. People, in general, did not feel a sense of immediate palpable relief that they had expected. To be fare to the administration of the time, they were faced with a huge task of rebuilding damaged and destroyed infrastructure – especially in the Valley – and the state administration did manage to put in some groundwork. Many such bridges, government schools and buildings were re-built. A substantial plan for this purpose was also put in operation, but the progress on the ground was such that it was perceived by the general public as not sufficient and much less than what had been expected or they were promised about. The people of the state had, in fact, great expectations from the newly installed democratic government and had expected that this would herald the complete return of normalcy and peace in the state; also that the remnants of terrorism would soon end. But this did not happen. To top it, the major initiative of this government to conduct Panchayat elections also floundered, as it was not seen through to its logical conclusion. In addition, the Kargil war of May-July 1999, three years after the Farooq government was sworn in, shook it so badly that the regime never really recovered its balance back. A further setback occurred in the form of a militant attack on the Legislative Complex at Srinagar on October 01, 2001. The Chief Minister's statement in the Assembly next day, where he practically broke down while speaking was seen as an expression of impotent rage by an ineffective political leader at the helm of affairs; one who had all the numbers in his favour. It was literally the last proverbial push to the incumbent government before the assembly election took place during the next year. Also, a new political entity had emerged in the state; more particularly in the Valley, in the form of Peoples Democratic Party (PDP).

In a free and frank interview with Rashme Sehgal of *The Times of India*, Omar Abdullah, apart from answering related questions about his almost imminent elevation to head the National Conference soon, made an appraisal of his father's tenure as Chief Minister by saying, "It's too early to make an assessment but he did provide a representative government. He also kept an administration moving, against tremendous odds. May be the development work in the state has not been as much as people would have expected but he has worked under very difficult circumstances. Being Chief Minister of J&K is one of the toughest – if not the toughest – jobs in India. He got it from both sides. He has had to fight militants and also face problems that were created by the security forces...."[5]

The new democratic government certainly inherited a largely stable security situation. Even though the militancy was still alive; it had lost the earlier dominating position in the Valley and was in the terminal stage south of Pir Panjal range. The security forces and the police were literally in a commanding position. The security scenario in the state did show some improvement during the next two years, but the change was much slower than generally expected. Also with the installation of the popular government and the violence graph steadily going down; the ISI increased its efforts to give a fillip to the stagnant level of terrorism in the state. Some of the favorable factors for the Pakistani operators included reduced deployment of security forces post elections; general sense of relaxation in every sphere leading to complacency and less effective coordination between the civil administration and security forces. This sort of negative fallout also adversely affected the functioning of the Unified Headquarters. The UHQ thus, and over time, ceased to be a focal centre and a place for pooling of resources by all agencies, central or state, for adequately meeting the challenge on hand and also planning and preparing for responding to the emerging threats and dangers. All these factors were adroitly exploited

---

5   *The Times of India*, dated February 25, 2002.

by ISI and Pakistani operators to up the *ante* and effectively raise the level of subversive activities in the state.

The Unified Headquarters was constituted in May 1993 in the backdrop of the difficult security scenario then prevailing. Even though this fell short of the initial concept to formulate a Unified Command, which was intended to be responsible for the command, control and direction of all security-related resources available within the state; still the UHQ was an appreciable improvement over the prevailing system where practically no mechanism of centralized coordination had existed other than personality of the Security Advisor and office of the Governor himself. The Unified Headquarters was able to achieve optimum synergy of anti-terrorism efforts of various organizations; as its conceptual framework had been worked out after careful considerations of the security requirements as well as keeping in mind the capabilities, sensitivities and peculiarities of different forces and organizations. This proved to be an extremely effective system whose working was further improved upon during the next three and half years; leading to the successful conduct of the two elections in 1996.

With the formation of the popular government; the UHQ was practically wound up with the Director General of the State Police being asked to chair its meetings. Within two months the State Government realized its folly and decided that there would be two UHQs at the divisional levels and the Chief Minister would chair the UHQ meetings and in his absence the two Corps Commanders would be the nodal points for coordination in respect of Kashmir and Jammu regions. The extreme preoccupation of the Chief Minister with affairs of the state and his involvement in running the day to day administration; coupled with the detached attitude of the civil administration further diluted the concept and functional effectiveness of the UHQ. It was not a policy making or advisory body; but a group which had to involve itself directly with the strategy and tactics of counterinsurgency operations on a continuing basis – meeting at least once a week - and when the situation so demanded, even on daily basis. This was not possible in the modified new set-up and it got converted to, more or less, a forum for debating and deliberating upon the functioning of different organs of the security apparatus. Thus the whole concept was reduced to a pale shadow of its earlier self and deviated considerably from the original idea with which it was created in the first place. Though technically this arrangement still continues; it can be said without any fear of contradiction that after October 1996, the level of coordination of forces and resources has considerably come down as compared to the earlier three and half year's functioning of the UHQ.

The change in policy and perceptions resulted in the overall decline of targeted operations, adversely affecting the result oriented outcomes and coordination mechanism. The efficacy of anti-militancy operations at the district level particularly became ineffective. As a result, the activities of disruptive and anti-national elements started picking up once again. In the midst of this see-saw scenario, Pakistan unleashed a storm of unprecedented magnitude in Kargil area of the state during the first week of May 1999. Even though India had been conditioned by the one-decade old Pakistan-inspired proxy war in the state; these belligerent incursions across the LoC came as a rude shock; taking both the governments and the security forces by complete surprise. It took India over two months to clear this transgression.

The confrontation between the Indian army and Pakistani forces, which commenced in early May, continued for two and a half months and even threatened a much wider conflagration at certain points before the situation was diffused in the second fortnight of July. During this period the Indian army, under *Operation Vijay*, used air power for the first time since 1971; although on a restricted scale and under considerable self-imposed constraints. The cost of conflict in monetary basis for India was estimated at around 11,000 crores. In terms of manpower, the most precious national resource, Indian losses were 527 all ranks killed and 1363 wounded. Pakistani casualties were estimated to be 1042 killed (Indian estimate); Pakistani official figure being 453 killed.[6]

Going by the deliberate nature of the defensive positions that the Pakistani troops had prepared in a number of places on the Indian side of the LoC, it became abundantly clear that the decision to cross the border and occupy territory on the Indian side was not taken in a hurry, but was a wilful and calculated move. An enterprise of such proportions, which was likely to have long-term and adverse implications on Indo-Pak relations - in addition to serious international diplomatic fallout - could only have been put in operation with the authority of the highest levels of civilian as well as military leadership in Pakistan. The apparently calculated strategy

---

6   www.wikipedia.org/wiki/Kargil War#Casualties. Accessed on May 24, 2016.

seemed to be aimed at flogging the dying militancy in Kashmir as also to put J&K back on the international agenda. The former intention succeeded but the latter flopped badly. Pakistan's adventure in Kargil was condemned by the world at large. The USA exerted pressure on Pakistan to withdraw its forces from the Indian territory, which it subsequently did in the later part of July 1999 marking the culmination of *Operation Vijay* for India.

It would be interesting to glance at and have a bird's eye view of the comments and views of Pakistani experts and political analysts that could come in the public domain. The first important reaction in the Pak media appeared immediately after the cessation of hostilities. It was a severe indictment of the system and makes interesting reading, as "The finest institution in this land, the bedrock of our existence, is now directly under attack because an initiative was not fully thought out as to possible consequences. More than a hundred officers and men of this magnificent army have paid a terrible price in blood for this negligence. On the other hand, though belated, we have begun to recognize the sacrifice and valour of the Northern Light Infantry (NLI). This was a must. ......, because of mishandling the Indians have turned their military disaster on the ground into a victory in the media"[7].

However, the most detailed, authentic and damning comments appeared in the monthly HERALD[8]. The write-up also carried two box items titled, 'Kargil – A Strategic History' and 'Minister Visits Hundur?' Both of these complement the main narrative which needs to be quoted at some length. Here are few excerpts. "There are over 500 flags flying across the entire Northern Areas, home to the Pakistan army's high- altitude warriors. The tombs are of the heroes of Kargil who fought valiantly in a war that seems to have many losers but no winners. Behind each of these tombs lie tales of struggle and valour, of neglect and disavowal, and of betrayal and unfaithfulness. But a year down the line these tales still remain untold....... By February 1999, the area was rich with its own version of events that were unfolding in Kargil. True to their tradition of glorifying soldiers, the people of the area were loathe to accept the government's claim that the militants had infiltrated deep into Indian

---

7   Ikram Sehgal, in The Nation, July 31, 1999; as reported in *The Times of India* dt. August 1, 1999.

8   M. Ilyas Khan in an article titled LIFE AFTER KARGIL in July 2000 issue of monthly HERALD.

territory. For the residents of Ghizer, Hunza and Baltistan, the districts which supply the bulk of NLI's manpower, it was only NLI soldiers who were involved in these heroic deeds..... The area was rife with rumors that there may soon be serious skirmishes in the Drass-Kargil sector. But there was no information on what was actually happening on the frozen heights. The uncertainty gave way to panic in early June last year when bodies of soldiers started arriving at the villages more frequently..... Over the next month, 105 bodies passed along the jeep track that leads up to Yasin, Punial and Ghizer valleys in the central Northern Areas. Similar traffic appeared in the valleys of Hunza, Nagar, Gilgit and Baltistan. Residents of the area claim that the NLI soldiers who accompanied the bodies took care to move them at night to avoid publicity. As a rule, only one soldier accompanied the body. Shakoor Jan's body, for instance, was brought by two soldiers in a private jeep which also carried the body of Sepoy Ibrahim. Both Ibrahim and Shakoor Jan were in track suits..... In both cases, there were no military honors at the funeral, no hoisting of the national flag and no gun salutes. The soldiers who brought the body did not even offer a simple salute..... The miseries of locals were compounded by the stories of starvation and shortage of ammunition at the frontline that emerged around this time..... According to circles close to the top military authorities in the NA, by mid-June 1999, almost the entire strength of 6 NLI on the Kargil front had been wiped out, while 12 NLI had also suffered heavy casualties. Though the Indians took more casualties than the NLI, they were able to clear the heights commanding the Srinagar – Leh highway by June 26, thereby taking the sting out of Kargil operation.... According to another veteran of the Kargil war, the NLI high command had made a specific promise of establishing supply lines to positions on the heights. But it was not fulfilled....... Many residents also alleged inaction on the part of commanding authorities of the NLI, claiming that an SOS was sent to the GHQ for reinforcements only after the troops in the forward positions had suffered a fatal setback. Even then, the hurriedly called regiments from Punjab could offer no help because they were not acclimatized..... On June 26, the anger of the people spilled into the streets of Hunza where activists of the Karakoram National Movement (KNM) held a peace march between Karimabad and Aliabad and openly raised slogans against the manner in which the Kargil operation was being handled. At least a dozen leaders of the march were later arrested on sedition charges and kept in Gilgit jail for three months".

The above-mentioned article comprehensively describes and records the feelings of disappointment and frustration of the NLI troops and the people of Northern Areas during the critical six months of 1999. This is something which hardly came to the notice of Indian population or reached rest of the world. Also elsewhere in the same publication, monthly HERALD of July 2000, Idrees Bakhtiar mentioned, "Mr. Nawaz Sharif's claims notwithstanding, the government insists that all the key players during the Kargil affair were kept fully informed of all developments.... However, independent observers feel that there is still a lot about the Kargil affair that has not come out in the open.... While India has already conducted a detailed post-mortem of the event and made its findings public, albeit with appropriate security deletions, it seems that this crucial chapter in Pakistan's history will continue to remain shrouded in controversy".

Add to this a very scathing condemnation in an article titled "Putting Our Children in Line of Fire" by Lt Gen (Retd) Shahid Aziz, a Pakistan Army officer and former Corps Commander[9]. The opening paragraph of this reads, "Kargil, like every other meaningless war that we have fought, brings home lessons we continue to refuse to learn. Instead, we proudly call it our history written in the blood of our children. Indeed, our children penning down our misdeed with their blood! Medals for some, few songs, a crossroad renamed, and of course annual remembrance day and a memorial for those who sacrificed their tomorrow for our today; thus preparing more war fodder for our continuing misadventures. Since nothing went wrong, so there is nothing to learn. We shall do it again. We decide. You die. We sing". He has also in the same article graphically and expressively described this desperate and reckless venture as, "An unsound military plan based on invalid assumptions, launched with little preparations and in total disregard to the regional and international environment, was bound to fail".

On the Indian side too there was considerable criticism of the failure of army and intelligence agencies to detect the occupation of Indian territory by Pakistan, and the handling of Kargil Operation, in all its manifestations, by the government. Some defense analysts and strategic thinkers maintained that the Indian response to the challenge posed by

---

9   The Nation, dated January 6, 2013. This article is also available in the Blog of Gen
     Aziz at: "gen-azizshahid.blogspot.com".

Pakistan was, once again, muted and lacking in the sting that such an adventure should have attracted.

It would also be worthwhile to quote the views of General V.P. Malik, who was then the Chief of Indian Army, about this war. In his book on the subject he says, "In India, the immediate impact of the Kargil war was reflected in the expression of overwhelming public opinion. The country rose as a nation putting aside all its internal differences.... A strong feeling of patriotism not only pervaded all parts of the country but also gripped Indians all over the world. India's self-imposed restraint and the measured response in the form of determinedly beating back the aggression won it universal acclaim."[10]

Notwithstanding the advantage of initial surprise gained by the other side, it does go to the credit of Indian army that after the details of infiltration became apparent and seriousness of the incursions evident, it reacted swiftly and decisively, without taking any more chances. According to an estimate, almost five additional brigades were moved into the area of conflict, almost post- haste, along with sufficient artillery components. The logistics for this big movement and maintenance thereafter were also managed competently.

The induction of such large body of troops into Kargil, within a short time, necessitated also shifting of a number of units as well as formation Headquarters from the Valley; including the famous 8 Mountain Division. These were successfully engaged in the counterinsurgency operations, against the militants and most of them were highly experienced and competent entities. Even though some additional units of BSF and CRPF were provided in lieu; but these were much less in numbers as well as effectiveness. Thus Pak moves in Kargil did seriously and adversely impact the security forces' drive against the militants. This gave the ultras time to regroup and rework their strategy leading to a marked increase in the level of violence over the next few years. In fact from 1990 onwards till 2010, as per records maintained by the J&K Police, the security forces casualties exceeded four hundred annually only during the four years from 1999 to 2002. The maximum spurt in the escalated levels of militant activities became evident during the year 2001, which recorded 4536 incidents of violence in which 1098 civilians died, 2020 militants were killed and also

---

10 General V.P. Malik, *KARGIL From Surprise To Victory,* HarperCollins *Publishers*, New Delhi, 2006, p. 352.

613 security forces' personnel laid down their lives. The counterinsurgency (CI) grid, so effectively established earlier by the forces; became strong and potent once again only in 2004 after the erection of Border Fence all along the Line of Control in 2003 - 04. The fact, however, remains that the thinning of the CI grid on ground and loosening of the grip of the security forces deployed in the Valley was a direct result of the Pakistani intrusion in Kargil and it took considerable time and effort to regain the earlier levels of effectiveness. These assertions are adequately and clearly reflected in the table below; which also gives a comprehensive view of the militancy violence of twenty years, starting from 1990, including the impact of the Kargil war on the internal security situation of the state.

| Year | Incidents | Killings | | Terrorists | Infiltration |
		Civilians	SF/ Police		
1990	4211	1000	155	550	1280
1991	3780	906	173	844	1400
1992	4842	1069	189	819	3045
1993	5273	1057	198	1310	3280
1994	5851	1069	200	1596	2625
1995	5946	1202	237	1332	3200
1996	5023	1424	189	1209	3230
1997	3437	1030	216	1075	3185
1998	2940	967	268	999	3720
1999	3073	937	407	1082	3050
2000	3091	942	482	1520	3455
2001	4536	1098	613	2020	3545
2002	4038	1050	539	1707	1729
2003	3401	836	384	1494	1313
2004	2565	733	330	976	516
2005	1990	556	244	917	231
2006	1667	410	151	591	691

Year	Incidents	Killings			Infiltration
		Civilians	SF/ Police	Terrorists	
2007	1092	170	110	472	232
2008	708	147	75	339	126
2009	499	71	79	239	113
2010	488	164	69	232	095

A tragic tale of misery, destruction and death could be woven around these figures; which included the cold-blooded murder of seven Kashmiri Pandits by militants in Sangrama of Badgam district on May 22, 1997, and equally tragic massacre of 35 Sikhs on March 20, 2000, in Chhati Singhpora village of Mattan area of Anantnag district. A fragile situation of peace prevailed in the state, particularly in the Valley, till the beginning of 2002; the year of another Assembly polls after the normal term of six years of the State Assembly came to an end. There was also, in between, a period of about one year of efforts of the central government which gave rise to all-round optimism. These exertions for peace began on July 24, 2000, with Hizb-ul-Mujahideen announcing a three-month cease-fire; and ended without any positive outcome almost exactly a year later at the end of July 2001 with the failure of Agra summit. This was followed by the terrorists' attacks in America on September 11, 2001, in which the iconic buildings of World Trade Centre in New York were destroyed and many hundreds of people were killed and injured. Close on the heels of this episode came the militants attack on the Legislative Complex in Srinagar on October 1, 2001. This happened less than two weeks after General Musharraf had publically aligned Pakistan with the Americans in his telecast to the nation on 17th September and made a resolve to root out terrorism from his country.

In the afternoon of 1st October the Legislative Assembly and Council sessions had concluded at 1230 and 1300 hrs respectively and most of the legislators and ministers, including the Chief Minister, had left the premises. However, the Speaker and the Chairman of the Assembly and Council, along with their staff and some members of both houses, were still present there; finalizing the agenda for the next sitting as the session had been extended by two days. Outside the Assembly complex events of a different nature were taking place and just after 1 pm a group of heavily armed militants managed to enter the premises after ramming and blasting their vehicle on the gate of the complex. The subsequent events have been described as, "Engaging the armed intruders by fire the security forces, Special Operations Group and the Fire Brigade rescued the trapped employees by creating an escape route from the rear of the building on the northern side. The whole operation to neutralize the militants lasted for over four hours resulting in the upper story of Council building catching fire in which one militant was charred to death. Two militants were killed in the Assembly compound. In this gruesome incident, 38 persons died including four militants, while 78 people received injuries. During the course of operations both the DGP and Addl DGP (Armed Police), had a miraculous escape when a burst of bullets fired by the militants went by in the space between them."[11] This was once more a clear assertion by Pakistan, if any such indication was required, that in relation to India there was to be no change in its stance and attitude and efforts to foment trouble in J&K and other parts of India would continue unabated.

With the beginning of the year 2002, preparations for the impending elections to the State Assembly also began with back-channel efforts to encourage and persuade some of the separatist elements to take part in the polling scheduled to be held later in the year. These endeavors did appear to have met with some success which considerably alarmed ISI and it quickly struck back. On May 21, 2002, Abdul Ghani Lone, a popular Kashmiri leader and head of the Peoples Conference – an important constituent of the Hurriyat – was gunned down in Srinagar in broad daylight in the midst of a huge public meeting organized by APHC to commemorate the death anniversary of Moulvi Farooq. His assassination was – and has been – a big blow to the political environs in the state. Lone was not only a founder member of the APHC; but also had in the past been a successful minister in the state cabinet and elected legislator more than once. He was always regarded as a thoughtful politician, an able legislator as well as a competent administrator. At that point of time it was generally believed that he and his associates may get persuaded to join the forthcoming electoral contest; and in that eventuality, this step might trigger a similar course of action by a good number of outfits and individuals. It was precisely to stall this

---

11 Dr. Sudhir S Bloeria, *The Men Who Served Jammu & Kashmir,* Vij Books India Pvt Ltd, New Delhi, 2016, pp.124-125.

kind of slide that the Pakistani handlers of militants must have decided to get him liquidated. The vice like grip of the ISI over separatist elements in J&K was once again brought to the fore and visibly demonstrated to be very effective – as the protests and condemnations were limited and muted - for everybody to see and draw appropriate conclusions. The death of Lone did not outwardly create many ripples in the separatist camp and practically sealed the prospects of any of these elements taking part in the forthcoming elections. The Central Government continued with its behind the scene efforts; including a veiled assurance of holding Assembly elections under the Governors Rule in case of credible participation by the separatist outfits. The Prime Minister himself guaranteed, on the occasion of his Independence Day address from the ramparts of the Red Fort, that elections to the Jammu and Kashmir Assembly would be absolutely free and fair. But there were hardly any takers, from this group, after Lone's death. The field was now exclusively open for the traditional political forces in the state, commonly called as the mainstream political elements. National Conference was, of course, a leading player in this category; and significant development was taking place in that camp.

On June 19, 2002, Omar Abdullah, the Lok Sabha MP from Srinagar constituency took over as President of the National Conference from his father and the Chief Minister Farooq Abdullah. This change of guards to the younger clan had a lot of significance on the political scene of the state as the party leadership passed on to the new generation with a manifestly modern and progressive approach to manage the affairs of the party and the government. It also meant the National Conference leadership passing to the third generation of the family; in line with the trend set in motion by the patriarch Sheikh Abdullah himself. Even though the acceptance speech of young Omar Abdullah, in the party convention that day, was not very impressive; the significance of this change was not lost to anybody and generated a lot of interest in the Valley.

The Election Commission of India announced the holding of elections to the State Assembly on August 2, 2002. This electoral exercise, like in 1996, was to be held in four phases spread over twenty-two days. The polling for the first phase was to take place on 16th September and date of completion of polling notified as October 8, 2002. With the announcement of the election schedule, political endeavors in the state got shifted into high gears, with feverish activity in all three regions. The security forces and the police put in place increased protection measures in Valley and the mountainous areas of Jammu region where the terrorists had started to intensify their efforts to thwart the elections. With the rising election fever, the terrorist violence too registered an upswing; which was also reflected in the daily and weekly data compiled by the J&K Police. There was a marked escalation in all militancy related incidents and parameters, also involving murderous attacks on important individuals and some candidates – including former as well as sitting ministers. The most important victim of the terrorists' violence was Mushtaq Ahmad lone, Minister of State of Law and Parliamentary Affairs - who was earlier the MOS in charge of Home Department of the State Government – a National Conference candidate from Lolab constituency in Kupwara district of Kashmir. He was killed by armed militants while addressing an election rally in his constituency on 11th September. In spite of such setbacks and sustained efforts by the terrorists, the political process even in the militancy-infested areas continued unabated.

"With the rising election fever the terrorist violence also registered an upswing; as between 1st August and September 10, 2002, there were 405 terrorist-related incidents in which 22 political activists were killed. The civilian casualties were 26 and 62 security personnel lost their lives. The main targets of terrorist attacks were National Conference ministers and activists followed by Congress, CPM and PDP leaders and workers"[12].

In spite of the efforts made by the militants and their overground sympathizers, the whole electoral process was successfully completed in the specified time frame. In statistical terms, a total number of 709 candidates, including 29 women contested the polls for 87 seats in the Assembly. The overall percentage of polling came to a respectable figure of 43.28. There were 7085 polling stations in the state and to provide adequate security cover for ensuring peaceful elections in the state, over 400 additional companies of para-military forces were deployed. The Election Commission had also deputed sixty-three Observers to oversee and ensure the free and fair conduct of elections. Since electronic voting machines were used all over the state for the first time, the counting process which used to take at least two days earlier, was over within seven-eight hours on the day of the counting on 10th October. By the

---

12 Jalil Ahmad Khan and Sudhir S. Bloeria, *The Dying Terrorism*, Manas publications, New Delhi, 2003, p. 218.

late afternoon that day all the election results were public; and people's mandate – the ultimate arbiter of political destinies in a democracy – did spring some surprises. The PDP, which came into being on the political horizon of J&K on July 28, 1999, made an impressive maiden entry into the legislature with sixteen seats. The largest single party was still the National Conference but, with twenty-eight seats, it was almost a pale shadow of its earlier self when in 1996 Assembly elections it had won in fifty-seven constituencies. Not only that; the party had to contend with a serious drubbing in matters of personalities also. Its President, young Omar Abdullah, lost in the Ganderbal constituency, considered almost a pocket-borough of the Abdullah family. The party was equally mortified with twelve of its ministers and the outgoing Speaker of the Assembly also loosing at the hustings. The Congress Party with twenty seats and Independents with a tally of fourteen; were other major winners in this contest. Rest of the nine seats was cornered by five smaller entities.

In view of the peculiar conditions existing in the state, and to ensure greater credence of the electoral process; the Election Commission had introduced an enhanced element of credibility in this exercise by allowing foreign diplomats to witness the conduct of these elections; in addition to providing unhindered access to the national and international media persons. Almost a record number of over four hundred media persons from rest of the country as well as abroad descended on the state to cover the electoral contests. Twenty-seven foreign diplomats also visited the Valley during this period. The comments of a leading national daily can be taken as a representative sample of the successful conduct of these elections. It said, "… That the polls were the fairest in the two decades became evident soon enough, a truth now being reinforced by the results …. Democracy places one key factor above all and that is performance, here, the National Conference, in particular, its former Chief Minister failed entirely…."[13] Even more importantly, the people all over the state, without exception, felt that these elections were completely free, fair and transparent.

The state had now a hung Assembly due to the fractured mandate of the people and no party by itself was in a position to form the government. With the National Conference making public pronouncements that it would prefer to play the role of a constructive opposition rather than cobble a majority to stake a claim to form the government; the next big

13 *The Times of India*, dated October 11, 2002.

players to attempt the same were Congress party with twenty seats and the PDP having sixteen members in the legislature. In a house of eighty-seven a government could be formed with the support of at least forty-four members. Even these two parties joining hands would fall short of that critical mark. Their initial efforts to attract splinter groups of sufficient numbers did not succeed and on 18th October; Governor's Rule was imposed in the state under Section 92 of the J&K Constitution to fill a constitutional void. Thereafter, in the wake of a series of discussions in Srinagar and New Delhi and political adjustments, both Congress and PDP reached an agreement on October 26, 2002. It was decided that with the support of four members of Panthers' Party, two of the CPI (M), and a requisite number of independents the two main constituents of the coalition – Congress and PDP – would stake claim to form the government on the basis of an agreed Common Minimum Programme (CMP). This CMP, it was said, "would aim at healing the wounds inflicted by militancy". The main highlights of CMP underlined four points; *inter alia,* that Prevention of Terrorism Act (POTA) will not be implemented; Prisoners languishing without trial will be released; Victims of militancy will be rehabilitated and All-round development in all three regions ensured. Added emphasis was laid on the salient features of the agenda for governance as reconciliation and initiation of unconditional dialogue with all parties.

It was also jointly agreed that during the six-year term of the Assembly, the Chief Ministership would be shared for three years each between PDP and Congress; with Mufti Mohammad Sayeed taking over as head of the State Government for the first three-year term. The Chief Minister and eight members of his cabinet were sworn on November 2, 2002, thereby bringing the whole process of elections in the state to a logical conclusion.

The era of Mufti Sayeed on the political horizon of the state had begun. He and Atal Bihari Vajpayee, who was already Prime Minister of India for the last three years, would together make sincere efforts to improve the situation over the next few years.

CHAPTER – VI

Enter Vajpayee

The political journey of Atal Bihari Vajpayee began seriously in 1952 when he became Political Secretary to Dr. Syama Prasad Mookerji, and was actively helping him to popularize the newly formed political party, Bharatiya Jana Sangh. His powerful oratory, tinged with a soaring flight of imagination of the poet in him, presentation of alternative parameters on various national issues – soon made him an important leader in the new party. He also became a very popular speaker and even those people who did not agree with his political thought, came to listen to him because of his oratory skills and mastery over the delivery of thoughts in Hindi; the language in which he spoke in public. He was elected to the Lok Sabha for the first time in 1957 and since then, for over five decades, his presence was always felt in the hallowed precincts of the Parliament. After the death of Dr. Mookerji in 1953 and then the demise of Deendayal Upadhya in 1968; Vajpayee always remained a central figure in his party.

He was arrested along with other important opposition leaders during 1975-77, the period when the internal emergency was declared in India by Indira Gandhi. On the call of Jayaprakash Narayan to form a joint opposition front against the Congress, Vajpayee was instrumental in merging the Jana Sangh into the newly formed Janata Party in 1977. Following the Janata Party victory in the national elections that year, Vajpayee became the Foreign Minister in the cabinet of Prime Minister Morarji Desai. However, the Janata Party government disintegrated within two years, but during this period he had made a reputation for himself as a competent political executive, an experienced statesman and a respected political leader. Soon after Morarji Desai resigned as Prime Minister in

1979, the Janata Party stood dissolved, creating a political crisis for its constituents including the Jana Sangh. He then played a significant role in the transformation of the Jana Sangh into its current identity as the BJP (Bharatiya Janata Party) in 1980. Since then the BJP organized and consolidated itself to be a national party; an alternative to the pan-Indian presence of the Congress.

In the middle of 1996, Atal Bihari Vajpayee became the 10th Prime Minister of India – on the basis of being leader of the single largest party - for a very short period of 13 days; but had to submit his resignation to the President as the alliance he was leading could not muster enough numbers in the Lok Sabha. For almost next year and a half India was governed by a minority coalition government, with the support of many parties – the main amongst them being the Congress.

Towards the end of 1997, in the month of November, the Congress withdrew support from the central government coalition then headed by I.K. Gujral. This left President K.R. Narayanan with no option but to dissolve the Lok Sabha and call for fresh elections; which were subsequently held during February and March next. The BJP contested these elections under the declared leadership of Vajpayee and emerged as the single largest party with 182 seats; while the Congress could register a victory in 141 constituencies and thus became the second largest party in the Lok Sabha. The BJP cobbled together the support of other smaller parties and groups to form National Democratic Alliance (NDA). This coalition staked a claim for power in the Centre, due to higher and sufficient numbers and was sworn to form the government, with Atal Bihari Vajpayee as the Prime Minister. The dream of BJP leadership to become an alternative to Congress had finally been realized in March 1998.

One of the priority item on the 'to do list' of BJP was to make India a nuclear weapons state; something that the party election manifesto had included right since 1967. This was achieved on May 11, 1998, with a series of successful nuclear explosions. The event is graphically described by L.K. Advani as[1], " Sitting in the Prime Minister's living room were seven of us – Atalji, Defence Minister George Fernandes, Deputy Chairman of the Planning Commission Jaswant Singh, Finance Minister Yashwant Sinha, the Prime Minister's Political advisor Promod Mahajan,

---

1   L.K. Advani, *My Country My Life,* Rupa & Co, New Delhi, 2008, p. 542.

his Principal Secretary Brijesh Mishra, and myself. We were eagerly awaiting a message from the deserts of Rajasthan – to be precise, from Pokharan. The message came, slightly before 4 pm, on a specially installed top-security phone line: 'Tests successful'. India's nuclear scientists had succeeded in conducting three simultaneous nuclear explosions, heralding India's emergence as a nuclear weapons state. None of us in the room could control our emotions". Shortly thereafter, the Prime Minister made the following statement before the assembled media at his residence, "Today at 1545 hours, India conducted three underground nuclear tests in the Pokharan range. The tests conducted today were with a fission device, a low yield device and a thermonuclear device. Measurements have also confirmed that there was no release of radioactivity into the atmosphere. These were contained explosions like the experiment conducted in May 1974. I warmly congratulate the scientists and engineers who have carried out these successful tests". Two more nuclear tests were conducted at Pokharan on 13th May, completing the planned series of tests. It was also remarkable, from India's point of view, that the American satellites were not able to detect the Indian preparations for these tests. The Prime Minister made a formal announcement to this effect in the Parliament on 27th May saying, "India is now a nuclear weapons state". He also outlined the broad contours of the country's policy in this regard by emphasizing that India would neither use nuclear weapons for aggression nor for mounting threats against any country but for self-defence and to "ensure that India is not subjected to nuclear threats or coercion".

Almost as if on a cue, within a fortnight, Pakistan also carried out its nuclear explosions in Chagai testing range in Baluchistan – conducting five simultaneous underground nuclear tests on May 28, 1998; and thus becoming an overt nuclear country before the world – notwithstanding its clandestine atomic efforts till then, though very thinly veiled, and also international nuclear poaching. Pakistan's second atomic test, code-named Chagai-ll, was carried out two days later on 30th May.

These tests by India and Pakistan resulted in the United Nations Security Council Resolution 1172 and sanctions were imposed on both nations by a number of major powers, particularly the US and Japan. The experts would forever keep debating about the comparative nuclear power of the two nations and relative impact of these tests on the economies of the respective countries. But the stated respective Nuclear Doctrines and public pronouncements since then make it very clear that whereas Pakistan's nuclear developments are explicitly India centric; the Indian endeavours in this direction are not solely aimed at Pakistan but cover a much wider spectrum; taking into account manifold challenges to its national security. It also encompasses the stated Indian policy of 'no first use'. However, the nuclear status of India and Pakistan has ever since cast its long shadow over the bilateral relations of the two countries; with Pakistan seemingly smugly carrying on its terrorist activities against India under a perceived safety net of nuclear over-hang.

Lahore Bus Yatra –Feb 1999

In a bold peace initiative, Atal Bihari Vajpayee undertook the Lahore Bus trip on February 20, 1999. It was, in fact, the inaugural Bus service between Amritsar and Lahore and he chose to travel the sixty-kilometer distance between the two cities in the first bus. Apart from the Prime Minister himself, this bus was full of celebrities belonging to different fields; including a couple of Hindi cinema personalities. The Pakistan government headed by Nawaz Sharief provided due courtesies and extended requisite protocol to the Indian Prime Minister and his team; except for the pointed absence and lack of appropriate behaviour of its Army Chief General Musharraf – for which the Pak government actually could not have been faulted as its absence of effective control over the army brass has been a well-known phenomenon for a long time. "On the following day, the two Prime Ministers signed the 'Lahore Declaration', containing three salient points. Firstly, it reiterated the determination of both countries to 'implementing the Simla Agreement in letter and spirit'. Secondly, it recognized that 'the nuclear dimension of the security environment of the two countries add to their responsibility for avoidance of conflict'. The third point was of special significance for India. Pakistan had agreed to join India in condemning 'terrorism in all its forms and manifestations' and affirming its 'determination to combat this menace'"[2]. Vajpayee also showed political acumen and statesman like sagacity by visiting Minar-e-Pakistan; a veritable symbol of the creation of Pakistan. This gesture of the Indian Prime Minister was widely appreciated by the people of Pakistan. No less relevant were the thoughts he penned in the visitor's book at this monument. He wrote, "A stable, secure and prosperous Pakistan is in India's interest. Let no one in Pakistan be in

---

2   *Ibid*, pp. 551-552.

doubt. India sincerely wishes Pakistan well". These thoughts went down very well with the general public of Pakistan.

The conspicuous signals of two events during this visit were duly noted by most political observers. The first was a resumption of road traffic between the two countries, which had remained suspended after the Indo-Pak war of 1965. This was now restored through the Wagah check-point. The second was Vajpayee's visit to Minar-e-Pakistan; a strong expression to demonstrate India's public acceptance of Pakistan's separate existence. It was all the more significant that such a measure came from someone heading the government in India led by the BJP; which had always promoted the idea of indivisible India – *Akhand Bharat.*

In a nutshell the bus journey to Lahore was a big step towards bilateral peace, as it was intended; and hopes on both sides of the border soared about the much improved prospects of peaceful resolution of outstanding issues. The bonhomie and camaraderie displayed by both sides amply indicated this. But, as it generally happens in the affairs of the sub-continent; two unforeseen events cast their shadows on this important initiative by Vajpayee. One was the unexpected fall of his government in New Delhi in April 1999 and the other was Pak-army generated conflict in Kargil during May-July that year. Both these developments were the results of political maneuvers in India and peculiar power dynamics in Pakistan respectively. A perceptive analyst commented on these developments as, "A reference in this regard may be made to the Prime Minister's Lahore visit in February 1999. Vajpayee had described it as a 'defining moment'. Nawaz Sharief, the then Pakistan Prime Minister, had said it was 'ice-breaking'. But the hoopla soon lost in Kargil heights, where the two countries used everything, short of nuclear bombs, against each other".[3]

The Indian political crisis started with the AIADMK withdrawing its support to the NDA on April 14, 1999 plunging the central government in an existential predicament and forcing it to undergo a test of strength on the floor of the House. This it lost by one solitary vote. Thus the government headed by Vajpayee fell. The Lok Sabha was dissolved on 26th April and the President asked Vajpayee to head the caretaker government till the next elections, to the 13th Lok Sabha, which were to take place within a period of six months, as mandated by the Constitution of India. The Kargil

---

3   *Border Affairs*, New Delhi, July – September 2001, p. 5.

war intervened in-between, diverting the Indian nation's attention from the electoral contest to focus on the national effort to successfully manage this conflict between India and Pakistan.

Kargil War – May-July 1999

Lot has been written about the Kargil War, which raged during May – July 1999, on the bleak and icy high- altitude peaks of Kargil. This clash of arms was primarily due to the Pakistani perfidy and in-satiated desire to cause damage to India as and when possible. Pakistan had once again proved to be unreliable and devious, and this time it had not only crossed the LoC but also transgressed the line of trust – this act of betrayal coming so soon after the Lahore Declaration, following a successful Bus *yatra* from Amritsar to Lahore. Vajpayee rightfully felt a great sense of outrage and hurt; as the turn of events unleashed by Nawaz Sharief and his government were diametrically opposite to the peace efforts initiated by the former. The Pakistani objectives in this military misadventure, code-named 'Operation Badr', were apparently multi-fold. The primary aim appeared to interdict and choke the main supply route to the Indian troops based in Ladakh region and also adversely impact the Indian forces deployed on the Siachen Glacier; and de-stabilize the entire deployment in these sectors. Another plausible goal could have been to improve its bargaining position in relation to India over future negotiations on Kashmir. In addition to further stoking the fires of militancy in the Valley; this Pakistani design could also be read as a ploy to project the crisis as a possible nuclear flashpoint and thus hope to trigger or incite international – American - involvement in the sub-continent. However, as the events were to unfold, Pakistan got nothing beyond all-round international condemnation for its churlish behavior and literally a bloody nose in the areas of conflict. According to L.K. Advani, "Finally, after seventy-four days, 'Operation Vijay' became *vijayi* (triumphant) on 26 July 1999, which is celebrated each year as Kargil Victory Day.... Kargil was also India's first war with television accessible to Indian homes. This enabled much of what was happening on the battlefield to be watched by people across the country. The mood of national unity, solidarity and self-confidence witnessed was truly unprecedented.... The martyrs belonged to all castes, creeds and religions of the country, and were a source of inspiration to one and all"[4].

---

4   n -1, p. 565.

In fact Batalik, Tololing and Tiger Hill almost became household names across the country those days.

The depressing and dark story of Pakistani intrusion in the Kargil sector took place during the winter and early summer months of 1998-1999. The Indian army, as a matter of normal practice, used to withdraw its high-altitude forward posts along the LoC during the winter months and reoccupy these in the summer. But due to Pakistan army clandestinely taking control of few such posts, this practice was abandoned during the 60s and 70s. All border posts were manned thereafter through-out the year in the whole of J&K, except Ladakh; and this is where the Pak military commanders found an opportunity. The posts vacated by the Indian troops, as per past practice, were occupied and further fortified by specially trained and acclimatized soldiers of some elite Pak units; coupled mainly with the troops of the Northern Light Infantry (NLI) who belonged to the Gilgit-Baltistan areas of PoK and were hence well used to operating at such heights. Another mistake made by Indian commanders, at the ground level, was not to trust early warnings given by the locals about this large-scale Pakistani incursion in the Drass and Batalik sectors of Kargil area. By the beginning of May, contours of Pakistani designs started becoming evident and serious counter measures were quickly and progressively put in place by India.

It may be useful to recall that the importance of Gilgit- Baltistan region, in fact, of the entire Northern Areas was not appreciated by our leaders in power right from the day India became independent. In stark contrast, most of the strategic region of Northern Areas consisting of a huge land mass of J&K territory, more than seventy thousand square Kilometers, was illegally occupied by Pakistan during the 1947-1948 Indo-Pak conflict. The successive governments of Pakistan have not only ruled this area directly by the central authority with a deliberate policy of suppression, deprivation as well as absence of civil rights and constitutional status; but also a large population of Pakhtoon settlers has been encouraged and inducted into this region with an effort to dilute, and ultimately change, the Shia majority demographic profile of the region.

Unfortunately, the policy makers of India did not appear to have sufficiently realized the huge strategic importance of Northern Areas from the national security point of view and practically made no efforts to wrest back Skardu and Gilgit region from Pakistan during the 1947-48 conflict.

In fact, even Leh and Kargil were saved from Pakistani occupation, literally by the skin of the teeth. Thus at the time of the U.N. brokered cease-fire coming into effect from January 01, 1949 - the existing position on the ground remained unchanged in the Ladakh region. Subsequently, also this area continued to be neglected and this resulted in major gaps in India's knowledge of Northern Areas and our intelligence agencies had difficulty in collecting credible human intelligence in this important sector. "Unfortunately, not only the successive governments but also the intelligence community itself gave low priority to this area even for strengthening the technical intelligence capabilities[5].

The Kargil Review Committee was set up by the government of India, immediately after the war was over, with the mandate to review the events leading up to the Pakistani intrusion and recommend measures to prevent it in future. After this Committee had submitted its report, some parts of it - not considered 'sensitive' from security point of view - were made public. "The review committee sifted through Pakistani writings on the subject and deduced that the political and strategic motives of the Kargil operation were:

> To internationalize Kashmir as a nuclear flashpoint requiring urgent third-party intervention;

> To alter the LoC and disrupt its sanctity by capturing unheld areas in Kargil;

> To achieve a better bargaining position for a possible trade-off against positions held by India in Siachen.

Musharraf is said to have committed himself to the proposal when he became Chief of Army Staff in October 1998; he even visited the Force Commander Northern Area (FCNA) in late October in pursuance of the plan".[6]

It is now evident that Pak army regulars, along with some elements of Lashkar-e-Toiba and Hizb-ul-Mujahideen were responsible for crossing the LoC and occupying important heights as well as areas of tactical importance right from Mushkoh Valley in Drass to Chorbat La in Batalik

5   Raman, B. Frontline, July 30, 1999.

6   A.S. Dulat, *Kashmir: The Vajpayee Years*, HarperCollins *Publishers* India, 2015, p. 24.

and beyond to Turtuk in the North – in Leh sector. The exact timing of this ingress and preparation of defences in each location is still not precisely determined; but one can safely premise that this was managed during the autumn of 1998 and the spring of 1999. The infiltration appears to have taken place in two phases. The first and the deliberate one must have commenced some time during the late summer of 1998 and culminated in the preparation of regular defences, stocking and arrangements for the occupation of these new posts during long and harsh winter. In the next phase, the intruders either took possession of some of the Indian positions unheld during the winter before these could be re-occupied by our troops as per established routine, or moved forward laterally from the prepared defences to enlarge the arc of infiltration. The Indian army patrols first confirmed the presence of intruding Pakistani troops in the Batalik sector on 7th May, Drass sector on 12th May and in the Mushkoh area on 14th May 1999. This is the time when alarm bells were sounded all round and countermeasures started to be put in place.

It is also a fact that, taken in totality, the Kargil episode was a failure of all intelligence agencies – RAW, IB, military as also the field intelligence units of the army deployed in this sector. Unfortunately, no one was held accountable or taken to task for this dereliction. It was also a laxity on the part of the local Brigade Commander, his staff officers and various unit commanders on the ground. If inter-battalion patrolling of large gaps in the defences had been properly carried out; intrusions would have been detected very much in time and appropriate counter-measures taken.

Even though by the beginning of May 1999, when our forces on ground became aware of the presence of Pak troops in own area and realized that the situation was pretty serious and grim; the broad contours of Pak designs and the extent of Pakistani ingress had not yet been fully comprehended. By the middle of May, the army was discovering fresh Pakistani held positions on an alarmingly regular basis spanning the entire Kargil sector. It also goes to the credit of the then Chief Minister of J&K, Dr. Farooq Abdullah that, apart from senior army commanders at various levels, he strongly and consistently took up and followed the matter of adequate military response to this threat with the central government very effectively. By the end of May, appropriately effectual military and diplomatic responses by India were put in place which began to wrest initiative from Pakistan.

Notwithstanding the advantage of initial surprise gained by the other side, it does go to the credit of Indian army that after the details of infiltration became apparent and seriousness of the incursions evident, it reacted swiftly and decisively, without taking any more chances. As immediate crisis management measure, some infantry battalions which had just been de-inducted from Siachen, were rushed in to plug the gaps and undertake counter operations. According to an estimate almost five additional brigades were moved into the area of conflict, almost post- haste, along with sufficient artillery components and supporting paraphernalia. This also included shifting of an entire division, then engaged in counter-infiltration measures in the Valley, thus diluting the security grid there.

In any military conflict it is almost impossible to find out the level of resources used, unless the figures are officially released and only estimates can be made based on informed sources. One report quoting the 15 Corps Commander mentioned that the Indian army had deployed nine battalions, including two teams of 9 Para, in Drass and Mushkoh sub-sectors; six battalions were positioned in Batalik area while one battalion was used in Kaksar[7]. The Pak manpower in this sector appeared to be about eleven battalions comprising elements of the regular army, Northern Light Infantry units, SSG troops and some militants of different outfits. The Indian army also reportedly deployed 300 artillery pieces, including 100 Bofor guns. The Airforce logged 550 strike missions, 150 reccee missions and 500 escort missions. In addition, 2185 helicopter sorties were also put into operations.

Apprehending the escalation of this crisis into a major conflict, the American efforts to defuse the tension between India and Pakistan and disengage the two armies started around middle of June - with a series of discussions between Deputy Assistant Secretary of State of America and Commander-in-Chief of the United States Central Command Anthony Zinni on one hand and General Musharraf on the other. Main thrust of these talks centered on the structure and timings of Pakistani withdrawal. As a consequence of these parleys, on 27th June Musharraf announced that the Pakistan Prime Minister would shortly be visiting the United States. Nawaz Sharief, in turn, cut short his visit to Beijing and returned home. He then headed for America – practically on urgent summons from there - to meet the US President, who reportedly altered the dates of his planned

---

7   Dinesh Kumar in *Times of India*, July 19, 1999.

vacations to enable the meeting with Sharief at Blair House. During this meeting, which took place on the 4th of July, President Clinton strongly urged Prime Minister Nawaz Sharief to withdraw Pakistan forces from the Indian territory, to which the latter agreed after emphasizing his non involvement and ignorance about the whole Kargil affair. He also strongly asserted lack of any knowledge about his own army chief having moved the nuclear weapons, as was reported in some sections of the press. He made a formal announcement of Pakistani forces starting withdrawal from India territories, on his return home. This was the beginning of the Indian diplomatic ascendency which resulted in intense diplomatic activity over the next few weeks. The American pressure, widespread condemnation from the world community including China, coupled with Indian forces increasingly gaining an upper hand on the ground, also practically forced the Pakistani army to start withdrawing its elements from the middle of July and fully vacate the Indian territory before the end of the month. "Operation Vijay" was declared a success by the Indian Prime Minister on July 26, 1999.

It would be useful to have a bird's eye view of the comments and views of experts on the other side that could come in the public domain. It almost became a public knowledge – particularly in the Gilgit-Baltistan area that the 4th, 5th, 6th, 11th and 12th battalions of NLI that took part in the operations had suffered a large number of casualties. When the dead bodies of these soldiers started reaching home; it led to a wave of consternation, unrest and some public demonstrations in parts of the Northern Areas.

In a searing comment in the DAWN dated June 21, 2000, M.H. Askari mentioned, "Even if Nawaz Sharief had actually been kept in the dark about the Kargil affair, as he has claimed, he should have known that this was not the first time that the Army had taken a major initiative concerning the nation's security by bypassing the political leadership. It appears that Nawaz Sharief learnt no lessons from the past two occasions when Army deposed a political government".

And enveloped in secrecy and unanswered questions the whole Kargil affair has remained in Pakistan over the last nineteen years. No inquiry was ever ordered by the Pakistan government and not even an in-house exercise carried out by the army there to absorb and benefit from the lessons learnt from this messy and totally avoidable conflict. This was so because the persons in authority there, particularly the all powerful army high command, were never interested in the truth coming out and relevant facts becoming public. To quote Lt. Gen (Retd) Shahid Aziz, in this context, "….Whatever little I know, took a while to emerge, since General Musharraf had put a tight lid on Kargil. Three years later, a study commenced by GHQ to identify issues of concern at the lowest levels of command, was forcefully stopped by him. 'What is your intent?' he asked"[8].

One of the leading Pakistani thinker and writer, Tariq Ali, has commented about this war as, "Looking back, it is truly staggering that Pakistan's military philosophers actually thought that they could defeat India. Once the latter realized that this was a full-fledged assault, it recovered and sent in heavy artillery with air and helicopter cover. A naval offensive, prelude to a blockade, was also set in motion. With only six days fuel left, the Napoleons in Pakistan's GHQ had no alternative but to accept a cease-fire. Sharif told Washington that he had been bounced into a war he didn't want, but did not oppose".[9]

The induction of such large body of troops by India into Kargil – to take part in the operations developing there - within a short time, necessitated shifting of a number of units, as well as formation Headquarters, from the Valley. These were successfully engaged in the counter-insurgency operations, being highly experienced and effective entities, against the militants. Even though some additional units of BSF and CRPF were provided in lieu, but these were much less in numbers as well as effectiveness. Thus Pak moves in Kargil did seriously and adversely impact the security forces' drive against the militants. This gave the ultras time to regroup and rework their strategy leading to a marked increase in the level of violence over the next few years. The security grid and other measures so effectively established earlier by the forces became strong and potent once again only in 2003. The CI measures were also significantly bolstered by the erection of Border Fence all along the Line of Control in 2003 - 04. The fact, however, remains that the thinning of the CI grid on ground and loosening of the grip of the security forces deployed in the Valley was a direct result of the Pakistani intrusion in

8   The Nation, Jan 6, 2013. This article is also available in the Blog of Gen Aziz at: "gen-azizshahid.blogspot.com".

9   Tariq Ali, *The Duel*, Simon & Schuster, London, 2008, p. 142.

Kargil and it took considerable time and efforts to regain the earlier levels of effectiveness.

During the months of May to September that year, the Kargil Operations gave rise to comments and analysis ranging from considerable admiration for the heroic performance of the Indian forces, in the face of very heavy odds, to the failure of the commanders and the units in not being able to track the enemy ingress well in time and take immediate countermeasures. Overall handling of the problem and emerging scenarios, both at the military as well as the political levels also came under criticism. The crying need for India to take urgent and effective steps to control Pakistan's mischief-making capacity was once again highlighted by the Kargil war. This issue was succinctly underlined by an editorial in the *Times of India,* in these words, "A society which does not feel a sense of threat after the loss of over twenty thousand lives over ten years of terrorism directed by a neighboring state, after having fought a limited war involving more than 450 fatalities, and after being continuously engaged in a proxy-war, is bound to be subjected to further acts of terrorism and aggression. Its complacency and casualness actually ask for it".[10]

It was only a natural consequence of the Kargil conflict coupled with the internal dynamics of Pakistani politics and army proclivities; that confrontation between the Prime Minister and the army chief was inevitable. It came to a head on October 12, 1999, through a dramatic turn of events which saw the military chief General Musharraf taking over the reins of power, in another army *coup*. Nawaz Sharief was ousted from power, jailed and then – under a political bargain – allowed to go to Saudi Arabia to seek asylum.

Looking back and also with the advantage of hindsight; some people believe that Nawaz Sahrief made a terrible mistake in 1998 by promoting Musharraf as the army chief by ignoring a more senior General, Ali Kuli Khan. Sharief may have thought, one can presume, that coming from a middle class refugee background, Musharraf would be easier to manage and manipulate as compared to the aristocratic Pathan background of Ali Kuli Khan. He seems to have made the same mistake as Bhutto did in the mid-seventies by promoting General Zia-ul-Haq as the army chief over the head of many senior generals.

---

10 *Times of India,* January 3, 2000.

The NDA Returns to Power

A couple of months after the Kargil war ended, and perhaps little delayed because of that, the elections for the 13th Lok Sabha were held during September – October 1999. The BJP under the declared leadership of Atal Bihari Vajpayee contested these elections putting before the people its twin successes in making India a nuclear power as also having secured victory in the Kargil war. The party won 182 seats and the political coalition of NDA it had put together was comfortably placed with a tally of 306 seats in a house of 545. In comparison, the Congress could get only 114 seats, 27 less than in 1998. Thus the new NDA government was more stable and secure; also expected to complete its full term in office – which it eventually did. Vajpayee was sworn in as the Prime Minister for the third time on 13th October. Ironically, a day before that, the army chief had usurped power in Pakistan. The contrast between the victory of democracy in India and strangulation of people's aspiration in Pakistan could not have been more stark and striking.

IC- 814 Hijack

An Indian Airlines plane – IC 814 - on a flight from Kathmandu, in Nepal, to New Delhi with an almost full load of passengers on board was hijacked by five armed men who ordered the pilot to fly it to Lahore. With airport authorities there refusing the permission to land and the plane running short on fuel, the plane landed in Amritsar where the hijackers demanded that it be refueled. According to the information available now, the authorities had decided to send the fuel bowser to the aircraft- along with some commandos who were expected to immobilize the aircraft. But before the bowser could reach the plane, the hijackers, probably alerted, ordered the captain to take off again for Lahore, where this time the plane was not only allowed to land but was also re-fueled and – in spite of India's requests - permitted to take off for a military airbase near Dubai. There the hijackers threw off-board the body of one person they had killed in cold blood and released 28 other passengers. The pilot was now ordered by the hijackers to fly the plane, with hostages on board, to Kandahar in southern Afghanistan. The episode of IC- 814, with full involvement of ISI and Pakistani militants, was to unfold in the next few days. A sad story indeed of Indian vulnerabilities and compromises; at least on this occasion. With mounting pressure from relatives of the hijacked passengers, so graphically telecast by most of the TV channels of India, and apprehensions of the hijackers resorting to some desperate and inhuman action; the government of India chose the easier way out of the crisis and opened negotiations from an inherently weak position. This ultimately resulted in the release of three hardcore terrorists, including Masood Azhar from Indian prisons, in exchange for the safe return of the passengers and the aircraft. The Indian negotiating team, headed by the External Affairs Minister Jaswant Singh could only have the face-saving satisfaction of being able to restrict the number of released prisoners.

An interesting analysis of the episode reads as, "If you were to ask me, Gen. Pervez Musharraf had to have a hand in the hijacking of Indian Airlines flight IC-814 on 24 December 1999. The reason one can say so is that such an operation could not have been undertaken without ISI support; a hijacking was no cakewalk, even in those pre-9/11 days. And Musharraf, being the army chief and that too in a country where the military had taken direct control, was all powerful. In fact, the story we heard was that when the hijackers took the plane to Lahore they were given a bag of weapons. Thus with three events in quick succession – the Kargil intrusion, the coup d'état, and the hijacking of IC-814 – there was every reason to be wary of Musharraf, who one suspected had a hand in all three incidents. The hijacking itself made for a harrowing final week of the final year of the century, what with the pressure upon the government from the families of the 176 passengers held hostage, and the international isolation in which India found herself, while the West celebrated Christmas".[11]

K.P.S. Gill, former Director General of Police Punjab, the man generally credited with eradicating militancy from that state in the early nineties; severely criticized handling of events at Amritsar as 'unforgivable blunder'. In an article titled "Terrorism, Institutional Collapse & Emergency Response Protocols", he sequentially and with characteristic thoroughness analyses the whole hijack episode. A very small part of his observations read as, "….The real failure, however, is not in the intelligence gathering mechanism, but in our inability to utilise large and discrete flow of intelligence to assess and evaluate the scale and direction of emerging threats, to maintain sustained vigilance in response to extended or diffuse threat perceptions, and to respond effectively when these are realised…. The fact is, the failure at Amritsar – and a majority of these emanated from New Delhi – were entirely avoidable and exemplify

---

11   n-6, p. 35.

in an extraordinary measure the institutional collapse that encounters each sudden or unforeseen crisis of internal security.... At this point of time, however, it is clear that no one person was in charge at the ATC Amritsar. The Cabinet Secretary was instructing the SSP, the PM's Principal Secretary was speaking to the DIG, the State DGP to the IG. The man actually talking to the pilots was the Airport Director V.S. Mulekar.... 8:15 p.m.: The NSG team lands at Amritsar – 26 minutes after IC 814 had flown out, one hour and fourteen minutes after it had landed at Amritsar, and a full three hours and twenty-three minutes after the first information of the hijack had been received at ATC Delhi....Simple but critical calculations – such as the available fuel in the plane – had clearly not been made. Nor were the technical and military options for immobilizing the plane adequately clarified or explored.... The situation is worsened infinitely by a long history of punishing officers who actually take action, while no penalties ever attach to 'sins of omission' and acts of outright dereliction... ."[12] There is a detailed sequential examination of the events and critical observations on various aspects of this and similar situations that would be immensely useful to those put in a critical situation to handle similar crisis in future. People in authority would be well advised to take into consideration this and similar advisories.

Dulat, who has had close links with some separatists, has this to say about the dismay of some of the important militants with Pakistan, "If terrorism suspects voluntarily returned from abroad during my time as the R&AW Chief (1999-2001), the main reason for doing so was their disappointment with Pakistan. Perhaps they had matured, grown older and wiser, and had developed familial responsibilities; perhaps it was exhaustion and a desire to come home and breathe easily, but what was undeniable in all cases was a sense of betrayal and the shattering of their dream that Pakistan would help liberate Kashmir from India. I had seen this repeatedly after 1994 and up close in great detail with Shabir's commander-in-chief, Babar Badr, whose real name was Firdous Syed.... Firdous then realized that Pakistan's priorities and Kashmir's priorities were two separate things. And in the bargain, Kashmiris were losing out, quite disastrously."[13]

---

12 K.P.S. Gill, *Faultlines*, The Institute for Conflict Management, New Delhi, February 2000, pp. 2-15.

13 n – 6, pp. 79 and 85.

The Hizb Cease Fire – July 2000

Majid Dar was the operational chief of the Hizbul Mujahideen, a very active militant group in Kashmir, also considered the armed wing of Jamaat-e-Islami. It took him over a decade to get disillusioned with Pakistan and the ISI and return to Kashmir, some people believe passing through Dubai. His exact date of arrival in Kashmir is not publically known as he had gone underground on reaching home. Then he all of a sudden surfaced in Srinagar and announced a unilateral cease-fire on July 24, 2000; also saying that the realities on the ground urge for a period of peace. A local political analyst, optimistically hoping about the peace initiative to succeed, said, "If this cease-fire holds for even three months, it will be difficult for even the Hizb to go back".

The reactions in Pakistan papers were on the expected lines, being full of negativity and pessimism. Pakistan Observer (26/7) wrote editorially: "It is hoped that the Hizb will not fall into the trap, and will reject the Indian position of talks within the framework of Indian Constitution." NEWS (26/7) mentioned, "Whether or not this attempt on the part of Hizb to reach out to Delhi will bear fruit depends entirely on how Indian policy makers respond." JANG (26/7) also said editorially, "The Hizb's offer will not succeed because without winning the confidence of the APHC any offer from the Hizb or another group will remain fruitless." AUSAF (26/7) opined, "The Hizb should review its talks offer with India because the cease-fire cannot lead to the resolution of the issue until all the concerned parties jointly try to resolve it." However, PAKISTAN (26/7) stressed positively, "We have complete faith that the issue can be resolved through peaceful talks and through war nothing can be achieved. For this, immediate trilateral talks are essential."

"The Union Home Secretary, Kamal Pandy, responded and on 3 August he and other home ministry officials flew in from Delhi and met four of Majid Dar's commanders, including his nominated interlocutor, Fazal Haq Qureshi, at the Nehru Guest House in Srinagar. It was a start. It looked as if a major breakthrough had taken place. Majid Dar himself became rather enthusiastic about the dialogue, and immediately began planning to broad-base it with the participation of other Kashmiri separatists and militants."[14]

---

14   *Ibid*, p117.

Those days in the Valley it was strongly rumored that Dar was to be joined by his supremo Syed Salahuddin, who was detained at the last moment by the ISI in Dubai, and thus prevented from joining his family back home in Kashmir. The ISI seemed to have panicked and, in addition to putting tremendous pressure on the APHC to work against the cessation of hostilities, literally forced Salahuddin to withdraw the cease-fire on 8th August. This announcement he made from Islamabad in the full media glare and also used the occasion as a big photo opportunity. Then, as if on a signal, a powerful car bomb was blasted by the militants in broad daylight on 10th August on the busy Residency Road Srinagar, in front of the main State Bank of India branch. This resulted in the death of twelve people, including ten policemen and a photographer of *The Hindustan Times*. A young IPS officer also received serious injuries. This effectively ended the cease-fire and put the security forces back on the anti-militancy drive; including seek-and-destroy mode.

Just a week before this incident, the militants had struck and inflicted a number of casualties on the pilgrims of *Amarnath Yatra*, which was then in full swing. Senseless violence and loss of life in these occurrences prompted condemnation from a number of prominent Muslim scholars and personalities in the country. Some representative statements, all dated between 4th and 14th August, are mentioned hereafter. Addressing the Friday 'Khutba' on 4th August, Syed Ahmed Bukhari, Naib Imam of Jama Masjid Delhi, described the killings in Kashmir valley as un-Islamic. On the same day Syed Shahabuddin, a former MP, appealed to the militant organizations in Kashmir to renounce terrorism and join the cease-fire to create an atmosphere for peaceful dialogue. Mohd. Jaffar, All India Secretary General of JEI-H, demanded the arrest and prosecution of those responsible for the killings. Condemning the car-bomb explosion, Maulana Rabi Hasni Nadvi – Reactor Darul Uloom Nadwatul Ulema Lucknow - said that it was an un-Islamic act. Maulana Kalbe Sadiq, Vice-President, All India Muslim Personal Law Board, described the incident as against the Shariat. This contrast between these statements and views expressed in the Pak media, as mentioned here-in-before, is too stark to be ignored and indicates the huge distance which would need to be traversed for bridging such a wide gap; to give the peace efforts any chance to succeed.

The developments in the first fortnight of August left Majid Dar literally out on a limb. But, he must have been made of a sterner stuff, with a very firm commitment to the establishment of peace in the Valley; as he resolutely carried on with this work. A report appearing in a local daily in the first week of July 2002, quoting Majid Dar, is really revealing. It says, "In his first interview to a local Urdu daily after he was expelled from Hizb-ul-Mujahideen, Abdul Majid Dar, considered to be an architect of July 2000 cease-fire, made sensational disclosures about the withdrawal of cease-fire. He said, 'a hidden hand in Pakistan was responsible for sabotaging the unilateral cease-fire declared by the outfit in July 2000…. After carefully weighing the option of a cease-fire in the meeting of commanders in POK, it was agreed that I will go to Kashmir and announce a truce. When I reached here, I was conveyed to make a formal announcement. But things changed suddenly. Secret parleys were held in Pakistan and the truce was withdrawn…. Hopefully, one day the truth would be unveiled and those who sabotaged the process will be exposed'."[15]

Majid Dar was got killed by the ISI, on March 23, 2003, in broad daylight at Sopore, when he had gone there to meet his mother. What loss his murder meant for the peace process in Kashmir and how much of 'acts of omission' in this incident involved the Indian intelligence agencies, are matters of unending speculation. In a tribute to Dar and thought-provoking statement on the prevailing uncertainty in the state, a veteran journalist wrote as, "One more vocal voice for peace in Jammu and Kashmir has been snuffed out with the killing of Abdul Majid Dar. A top leader of Hizbul Mujahideen, once the dreaded militant outfit, Dar appeared to have realized two years ago that violence would not yield any positive result. In a bold move, he had settled for a dialogue with the Central Government. That the dialogue did not lead to any positive breakthrough was because of a combination of factors which have become a part of the murky political environment of the State. What was more credible was that before opting for the dialogue Dar had shown the rare courage of conviction and met top militant and secessionist leaders to personally convey to them his decision. His assassination has taken place in less than a year after Abdul Ghani Lone was killed while striving for amity and peace. How long will the voices of sanity be not allowed to be heard in Kashmir?"[16]

Ramzan Ceasefire (NICO) – Nov 2000 to May 01

The Non Initiation of Combat Operations (NICO) was a unilateral gesture on the part of India to address the internal dimensions of the festering

15 *Kashmir Times*, Jammu, July 6, 2002.

16 Pushp Saraf in *Border Affairs*, New Delhi, April- June 2003, p.4.

Kashmir issue as well as a positive signal to the concerned countries – primarily Pakistan - of its constructive intentions. The beginning was made by an official announcement on behalf of Prime Minister Vajpayee, on November 19, 2000, that the security forces had been asked not to initiate combat operations against terrorists in J&K for the month of Ramazan. The order was to come into operation from 23rd November. Parts of this release read as, "During my visit to Srinagar on August three this year, I had underscored the need for resolving all issue in the spirit of *Insaniyat* (humanism). Mine was a sincere appeal for cooperation to bring an end to the long trail of violence, which has claimed so many precious lives and inflicted untold misery on all sections of the State's population.... The holy month of Ramazan, during which Prophet Mohammed exhorted one and all to live in peace and harmony is soon approaching. The Government has therefore instructed the security forces not to initiate combat operations against militants in Jammu and Kashmir during this most pious month in the Islamic calendar.... I hope that our gesture will be fully appreciated and all violence in the State and infiltration across the Line of Control and the International Border will cease and peace prevails".

The Hurriyat response to the cease-fire was luke-warm, somewhat ambivalent and guarded; laden with 'ifs' and 'buts'. However, within a month all notable leaders of this amalgam sounded positive and formally welcomed it in a meeting held at the residence of Mirwaiz Umar Farooq on 21st December. But, the militant groups in the State, not surprisingly rejected the NICO offer. Further, as if to prove their point, on the very first day Hizbul Mujahideen blew up an army vehicle in south Kashmir's Kokernag belt killing half a dozen soldiers and wounding ten others. This action was soon followed by the cadres of LeT striking a unit of CRPF in Anantnag which resulted in the death of six men of the force.

Despite the lack of positive response from Pakistan and its proxies, this peace offer was extended by a month more on January 23, 2001. It was a short statement, portions of which read, "It is regrettable that Pakistan has not recognized the demand of time for peace and continues to promote, encourage and abet cross-border terrorism.... The government believes violence must be ended by peace – which has been welcomed by the people of Jammu and Kashmir. The present phase of peace in J&K is being, in that hope, extended by another month".

B. Raman, a retired Additional Secretary of the Cabinet Secretariat, in an on-line interview[17] termed the cease-fire as a "wise decision." He further accused General Musharraf of eight main acts of commission and omission, as follows, and all his insinuations were based on solid facts and happenings:

1. General Musharraf's attitude towards the 'Army of Islam' and its patron Osama bin Laden was deliberately ambivalent.

2. He has not taken any action against HuM, despite its being declared by the US as an international terrorist organization.

3. He has resisted US pressure to co-operate in tracing and arresting hijackers of the IAC aircraft to Kandahar in December, 1999.

4. He reportedly promised the US President in March last year that he would himself meet the Amir of the Taliban, Mullah Mohammed Omar, in Kandahar and persuade him to moderate the Taliban's policies and co-operate with the US on the bin Laden issue, but has not done so.

5. He launched with fanfare last year a programme for the disarming of Pakistani society, but, subsequently, slowed down its implementation under pressure from the 'Army of Islam'.

6. His Interior Minister, Lt. Gen. (retd) Moinuddin Haider, announced a plan for the documentation of the madrasas' and for greater government control over their curriculum, but the implementation of this too has been slowed down under similar pressure.

7. Under US pressure, he initially imposed restrictions on the movements of Maulana Masood Azhar, but subsequently relaxed them and allowed the Jaish-e-Mohammed to operate freely from Pakistan territory.

8. Previous Pakistani rulers covertly supported the jihad of the 'Army of Islam' against India, but he is the first Pakistani ruler to have openly justified the jihad.

17 www. stratmag.com dated February 1, 2001, accessed on March 7, 2010.

This is a long list of serious charges which no one in charge of a nation's destiny would want to be accused of. But, truth does remain that all that is mentioned therein happen to be based on incontrovertible facts; in spite of Indian exertions to find a middle ground and peaceful overtures. These details also clearly show the finesse and expertise with which the Pakistan Government and the Establishment - some commentators like to call it the 'deep state' - were able to hoodwink the international community, particularly America, about its double dealings, subterfuge and obfuscation attempts in matters related to security and declared commitments.

Continuing the NICO initiative a notch further by extending it a third time, the Prime Minister made a statement in Lok Sabha on February 22, 2001. In this, he reminded the members that the President in his address earlier to the joint sitting of both Houses of Parliament had outlined the government's approach to the matter of Jammu and Kashmir and that the government was pursuing a multi-pronged strategy to bring peace and normalcy in the state. This address of Vajpayee further included new initiative of the government of India and highlighted some issues as, "The government has decided to pursue this path by initiating talks with various groups in J&K.... In this regard, the government has benefited by the detailed briefing of and consultations with all political parties that it had on February 21, 2001.... Having examined all aspects of the question in its totality, the government has decided to further extend the period up till the end of May. Let this opportunity be not missed by all those that desire peace, for our patience is not infinite". He concluded this well-rounded and comprehensive policy relating to the peace process initiatives by saying, "It is my hope that Pakistan will act, even now, and abjure violence, give up their continuous hostile propaganda against India, stop promoting and aiding cross-border terrorism, take the path of peace through bilateral talks as enshrined in the Simla Agreement and the Lahore Declaration".

The Government of India once again held out a hand of peace in a major policy statement on April 5, 2001. This initiative was intended to address both the internal as well as external dimensions of the Kashmir issue. It invited representatives from all walks of life in the state to hold dialogue with the Centre's nominee, K.C. Pant, Deputy Chairman of the Planning Commission. About Pakistan, the press release mentioned, "The Government of India takes note of the frequently repeated requests from Pakistan that they are eager for a dialogue with India on J&K. The

Government of India reaffirms its faith in such a bilateral dialogue and hopes that Pakistan will help in its resumption by curbing cross-border terrorism and putting an end to the vicious anti-India propaganda emanating from Pakistan….." The statement concluded with reiteration of the talks offer and a note of optimism, with this hope, "The Government expects that all right-thinking people in the State will join hands with the Government and march purposefully in quest of the peace which has eluded them for the last 12 years. It is only in an atmosphere of peace that an agreed solution for the J&K issue can be evolved".

Some people and critics of this unilateral move felt that the one-sided cease-fire did not prove successful militarily. Some army and para-military forces commanders not only reportedly shared their concerns about the efficacy of this step; a number of commanders in the field were against the extension announced in the second fortnight of January 2001. The forces felt that NICO had restricted their freedom to strike; as no pre-emptive action could be taken against the terrorists, even based on credible information; nor could they chase militants to areas other than incident sites. The statistical data also does not indicate outright success of this measure:[18]

	150 days before cease-fire	150 days after cease-fire
Militants Killed	415	410
SFs Killed	154	119
Policemen Killed	60	32
Civilians Killed	348	151

Seen in totality, however, this initiative did introduce an element and hope of peace in the State and became a very promising gesture in the recent history of Kashmir.

For almost one year, from Hizb cease-fire in July 2000 to the NICO measures and extensions thereof; Vajpayee and his government had made strenuous exertions for bringing peace to the strife-torn Valley and one would give them credit for making sincere efforts towards this end. These initiatives were also in sync with the Kumarakom Musings of Vajpayee, released to the media on January 1, 2001, wherein he had promised, "to

18 *Border Affairs*, New Delhi, April- June 2002, p.11.

seek a lasting solution to the Kashmir problem". It appeared that he was keen to show visibly tangible progress on J&K during the current tenure of his government in the Centre; as also prepare the ground for wider participation in the state assembly elections which were scheduled to take place towards the second half of 2002. Seen in this light, Vajpayee's moves appeared suffused with political sagacity and statesman-like farsightedness.

Agra Summit – July 2001

By ending May 2001, the six months period of non initiation of combat operations by the security forces – announced by the Prime Minister on the eve of Ramzan for one month and extended in installments later – was about to end. Response to it by the terrorist organizations had been quite disappointing; and to that extent, a need was felt in the policymaking circles in New Delhi to try and again engage with Pakistan directly. This line of action also underlined the Indian desire to sincerely find a way out of the existing impasse. It has been well recorded by both L.K. Advani and Jaswant Singh in their respective *memoirs* that the decision to invite General Musharraf for talks was taken over luncheon discussions between Vajpayee, Advani and Jaswant Singh towards the end of May 2001. It was a kind of brain storming session by these three stalwarts of Indian policy formulation and its implementation towards Pakistan. The unanimous opinion veered around the fact that even though the developments that had taken place since the Lahore bus *Yatra* in February 1999 had not been very positive from India's point of view; these had generated considerable optimism and hope amongst the people on both sides of the divide. Particularly the population of Valley had a sigh of collective relief for the short duration, of little over two weeks, while the Hizb cease-fire lasted. Also during the past six months when NICO instructions were in place, the general public in J&K appreciated the gesture a lot, as it made their lives so much easier. The loud thinking of this nature prompted the trio to decide and take another chance in the journey towards peace by inviting General Musharraf for summit talks in India. That settled; administrative details and issue of formal invitation plus related matters were left to be worked out by the respective ministries. Agra was chosen as the venue of the meeting, with the fond hope that as a well-known symbol of love and affection, this location may inspire a new beginning of peaceful co-existence amongst the two neighbors.

The period of a month and a half between the invitation and Agra talks was full of intense preparations, political activity as also media speculations – in print as well as in electronic circles – in both countries. Amongst erudite and speculative comments in the Indian media was this thought-provoking analysis of the situation, which included "....More importantly, while India seeks an end to violence in Kashmir as an essential need for a peace process, Pakistan seems determined to use violence as a catalyst to coerce India into a solution. These obviously irreconcilable positions will need to be tackled if the summit is to succeed....The possibility of the two Governments cooperating on finding resolution of the Kashmir issue will put out of reckoning numerous groups, who have assumed roles disproportionate to their marginal capabilities..."[19] The media comments across Pakistan were generally not optimistic in nature; and few positive projections were also laced with conditions and pessimism.

On 27th June, Musharraf called a meeting of important political representatives to work out, what was called national consensus in the Pak media, the contours of his plans for the forthcoming meeting in Agra. Those present on this occasion included; Asfandyar Wali Khan of the Awami National Party (ANP), Aftab Ahmed Shaikh of the Muttahida Quami Movement (MQM), Qazi Hussain Ahmed of the Jammat-e-Islami (JEI), Maulana Fazlur Rehman of the Jammat-ul-Ulema Islam (JUI), Maulana Shah Ahmed Noorani of the Jammat-ul-Ulema Pakistan (JUP), Dr. Tahirul Qadri of the Pakistan Awami Tehriq (PAT), Imran Khan of the Tehriq-e-Insaaf (TEI), Dr. Abdul Hayee Baloch of the Balochistan National Movement (BNM), Air Marshal (retd.) Asghar Khan of the Tehriq-e-Istaqlal. However, the PML of Nawaz Sharief and PPP of Benazir Bhutto, the two main political entities in Pakistan, boycotted this meeting. It was reported that General Musharraf had established secret contacts with some of the major *jihadi* groups also.

As the date of meeting approached nearer, activities on both sides picked up notably and public pronouncements considerably laid emphasis on the combined good intentions and efforts to make the forthcoming parleys a success. However, doubts did persist in the minds of many people across the divide, with a general consensus that if both sides agreed to continue talking; that itself would be seen as a major achievement.

---

19 V.R. Raghavan in *Hindu* dated June 20, 2001.

Almost two months after the invitation was extended to him the General, along with his entourage, arrived in the Indian capital on the morning of 14th July. The Indian media both print, as well as electronic, went overboard in covering Musharraf's visit to his ancestral house in Old Delhi. After a formal banquet in Rashtrapati Bhavan that evening, both delegations reached Agra by the late night. The talks were slated to be held over the next two days, after which Musharraf had planned to visit *Ajmer Sharief* Shrine, before heading back to Pakistan.

The Agra summit opened with delegation-level talks, without a structured agenda as per the wishes of General Musharraf. He also had one to one extensive talks with Vajpayee. After their first day round of talks, both sides decided to issue a mutually acceptable joint declaration. And this is where the rub came in, as none of the drafts prepared by either side was acceptable to the other – the diplomatic finesse and subtleties notwithstanding. The prevailing situation is graphically described by Advani as, "From India's point of view, two unwelcome things happened at Agra. Firstly, the exercise of drafting a joint statement proved highly unsatisfactory. The inconclusive draft which Jaswant Singh brought from his meeting with Pakistan's Foreign Minister, Abdul Sattar, was discussed at the informal meeting of the CCS that the Prime Minister convened in his suite on the evening of 15th. I noticed that there was no reference to cross-border terrorism in the draft. 'This cannot be accepted' I said. My view was unanimously endorsed by all present in the room. We also noticed the absence of any reference to the Simla Accord (1972) and the Lahore Declaration (1999) in the text. Musharraf seemed allergic to these pacts, as these were associated with his political rivals. He probably wanted to send a signal to his people back home that he wanted to start Indo-Pak engagement on a clean slate, all on his own terms and bearing his exclusive imprint. On our part, we conveyed that the Simla and Lahore agreements should continue to remain the cornerstones of Indo-Pak dialogue. Our rejection of the draft was communicated to the Pakistani side, after which efforts continued at the official level to rework it until 4.30 am on 16 July".[20]

Musharraf, on his own part, made things even more difficult by turning his hour-long informal breakfast meeting with a group of prominent Indian media journalists into a virtual one-sided press conference which

20   n-1, p. 702.

was telecast live in India and Pakistan for over an hour. This show of defiance and bluster virtually finished whatever was left of the Agra Peace Conference. A peeved Musharraf paid a short courtesy call on Vajpayee that evening before heading home. He also cancelled his scheduled visit to the Ajmer Sharief Dargah. Some devout observers believe that the moment he decided to cancel his visit to pay obeisance at the Dargah of Khwaja Moinuddin Chisti at Ajmer, his efforts at Agra were doomed to fail. Also, a good number of people in India and Pakistan – including Musharraf – have held this impression that Advani as the Deputy Prime Minister and Home Minister and Vivek Katju, an IFS officer of the rank of Joint Secretary with a hawkish reputation, were the two persons mainly responsible from the Indian side for the failure at Agra.

An astute observer summed up the unsuccessful Agra Summit very aptly; observing that Musharraf the commando could not fathom Vajpayee the Chanakya.

Even though the talks between the two countries apparently appeared to have dead locked, in fact, many observers did not view this as an exercise in futility and were sanguine about the future. The basic logic behind this belief was a simple assumption that the Summit had taken place and this fact alone was a good enough reason to be optimistic about the future. The meeting in itself was also a sign of forward movement in the Indo-Pak relations which had been besotted by mutual suspicion, mistrust and a degree of hostility. Another positive outcome of this event was a number of one to one exchanges between Vajpayee and Musharraf during which both appeared to have struck a cordial relationship; with the latter acknowledging regards and admiration for his Indian counterpart. Even the Pakistan Foreign Minister, Abdul Sattar, in his post-Summit statement mentioned the talks as having "remained inconclusive....but did not fail". He told the news persons that both leaders had succeeded in covering a lot of ground and that the two shared a common vision of peace, progress and prosperity for their people; also asserting, "....the goodwill between them is an asset for better relations between the two countries". In his address to the news persons, the Indian External Affairs Minister Jaswant Singh did make a polite but pointed attack on Musharraf; who had aired his views freely to editors before an agreement could be reached. But, Jaswant Singh also did not term the parleys as an exercise in futility, saying "I don't characterize it as a failure. It is yet another step to improve bilateral relations....we will pick up the threads from the visit of the President of Pakistan....India remains committed to talks". This was not merely an expression of diplomatic finesse and political maneuvering by the Indian Foreign Minister, but reflected a positive outlook for the future. Also the fact that Musharraf spent more than an hour in saying goodbye to Vajpayee was an adequate indication that all was not lost.

After his return home, General Musharraf addressed a press conference on 20th July outlining the events at Agra; including his broad approach at the Summit and also declaring the intention to carry forward the dialogue process. What he said there indicated a positive attitude for the future and included, "I returned from India empty-handed, but not disappointed, as the Agra Summit had generated tremendous goodwill and understanding....The wide gulf between India and Pakistan has in fact narrowed as a result of the Summit, though twice we were close to signing the declaration....It is not time to throw blame on each other". The next day, while reporting the press conference, DAWN (21/7) added, "The President praised Indian Prime Minister Atal Bihari Vajpayee for taking much interest in narrowing down the differences between the two countries. He said Mr. Jaswant Singh also deserves commendation for showing wisdom and sagacity to resolve disputes between the two sides".

In J&K State, particularly in the Valley, the Summit generated lot of hope and expectations among the people. They were hopefully looking forward to a positive outcome which would significantly scale down the militancy related violence and reduction in the tension level of day to day life. A general optimism prevailed regarding steps to ease travel restrictions across the line of control and the resultant hope for a tourist boom in the next year. The breakdown of talks in Agra dashed all such presumptive expectations; at least in the short term.

The curtain on the Agra Summit was literally brought down by Vajpayee's statement in both Houses of Parliament on July 24, 2001. Excerpts from this address read as, "....During these discussions, I emphasized the importance of creating an atmosphere of trust for progress on all outstanding issues, including Jammu and Kashmir....I conveyed in clear terms that India has the resolve, strength and stamina to counter terrorism and violence until it is decisively crushed....We are also willing to listen to all other streams of Kashmiri opinion, however small the majority they represent, as long as they abjure violence.." The concluding portion of this statement pointed to a positive future scenario, and included, "Thus our bilateral engagement with Pakistan will continue. We will continue to seek dialogue and reconciliation....We will engage in quiet, serious diplomacy. Our endeavor for a relationship of peace, friendship and cooperation will be pursued vigorously."

But, the cataclysmic events of eleventh September in America, followed by the insurgent attack on the J&K Legislative Complex Srinagar on 1st October and the militant strike on the Parliament in New Delhi on 13th December same year plus the subsequent developments, badly ruined the chances of any rapprochement between India and Pakistan. The consolation from all these developments that came in India's way was that many countries, particularly the US and the UK, now started looking at the terrorists' threat to India more realistically and also with greater sympathy and understanding. After all, the western world was now getting badly affected by the international terror network and Pakistan was being increasingly recognized as one of the major breeding grounds of this menace. However, the American ambivalence and its need for Pakistan support in Afghanistan would continue to remain a hindrance for India to fully lean on Pakistan for a meaningful change in that country's stance and proclivities to create problems.

11/9 of September 2001

In the aftermath of 9/11 incidents, Musharraf was literally bull-dozed into making public pronouncements of Pakistan joining with America in its fight against terrorism. This made some Kashmiris to publically wonder as to how the same country could sponsor and fight terrorism simultaneously. Despite Musharraf's public pronouncements of being an ally of America in its fight against global terrorism, Pakistan continued to provide military assistance and guidance to militant groups in J&K. Within that country most of the far-right organizations banned in the wake of September 11, 2001 incidents became active in a short time under new names; and with full knowledge of the state authorities. The state was so helpful that a person like Tariq Aziz, head of the banned terrorist group Sipaha-e-Sahaba and in jail for involvement in many sectarian killings, was allowed to contest the general elections in October 2002 from the prison. He won a seat in the National Assembly and was released subsequently. Musharraf also set-free another known terrorist Hafiz Saeed. Both Saeed and Tariq, on being released from Jail, went on to make fiery public speeches against India and the US. It appeared that in the aftermath of 9/11 events Pakistan army and the ISI had further fine-tuned their operations and involvement in Indian and J&K affairs and calibrated these to effectively assure the Americans of Pak positive intentions; while keeping the pot on a high temperature in J&K. The US Administration, though badly singed by the terrorist attacks inside America, appeared quite satisfied with Pakistani cooperation in the Afghan operations and related issues. It actually behaved as if the problems in Kashmir and the rest of India did not concern the US as long as the confrontation between the two countries did not blow up into a major crisis. The American attitude during the entire year of 2002, a period of considerable crisis for India, its continuous diplomatic pressure on India counseling restraint while appearing to support Pakistan betrayed this partisan perspective.

Attacks on J&K Assembly Complex, 01 Oct and on Parliament, 13 Dec. 2001

In less than a month after the 9/11 episode and Pakistan's stated policy of joining the American 'war on terror'; for the ISI its anti-India machinations were back in the reckoning with a terrorist attack on the J&K Legislative complex in Srinagar on October 1, 2001. A group of five heavily armed militants hijacked a vehicle of the P&T department in the downtown of Srinagar and rammed it into the main entry gate of the Assembly, blowing it to pieces, and thus entering the Legislative Complex. It took over four hours for the security forces to neutralize the militants and also try and securely evacuate the inmates. In this tragic event, 38 persons died, while 78 people received injuries. A number of important persons, employees and senior security officers had miraculous escape during the episode.

As if this was not sufficient - and may be emboldened by the mayhem they had managed to create in terms of loss to life and property in Srinagar - the ISI backed militants carried out even a more sinister assault in the form of a suicide attack on the Indian Parliament in New Delhi, around noon, on December 13, 2001. The five terrorists had managed to enter the premises from the main entrance in a white ambassador car, usually taken to be an official vehicle, with a forged Home Ministry label and entry pass.

Fortunately for all concerned, the policemen and security staff deployed on duty reacted with alacrity and effectively neutralized all the five intruders, by killing them, before any on these could enter the main building and cause harm to the MPs and staff still inside. In this action nine security personnel lost their lives. The death toll also included one TV cameraman. This time the militants had dared to attack the temple of democracy in India – the Parliament itself. A visibly angered and distressed Prime Minister Vajpayee addressed the nation the same afternoon, in which he resolutely said, "Now the battle against terrorism has reached a decisive moment. This is going to be a fight to the finish". Subsequent actions by the Indian government following this attack on Parliament resulted in the massive mobilization of the armed forces, including deployment in forward locations. The whole military posture of India appeared to be ready for an open engagement, but in time it stopped just short of precipitating a crisis situation. However, this restraint was never due to any Pakistani overtures or downplaying of its designs. There were no signs of Pakistan backing off at any moment of time during this period.

The attack on the Indian Parliament, followed by mobilization of Indian armed forces, under the code name Op – Parakaram, appeared to have increased the American apprehensions about a possible clash of arms in the sub-continent considerably. Realizing that Pakistan had crossed the threshold of Indian tolerance, they tried to do what they were adept at, that is, put successful pressure on India to not precipitate matters and also counsel Pakistan to behave more responsibly. Since the Americans needed the support of Pakistan in their ongoing operational involvement in Afghanistan; the bottom line in their dealings with Pakistan was well understood by the U.S. administration – which they reckoned would not go much beyond rhetoric and some cosmetic actions. The much-touted televised speech of General Musharraf, on January 12, 2002, should be seen in this context. On this occasion, the General declared that Pakistan will not allow its territory to be used for terrorist activities. Based on this exertion, some cosmetic control of cross-border terrorism was carried out for all round and general consumption; even though this did not mean much in real terms. This time again Pakistan seemed to have successfully pulled wool over the eyes of America and India as neither of them achieved their stated aims; whereas the General was apparently quite smug with all that he had managed to get in his kitty.

Operation Parakram, Dec 2001 to Oct 2002

It would be useful to quote the relevant portions from the reminiscences of General Padmanabhan, the then Chief of Indian Army, which reads as follows, "From 11th September 2001 onwards, Pakistan, which by then was in a parlous economic and political state, became once again a front-line state and ally of the USA in their invasion of Afghanistan and the continuing 'search' for the elusive Osama bin Laden and his followers. At about the same time (13th December 2001), a group of suicide bombers dispatched by a Pakistan controlled terrorist outfits, attacked the Indian Parliament. The terrorists were duly killed before they could cause any real damage but India's patience with Pakistan's abetment of cross-border terrorism had run out. Indian armed forces mobilized fully and were placed in what could only be read as offensive dispositions. With this, Pakistan's 'cup of misery', as it were, flowed over. It decided to accede to the US requests for air bases, passage facilitation for US ships and aircraft and full support including intelligence support to them against Afghanistan. What the US promised Pakistan as *'quid pro quo'* can only be guessed. But the Indian forces did not attack, nor did Pakistan actually comply with Indian demands to stop cross-border terrorism and hand over some 'wanted terrorists' etc. The USA for its part, got what they wanted – or at least appeared to have.... And so, with the USA re-charging its coffers and rescheduling the debts, giving it military equipment/spares and praising Pakistan's contributions to the USA's war against Terrorism, Pakistan continued with the proxy war against India in a 'business as usual' mode.

And, it was 'business as usual' too as India discovered on 14th May, 2002, when Pakistan trained and inspired terrorists attacked the Army's family quarters in Kaluchak (J&K) and killed 29 men, women and children in a barbaric act of terror. With Indian forces still deployed in forward positions and fighting rhetoric emanating from top Indian leaders, it seemed that war was imminent again. But with the USA by now heavily depended on Pakistani support in its operations in Afghanistan, the Indians were counseled restraint and they duly obliged. Rather intriguingly, within one month of the Kaluchak massacre, India 'magnanimously' cleared overflights of India by Pakistani airlines, a ban that was enforced in December 2001 in the wake of the attack on the Indian Parliament! Strange are the ways of Indian politicians! With no compliance from Pakistan of our demands, President Musharraf's telecast speech of 27th May, 2002, sounding more bellicose and intransigent than ever before, India's action in allowing overflights of our airspace by Pakistani aircraft is, to say the least, curious."[21]

Just after the very provocative terrorist attack on the Indian Parliament and finding that Indian army had been fully mobilized and committed on the borders with Pakistan under Operation Parakram; the American diplomatic exertions in the sub-continent were literally shifted into the top gear. The US did what it was best at; it counseled restraint on India reassuring to put adequate pressure on Pakistan and on the other hand leaned heavily on rulers of Pakistan. It is generally believed that Musharraf was constrained to make his lengthy nationwide speech on January 12, 2002, under the US coercion. In this 'landmark' statement, he offered India a no-war pact, making South Asia a nuclear-free region, pledged to 'reform madrasas in Pakistan' banned five jihadi groups including infamous LeT and JeM. In short, he departed from his earlier public pronouncements. Also for the first time, he condemned the attack on Parliament and termed it as a 'terrorist act'. India did not buy his promise of total transformation of Indo-Pak relations, it was wary of his oft-changing stances; and rightly so. On the other hand, the US was constantly imploring India not to do something which would undermine the war efforts in Afghanistan.

However, the terrorist attack on the army family lines in Kaluchak, near Jammu was almost too much for the army, Indian policymakers and the public to stomach. There was a legitimate consternation all round and calls for revenge getting louder by the day. The prevailing situation has been succinctly described by Jaswant Singh as, "To my mind this Kaluchak attack was almost the 'last straw', following as it did that attack on our Parliament of five months earlier. Despite this, or perhaps because of the sharpness of this provocation, I counseled restraint. This was based on my assessment that a retaliatory action then would be strategically faulty, the region was already embroiled in a major conflict in Afghanistan. Militarily this would amount to falling into a classical trap: deliberate provocation launched for inviting a predictable retaliation; thus both time and place being of the adversary's choice.... These two attacks, on the Parliament and in Kaluchak, then constituted the principal 'set-backs'

---

21 General S. Padmanabhan, *A General Speaks,* Manas Publications, New Delhi, 2005, pp. 191-193.

to normalization. The government, in such a near impossible situation, remained calm, it continued to counsel restraint. This was a very difficult time, painful even in a recalling of it. No doubt, however, that this restraint was yet another act of great courage and challenging statesmanship by Prime Minister Vajpayee".[22]

A leading newspaper of India echoed similar views, during the same month of the Kaluchak outrage and two days after General Musharraf's jingoistic speech on 27th May. It said, "….the only guaranteed strategy can be a policy of economic, political and military containment of Pakistan by all coalition partners…, a coherent international framework to deal with Pakistan needs to be finalized…. The extremely dangerous and delicate situation created by General Musharraf's intransigence has to be met through astute strategic diplomacy and not by angry rhetoric".[23]

Thus India achieved nothing substantial during the year following the terrorist attack on the Parliament; except keeping its entire army mobilized and action-ready for over ten months. The cross-border infiltration and terrorism continued unabated; also India was not able to 'teach Pakistan a lesson'. In fact, the killing of security forces personnel, number of attacks on security forces and the number of civilians killed remained comparatively high. India and Pakistan came close to war on two occasions; once resulting in the post haste change of an Indian army officer of the rank of Lt. General, a Corps Commander. Even the reported shifting of three army divisions from the eastern sector did not materially change the ground situation.

It was only after a meeting of the National Security Advisory Board on October 16, 2002, that the army was asked to pull back from the enhanced forward deployment. In totality the army remained deployed on the borders and in a state of heightened readiness during this entire period of almost ten months; and that the USA had effectively prevented India from exercising its options in the arena of foreign policy, in relation to Pakistan. Op-Parakram was estimated to have cost India around 800 crore rupees, apart from 300 crores paid as compensation. Taken in entirety, it was almost an exercise in futility.

---

22 Jaswant Singh, *A Call To Honour*, Rupa & Co, New Delhi, 2006, p. 347.

23 *The Times of India*, May 29, 2002.

The Musings From Kumarakom Plus

What was driving the Indian Prime Minister, Atal Bihari Vajpayee to seek accommodation with Pakistan and usher in an era of peace in the sub-continent; even when that country's belligerence and continued exertions to foment trouble in J&K did not come anywhere near the overtures held out by India? In order to understand the philosophical contours of this urge and the ideological underpinnings of Indian peace initiatives; one should take a look at and soak in the two New Years messages of Vajpayee, addressed to the people of India, at the beginning of 2001 and 2002.

Vajpayee spent a week of vacations from December 26, 2000, at the famous Kumarakom resort located on the backwaters of Kerala and started the New Year of 2001 in that place only. There the poet in him probably overshadowed the official persona as he contemplated on the ancient heritage of India, the problems inherited by the country which still kept it bogged down and also the challenges and opportunities of the future. These thoughts, which he preferred to call "My Musings from Kumarakom", appeared in two installments and were widely acknowledged as his New Year greetings and message to the countrymen. He took a broad sweep of the issues confronting the nation and determination of the country to face and try to resolve these problems; and hence strive to move towards a better future. He also emphasized the fact that progress of India would be judged on basically two counts. One being how many problems inherited from the past it has been able to resolve; and the second being how much strong foundation is laid for the future development of the nation. It would be interesting to note his views on focal issues, which naturally included J&K; and some of them read as, "As we bid goodbye to 2000 and usher in 2001, I send my hearty New Year greetings to all my fellow countrymen, as also to the large Diaspora of Indians abroad.... A year is but a speck in the life of an ancient nation like India, which is ever youthful in spite of her great antiquity.... India is willing and ready to seek a lasting solution to the Kashmir problem. Towards this end, we are prepared to re-commence talks with Pakistan at any level, including the highest level, provided Islamabad gives sufficient proof of its preparedness to create a conducive atmosphere for a meaningful dialogue. I am sad to note, however, that the Government of Pakistan is not doing enough to rein in terrorist organizations based on its soil that are continuing their killing spree, targeting both innocent civilians and our security personnel in Kashmir and other parts of India.... In our search for a lasting solution to the Kashmir problem, both in its external and internal dimensions, we shall not traverse solely on the beaten track of the past. Rather, we shall be bold and innovative designers of a future architecture of peace and prosperity for the entire South Asia region. In this search, the sole light that will guide us is our commitment to peace, justice and the vital interests of the nation". Looking over the horizon perhaps, he wrote "India must move on. The best of India resides not in the past. Rather, it belongs to the future that we all must collectively build. Glorious though our past was, a more glorious destiny beckons India. However, its realization calls for a radical shift from contention to conciliation, from discord to concord, and from confrontation to consensus and cooperative action".

The second part of his 'Musings'; he begins with paying a great tribute to the power of India's democracy where an ordinary person like him, son of a village teacher, could become Prime Minister of the country. Thereupon he goes on to outline the broad contours of India, as he sees it, and emphasizes on three distinctive features;

➤ "Sometimes, however, we get so involved in our own narrow concerns and so obsessed with our own specific identities, that we tend to ignore the chief source of our national pride and strength – namely, India's diversity and her essential unity.

➤ Diversity does not permit divisiveness or exclusiveness. Similarly, unity cannot be achieved through uniformity.

➤ Secularism is not an alien concept that we imported out of compulsion after Independence. Rather, it is an integral and natural feature of our national culture and ethos".

He concluded by pointing out the future prospects of India as, "We are inheritors of an ancient civilization which is also forever young. Guided by the light of the eternal and universal values of our civilization, inspired by a modernizing vision of national development, and powered by the youthful energy of one billion children of Bharat Mata, we can certainly make the 21st Century India's Century".

The year 2001 saw a number of developments; important ones being the conclusion of six months of NICO instructions, the failed Agra Summit, 9/11 events in America and their fallout, militant attack on the Legislative Complex in Srinagar and the terrorist strike on the Parliament. Like the previous year's Musings from Kumarakom, an article written by Vajpayee was released on the New Year of 2002. This time the text was short, less philosophical, crisp and shorn of rhetoric. Most of the write-up was devoted to Pakistan's continuing perfidy and a bright future beckoning to India. After pointing out Pakistani provocative involvements in the three Indo-Pak wars of 1947-48, 1965 and 1971; he concentrated on the current Pakistan designs on J&K and, in parts, said, "I must say that they are nursing a dangerous illusion.... They failed miserably in their designs in Punjab. Terrorism bled Punjab; but, in the end, it fled Punjab.... Although India has been a victim of cross-border terrorism for the past nearly two decades and has lost tens of thousands of innocent men and women and security forces, the outrage of December 13 has breached the limit of the nation's endurance.... our oft-extended 'cease-fire' in Jammu and Kashmir are a testimony to India's sincere, bold and innovative search for peace. This search continued even after the betrayal in Kargil. Our efforts will be further intensified if Pakistan demonstrates its matching sincerity to have peace with India." In the later part of the piece, Vajpayee made references to the search for finding a lasting solution to the Kashmir problem and his musings from Kumarakom the previous year. In that context and also looking into the future of India, he confidently and optimistically predicted, "Dear fellow countrymen, the situation we are facing is unprecedented. I would like you to be prepared for any eventuality.... True, we cannot predict what may happen to our individual destinies. But, in my mind, there is no uncertainty whatsoever about India's destiny.... It is also a future when the fabled richness of India's culture, arts, intellectual exploration, and spiritual pursuit will begin to show its full radiance, bringing much succor to the troubled spirit of the modern man.... We shall triumph against terrorism – to defend India, to defend humanity. Let this be every Indian's New Year resolve. May the Almighty give us the strength to redeem this resolve". Thus, on a positive note ended the message of Atal Bihari Vajpayee at the very beginning of 2002.

To be sanguine about the future when less than three weeks ago the country's Parliament was under terrorist attack and at a time when India's armed forces stood fully mobilized under Operation Parakram; really needed a strong conviction, firm stability of mind, deep-rooted spiritual moorings and, above all, an unshakeable faith in the glorious future that lay ahead for the country. All this Vajpayee seemed to have in ample measure. He was also determined to pursue the peace initiatives and, even if not adequately responded by Pakistan, quite prepared to travel on that road alone. After a year, fate will give him openings to follow his determined path.

CHAPTER – VII

Vajpayee Reasserts

During the entire year of 2002, the internal political climate as well as strained relations with Pakistan, conditions were hardly conducive to embark upon any new peace initiative. The already tense situation was further muddled by the terrorist attack on the army family lines in Kaluchak, in the month of May. But Vajpayee, the eternal optimist that he was – and also endowed with the vision of a farsighted politician and reputation of a matured statesman – was patiently waiting for an opportunity to come his way. He also could not have been oblivious to the fact that the NDA government at the centre, headed by him was entering the second half of its tenure by the middle of 2002 and hence also the need to take initiative at an early date. He sincerely believed in the commitment and ideology that he had outlined in his message to the people of India, released on the first day of January 2002. A part of it relating to Pakistan mentioned significantly as, "Together, let us leave the past of futile hostilities behind us and embrace a future free of tension and full of mutually beneficial possibilities. The common enemy that both our countries face is poverty, illiteracy, disease and unemployment.... This is the challenge of the New Year and of the New Century. Let us accept it in a spirit of cooperation." It is with this sense of realism that he wanted to proceed ahead with determination. But conditions on the ground did not appear conducive for any new peace efforts till the fully mobilized armed forces of India were not asked to revert to the peace-time locations. This happened only after the Op Parakram was called off in the second half of October. Almost side by side, a lot of developments of far-reaching consequences had taken place in the political landscape of Kashmir and the dust of these events took time to fully settle.

The important happenings on the political scene in the state included a change of guards at the top of the National Conference, the oldest, most visible and dominant regional political party in J&K. Omar Abdullah took over as President of the National Conference from his father on June 19, 2002. This change of baton had very meaningful significance as the party leadership passed to the new generation – the third from Sheikh Abdullah to Farooq Abdullah and then to Omar Abdullah – with expectedly a modern and new approach to the problems of the party and the state. Contrary to the widely held belief in the knowledgeable circles in the State and in New Delhi; Farooq Abdullah neither became the next Vice President of India nor moved to the Centre as an important Cabinet Minister. Thus Omar Abdullah as the party President and his father as the Chief Minister of the State; faced the forthcoming Assembly elections. Omar Abdullah was also the declared candidate of the party as the next Chief Minister.

Simultaneously, another regional party was rising on the political horizon of J&K in the form of People's Democratic Party (PDP), an outfit headed by Mufti Mohammad Sayeed. The political journey of Mufti Sayeed makes an interesting reading. He had all along been a Congress stalwart; was a Minister in the Cabinet of Mir Qasim in early 70s, except when he joined the Jan Morcha in 1987 and became the Union Home Minister at the Centre in the V.P. Singh Government in December 1989 for one year. Later, he re-joined the Congress when it was headed by P.V. Narasimha Rao; but left it again to launch his own organization, the PDP on July 28, 1999. The stated objectives of this party included, "…mobilizing public opinion in the state and the country in favor of persuading the Government of India to adopt a policy of understanding and reconciliation and initiate a comprehensive and unconditional dialogue with the people of Kashmir to resolution of Kashmir problem….also to wage a struggle for restoration of normalcy, democracy and rule of law in the state so that human rights of the people can be duly respected and protected."

Mufti had realized that the militancy since 1989 had brought calamitous changes in the socio-political landscape of the state; in which the economy, the education and the much adored "Kashmiriyat" received a serious setback. It was also a fact that towards the late 90s, the euphoria of 'Azadi' and the writ of separatists had started waning away. As an astute political observer, Mufti Sayeed understood the paradigm shift in J&K politics caused due to the twin factors of militancy and alienation of people from the national mainstream; a scenario where even persons and parties who had no separatist tendencies strived for their personal safety and political relevance. He well realized the need for a 'regional political party' which would fill the existing political void effectively; a space caused due to the abdication or irrelevance of various political elements in the state. He firmly believed that a regional party which would ventilate the sentiments and aspirations of the people, especially the majority community, would eventually replace the National Conference – and the dynastic rule represented by it – and would also dilute the efficacy of Hurriyat conference. With these thoughts in mind, he launched his PDP and used his experience and expertise as a sound political organizer to build a strong cadre and raise an effective party organization; not only in the Valley but also in some parts of Jammu division. Thus he started pleading for - as the main political planks of his party – Self-Rule for political empowerment, safeguards against Human Rights violations, rehabilitation of militancy-affected victims, return of Kashmiri Pandits, opening of routes and establishing trade across the LoC and dialogue with all stakeholders of Kashmir problem. In a way, he not only hijacked the agenda of National Conference as well as the overground separatist organizations; but, equally importantly, people found some hope and optimism in this new party.

The election symbol of the party, "Ink Pot and Pen" as approved by the Election Commission of India, soon became a popular label and mark amongst the people. Some of his close associates, who helped him to organize the new party well, included established political personalities of the state like Mehbooba Mufti – his daughter – Ghulam Hasan Mir, Muzzaffar Hussain Baig, Abdul Aziz Zargar, Tariq Hamid Karra and Mohammad Dilawar Mir. However, the PDP made a very strong base in South Kashmir, registered less of strength in the Central part of the Valley and had a weak presence in North Kashmir. It was rumored that its efforts to forge alliance there with A.G. Lone's Peoples Conference had not been successful. Thus with fairly sufficient time of three years to organize itself; the new party was well poised to take on the National Conference in the 2002 Assembly elections. The PDP hurled itself into the electoral fray with a lot of enthusiasm and also confidence; both backed by the charisma and organizing skills of Mufti Sayeed and his trusted aides. Some political observers have been of the opinion that in some pockets, especially in South Kashmir, this party was extended covert support by certain separatist elements.

However, two significant – though unrelated – events happened before the elections were held. The first one related to an opinion poll conducted in Kashmir by a well-known British organization; which showed Pakistan in a poor light in the eyes of Kashmiris. Details of this were prominently carried by the Indian print media. Manoj Joshi wrote about it in an article titled "The Mori Message; Silver lining in Kashmir's Cloud." This piece, in parts, mentioned "....Last week, the findings of a poll conducted by Britain's largest independent market research agency, *Mori*, have turned conventional wisdom on its head. This is all the more remarkable considering that the poll was commissioned by Lord Eric Avebury, a British human rights activist who backs virtually every separatist movement in the world, not excluding those in Kashmir and Punjab.... The prominent finding of the poll, as reported by Indian newspapers, has been that 61 per cent of the respondents would like to remain Indian citizens with just 6 per cent opting for Pakistan.... The Hizbul Mujahideen found favor with 11 per cent and the jehadi groups just 9 per cent support from the respondents.... The surprise finding of the poll is Pakistan's poor image in Kashmir. Distrust of Islamabad and its motives show up repeatedly in responses to the questions...."[1] As the sponsoring agency of this poll could not be accused of a bias; the separatist elements generally reacted with silence and, as it happens with such news items, after some time everyone conveniently forgot about it. More attention grabbing things were happening around.

In another development; Prime Minister Vajpayee in his Independence Day address, from the ramparts of the Red Fort in Delhi on August 15, 2002, categorically stated that the forthcoming Assembly elections in J&K would be absolutely fair and free; and called upon the voters of the State to exercise their franchise in good numbers with this assurance in mind. Probably he realized that in the Kashmiri psyche perceptions play an important role. The people of Kashmir had always regarded the 1977 Assembly elections to be the fairest of all, till then. Morarji Desai, as the incumbent Prime Minister, had successfully resisted local pressures from his party men and steadfastly refused to influence the elections. Vajpayee as a Cabinet Minister in that government must have understood the huge

1   The *Times of India,* dated June 10, 2002.

positive impact this non-partisan approach had on the Kashmiri mind; and probably decided to win the trust and confidence of the local population by remaining aloof. This stance of the Prime Minister was widely appreciated by the general public and major political parties in the state. Also by that time, the stage had been set for the elections in the State. Apart from this promise of the free and fair polls, the other events which also played a role in creating conducive atmosphere for these Assembly elections included – in varying degrees – Majid Dar's coming back from Pakistan and announcing a cease-fire in July 2000; unilateral NICO announcement in November 2000 and the Agra summit in July 2001.

The elections to the State Assembly were announced by the ECI on August 2, 2002. According to the notified schedule, the election was to be held in four phases – almost on the pattern of 1996 Assembly Elections – covering a period of twenty-two days and spread over the months of September and October. Even though enhanced security arrangements were put in place throughout the state by official agencies; with the rising election fever, the terrorist violence also registered an upswing. Between August 1 and September 10, 2002, there were 405 terrorist-related incidents in which 22 political activists were killed. The civilian casualties were 26 and 62 security personnel lost their lives. However, in spite of these setbacks and sustained efforts by the terrorists, the political process – even in the militancy-infested areas continued unabated. One of the important developments during the election period and certainly spurred by the killing of Abdul Ghani Lone by terrorists during May 2002, was a mood of defiance in the Peoples Conference now headed by the slain leader's younger son Sajjad Lone. Three members quitted the party; it was rumored, with the support of Sajjad Lone to take part in the elections as Independent candidates. This development did add a new dimension in the election process in Kupwara district and ultimately ensured a very high turnout and keen contests in the three constituencies of Handwara, Kupwara and Lolab.

The electoral exercise began on the 16th of September and the last phase of polling was held on the 8th of October. According to the directions of the ECI, re-polls took place for six polling stations each on 1st October and 8th October and for 4 polling stations on 9th October. Notwithstanding considerable variation in the polling percentage in different districts and constituencies, the overall percentage of votes polled in the State was a respectable figure of 43.28 %. Since electronic voting machines were used here for the first time; the counting process was over within few hours on the day of the counting on 10th October and by the late afternoon all the poll results became known. The National Conference emerged as the single largest party with twenty-eight seats, as compared to its winning fifty-seven seats in the 1996 assembly elections. This electoral set-back to the party was heightened even more because Omar Abdullah lost his election in its traditional Ganderbal constituency. Also, twelve National Conference ministers lost in their respective constituencies. In term of numbers; the next slot was taken by the Congress with twenty seats, followed by the PDP making an impressive maiden entry into the Legislature with sixteen seats. The other winners included four candidates of Panther's Party, two of the CPM, one each of BJP and BSP. The Independents and others bagged a large number of fifteen seats.

In totality, it was a fractured mandate delivered by the electorate of the State and no single party, by itself, was in a position to form the government. Following a series of discussions between Congress and PDP, in Srinagar and Delhi, an agreement was reached on 26th October; wherein it was decided that they would, with the support of Panther's Party, the CPM and a requisite number of Independents would stake a claim to form the government on the basis of a Common Minimum Programme (CMP) agreed by the two main constituents of the coalition. It was also resolved that during the six-year term of the Assembly the Chief Ministership would be shared for three years each between PDP and the Congress, with Mufti Sayeed taking over as the Chief Minister for the first three-year term. The Chief Minister and eight members of his Cabinet were sworn on November 2, 2002, thereby bringing the process of Assembly elections in the State to a logical conclusion.

This sequence of events has been interestingly described, by Dulat in his book, as "Though the National Conference had the maximum number of seats in the assembly there was nowhere for the party to turn to, because at that time the Congress was not going to support the NC. The Congress plus PDP together tallied 36 seats and it was enough because they were sure to get the support of some of the smaller parties and independents to cross the halfway mark of 44 seats (in fact, the Congress-PDP combine mustered a total strength of 57 seats when it went to the governor to stake claim to forming the next government). The tie-up was natural in many ways for, after all, Mufti was originally a Congressman.... Interestingly, Delhi preferred that the senior partner in the tie-up, the Congress with its 20 seats, form the government. The BJP was distrustful of Mufti.... She (Sonia Gandhi) thought that Mufti should rule, and overruled the idea. And so Mufti Mohammad Sayeed's life ambition came true. He became Chief Minister of J&K."[2]

The CMP document was released to the press in New Delhi on October 26, 2002, by Mufti and senior leaders of Congress headed by Dr. Manmohan Singh; in the presence of other senior party functionaries. Those present on the occasion also included Prof. Bhim Singh of Panther's Party and CPM leader Yusuf Tarigami. This document laid down the broad parameters which were to be followed by the coalition State Government. This Common Minimum Programme aimed at healing the wounds inflicted by long years of militancy and laid considerable emphasis on the process of reconciliation and initiation of unconditional dialogue with all parties. The CMP made bold, specific promises to usher in peace and one of the important items mentioned therein assured that "Full powers would be given to the Ladakh Autonomous Hill Development Council (LAHDC) and a similar council for Kargil would be formed."This certainly was a sourly needed measure for the people of Ladakh region and greatly helped in assuaging their collective feeling of neglect

The State Government headed by Mufti Sayeed began well and within a matter of few months the people started feeling the difference. Even though there was not much let up in the militancy related violence; the common people began experiencing a more relaxed atmosphere. The new measures also included, in time, allowing round the clock traffic on the Jammu-Srinagar national highway; which was till then blocked at the Jawahar Tunnel, on the Pir Panjal Range, for the night hours. In this overall improvement in the environment; catchy slogans of the PDP like *Grenade se na goli se, baat banegi boli se* and *Aman ki baat Izzat ke saath* played a considerable role. The new administration also concentrated on giving a fillip to the developmental activities and studiously avoided finding faults with or launching probes against their predecessors. This attitude of not wasting efforts on non-productive ventures and instead concentrating on the essentials did not go unnoticed by the public. Mufti also enunciated and

---

2   A.S. Dulat, *KASHMIR The Vajpayee Years,* HarperCollins *Publishers* India, 2015, pp. 239-240.

implemented the 'healing touch policy', aimed at making the common man feel more comfortable and the security forces increasingly accountable to the established hierarchy; for which the district administration was made answerable at the local levels. As an extended part of this initiative, the much talked about Task Force of the J&K Police, till then operating under a separate chain of command, was converted into Special Operations Groups as a part of each District Police and answerable to the respective district SPs. The new Chief Minister also reached out to the victims of militancy for providing sympathy, help and support to them. He appeared to be a person who understood the Kashmiri mind very well and tried hard enough to make a general positive impression during the three years of his tenure. Towards this end he started striving earnestly right from the very beginning.

The results of his exertions became quite noticeable on the Republic Day functions on January 26, 2003, barely less than three months of his becoming the Chief Minister. For the first time after the militancy started, a gathering of around ten thousand witnessed the function in the Bakshi Stadium at Srinagar. Similarly, in all district headquarters of the Valley, the local response was impressive. This by itself was a positive development in favour of the new regime.

The 'healing touch policy' and commitment to start 'talks with all' by the new regime in J&K, were in tune with the general approach of peace and rapprochement with Pakistan; so consistently advocated and followed by Vajpayee. The latter also appreciated the overall positive trends and improvements in the atmospherics in the State. But, the BJP and certainly the two people very close to Vajpayee – and also very important members of his Cabinet – Advani and Jaswant Singh - did not fully trust Mufti Sayeed; at least not yet. New Delhi had not still fully sized up this man. To make matters worse, the first encounter between Mufti and Jaswant Singh was anything but friendly. An official meeting was convened in the first fortnight of December 2002 in the Parliament House office of Jaswant Singh, who was then the Union Finance Minister, to discuss about the finances of J&K. While the deliberations were useful from the State and official point of view; the political chemistry between the two principals was cold and less than cordial – and once almost reached a breaking point.

From Prime Minister Vajpayee's point of view, the sands of time were running out. The year 2002 turned out to be barren in so far as improvement in the Indo-Pak relations was concerned. The Assembly polls in J&K had been conducted in free and fair manner as had been promised by him. To what extent could he depend on the new Chief Minister of the State, who as a trusted ally could be a huge asset in the peace process; was an unanswered question that must have bothered him. Also, he was to face another Parliament election by the middle of 2004 and was determined to make more attempts at the peace process between the two countries. Vajpayee's mental condition could have been somewhat similar to that of the protagonist mentioned in *The Story of My Heart* (1883) by Richard Jefferies, as "My heart was dusty, mind arid and dry, for there is a dust which settles on the heart as well as that which falls on a ledge. It is injurious to the mind as well as to the body to be always in one place and always surrounded by the same circumstances.... I felt eager to escape from it, to throw it off like heavy clothing, to drink deeply once more at the fresh fountains of life. An inspiration – a long, deep breath of pure air of thought – could alone give health to the heart."[3]

Vajpayee was slated to come to Srinagar on April 18, 2003, and address a public meeting. Mufti Sayeed wanted to make this event a big success; also as a part of his larger scheme of things to effect visible positive change in the internal as well as external dimensions of the Kashmir situation. He took personal charge of the preparations for this event and supervised political and administrative arrangements right from the beginning of March. In the meanwhile a high-level meeting was convened by the Union Ministry of Home Affairs in New Delhi, on 31st March, to review the security scenario in the state. This meeting was chaired by Deputy Prime Minister and Home Minister Advani and attended among others by J&K Governor Saxena, Chief Minister Mufti Sayeed, Defence Minister George Fernandes and External Affairs Minister Yashwant Sinha; along with a number of high ranking central and state civil, intelligence and security officers. Whereas for the senior officials accompanying him, it was a very important security-related meeting in the MHA; but Mufti probably understood the political implications behind this round of deliberations. The central leadership at the apex level was perhaps trying to finally make up its mind about him; more particularly in view of the Prime Minister's forthcoming visit to Srinagar. In a way, Advani was to probably size up Mufti for the plans he and Vajpayee had in mind.

---

3   Ruskin Bond, *Love Among the Bookshelves*, Penguin Books India Pvt. Ltd, New Delhi, 2014, pp. 165-166.

The meeting began formally and a round of serious discussions started as per the agenda. The J&K Chief Minister's interventions were short, crisp and at times caustic. His senior official aides present there started feeling uncomfortable; apprehensive about him spilling over the edges any moment and thus vitiating the serious businesslike atmosphere of the conference. Suddenly, there was a change in the tone and tenor of his talk which took every one present by surprise. As per one of the senior officers present in the meeting, Mufti Sayeed spoke for about five minutes with lot of feelings and frankness about his political beliefs aimed at ending the militancy and working towards peace and reconciliation; also expressing mental anguish on certain events of the past. At the end of discussions which lasted for a few hours, there was a palpable bonhomie all round. Union Home Secretary N. Gopalaswamy mentioned in his press briefing after the conference, that a group headed by Special Secretary J&K Affairs in the Home Ministry would review the strategies of the security forces and intelligence agencies in the state. He also said that the meeting resolved all issues with complete harmony between the centre and the state on security-related matters. But, beyond the official briefing and recording of proceedings of the conference; a sort of bridge of understanding and commonality of views had been built between Mufti and Advani – and through the latter – between Mufti and Vajpayee. He had become, and was to remain, an important player of the Vajpayee team for the peace initiatives with Pakistan.

From that day onwards there was no doubt about the visit of the Prime Minister to Srinagar being hugely successful. The Chief Minister and his political associates worked very hard towards that end. The show, after all, had been reduced to be a measure of the PDP's ability to mobilize the general public. The National Conference, which was a part of the NDA at the Centre, had already decided not to attend this rally. The Congress which was a major partner of the PDP in running the State Government had also conveyed its decision, presumably under instructions from the high-command in Delhi, of not sending its supporters to this meeting. Mufti's senior lieutenants like Muzzaffar Baig, Ghulam Hassan Mir, Qazi Afzal, Mehbooba Mufti and others spent days in their areas to motivate their cadres and supporters to reach Srinagar and attend the function and on the due date brought bus loads of them from their respective constituencies. More than 90 per cent participation in the public meeting was from the rural areas.

On 18th April, the Prime Minister landed at the Srinagar airport, and after a brief ceremony there for the expansion of the terminal building, he headed for the public meeting which was organized at the secured ground of Sonawar, next to the picturesque Cricket Stadium, arriving there just before noon. At the venue, he first laid the foundation stone of the North-South railway corridor for the Valley – a trailblazing railway line between Baramulla and Qazigund – and then addressed the large public gathering. Over thirty thousand enthusiastic people had gathered there to welcome and listen to him; the first public meeting of the Prime Minister in the last fifteen years. The spring time pleasant weather, large gathering and visible interest of the crowd all seemed to have had the effect of invoking the poet in him and he began by mentioning the sparkling crisp air, tall Chinar trees around the ground, and the chirruping birds. His oration reflected the flight of imagination of a poet as well as hard ground realism of a seasoned politician and statesman, appreciating the present and looking hopefully at the future. In his twenty minutes extempore address; he said the Centre would work in close coordination with the State Government for enhanced development and to root out unemployment. He assured the Chief Minister that the NDA government in New Delhi would leave no stone unturned to make his programme of restoration of peace with dignity a success; pointing out that the path of peace and brotherhood may be time-consuming but by far a worthwhile course to follow with patience. Vajpayee referred to his Independence Day speech the previous year and took full credit for the free and fair Assembly elections in the state; also congratulating the people to have exercised their democratic right of the franchise so well and demonstrably in spite of militant threats. He added, with good effect, "I can see the change in the situation in the Valley. I am sure that once again there will be normalcy in the State. We should protect the democracy (*Jamhooriyat*), humanity (*Insaniyat*) and *Kashmiriyat* to achieve this goal." He emphasized to the delight of the audience that all talks should be based on these fundamentals.

Extending a hand of friendship to Pakistan, he said this feeling should be reciprocated appropriately; and emphasized that the time had come for ushering in a sea change in the sub-continental scenario as both countries had so many things in common ranging from nature to civilization. The whole speech was an example of his oratorical skills and the capacity of the poet in him to so beautifully craft sentences.

It was a very successful and well managed public meeting which made Vajpayee and Mufti both happy. After 1988, more than fifteen thousand people had never participated in any mainstream political rally in the Valley. There was understandable jubilation in the PDP camp for creating a history of sorts by successfully organizing this big a public meeting. Some analysts believed that such large number of people who had come to listen to the Prime Minister signified the Kashmiri's changing aspirations.

The next day, Vajpayee was to fly to Qazigund for laying the foundation stone of an important railway bridge there. This engagement had to be cancelled due to heavy rains and bad weather and the ceremony was instead carried out by remote control at the airport before he left Srinagar. Both P.M. and the Chief Minister appeared more than satisfied with this visit. Vajpayee had been able to reach out to the people of the Valley effectively; as also extend a hand of friendship to Pakistan – once again and this time from Srinagar in the midst of a large public gathering, which had its own significance. Mufti Sayeed was also pleased as Vajpayee's two days engagements not only went off very well, but also amounted to a strong backing of New Delhi to his regime and signaled support for the policies he was pursuing.

Vajpayee followed up his peace initiatives by making a statement in both Houses of Parliament on May 2, 2003, wherein he gave details of his Srinagar visit a fortnight ago and also a gist of his telephonic conversation with Pakistan Prime Minister Zaffarullah Khan Jamali on April 28th. He also announced the decision to appoint a High Commissioner to Islamabad and restore civil aviation links on reciprocal basis. Underlining commitment to improve relations with Pakistan, Vajpayee said in an emotionally charged voice "….this would be my third and final effort at improving bilateral relations with Pakistan….Now whatever happens will be decisive."

The response from Pakistan was prompt, almost immediate. The Pakistani Foreign Ministry announced that it had agreed to restore full diplomatic ties with India. Their Information Minister, Sheikh Rashid said, "It is a good gesture, a good start and hope for good future….I cannot say right now when talks are going to start but it should be soon as things are moving quite fast."

Four significant reactions to these developments, indicating their actual and perceived importance, were printed as a 'box item' in the 3rd May issue of Greater Kashmir, a Srinagar based Daily;

➤ US, UK, Russia welcome initiative.

➤ No third party can impose solutions on Indo-Pak issues, says Sinha.

➤ Meaningful talks only way to resolve Kashmir: Musharraf.

➤ Mufti says no US pressure behind the resumption of diplomatic relations.

An interesting article by the noted Pakistani columnist, Dr. Ayesha Siddiqa indicated the view from Pakistan; and she also proffered some thoughtful advice. Excerpts from this write-up read as, "India's Prime Minister A.B. Vajpayee has indicated New Delhi is prepared to talk to Pakistan. That's a welcome development and addresses the concerns of those on both sides who were troubled by an absolute lack of dialogue between the two countries for over a year.... one hopes the two governments must realize that discussions must not start with a lot of fanfare. In fact, this time around there is a need for India and Pakistan to conduct discussions with little media hype. Excessive publicity raises expectations that are often counterproductive. One would like to remind policymakers that most of the US-USSR negotiations on long-term and major agreements were conducted relatively quietly."[4] A very sound advice indeed as the last serious engagement between India and Pakistan, at Agra in July 2001, had actually been undermined by an over exposure to the media, both print as well as electronic. Similarly, laudatory and appreciative assessment of the Vajpayee initiative was recorded by Karl F. Inderfurth, former American Assistant Secretary of State for South Asian Affairs from 1997-2001; in 6th May issue of *The Hindu* daily.

The events of the past few months also indicated that the Indian Government had realized that the current head of Pakistan, General Musharraf was the person well suited for the peace process to really pick up and go forward. There was no other personality in Pakistan who could do better than him in the two critical areas; effectively neutralize the

---

4   *Kashmir Times*, Jammu, dated May 3, 2003.

opposition of the 'Jihadi' elements to the peace process and also ensure that the army in Pakistan accepted his decisions. India's moral dilemma of not negotiating with a dictator had also got resolved with the installation of an elected Government in Pakistan. However, having taken the first step, India was to wait for Pakistan to respond meaningfully to the peace initiative. In the meantime, both central and the state governments busied themselves with improving the internal situation in the State; making it more development oriented and life increasingly stress-free for the common man. Good governance and 'healing touch' were the two main policy planks of the state government and these measures helped considerably in reducing the day to day tensions in the life of general public.

Mufti Sayeed also persuaded the army to help in improving infrastructure facilities in the state. Two of the schemes implemented by the army are worth mentioning. One related to launching of four *'bailey bridges'* in the Valley at locations decided in consultation with the Chief Minister. All these connected significant population centers which remained cut-off during the summer and rainy seasons when water level in the local streams rose menacingly. This provided lot of satisfaction in the benefitted areas. The second initiative was to locate, construct and operate two fully residential schools by the army near Pahalgam in the Valley and Rajouri in Jammu division. Both these facilities were fully funded by the army and meant to provide quality education to local children. Such schemes not only proved useful to the local population but also helped in bringing the army that much closer to the general public. It was a win-win situation for both sides. Those days it was a common sight to see senior civil, police and army officers travelling together and engaged in consultation to find ways and means to help the local people. The benefits of this approach, though not exactly quantifiable, were huge and made a considerable positive change in the general mood.

This change was also reflected in the figures released by the State Tourism Department regarding the domestic and foreign tourist arrivals in the Valley. A comparative table for the first seven months of 2002 and 2003 indicated that for the month of May this figure was 9008 and 23679; for June it was 10322 and 74775 and for July it stood as 10350 and 76360 respectively. Commenting on this improved environment a noted journalist of the state observed, "Mufti has said that the present spell of peace in the Valley is by 'design'; …. The Chief Minister's observation should ensure that his government does not become complacent. Having made peace with Leh and Kargil and left Jammu largely to the Congress, which is the major partner in his coalition government, Mufti is concentrating mainly on governance which, if he continues the present good work, is bound to yield badly-needed political gains." A very perceptive assessment and apt description of the overall situation in the state. He further goes on to say, "There is presently a feel-good environment which has been further strengthened by the high-profile visits of President Abdul Kalam, Prime Minister Atal Bihari Vajpayee and Congress president Sonia Gandhi. The top leaders have conveyed to the people of Kashmir the national mood that the country cares for them....Doubtless, there is an air of expectancy in the Valley because of two more reasons: the global dislike for terrorism and the possibility of improvement in the India- Pakistan relations. On its part, the State Government has definitely helped lower tensions. The Chief Minister Mufti Mohammad Sayeed has been working hard to reach all sections of society and in all the regions....It is good that of late a large number of politicians and Parliamentary committees have been visiting the Valley. Domestic tourists are also making decent contribution. They should keep a regular date with the Valley. Their role is the most important in the meeting of hearts of the people of Kashmir and the rest of the country."[5]

Also, apart from the efforts of the State Government, the Central Government too contributed to the developmental push and overall improvement in the ground level situation. New Delhi's efforts to make friends with the local population and make a positive difference in the atmospherics need special mention in respect of three schemes and initiatives. These related to the speedy land acquisition for the Qazigund–Baramulla railway line in the Valley; erection of the LoC fencing and the holding of Inter-State Council meeting in Srinagar towards the end of August 2003.

During his visit to Srinagar in the summer of 2003, the Union Railways Minister and the State Chief Minister jointly reviewed the progress of Udhampur- Baramulla railway line. They were given detailed briefing about the current engineering and land acquisition status of the project. After taking into consideration all the pros and cons of the recommended measures, the Railways Minister emphasized to expedite the process of land

---

5   Pushp Saraf in *Border Affairs*, New Delhi, July-Sept 2003, pp. 1-4.

acquisition, which was the crucial component to accelerate the progress of the project; particularly in relation to the north-south connectivity in the Valley sector. To achieve quick progress he agreed to take recourse to private negotiations also, where ever required, within the ambit of the Land Acquisition Act. This go-ahead approval provided considerable momentum to the land acquisition progress and personal involvement of the Railway Minister himself in the project gave requisite impetus and motivated the entire team - both officials of the central as well as state governments - to compress the completion time as much as possible. More than ninety percent land acquisition work on the 117 kilometers of Valley section was completed in the record time of two years in 2003 and 2004.

Payments in all cases were made to the landowners by cheques only. As the work progressed it was quite normal to find an elated group getting full compensation of their lands paid through cheques and deposited in their bank accounts. A good number of them had also turned entrepreneurs and purchased trucks and tractor-trolleys out of the money received, turning these into earning assets by hiring them to the construction contractors. A large amount of money, as the land compensation, went into the hands of the local population and thus added to their level of satisfaction; which was an important consideration from the political point of view. It is also remarkable that all this was achieved under the shadow of militants' threat and violence.

An important initiative to improve the internal security situation in the state was the erection of fencing, an effective wire-obstacle, along the LoC. It was an admirable achievement for the army to successfully complete around 750 kms of this difficult work, in an extremely mountainous terrain, in a short period of little over one year in 2003-04. Of this length, 550 kms were covered with the actual specially designed fencing; and small stretches of land between – the gaps – were virtually saturated with landmines. For the first few months, in the beginning, construction work on this project was slow and hampered by repeated exchange of fire, including artillery, on the borders; but after the declaration of cease-fire ending November 2003 the process of laying the wire-obstacle picked up considerably. The results soon became obvious and also very telling in statistical terms. Right from 1990 to 2002 the estimated infiltration had every year been more than the number of militants killed. It was only after 2003 that this ratio became inverse, with appreciable gap between the number of militants eliminated and those estimated to have crossed over to this side. Therefore, while the terrorists still retained some capacity to launch strikes and undertake acts of violence with high news value; their capability to disrupt the normal life in the state had been seriously blunted. This step also added another dimension the Vajpayee efforts in progressively making a positive difference in the internal security situation in the state and to reach out to the local people.

A two-day meeting of the Inter-State Council was held in Srinagar from August 27, 2003. It was attended by the Prime Minister, Deputy Prime Minister and the Home Minister, some of the Union Ministers and all the Chief Ministers in the country. It was the first time that this meeting was held outside Delhi. It was another significant gesture on the part of the Prime Minister to show solidarity with the people and government of J&K; as well as the confidence of the Union Government about the ability of the state administration to successfully manage the administrative and security related arrangements required for such a big event. The venue of this meeting and all other related functions was Sher-e-Kashmir International Convention Complex (SKICC) and the adjoining building of Centaur Hotel at a picturesque location on the banks of famous Dal Lake. Considering the galaxy of participating VIPs, very elaborate security arrangements were made for kilometers around the location, including round the clock water patrolling of the Dal Lake. While the meeting was in progress, towards the evening, information came of a grenade attack outside Green Hotel on the Exchange Road Srinagar, more than five kilometers away. It was obviously an attempt by the militants to mark a presence. The DGP, who was personally supervising security details around the Lake, thought this to be a diversionary move with the main target being the venue of the meeting where the PM, and other dignitaries were present. He therefore immediately sent the IGP, Kashmir, to the scene and himself held the fort at the SKICC, the venue of the meeting. The next message was about firing at the site, signifying a suicide attack. In the ongoing encounter with security forces, the hotel building had caught fire; a former member of the Legislative Council was killed and a number of innocent civilians were trapped in the hotel and an adjoining building. After the day's proceedings finished at the meeting, the DGP rushed to the site of the incident where encounter was still going on and intermittent firing was taking place. He was there till almost wee hours of the next morning, first ensuring that all civilians were brought out of the two structures without any harm and then neutralizing all the attackers, followed by the mandatory search and mopping up operations. All this, however, did not in any way affect the deliberations of the Inter State Council Meeting which carried on with its proceedings, including a major press conference the next day.

The successful management of administrative and security arrangements for this major conference – attended by a large galaxy of VIPs from the entire country – including clinical handling of the militant strike during the night of 27-28 August, justified the confidence reposed by the Prime Minister in the state administration headed by Mufti Sayeed. This gesture of holding the Inter-State Council meeting in Srinagar, in the contemporary scenario, was hugely appreciated by the people of the State and was a very significant measure to reach out to the common man of J&K.

Vajpayee went through all his scheduled engagements in the State in a very cool and composed manner and returned to Delhi, as planned through a short stopover in Jammu, by the afternoon of the 29th August. There the militant incident at Srinagar came under a sharp attack by him. He seemed visibly upset and told the reporters that the continuous violence in the State was holding back the two countries from starting an exercise of meaningful dialogue. He said, "Normalcy is still to return to the State and incidents like the Srinagar attack are ample proof of it. The support from across the border should cease and a conducive environment should be created for the talks to start....there cannot be any headway in normalizing relations between India and Pakistan until terrorist violence aided from across the border comes to a halt." The Prime Minister had clearly indicated his displeasure and impatience at the less than expected response from the other side over his peace efforts; and many political observers felt that the process of normalizing relations with Pakistan was virtually reaching a dead-end.

But, may be due to some positive signals from Pakistan side or due to his abiding faith in improving bilateral relations; or possibly a combination of both factors, the situation changed again in less than two months time. After a meeting of the Cabinet Committee on Security (CCS) on 22nd October; India announced a number of measures to improve the external and internal dimensions of the Kashmir issue. For improving relations with Pakistan, India proposed some steps of far-reaching consequences. The important ones included; a bus service between Srinagar and Muzaffarabad, a Mumbai-Karachi ferry service and resumption of bilateral sporting links – including cricket. The announcement of these and other offers was made by the External Affairs Minister, Yashwant Sinha in a press conference in which he emphasized that all the proposals will lead to a greater level of people to people contacts which process is in favor of both the countries.

In the same meeting of the CCS, it was decided to take forward the internal peace process also and the Deputy Prime Minister Advani was designated to start a dialogue with the Hurriyat Conference. Incidentally, the APHC had undergone a vertical split on 6th of September, with Geelani leading the rebel faction and the main Hurriyat electing Maulana Abbas Ansari as the new president. The nomination of Advani leading talks on behalf of the Government of India was a very shrewd move by Vajpayee with twin benefits in mind. It ensured greater involvement of the top BJP hierarchy in the ongoing peace process; as also aimed at deriving optimum advantage from the good equation that had been established between L.K. Advani and Mufti Sayeed.

The Pak response to the Indian peace overtures came in the form of a statement from Pakistani Prime Minister Jamali, on 23rd November offering a cease-fire from the Eid, three days later, along the LoC. After urgent consultations between the two countries, this step was extended to the other borders also; and this cease-fire held effectively for a number of years. This was probably the most successful cessation of hostilities between the two countries, over a considerable period. A report appearing in the daily NEWS from Islamabad, dated 26 November, mentioned this development as, "Pakistan and India agreed to implement the ceasefire along the Line of Control (LoC), the Working Boundary and the line of Actual Contact in the Siachen sector from midnight between November 25 and November 26....The ceasefire, the first in at least 14 years, will cover the 230-km section of the Working Boundary, the 760-km Line of Control and the Northern Siachen Glacier....Pakistan hoped the ceasefire 'for an indefinite period' will lead to dialogue on disputes between the two countries." Thus, with the guns falling silent and no firing taking place along the borders; people on both sides of the divide – particularly those staying close to the boundary – heaved a sigh of relief. Their day to day life became much more comfortable and relaxed and general public in the two countries started looking forward to improved bilateral relations and easing of the tensions; something that had been hoped for during the past quite some time.

General Pervez Musharraf, in a televised interview on December 18, 2003, offered to give up Pakistan's traditional policy of insistence on the implementation of the UN resolutions on Kashmir and said that both countries would need to take courageous steps to improve relations. The very next day he surprised everyone saying Pakistan was prepared to drop the demand of referendum in Kashmir and India should come half way to solve the problem. The two statements coming in a span of two days were very significant; whatever may have been reasons and factors behind them. The developments of the last one month, and remarks of important authorities emanating from Pakistan were not palatable to the 'Jihadi' elements in that country and these reacted in the only manner known to them – violence. Two suicide squads with explosive-laden cars exploded near the motorcade of General Musharraf in Rawalpindi, on 25th December. Though he and his entourage were not hurt, fourteen other people got killed. This was the second attempt on his life in eleven days. Such reaction by the extremist elements probably increased his determination to pursue the path of peace with India and try to look for a long-term solution to the festering issues amongst the two neighbors.

Some political analysts believe that three events in 2003 broke the impasse between India and Pakistan. The first was the speech of Vajpayee in Srinagar on 18th of April wherein he offered a hand of friendship to Pakistan. The second was the statement by Pakistan Prime Minister Mir Zafarullah Khan Jamali offering ceasefire on the LoC, which India accepted and enlarged. The ceasefire on the borders was actualized on the ground from November 26, 2003. The third development in this behalf was the televised announcement of General Musharraf that Pakistan was conditionally prepared to give up its traditional stand of implementing UN Resolutions on Kashmir. All these evolutionary happenings unfolding within a period of nine months heralded well for the bilateral relations in the sub-continent. With Vajpayee deciding to spend three days in Islamabad to attend the 12th SAARC summit and interact with his hosts there, in the first week of January 2004; the stage was set for an upswing in the relations between India and Pakistan.

Some interesting observations on these issues and generally about the sub-continent were made in an article by Afzaal Mahmood which appeared in the DAWN of December 20, 2003. Parts of this write-up read as, "Few regions in the world can compete with South Asia in springing surprises. Important developments can take place in this part of the world when they are least expected. When the guns fell silent on the LoC and the Siachen Glacier at midnight on November 25, even the most inveterate optimists were taken by surprise…. What is baffling is that only a few weeks ago, Vajpayee's 12- point initiative had not received quite a positive response from Pakistan. Yet his proposals have now been accepted by Islamabad – almost totally. What has caused this amazing change of heart?...." Keeping a date with the unexpected and the intriguing developments, was the visit of the Indian Prime Minister to Islamabad. But, his aides had been busy in preparing the ground well in advance. Apart from quiet and useful background work done by the competent Indian High Commissioner Shiv Shankar Menon; the National Security Advisor Brijesh Mishra came to the Pakistan capital three days in advance. He was there to see that the visit was productive and went off well; as also to 'tie up loose ends'. Major political parties in Pakistan like the PPP and PML-N also supported these peace initiatives – though from the sidelines - and this was a big plus point for both sides.

Vajpayee arrived in Pakistan on the afternoon of January 3, 2004, on a three-day visit and he was received at the airport by his Pakistani counterpart, Mir Zafarullah Khan Jamali. The body language of both dignitaries and the chemistry between them was enough to assure those present there of very fruitful days of negotiations ahead. In his remarks there, the Indian Prime Minister said that India and Pakistan must keep talking and that it had been his endeavor to make peace with Pakistan ever since his first visit to Islamabad 25 years ago as the External Affairs Minister in the Janata Party Government. In an interview with Pakistan Television the same evening, he expressed the belief that India could gainfully talk to the Pakistan President Pervez Musharraf, and hoped that the mutual discussions would lead to concrete achievements.

The next day the SAARC summit formally started its deliberations after the ceremonial opening and transacted the business on agenda for the ensuing couple of days, but the Indian and Pakistani media was mostly concentrating on and remained busy in covering the unfolding rapprochement between the two countries. In his address to the heads of states assembled at the summit, Vajpayee implied his continuing efforts at improving relations with Pakistan, in reference to the earlier failed attempts, and philosophically observed, "History can remind us, guide us, teach us or warn us. It should not shackle us." The same evening, delegations of the ruling Pakistan Muslim League and the Pakistan People's Party met Vajpayee at a reception hosted in his honor by the Indian High commissioner. On 5th January, he laid the foundation stone for a residential complex for the staff of Indian High Commission in Islamabad; reiterated his views and said the dialogue between India and Pakistan should continue and both countries should understand each other's problems to find a way out.

But the most important and also news worthy meetings were between the two Prime Ministers and between Vajpayee and President Musharraf on 5th January. Even though not many details of these interactions were shared with the media; the fact that such meetings had taken place was a good sign in itself. Particularly his "courtesy call" on General Musharraf, which lasted for an hour, was interpreted as sort of path-breaking and heralding a new era of better ties between India and Pakistan. Learning from their respective mistakes in Agra, the officials of both sides appeared determined not to share anything with the waiting newsmen till the last word in the joint statement had been approved by the respective principals. The two Foreign Ministers and the two National Security Advisors worked very hard on the joint press statement and were able to finalize the approved text by the evening of 6th January. This was read by both Foreign Ministers in the press conference. The spirit of bonhomie was evident as the Pakistan Foreign Minister Khurshid Mahmud Kasuri invited his Indian counterpart to lead in this; whereas being the host country it was the former's privilege to do so. In the joint statement, Musharraf's assurance to Vajpayee was highlighted that he "will not permit any territory under Pakistan's control to be used to support terrorism in any manner". In response, India agreed to begin a composite dialogue in February that "will lead to peaceful settlement of all bilateral issues, including Jammu and Kashmir, to the satisfaction of both sides". It was a breakthrough which not many had imagined would take place.

This Islamabad initiative was hailed as the best chance till then for peace in the sub-continent and something that could leave everyone feeling as the winner. Whereas, Musharraf was reportedly happy at the outcome and said history had been made; in New Delhi, Deputy Prime Minister Advani congratulated the people of India and Pakistan on a breakthrough. Major foreign powers also hailed this joint effort. The US welcomed these meetings between leaders of India and Pakistan hoping this interaction would "lead to further engagement and dialogue". A spokesman of the Russian Foreign Ministry, while welcoming the historic meeting between the two leaders, expressed the hope that this would lead to further talks between the two countries. A representative of Britain's External Affairs Ministry said, "We hope that this will lead to increased momentum in the process of normalization of relations between the two countries and addressing each other's core concerns." In a similar vein, the Chinese Foreign Ministry spokesman appreciated the efforts made by the leadership of the two countries to improve bilateral relations. One of the most apt comments on this new initiative, by both sides, was made by the former foreign secretary of Pakistan, Niaz Naik, who said, "The door has opened again and we must seize the opportunity." One Indian fortnightly succinctly described the whole scenario as, "The SAARC communiqué, in retrospect, was hardly an event. The suspense was all about the communication process between the Indian Prime Minister and the Pakistani General – the democrat and the dictator: one looking for a place in history, the other postponing its wrath. The SAARC multilateralism was subordinated to Indo-Pak bilateralism."[6]

One of India's finest soldiers recollected this event in his memoirs as, "Thus, it would appear that the 5th January, 2004, summit meeting between India and Pakistan at Islamabad took place under very propitious conditions in India (including J&K) and Pakistan. It clearly had all the ingredients that make for success in such matters. Above all, the people of India and Pakistan, as well as the people of J&K on both sides of the Line of control, were tired of the constant tension between the two neighbors. This tension has affected our lives in every possible way – from national security to playing cricket matches, from our economies to our performing arts – you name any field of human endeavor and the oppressive Indo-Pak tension had given it a skew, distorted it and made it unattainable or enjoyable. The relations between our two countries have so far been an example of how two neighboring countries should not behave with each other. Perhaps the summit has set afoot new dynamics which will gather momentum...."[7]

---

6 *India Today*, New Delhi, January 19, 2004, p.33.

7 General S. Padmanabhan (Retd), *A General Speaks*, Manas Publications, New Delhi, 2005, pp. 198-199.

Thus, the happiest person around must have been undoubtedly Vajpayee himself; as he could see his latest attempt at improving relations with Pakistan fructifying and promising to deliver substantive results. The months ahead would be full of work for the senior functionaries on both sides if progress was to be achieved to put bilateral relations on more sound footings. A beginning was made almost immediately and quite a distance covered. As per a news report in the daily *Times of India* of February 8, 2004, a hotline was established between the two National Security Advisors, Brijesh Mishra and Tariq Aziz. Also, for the first time, a similar facility came up for the two intelligence chiefs of RAW and ISI to keep in touch with each other. There was also a talk of Government of India agreeing in principal to allow Hurriyat leaders for a Pakistan visit. It was significant that these and some other confidence enhancing measures were put in place before the Foreign Secretaries of two countries met on 16th February for the official first round of bilateral talks.

As a part of this expanding new relationship, nearly a month-long engagement of five one-day cricket matches was held in Pakistan between the two national teams. This was almost a bonanza for the huge followers of this game in both countries. All the matches were played in a cordial and sporting atmosphere and the game of cricket was appreciated irrespective of which side won. Though for record it may be mentioned that the last, fifth and final, ODI was held in Lahore on 24th March. It was an exciting match with India winning the fixture and the series with a 3-2 lead. The important thing was that this contest was held at all and the appreciable sportsmen spirit displayed by the spectators in all the five engagements.

Advani Opens a Line

A lot of success about these initiatives depended upon the premise of the victory of Vajpayee regime in the forthcoming Parliament elections in India. But, that was a few months away from the Islamabad parleys in the first week of January 2004. During this month, Advani took the initiative to address the internal dimensions of Kashmir issue.

It was after the meeting of the CCS on October 22, 2003, that the Union Home Secretary announced, "The Deputy Prime Minister will meet Ansari (the then chairman of the APHC) in response to his statement of August 25 that they are interested in talks with the centre." In a separate press conference held by the External Affairs Minister to announce Pakistan related initiatives endorsed in the same meeting of the CCS, he clarified that this move was part of India's internal process and had nothing to do with Pakistan. Thus, it was very clear that the Prime Minister was keen to address the internal as well as external dimensions of the Kashmir issue simultaneously; and not waiting for one to fructify first to take initiative on the other side. Apparently, this was just an announcement of intent on the part of Government of India and the dates of actual meeting were to be decided later. Interesting and thoughtful set of editorial comments, on this issue, appeared in a national daily the next day. Excerpts from this piece read as, "A new breeze has been blowing across the hills and vales of Jammu and Kashmir and this has become more noticeable after the last year's elections....It is in this context that we need to view the new decision of the cabinet to ask Deputy Prime Minister L.K. Advani to talk to the Hurriyat. There can always be questions whether this should have taken place earlier or not. But the fact is that the success of a dialogue at the political level requires that sufficient ground for such a step is first thoroughly prepared.... Mercifully, this time Advani would also have the benefit of extensive preparation carried out with great attention by the present interlocutor N.N. Vohra.... There is both a limit and an opportunity in this attempt to chart a new course for J&K."[8]

Two days after the CCS meeting, when the country's print and electronic media was becoming hyper-active on this issue of the Centre's talk with the Hurriyat; Advani spoke further about this matter on the occasion of the Raising Day of the Indo-Tibetan Border Police. He said that the discussions were envisaged on "decentralization" of power in Kashmir and not on any issue which might compromise India's national sovereignty and integrity. While not elaborating the concept of "decentralization"; he emphasized that the offer of talks by the Vajpayee government to find a solution to the Kashmir issue should not be seen either as any change in India's policy towards Kashmir or a product of weakness. Thus, quite adroitly the broad contours of the future deliberations were being laid down. The APHC reaction to this statement was relatively subdued and not very negative; raising hopes of an early beginning of the talks.

After successful visit of the Prime Minister to Islamabad, in the beginning of January 2004 and a very encouraging joint press statement indicating the restarting of the stalled Composite Dialogue; it may have

---

8   *The Indian Express*, dated October 23, 2003.

been thought that the time was opportune to address the internal issues also. A beginning was made with APHC meeting Advani on 22nd of January. A five-member Hurriyat delegation, led by its chairman Moulvi Abbas Ansari and comprising Abdul Gani Bhat, Mirwaiz Umar Farooq, Bilal Lone and Fazl-ul-Haq Qureshi called on Advani, in New Delhi, and spent over two and half hours with him. It was a promising start of the dialogue process; with this first meeting mostly restricted to the pleasantries and broad common parameters underlining the need for all forms of violence to come to an end and a step by step approach for resolution of the Kashmir issue. That this contact was preliminary and exploratory in nature was also evident from the joint statement issued after the meeting. In this document, in which three main issues were highlighted, it was emphasized that, "an honourable and durable solution should be found through dialogue....cases of prisoners who have not committed heinous crimes will be reviewed.... All forms of violence at all levels should end and the scope of dialogue be enlarged to cover all regions and communities." While Advani termed this meeting as a good beginning; Abdul Gani Bhat said, "We have had amicable, free, frank, fair and fruitful discussions."

Next day, this delegation also called on Vajpayee and spent about forty minutes with him. Most of the talking was done by the visitors, who conveyed that they appreciated and fully backed his efforts to improve relations with Pakistan and find mutually agreeable solution to all outstanding problems, including Kashmir. As usual, Vajpayee spoke very little and most of the time he quietly heard his guests. After the meeting, Mirwaiz Umar Farooq told the reporters "The Prime Minister listened to us patiently and asked us to continue with the peace process." It was good that this contact was established, as this was the first-ever dialogue of the Hurriyat with the political leadership at the centre – and that too at such a high level. This also signaled the willingness of New Delhi to address the internal dimensions of Kashmir issue as seriously as it was pursuing improving relations with Pakistan. That both sides agreed to meet for the next round in March, also showed that the January parleys were not a one-time event but a beginning of a serious effort to find a solution. General Musharraf welcoming these talks was an additional source of satisfaction to both parties.

The second set of discussions between Advani and the APHC took place on 27th March in New Delhi. That it happened in the midst of signs of further improvement in Indo-Pak relations was another positive factor. This time Fazl-ul-Haq Qureshi had not joined the delegation to register his protest against the continuance of alleged human rights violations of the common man. Perhaps, he had not been able to withstand the pressure exerted on him on this issue by 'the invisible hand'. Also, after the last meeting, Hurriyat members had given a list of thirty people whom they wanted to be released. Out of this, twelve had been set free with the promise that the government was considering favorably other cases also; in addition to the general promise made earlier in this respect. Nothing substantive came out of this meeting in the public domain – probably no specific issues were put on the table by the Hurriyat. Both sides reiterated their determination to cooperate in order to restore peace in the state; expressed satisfaction over the progress achieved so far and decided to meet again for the third round in June. It was evident from their cautious approach that both sides wanted to give each other sufficient time before taking up substantive matters.

The next statement on this topic came from Centre's interlocutor on Kashmir N.N. Vohra, after his hour-long meeting with Deputy Prime Minister Advani on 23rd April. He indicated the possibility of widening the base of this dialogue process, in his interaction with the reporters, saying that all political elements would be roped into the dialogue process but added this could happen only after the election process was completed in the country and new government installed. He also confirmed that the third round of talks with the Hurriyat would be held in the end of June. However, contours of the plan to broad-base the consultation process could not become evident as the Parliament election results in the middle of May brought in a change of government in the Centre. With that, this process also got stalled. Incisive comments about this subject came from someone having a ringside view, as "The UPA instead got bogged down in what was right and what was wrong. Such initiatives have to come from within; that is what is political will. And the UPA had it on a platter. All it had to do was to follow up on the process that Vajpayee started. Since Advani had started talking to the Hurriyat, that should have been the starting point. It just needed following up, patience, time and understanding. It would have been impossible for the Hurriyat to wriggle out, or for the BJP to backtrack on. But these things never happened."[9]

---

9   n-2, p. 276.

Appointment of Interlocutors

The quest of Atal Bihari Vajpayee to improve relations with Pakistan was not a unidirectional policy but a part of an overall strategy to tackle the Kashmir problem in its entirety and in a comprehensive manner. In this urge to create a peaceful atmosphere, he showed equal keenness to address the internal aspects of this issue also. Though efforts in this direction had been taking place in an undeclared and unobtrusive manner ever since he became the Prime Minister, but he made a formal reference to these exertions over a year later during his speech in the Parliament, on February 22, 2001, in connection with the extension of NICO offer a third time. He said "The government has decided to pursue this path by initiating talks with various groups in J&K.... In this regard, the government has benefited by the detailed briefing of and consultations with all political parties that it had on February 21, 2001...."

The Government of India once again outlined its policy to address both internal as well as external dimensions of the Kashmir issue in a major policy statement on April 5, 2001. As a part of this initiative, it invited representatives from all walks of life in the state to hold dialogue with the Centre's nominee, K.C. Pant, Deputy Chairman of the Planning Commission. Thus Pant became the first Interlocutor of the centre in J&K, in a well publicized bid to break the political impasse in the Valley. The official announcement in this regard mentioned, "The Government invites the people of good-will, who desire the restoration of peace and normalcy in the State to come forward and participate in the dialogue. The doors are also not closed for Kashmiri organizations which are currently engaged in militancy but are desirous of peace." Pant, it must be said to his credit, did try to open channels of communications with separatist elements, including some Hurriyat leaders but did not succeed in meeting anyone of value except Shabir Ahmad Shah, the chief of Democratic Freedom Party. In the process he met other leaders in J&K, including some belonging to Jammu and Ladakh; but the initiative did not cut much ice. His work as Interlocutor was also impeded by the fact that he continued with his full time assignment in the Planning Commission; and also did not understand the intricacies of the Kashmir situation. In short, the Pant initiative failed to make any headway in changing the ground situation in the State.

By the beginning of 2002, it was clear that after few months the Assembly election fever will pick up in the State. In this scenario, consistent reports started appearing in the media that intelligence agencies were making considerable efforts to encourage and persuade separatist elements and at least some of the terrorist outfits to take part in the coming elections. The Central Government announced the formation of a Kashmir Committee headed by Ram Jethmalani, the former Law Minister and an eminent lawyer, to start a dialogue with the broad spectrum of opinion leaders in the State. To boost these efforts further, the Prime Minister appointed Arun Jaitley, Union Law Minister as an Interlocutor to start negotiations with separatist elements. With increased efforts to engage the dissatisfied groups and also exertions of the intelligence agencies; by the beginning of the summer it had started becoming plausible that some terrorist outfits as well as a part of the Hurriyat could be willing to take part in the elections provided there was an assurance of free and fair elections to be held under the Governor's Rule. But, two events intervened. One was the assassination of A.G. Lone by terrorists in broad daylight on May 21, 2002; and the other refusal of the State Chief Minister Dr. Farooq Abdullah for the elections to take place under Governor's Rule. Thereafter, not much was heard either of the Kashmir Committee or the efforts of Arun Jaitley. As a matter of fact, both these initiatives suffered from the basic flaw noticed in the case of K.C. Pant, that these two gentlemen also had to first take care of their respective primary occupations and the involvement in matters of J&K became only of a secondary interest.

In the third attempt, the Central Government appointed N.N. Vohra, a retired bureaucrat, as the Interlocutor in February 2003. Vohra not only brought considerable administrative experience with him, having been a former Defence Secretary, Union Home Secretary and also Principal Secretary to the Prime Minister; he took up this assignment as a full time job. He established his office in the premises of Vigyan Bhawan, New Delhi and his secretariat was headed by a senior J&K cadre IAS officer. He began his work methodically and with full zeal; also starting with the advantage of knowing a good deal about most of the major groups, players and organizations working in J&K. Though, a prominent publication having expertise about the developments in J&K expressed doubts about this appointment as, "The new Central Government interlocutor, N.N. Vohra, on Jammu and Kashmir is an able man. A former Union Home and Defence Secretary, he has the well earned reputation of being an efficient administrator....Does the experience of the previous interlocutors, K.C. Pant and Arun Jaitley, not show that they are not even listening posts? The country has not been informed whether, and if at all, Pant and Jaitley made any credible achievement. With Vohra's appointment, the impression, on the other hand, has been confirmed that both have proved unequal to their assigned task.....One hopes that Vohra's fate is different."[10]

The new Interlocutor began his job in a systematic and focused manner. This was evident during his first two day visit to Jammu, the summer capital of the State, beginning on 5th March. During the first day he met and held wide ranging discussions with the Governor, Speaker of the Assembly, Chairman of the Legislative Council, Deputy Chief Minister, leader of the opposition in the Assembly as well as leader of the opposition in the Council. He joined the Chief Minister and the Chief Secretary for dinner and the three talked generally about economic development of the state and its bearing in turning mood of the people; which was already showing signs of change. Next day he left for New Delhi and before departure shared with one of his confidants in Jammu that he would try for the constitution of an expert group at the Centre, which would work as a collateral to his own efforts. He also confided that there have been differences between North Block and South Block in New Delhi that he would very much like these to be removed or at least reduced. His next visit to the state was a weeklong sojourn in Srinagar beginning from 21st April. This time he utilized in establishing contacts with individuals and organizations which would be useful in the line of his work; also getting the ground level briefing from various senior officers and intelligence agencies working there. Thus, with hard work, previous experience and extensive contacts established; he became a useful supplement at the apex level about J&K, within a couple of months of his appointment.

Vohra worked in an unobtrusive manner and maintained a low profile; all the same becoming an organic part of the decision making process at the highest quarters. He periodically briefed the Principals on matters related with J&K; as also coordinated with the chiefs of different intelligence agencies and their important field functionaries. The list of his expanding contacts and acquaintances included not only separatist elements, but also senior officers of the State Government, J&K Police, security forces and intelligence agencies working in the state. Also, the credit for two successful meetings of the Deputy Prime Minister with Hurriyat leaders in January and March 2004 was in no small measure due to his detailed

---

10 *Border Affairs*, New Delhi, April- June 2003, p. 3-4.

background work. In one of his infrequent meetings with press reporters on April 23, 2004, after his hour-long briefing session with Advani, he gave a hint about the direction of his efforts by saying, "We have already held talks with various sections of people in Jammu, Kashmir and Ladakh including professional groups of doctors and lawyers. Consultations with these sections will be carried forward." He also added that further round of dialogue and process of engaging all sections of political elements could be made only after the Parliament election results in the month of May. As it happened, after the national elections the NDA government was replaced by the UPA. However, Vohra was to continue as the Interlocutor in the new regime also and a useful help in furthering the peace efforts, till he was elevated to the post of Governor of J&K in June 2008.

Assessment of the Vajpayee Initiatives

The Parliament polls took place in the country during the latter half of April and the first fortnight of May 2004. In J&K these were held in four phases from 20th April to 10th May. The Prime Minister paid one visit to the State during this period. He arrived in Jammu on 14th April, and in a public gathering spoke more like an elderly statesman, that he was, than a senior political leader of his party. He promised free and fair polls and asked people of the State to exercise their right of franchise without fear and in large numbers. In the first phase on 20th April, elections took place for the Jammu and Baramulla seats, on 26th for Srinagar; whereas for Anantnag the votes were polled on 5th May and in the last and fourth phase for Ladakh and Udhampur constituencies polling was held on 10th May. The overall voting percentage in the State was higher than what was registered in 1999 elections and this was a matter of considerable satisfaction. The counting took place three days later on 13th May and in J&K the results were on the expected lines; with Congress taking both the Jammu seats, National Conference winning in Srinagar and Baramulla constituencies; with the third seat of the Valley going to Mehbooba Mufti of the PDP. The lone Ladakh seat was cornered by the Ladakh Union Territory Front candidate Chewang Thupstan. However, it was at the national level that the results of this public mandate were different than general expectations and poll predictions. The BJP tally had shrunk to 188 and Congress surged ahead with the win in 223 seats. Pronnoy Roy, a leading commentator on the NDTV channel, termed the mandate as 'cataclysmic.' These results lead to a change of government at the Centre and Dr. Manmohan Singh became next Prime Minister of the country, heading a UPA government.

The Vajpayee era had passed and it was right time to undertake a dispassionate analysis of his efforts to improve relations with Pakistan as well as make a positive difference in the internal dimensions of J&K. To start with, his basic philosophy cannot be faulted with; that dialogue is always a better way as compared to bitter exchanges and acrimonious debates. By the time his regime ended, middle of 2004, circumstances for a comprehensive peace appeared very favorable. The infiltration from across the LoC had come down considerably and the ceasefire along the border was holding; making the life of the people residing on both sides of the divide so much more relaxed. The level of hostility amongst people of India and Pakistan had also come down; as became evident from behaviour of the crowd – and fans from both sides - during the Indo-Pak cricket matches played in Pakistan. The spectators had sided with the quality of the game rather than with teams of their respective countries. Every gem of the game was applauded rather than the nationality of the player. Another important issue which had positively impacted on the peace process was Pakistan's recent deviation from its traditional stand relating to the UN resolutions on Kashmir. This had made the prospects of talks so much more meaningful. During the Vajpayee visit of Pakistan in January 2004, General Musharraf had started talking about 'out of the box solutions' and subsequently put on table his four-point formula; for taking the negotiations fruitfully forward. This opportunity could have been gainfully used by Vajpayee, if he had got a second term, as by then he had sufficiently sized up Musharraf so as to negotiate with him purposefully and with positive results. Just possible, that both sides could have reached a formula or settlement that could meet the core interests of India, Pakistan (army) and separatists leadership represented by the APHC.

It also goes to Vajpayee's credit that he placed principles over party and national interests over narrow political considerations. Just consider the facts that in the J&K assembly elections of 2002 the BJP got only one seat in a house of eighty-seven; and in the Parliament elections two years later, it won in none of the six constituencies of the state. These statistics prove the point of his wider vision and capacity to stand on the principles. He had rightly come to the conclusion that interests of the Jammu and Kashmir state took precedence over the fortunes of his party – BJP - there.

He may not have succeeded to the extent he had desired and striven for, but his exertions certainly made a difference. He left the process of normalization of Indo-Pak relations at a point where his successor could build upon the break-through he had made. As a statesman he had tried to mark his footprints on the sands of history; and history would one day give a decisive verdict about his contributions. The future generations of India and Pakistan – both countries – will remember him for the sincere and conscientious efforts he made; consistently over the five years plus of his tenure as the Prime Minister of India to improve the Indo-Pak relations.

Vajpayee had once famously said about his poetry, "….It is not the defeated soldier's drumbeat of despair, but the fighting warrior's will to win. It is not the dispirited voice of dejection but the stirring shout of victory." His consistent efforts as the highest political executive of the Indian nation do ring true to his poetical philosophy and mysticism.

CHAPTER – VIII

Efforts Continue

S oon after the well-publicized and successful "Summit Meeting" between Vajpayee and Musharraf in January, the clogged process of dialogue and forward movement resumed with some new vigor. This gave rise to begin the process of a series of official level talks as also prepare for an early ministerial-level talks. In the meantime the General Elections for Lok Sabha commenced in India during the month of April and the results were declared on May 13, 2004. This election saw defeat of the incumbent National Democratic Alliance government, which many political analysts in both countries saw as a setback to the resumed dialogue. In the first few days after the polls public statements and views flew back and forth on the possibility of Sonia Gandhi, the acknowledged leader of the single largest party in Lok Sabha – the Indian National Congress – becoming the country's Prime Minister. But she sprang a surprise by announcing the party's choice for this post. On 19th May, the President of India invited Dr. Manmohan Singh to form the government of a new coalition of parties termed as, "United Progressive Alliance (UPA)", led by the Congress.

Dr. Manmohan Singh came to occupy this high office with a solid reputation as a leading economist of world repute and also the man credited with initiating the economic reforms in the early nineties, as the Union Finance Minister, under the premiership of P.V. Narasimha Rao. In addition, he was also Leader of the Congress party in the Rajya Sabha till then. Those familiar with the style of functioning of Vajpayee could make a fair guess that he must have kept influential opposition leaders like Dr. Manmohan Singh informed of his important initiatives, including renewed efforts to reach out to Pakistan. Also, the media highlighted that the place of his birth was now in Pakistan and gave wide coverage to struggles in early life, as a refugee, to acquire education and then settle down in his chosen profession. Thus his credentials sufficiently proved to any skeptical that the current Indian Prime Minister not only knew the contours of his job well, but was also reasonably familiar with the nuances of the developments in the sub-continent over the last six decades, including the recent progress made. In his interview to a British journalist Jonathan Power, published on the day he took over, he said, "… Then we have to find a way to stop talking of war with Pakistan. This is stopping us from realizing our potential. Two nuclear-armed powers living in such close proximity is a big problem. We have an obligation to ourselves to solve the problem….. Short of succession, short of redrawing boundaries, the Indian establishment can live with anything. Meanwhile, we need soft borders – the borders are not so important"[1]. This very much indicated his mature understanding of the issues involved, the progress made so far as well as the continuation of the existing policy framework towards Pakistan.

Natwar Singh, an erstwhile career diplomat of consummate skills and also a former External Affairs Minister, was once again assigned the same portfolio. These developments, from Pakistan's point of view, also augured well for the bilateral relationship. The optimism further built up when he met the Pakistani counterpart Kasuri in Quingdoo, China, where both had gone for a conference, and assured that his government valued the process of dialogue to address all bilateral issues. This ministerial contact was a good beginning, particularly after the recent Foreign Secretary level talks in New Delhi on June 27-28, 2004. Also, notwithstanding the fact that, while in New Delhi, the Pakistan FS, Riaz Khokhar, had queered the pitch by inviting Geelani and other separatist leaders for a meeting. It was an almost crude attempt to tell New Delhi that the road to Srinagar passed through Islamabad; as if the Indian Establishment did not understand the importance or the lack of it, of the few favourite lackeys and henchmen of Pakistan. The environment in the Valley had been muddled earlier during the month of May by an attack on the residence of Maulavi Umar Farooq and the killing of his uncle Maulvi Mushtaq.

In spite of such pin-pricks, the relations between two countries and the process of normalization did not suffer due to the change in the

---

1   *The Statesman*; May 20, 2004.

government in New Delhi and Dr. Manmohan Singh continued with the policy of improving relations initiated by the previous regime. In the month of September, meetings of the two Foreign Ministers followed by parleys between Manmohan Singh and Parvez Musharraf in New York set the tone and tenor of further improvements in bilateral relations. Political analysts did not fail to note that they refrained from criticizing each other's policies in their addresses to the U.N. general assembly and rather expressed strong desire to pursue bilateral dialogue on contentious issues in a "sincere and purposeful manner". The contours of this meeting gave indications that the ongoing exchanges at different levels would be further enhanced and influence the nature and direction of dialogue in the future, reinforcing it with the current and new CBMs.

A comprehensive analysis of the Indo –Pak relations and the direction these were set on, was reported in the Sunday Times of India, New Delhi / Chandigarh, dated November 21, 2004, under four categories,

Measures Implemented by Both Sides

➢ Appointment of High Commissioner to Pakistan.

➢ Restoration of civil aviation links on reciprocal basis.

➢ Resumption of Samjahuta train service and the Delhi – Lahore bus service.

Being Unilaterally Implemented by India

➢ Free medical treatment to a second lot of 20 Pakistani children.

➢ Liberal visa regime for performing artists, film personalities.

➢ Exchange of youth delegations.

Under Discussion

➢ A bus or rail link between Khokrapar and Munnabao.

➢ A bus service between Srinagar and Muzaffarabad.

➢ A dedicated and secure hot-line between the two foreign secretaries.

No Response From Pakistan

> ➢ Holding of visa camps by the respective High Commissions in different countries.

> ➢ Develop links and exchange of visits between the armed forces.

> ➢ Opening of Jammu – Sialkot route.

In addition, there were certain other developments which, though not very spectacular or significant in themselves but all the same, helped in improving the atmospherics and perceptions in the two countries. These included the start of survey of Sir Creek in Kutch area, agreement to work out an arrangement on the "disengagement and redeployment" of their troops in Siachin, holding of World Punjabi Conference and First Indo – Pak Punjab Games in December 2004 as also Pakistani Cricket team touring India in March – April 2005 which was in response to the Indian tour to Pakistan a year before.

Simultaneously, within Kashmir, certain steps were taken to lower the temperature. In order to reduce the visibility of troops presence in Srinagar and give a fillip to tourism, during the summer of 2004, about 200 rooms of seven hotels were vacated by the CPMFs. In the similar vein, Political Protectees were shifted from 67 rooms of three hotels in the city. Also a thinning out of troops from J&K was started by the government which was estimated to be around two brigades in strength. The Prime Minister undertook his first visit of the state on 17-18 November 2004 and at the end of this important journey, the Media Advisor to The Prime Minister issued an exhaustive five-page Press Release, with following descriptive headings;

" Manmohan Singh Calls For a New Beginning in Kashmir

High Power Advisory Council to Oversee Implementation of Rs 24,000 crore Development and Reconstruction Plan for Jammu and Kashmir for 2004 – 2008.

Immediate creation of 24,000 new jobs. Over a Lakh jobs in new projects."

Dr. Singh reiterated his government's commitment to "an unconditional dialogue with anyone and everyone in the State who abjures violence." However, he said "Kashmir cannot wait until these dialogues arrive at a satisfactory solution. The challenge is to begin peace building in Kashmir now. I want the journey of development to begin here and now." He further said he was visiting Kashmir not with a "package" but with a "plan". A plan "to reconstruct the economy, reform the government, regenerate entrepreneurship, revitalize the institutions of civil society and redefine the political paradigm and context in the sub-continent". During his two days stay in the state, the Prime Minister had correctly and effectively emphasized on the nine important issues so relevant for J&K; these included Accelerating economic development of the three regions, Follow process of dialogue, Interaction with people of Pakistan, Promoting culture of J&K, Tackling unemployment, Redressal of public grievances, Enhancing security measures, Avoiding human right violations and More effective perception management.

This visit of the Prime Minister and its comprehensive media coverage including his engagements and sayings fitted very well with the Pakistan policy of his government and closed the year 2004 on a positive and optimistic note. Also during this period, certain measures initiated by the earlier regime were reaching towards fruitful conclusion bilaterally and loose ends were being tied up internally. The most significant of these policy initiatives related to starting a bus service between Srinagar and Muzaffarabad. An agreement about the date and modalities of this important, almost momentous, initiative was reached between the India Foreign Minister Natwar Singh and his Pakistani counterpart Khurshid Mehmood Kasuri, in Islamabad. An official announcement made on February 16, 2005 read as,

"Both governments have agreed to allow travel across the LoC (Line of Control) between Srinagar and Muzaffarabad by bus. Travel will be by an entry permit system, once the identities are verified. Application forms for travel will be available with the designated authorities in Srinagar and Muzaffarabad. The bus service is expected to commence from April 7, 2005". It was indeed a historical agreement. A report on this event, emanating from Islamabad mentioned, "…with a 53-word joint statement the two Ministers have contributed their bit to the making of history in the relations between the two countries"[2]. This agreement was an extraordinary gesture on the part of both governments which also reflected, in ample

---

2   FRONTLINE, March 11, 2005, p- 31.

measure, the changed ground realities and justified anticipation of even better things to come.

This was certainly the biggest CBM since India and Pakistan announced and implemented a ceasefire in November 2003. On the Indian side preparations for this event had started much before the official announcement, as not only the issues pertaining to travel documents and border crossing had to be discussed and finalized, but the infrastructural development on the ground was also to be put in place in a time-bound manner. The latter was not an easy task. The last 18 kilometer stretch between Uri and the border point at Kaman Bridge was extensively repaired and practically re-laid. The last three-kilometer section was heavily mined, especially during the past few years, and the process of painstakingly removing the mines also had to be completed before commencing the work on the road. One bridge on this road as well as the Kaman Bridge was reconstructed in a record time by the Indian Army Engineers. As the final date approached, activities of all concerned departments and agencies reached a feverish pitch, this side of the border, as if each individual was enthused with a spirit of completing the job at hand in time so as to ensure smooth conduct of the event. At the state headquarters; all arrangements at Srinagar and the crossing point were monitored regularly at the highest political and administrative levels.

On April 7, 2005, the Prime Minister was to visit Srinagar for flagging off the first bus service to Muzaffarabad. The selected passengers for that bus were brought, in advance, to Srinagar and housed in the Tourist Reception Centre, in the heart of the city and not far away from the venue of the main function. A day before, around 4 pm, the militants managed to gain entry due to laxity and lack of alertness on the part of the CPMF unit guarding the complex; and executed a suicide attack on the complex. The DGP of the state himself rushed to the spot on receiving this disturbing information, reaching the site within about 10 minutes of the first shot. Exposing himself to the danger of being fired upon by the militants holed up inside the main TRC building, his main effort was to isolate them in that structure and deny the opportunity of going deeper into the complex, near the travelers. All the three militants were eliminated in the counter operations within an hour while seven persons received injuries in the attack. The beautifully architectured main building of the TRC complex was fully gutted in the ensuing encounter, after catching fire. However, all the passengers of the bus were safe as they were housed in a structure some distance away from the TRC building. Still to make them more secure; the entire group was immediately shifted to the greater safety premises of the Centaur Hotel, on the banks of Dal Lake. Notwithstanding the fact that responsibility of this reprehensible act was claimed by four militant groups, the fact remains that it did leave a bad taste in the mouth of all concerned and almost derailed the Prime Ministerial visit.

However, fully realizing the unique importance of this event Dr. Manmohan Singh did come to Srinagar, as planned and flagged off the first bus to Muzaffarabad, to the thunderous applause of thousands of people gathered at the venue. During the speech, he also praised his counterpart and said "It is a small step but it will enable the divided families to meet each other and strengthen the relationship between the two countries. The role played by the Pakistani Government, particularly its President Pervez Musharraf is commendable". He also hoped that nothing would stop this caravan of peace. The U.N. Secretary-General Kofi Annan, U.S. Ambassador David Mulford and the Russian Foreign Ministry hailed this peace initiative and expressed hope for similar mutual understanding and spirit of conciliation in other matters also.

A total of 49 passengers, 30 from the PoK and 19 from J&K, had crossed over the LoC. These were the lucky ones from amongst thousands who had fondly applied for the permission. The Deputy Commissioner of Muzaffarabad said that he had received twelve thousand applications for this trip. The enthusiasm this side was no less intense. Whereas passengers who went across from Srinagar reported of cordial reception and hospitable treatment; first to welcome the visitors from Muzzafarabad was the J&K Chief Minister Mufti Mohammad Sayeed. They were treated as official guests for the day and in the evening the state government had arranged a special cultural programme for the visitors where they were formally felicitated before heading for respective destinations next morning.

It would be worthwhile to record the feelings and emotional outpourings of some of these passengers. An elderly Sharief Hussain Bukhari, a retired High Court Judge from Muzaffarabad and the bulk of whose family lived in Kreeri town of the Valley said, "I am coming here after such a long time... I have looked forward to this day for decades". Another man from PoK, Ghulam Haidar Khan enthused, "I have not met my relatives here after 1947. It is a blessing of God that I am here today....

I am eighty years old, but now I feel like a twelve-year-old". In the similar vein Ghulam Fatima, who traveled from Srinagar along with her husband to meet their daughter and her four children, said "I have brought loads of gifts for my grand children. I am very eager to see them for the first time". It is also a matter of record that the majority of passengers from PoK belonged to the Poonch district of Jammu division of the state and had come to meet their long-separated family members.

The essence and importance of this step was wholesomely captured by a national daily as, "Divided families were reunited; tears and rose petals flecked their faces. The significance of this extra-ordinary moment lay perhaps in the ordinariness of the backdrop: two buses with 49 passengers had crossed over and blurred a line that has divided Kashmir for over five decades in blood and prejudice... Other confidence-building measures undertaken by the two countries may have made academic sense to the people of the region, this one touches their lives. It does more than that, in it lies a method – however inchoate it may appear at this moment – of transforming the Kashmir question by informing it with a new dynamic and energy. Listen to the talk of travelers. They want not just one bus but many busses, not one border crossing but many border crossings".[3] Sadly though till today, this single number has been increased to merely two; and many more similar transit points remain under discussion – prolonged and seemingly unending.

Another link of this kind was agreed to during the Indo-Pak talks at different levels over the next one year. The two countries decided to open second cross-border link, 47-kilometer long road connecting Poonch in J&K with Rawalakot on the PoK side. It was meeting of a long-standing demand of the people from both sides, as Poonch and Rajouri districts of Jammu division have more divided families across the LoC than Uri and Muzaffarabad. The Poonch – Rawalakot bus service was ceremonially flagged off, on June 20, 2006, by Sonia Gandhi, Chairperson of the UPA, in the company of two Union Ministers and the Chief Minister of J&K. Though shorn of the media hype and international significance of a similar happening in April 2005 in Srinagar, this was of even greater value to the people on both sides of the divide. A newspaper report graphically described this event as, "The 'invisible line of sorrow'- which has kept thousands of souls away from their family members and relatives for the

---

3   *The Indian* EXPRESS, April 8, 2005.

last 58 years, today turned up into a 'road of happiness' for these divided families as this link is going to end their long separation"[4].

In this context, it would be interesting to also mention excerpts from the monthly Epilogue, published from Jammu, which wrote, "The Srinagar – Muzaffarabad bus service had attracted a whole international attraction as the world media prominently reported the event. However, the Poonch - Rawalakot bus service did not find mention in the media. While the world media did not take note of the event at all, the Indian national media hardly mentioned about it in a mere passing reference. One of the reasons for lack of media interest in this event can be seen in the fact that the route of this bus service was outside the Kashmir Valley.... Farooq Sikander, son of the former Prime Minister of Pakistan administered Kashmir (*sic*), Sardar Sikander Hayat Khan, who showed up at a LoC crossing point in Poonch district on May, 2005, strongly advocated that more points should be opened in Jammu region rather than in Kashmir Valley. 'As far as our Kashmir is concerned there are only a few Kashmiri speaking families who have their relations in Kashmir while as on the other hand there are lakhs of separated families who have blood relations in Poonch and Rajouri', he said and informed that in Pakistan there were approximately about 25,000 Kashmiri people while as five lakh Pahari speaking divided families, who have blood relations this side, have been living in Pakistan administered Kashmir (*sic*)"[5].

The period of fourteen months, which separated starting of these two bus services, was marked by considerable diplomatic activity and forward movement towards the improvement of relations between India and Pakistan. Almost immediately after the 7th April big function in Srinagar, "The President of Pakistan, His Excellency General Pervez Musharraf and Begum Saheba Musharraf visited New Delhi as guests of the Prime Minister of India and Shrimati Gursharan Kaur on 16 to 18 April, 2005. While in New Delhi, The President of Pakistan called on the President of India, who hosted a dinner in his honour. The President also watched the last one-day international cricket match between India and Pakistan..." (paras 1 and 2 of the Joint Statement issued from New Delhi on April 18, 2005). Based on this Joint Statement which categorically declared the peace process between India and Pakistan to be "irreversible" and

---

4   Daily Excelsior, Jammu, June 21, 2006.

5   Epilogue, Jammu. J&K: Book of Year-2007, pp. 58-60.

pledged to further "soften" the border, this meeting was seen as a major step forward. Most of the political analysts and commentators were almost unanimous that the important points on which the two leaders agreed, related to;

➢ Peace process is now irreversible.

➢ Discussions on Jammu and Kashmir to continue.

➢ More measures to enhance interaction and cooperation across the LoC.

➢ Terror can't be allowed to impede the peace process.

➢ Frequency of Srinagar – Muzaffarabad bus service to be increased. Allow trucks to use this route to promote trade

➢ Open more route like Poonch – Rawalakot and Amritsar to Lahore.

➢ Khokhrapar – Munabao rail link by January 1, 2006.

➢ Consulates in Bombay and Karachi to be opened before the year-end.

➢ Discussions to continue on Sir Creek and Siachin.

➢ Ministers of Petroleum and Natural Gas to meet in May to explore cooperation in the sector including the issue of pipelines.

➢ Joint Economic Commission to be reactivated as early as possible.

By any standard, these were almost path-breaking parleys and announcements, which firmly set the course of the future relations between the two countries. At least it appeared so at that point in time. By the virtue of two well-publicized engagements, General Musharraf played his cards even more deftly and effectively on the last day of his stay in New Delhi. Setting aside the established protocol on such visits, he took time to call on the former Prime Minister Atal Bihari Vajpayee. At the end of this meeting, he secured the endorsement of the latter, by now a recognized persona of an elder statesman of national stature in India, of his latest peace initiatives. In fact, this helped the ruling Congress more in better managing the BJP criticism on these issues. Also, perceptive observers did not fail to notice that the date of 18th April coincided with the day, two years ago when Vajpayee, as the then Prime Minister, had famously extended a hand of friendship to Pakistan from Srinagar; an initiative that led to ceasefire along the LoC seven months later.

The General's second notable engagement that day was a televised breakfast interaction with the Indian Editors, which reminded some of a similar meeting almost four years ago in Agra, which turned into a fiasco. But this time the Indian Editors were in the presence of a different man who diligently explained the rationale and significance of the new peace initiatives between the two countries. He was both patient and convincing in the answers he gave to their questions and also delved into some details about his proposal and concept of soft borders. In the analysis of a leading political commentator, "It is my belief that the Indian side – our leadership and the bulk of our media – has not yet understood the huge shift that the General's endorsement of the soft borders along the LoC implies. To drive home the point, he reminded the editors of Pakistan's position that the LoC should not become the border, India's position that there could be no redrawing of borders and the only possible via media between these two positions: 'The LoC cannot be permanent, borders must be made irrelevant and boundaries cannot be altered. Take the three together and now discuss the solution,' he said.

A soft border is the only administrative arrangement that allows India and Pakistan to maintain their respective de jure or de facto sovereignties in Kashmir while not coming in the way of the people of the divided state enjoying the fruits of a unified territory. The LoC need not be made permanent or redrawn; the solution is to make it irrelevant"[6].

Though the expression "soft borders" did not specifically find a mention in the Joint Statement and officially both sides avoided using these words, but it was largely understood, and rightly so, by all concerned that the focus of both countries had now shifted from the territorial jurisdiction to being practically public-centric. However, its importance was understood as a concept by both sides as well as the need for a larger public debate to flesh out broader contours of this new shift. The new measures were generally welcomed across the board and the only opposition seemed to come from the militant outfits as well as their handlers and complex control hierarchy; separatist leaders and their over ground supporters.

---

6   Siddharth Varadarajan in Kashmir Images dt. April 20, 2005.

It could also be assumed that some sections of the Pakistan Army were certainly unhappy with this turn of events. But President Musharraf was also the Army Chief there and any opposition to his initiatives had to be carefully calibrated and diligently planned and executed.

It is noteworthy that as a sequel to the peace efforts, there was no let up in the terrorist activities, and in fact, the tempo seemed to have picked up. This becomes evident from the compilation of J&K Police about such actions, pertaining to April 27, 2005 – barely nine days later;

"Srinagar – Terrorists kidnapped ASI Ali Mohd, from his residence at Nishat and killed him by slitting his throat.....

In the evening, terrorists fired upon Police Naka party at Kathi Darwaza Rainawari, causing serious injuries to Constable Bilal Ahmed, who later succumbed to his injuries.

Anantnag – An encounter took place between terrorists and Army at Kokernag in which one terrorist got killed.....

Terrorists kidnapped a teacher Mohd Yaqoob Mir from a primary school near Pahalgam and shot him dead.....

An encounter took place between terrorists and Army near Kulgam in which one terrorist got killed....

The terrorists shot dead Mohd Yusuf Magray an employee of irrigation department, near Bus Stand Wathoo.

Kupwara – Four terrorists got killed in an encounter with the BSF near a border post in Trehgam area....

Baramulla – Terrorists fired upon SGCT Maqbool Lone, posted in Magam Court, near his house. He succumbed to his injuries on way to the hospital.

Pulwama – Terrorists shot dead Mohd Yusuf Gujjar, a laborer by profession, at his rented accommodation at Tral Payen......

Terrorists kidnapped a released militant Mushtaq Ahmed Mantoo of Aglar Litter and later killed him.

Doda - An encounter took place between terrorists and Army at Bharat area, in which one terrorist got killed....

In another encounter with Army at Drang one terrorist of LeT, a Pak national, got killed.....

Army / Police busted a hideout of terrorists at Arenag Mangit, near Banihal, and recovered arms and ammunition.

Rajouri – A search party of J&K Police busted a terrorist's hideout at Chicka Kheit near Kandi and recovered large quantities of arms and ammunition. However, the terrorists managed to escape after an exchange of fire with the Police."

This routine and the daily report does tell a story of its kind about impact of the peace initiatives at the ground and the distance that needed to be traveled by both sides. At another level, these details also indicated acts of duplicity and games being played by organs and outfits controlled by the military at various levels in Pakistan. A simple question that arises in mind is about a doubt that the man at the top there was, at best, not in sync with his systems which seemed to be pulling in a different direction.

As the events leading to peace between India and Pakistan appeared to be moving fast, the separatist leaders were feeling left out and irrelevant. The J&K government came to know around the fourth week of May that the "moderate" faction of APHC was planning to visit PoK and Pakistan, after having received an invitation, to assert their credentials and pertinence as a component of the ongoing peace moves. The underlying intention appeared to be to make a media hype about this visit and capture the public attention in the Valley, notwithstanding the fact that the faction led by Geelani – for its own reasons - did not support this move. After taking various factors into consideration and keeping in view the ongoing CBMs, particularly as a sequel to the Joint Statement of 18th April issued from New Delhi, the state government decided to clear eleven separatist leaders to visit Pok and Pakistan. However, two persons out the list of eleven approved by the J&K government did not get clearance from the PoK authorities. The important ones in the nine names agreed to by both sides included Mirwaiz Umar Farooq (AAC), Prof Abdul Gani Bhat (MC), Bilal Gani Lone (PC) and Yasin Malik (JKLF). Reports reaching the state establishment indicated that the PoK government wanted to capitalize on this visit and was contemplating to give considerable media hype to the event, including plans to telecast some engagements live on few TV channels.

This group's visit to PoK and Pakistan lasted for a fortnight, from June 02 to June 16, 2005. During this period they were hosted for lunches and dinners by the PoK President and Prime Minister, Governor and Chief Minister of Sindh, as also the Pakistan Prime Minister Shaukat Aziz; the itinerary included a meeting with Pak Foreign Minister Khursheed Mehmood Kasuri. However, main highlight of the trip was their calling on Pervez Musharraf on 7th June. Also, reactions of various organizations and groups were mostly on the expected lines. While the ruling establishment in PoK, including its President and Prime Minister, as well as other significant organizations and individuals, welcomed the visitors and actively participated in the functions; the hardliner factions, terrorist groups and persons opposed the visit did stay away from the visitors. Similarly, coverage in Pakistan media and reactions in the government circles was on the expected lines as the official circles stuck to the clichés of support for the, so called, Kashmir cause and making efforts towards the inclusion of Kashmiris in the Indo – Pak dialogue. Pakistan President and Prime Minister went out of their way to lend credibility to the visiting group, assuring them of Pak support. However, on the other hand, the Pakistan Foreign Minister's statement that Pak cannot force India to include Kashmiris in talks and the questioning of visiting leaders' representative character by two Senators of Pakistan Parliament's Foreign Relations Committee strongly underlined the point that the APHC leaders cannot blindly take Pak support for granted without proving their credentials in elections.

Back in the state, the responses of various groups were on the expected lines. The hardliners circles represented by Geelani and his likes, as also terrorist outfits rejected the visit as insignificant and termed it as "betrayal". Similarly, while as majority of the Kashmir press highlighted the visit; Jammu based papers generally played down the trip and expressed Jammu people's opposition to such undertakings. Amongst the political circles, except the PDP, no state party looked at this initiative favorably. Some also pointedly questioned the representative credentials of the APHC.

At the individual level, each person was happy to have got an opportunity to visit Pakistan and get feted by the mighty and successful there. On the whole, this outing could be termed successful as the group was able to get much sought after endorsement from the Pakistani President. It was reported that Pervez Musharraf, during their meeting in which some generals were also present, told Umar Farooq and his associates that henceforth he would treat them as the real "Hurriyat" in Kashmir rather than Geelani and deal with them accordingly. This was a big gain for Umar and his associates. Another news also filtered through to India that the ISI head, Lt. General Kiyani, had managed to arrange a meeting between two important members of this group and the PoK based UJC chief Syed Salahuddin, in which the latter emphasized the importance of armed struggle and the need to include Geelani in future talks. Apparently, there were chinks in the armor on the other side and a lack of unity of purpose, at least about the initiated peace process. Happenings over the next one year would underline the significance of both events.

Almost three months later, Umar Farooq led five-member APHC team, which included Bilal Lone, Prof Abdul Ghani, Fazal Qureshi and Moulvi Abbas Ansari, had two and half hours long meeting with Prime Minister Manmohan Singh in New Delhi on September 5, 2005. The next day almost all newspapers prominently carried this story in headlines. Last time the Hurriyat leaders had traveled to New Delhi, over a year and a half ago to meet the then Deputy Prime Minister and Home Minister, L.K. Advani and exchange views with him. Since then the Center had no formal contact with them, and even though no major break-through was reported in these talks; it was seen as picking up of an important thread, like restoring a snapped link. A press release issued by the PMO underlined the Prime Minister's commitment to "ensuring a life of peace, self-respect and dignity for the people of Kashmir and ensuring that human rights violations would not be tolerated". Mirwaiz Umar Farooq called this meeting a historic start and said that Prime Minister had assured of an honorable and durable resolution of the Kashmir problem. He also mentioned, "We are very excited.... It transcended our expectations. The peace process finally seems on track." Also, both sides agreed to review of all cases of detention as well as have a fresh look at cases under PSA and POTA in a time-bound manner. The next round of discussions was expected to take place in a few months.

This interaction with an important faction of APHC was hailed by most of the commentators in the media, with one important observer describing the meeting as, "Mirwaiz and his colleagues have made no secret of the fact that they wholeheartedly endorse the framework for a dialogue on Kashmir that was forged by Musharraf and Manmohan Singh in Delhi, and believe that the way ahead lies making the LoC progressively less relevant. This is a solid platform to build upon"[7]. This step by New Delhi amply demonstrated the desire of the central government to not only bring down the temperature in the Valley considerably but also to match the external dimensions of the ongoing peace initiatives with equally perceptible and viable internal initiatives. In this quest, it showed the willingness to engage with any group that was prepared to come forward and participate in the quest for reducing, if not eliminating, the level of violence in the state.

It was in pursuance to this line of action as also efforts to "reach hearts and minds" of the people of Jammu and Kashmir, that the Centre held its first meeting with Kashmir leaders outside the pale of moderate faction of APHC on January 14, 2006. This group was led by Sajjad Lone, son of late Abdul Ghani Lone and younger brother of Bilal Lone, heading a faction of his father's People's Conference. Other influential members of his team included a close associate of senior Lone, Peer Hafeezullah Makhdoomi, as also Qazi Yaseer, and the son of late Qazi Nissar of Anantnag. The very invitation to Sajjad Lone for talks reflected a desire on the part of New Delhi to broad base the internal dimensions of the peace process and involve as many people of substance as possible. His restrained approach and careful composition of public statements, emphasizing the involvement of all relevant players as also adequate stress on the process of dialogue further enhanced his image. Sajjad Lone emerged as a leader in his own right after the conclusion of this meeting. It is also worth mentioning that he contested the 2014 Lok Sabha elections unsuccessfully and also participated in the State Assembly elections a few months later. This time he was declared successful and became a M.L.A. Not only that, he was also sworn in as a Minister in the state government headed by Mufti Sayeed in March 2015 and later also, after Mufti's demise he joined in the similar rank, the government of Mehbooba Mufti in April 2016. However, back in the month of January 2006 the New Delhi meeting with this group was certainly an innovative step in the right direction.

---

7   Prem Shankar Jha in *Outlook* dt. September 12, 2005.

Reverting back to PM's meeting with Mirwaiz led APHC in September 2005; the only other event of consequence in the Indo – Pak context, during last three months of the year, was a joint declaration of the two Foreign Ministers, issued from Islamabad on October 4, 2005. Apart from mentioning the usual points, this statement included the following four notable matters;

➤ India and Pakistan agreed to hold an expert-level meeting in Islamabad on 25-26 October 2005 to start the Nankana Sahib-Amritsar bus service at an early date.

➤ Agreed to hold technical-level talks before the end of this year for operationalising the Rawalakot- Poonch bus service.

➤ Technical-level talks for starting truck service on Muzaffarabad-Srinagar route before December.

➤ Both sides reiterated their commitment to the Iran-Pakistan-India gas pipeline.

However, on the flip side two developments need a mention, and both happened during the month of October. A massive earthquake, with its epicenter near Muzaffarabad, devastated both sides of the LoC on 8th October, causing large-scale loss of life, property and extensive damage to the infrastructure. The casualties on the Indian side in the Poonch-Uri-Tangdhar belt were reported to be around 1300; the PoK losses were staggering with almost 70,000 killed and many more wounded. The consequent damages to private and public property can only be imagined. Whereas the central and provincial governments on both sides reacted, with varying degrees of alacrity and success – and the respective efficacy of these efforts is not the point of analysis here – the fact remains that both sides lost a big and nature given opportunity to actually make the borders / LoC irrelevant and permit rescue teams to help people in distress. With roads and tracks for reaching to the affected people badly damaged; the Indians could have effectively extended a helping hand, across Uri sector, to the population in the Muzaffarabad sector. Similarly, the teams from Pakistani side could provide succour to the suffering ones on the Indian side in Poonch and Karnah belts. But, indeed that did not happen and a golden opportunity was lost by both sides to put in practice the concept of caring more for the people rather than the imaginary dividing line between the two sides. It is a futile exercise to apportion the degrees of blame to either party. However, as per the international media reports, the front organizations of some militant groups were allowed to undertake relief works in the PoK, a legitimate concern and responsibility of the official establishment itself, with the ostensible purpose of garnering local support.

Another setback to the ongoing peace process was the series of blasts that took place in the Indian capital on 29th October when people were busy shopping there for the coming Diwali and Id-ul-Fitr festivals. This mindless violence resulted in sixty deaths and many injuries. It also bared the ugly face of terrorism and made it abundantly clear that the ongoing peace process in the sub-continent is not to the liking of terrorist organizations and also to their handlers. The involvement of the latter in such wanton acts was not only duplicitous but also more dangerous. It was yet too early to pass a judgment on this issue, but clearly there was a divergence of opinion at the decision making levels in Pakistan. Keeping the overall situation in mind, New Delhi correctly took this aberration in its stride and did not over react.

Thus, on the whole, the year 2005 closed on a positive and optimistic note with chances of peace prevailing in the sub-continent brighter than ever before. Considerable positive achievements were discernible on both sides, along with sincere efforts to reach to the other party. Starting of Srinagar- Muzaffarabad bus service on 7th April, New Delhi Joint Statement of 18th April, APHC visit to PoK and Pakistan during June, APHC and other delegations meeting the Prime Minister in New Delhi on 5th September and January 14, 2006, as also the Joint Statement of the two Foreign Ministers issued from Islamabad on 4th October; were all parts of the same sequence of events. Notwithstanding the lost opportunity of earth quake on 5th October and the Delhi blasts on 29th October; on the whole, the year 2005 had been a period of hope and satisfaction.

Dr. Manmohan Singh took another notable initiative as an important part of seriously addressing the internal dimensions of reaching out to the people of the state. Assisted by a set of advisors including the Home Minister Shivraj Patil, Centre's Interlocutor on J&K N.N. Vohra and National Security Advisor M.K. Narayanan, he held the first Round Table Conference (RTC), in New Delhi on February 25, 2006. It was a seven-hour long session attended by 52 delegates representing various shades of political opinion in the state and belonging to all major mainstream political parties. All factions of APHC refused to participate terming it against the spirit of tripartite talks between itself, India and Pakistan. All the same, it was a major step forward which amply indicated the Government of India's desire to seriously engage all stakeholders of the state. The underlying philosophy was aptly described by the PM as, "To build a better tomorrow for the people of Jammu and Kashmir we need to explore jointly new pathways". Comprehensive analysis of this initiative will be attempted at a later stage, however, it may be mentioned here that the second RTC was held at Srinagar on 24th May and the third, also the last one, in the series again in New Delhi on April 24, 2007.

Coming back to the year 2006, the first big event involving the goodwill of Pakistan took place on 24th March. On this day the Prime Minister Manmohan Singh flagged off the first Amritsar – Nankana Sahib Bus service, from Amritsar in the presence of Punjab Chief Minister and Deputy Chief Minister. His speech on this important occasion not only reflected his happiness and satisfaction on behalf of the local audience but also addressed himself to the people and policymakers across the border. He said, "I have a vision that the peacemaking process must ultimately culminate in our two countries entering into a treaty of Peace, Security and Friendship to give meaning and substance to our quest for shared goals.... The time has come to leave behind the animosities and misgivings of the past and *to think the unthinkable*" (emphasis added). His statement only elicited a cautious welcome from the official spokesperson of Pakistan Foreign Office. Eyewitnesses present on the occasion and perceptive observers were unanimous in their opinion that Dr. Singh that day spoke from his heart and his speech was emotionally charged. It was singularly unfortunate that his offer of a treaty of peace, friendship and security, which raised the peace process to a new high level, was not suitably responded to at the appropriate political level.

Commenting on this occasion as well as the overall pattern of relations between the two nations, the veteran journalist B.G. Verghese very thoughtfully analyzed, "Pakistan has studiously avoided any discussion or introspection regarding governance on its side of J&K while making strident comments about and demands on the Indian-controlled part of the state. This is a totally unreal position, which the Hurriyat too has masterfully sidestepped, unmindful of the huge contradictions under which it labours..... India can and should help General Musharraf, but there are certain limits which none can cross..... Dr. Manmohan Singh in his own quiet way outlined a grand vision of 'a cooperative common future'. He saw an Indo-Pak Treaty of Peace, Security and Friendship as setting the seal on this arrangement and giving meaning and substance to a shared quest to overcome chronic poverty and to foster economic cooperation...[8].

The only development of positive nature after the Amritsar bus service in the month of March was flagging off the Poonch – Rawalakot bus service by Sonia Gandhi, Chairperson of the UPA, on June 20, 2006; details of which have already been covered.

In an obvious bid to push back the peace process, as also affect the forthcoming second round of RTC in Srinagar, militants suspected to be belonging to the LeT group, struck in the Kulhand village of Doda district killing 29 persons and injuring 10, on 1st May. It was a pre-planned act with definitive purpose. However, another very serious setback to the improving relations took place on 11th of July with, what appeared to be a coordinated strike by militant groups in Srinagar and Mumbai. In Srinagar, five grenade attacks claimed eight lives and left 37 persons injured. But the more vicious episodes happened in Mumbai, where blasts ripped through the local train compartments at the evening peak rush hour at seven different places. According to the Police Control Room, 147 passengers were killed and 439 reported injured in these explosions. The whole of India was outraged at this brutal action. As was expected, and also probably intended, the Mumbai blasts put a question mark over the peace initiatives with Pakistan. Four days later, in New Delhi the Foreign Secretary Shyam Saran practically put a stop to further deliberations on the subject, saying "as a result of this terrible terrorist incident, it is becoming difficult to take the peace process forward." In a similar vein, the Minister of State for External Affairs Anand Sharma said the Mumbai terror attack has vitiated the atmosphere for talks and that the parleys can only be held at an "appropriate time". Few days afterwards, the Prime Minister echoed similar sentiments, while keeping a window of opportunity open, when he said, "...For the time being, I think the dialogue process has suffered but I won't say it is a setback. I think it's inevitable that in the light of this

---

8   B.G. Verghese "Cooperative Common Future", in Tribune, Chandigarh, dt. April 10, 2006.

ghastly tragedy, we need to reflect on our relations with Pakistan."Anyway, the heady days of April 2005 already seemed a long time ago. The thread of goodwill and confidence had been broken, and even if the loose ends were tied together again, the proverbial knot would remain.

It took another two months of back-channel activities and also, as it became clear with the passage of time, strong leaning on the government of India by the United State of America to get the peace efforts back on the rails. The American Secretary of State Condoleezza Rice meeting the Indian Prime Minister in New York, at the latter's hotel, on 15th September, was probably the most visible manifestation of these exertions. It was reported that she had requested Dr. Manmohan Singh to not only help restart the stalled dialogue but also make visible and positive moves in Kashmir to help General Musharraf sell his side of the peace process bargains to the local elements in Pakistan. Even otherwise it was becoming quite clear in India that the General was increasingly coming under pressure in his own country from the enhanced activities of political parties, in addition to the highly vocal segments of the religious groups and overground supporters of militant outfits. Also what was not being mentioned in public, but mattered perhaps most in the context of Pakistan, was the combined feeling of restlessness and negativity amongst the senior Army Commanders about Musharraf's peace initiatives. Seen from their respective standpoint; the General appeared to be conceding more than what he was getting in return. But also across the board, the Indian Prime Minister was functioning within the defined limits of his country's democracy and had to take into consideration not only the public opinion but also keep in mind the red lines drawn and limits imposed in respect of a hugely emotive issue like the J&K.

It was in this background that the two leaders met for an hour in Havana, on September 17, 2006, on the sidelines of the NAM Summit being held there. Both stressed early resumption of the Foreign Secretary level talks as part of the overall composite dialogue process. The outcome was broadly reiteration of the contours of New Delhi Joint Statement of April 18, 2005; except the new element of setting up of anti-terrorism mechanism. This provided justification for India to be on board once again. Dr. Manmohan Singh read out the joint statement, which partly contained, "The two leaders met in the aftermath of Mumbai blasts. They strongly condemned all acts of terrorism and agreed terrorism is a scourge that needs to be effectively dealt with. They decided to put in place an India-Pakistan anti-terrorism institutional mechanism to identify and implement counter-terrorism initiatives and investigations". For the benefit of his audience back home, Pervez Musharraf said about this meeting as, "We agreed to narrow down the divergences and strengthen convergences. *The road forward is the willingness to discuss and resolve the Jammu and Kashmir dispute"* (emphasis added). In short by agreeing that the peace process must be maintained and its success was important for both countries and the future of the entire region; the joint statement made all the right noises for improved bilateral relations.

A direct early outcome of this interaction was two days Foreign Secretary level meeting held in New Delhi on 14th and 15th November. Of the decisions taken in this forum, apart from agreeing to meet again in February 2007 in Islamabad, two items stood out in importance. One dealt with setting up of a three-member anti-terror mechanism headed by respective Additional Secretary level officers. Also the two sides "agreed to fully implement measures to enhance interaction and cooperation across the LoC, including the early operationalisation of truck service for trade on agreed items".

As agreed, the FS level meeting did take place in Islamabad, not in February but on 13th March next year and it was termed as the fourth round of the composite dialogue. But apart from civilities and diplomatic niceties, nothing substantial came out of these parleys. But almost three months before this official interaction, President Musharraf gave an interview to the Indian NDTV, and all major newspapers and TV channels gave prominent headlines to his views, on December 5, 2006. He was reported to have famously said that if the four-point solution, which includes no change in boundaries of Kashmir, making borders and LoC irrelevant, staggered demilitarization and autonomy or self-governance with a joint supervision mechanism, is agreed upon; Pakistan would also give up on the UN resolutions and its long-standing demand for a plebiscite. Notwithstanding the fact that the proposals did not come through an official channel and were neither followed up seriously in Pakistan; the reality remains that during the period this interview did create waves in the Indian media. The Times of India in its editorial titled "A New Kashmir" dated December 7, 2006, conducted interesting diagnosis of this stipulation. In part it mentioned, "Moderates among separatists in the Valley as well as the political mainstream in Jammu and Kashmir including NCP and PDP, have welcomed the general's proposals. New Delhi's mistrust of Musharraf is understandable and the general has to share a large part of the blame for it. That said, it is in India's interest to see if it could improve upon Musharraf's formula". However, the official efficacy of the formulation was hardly ever substantiated and it was little wonder that this four-point formula was not discussed at the FS level meeting little over three months later.

By the time world was well into the year 2007, it was becoming increasingly apparent that the upswing in the bilateral relations which had peaked in April 2005 and created lot of expectations in the minds of the general public of the two countries, was fast losing steam and that no new initiatives could be expected from Pakistan side any longer. There were a number of reasons for this; but the most obvious one related to the considerable, and also continuing, decline in the personal prestige and hold of General Musharraf over all organs of the establishment there. Bus service from two points between J&K and PoK was the only significant CBM that had effectively materialized and was also likely to hold for future. This was so because of the pressure generated by the people, effectively and in ample measure, from both sides of the divide. Dr. Manmohan Singh made another valiant effort in the middle of July, during his convocation address in the Jammu University, by taking the concept of cooperative and consultative mechanisms between two parts of the state a notch higher. He said during the speech, "....We could, for example, use the land and water resources of the region jointly for the benefit of all the people living on both sides of the Line of Control". This was certainly an attractive offer, with huge underlying and latent possibilities. But no one across the border seemed to be interested any longer. It appeared that New Delhi would have to wait for the new dispensation to emerge in Pakistan, probably by early next year to take the peace agenda forward. In the meantime, the internal dynamics inside Pakistan were changing fast resulting in loosening of the General's hold over systems there.

The difficulties for Pervez Musharraf started with a spat with the higher judiciary in Pakistan. The first major showdown took place on 9th of March in a meeting with Chief Justice Iftikhar Chaudhary of Supreme Court of Pakistan. This well publicized meeting, in which Musharraf was accompanied by some top generals of the Army, ended with the suspension of the Chief Justice, after the later refused to resign as demanded. This was just the beginning of Musharraf's difficulties; as Justice Iftikhar Chaudhary was not a person to take such insults lying down. He fought back, in his own way and time, as also staged a comeback as the Chief Justice of Supreme Court during the next regime. But this followed an unexpected and avoidable trajectory of events which saw his reinstatement – following lawyers' agitation – on 20th July that year and again his arrest along with some more judges in November 2007 when Musharraf declared Emergency in Pakistan. The antagonism of the Supreme Court, as also the higher judiciary of Pakistan was to haunt the General for more than a decade. Another notable episode which worked against him took place during 3-11 July that year and came to be known as the Siege of Lal Masjid in Islamabad. To be fair to Pervez Musharraf the sequence of activities taking place within those premises, which also included a Madrasah or seminary each for boys and girls, as well as the highly charged and provocative statements issued by the leading clerics there, had left him with no choice but to deal with this menace decisively. That is exactly what he proceeded to do in the first week of July. Many observers did accuse him in this case of different acts of commission and omission, ranging from waiting and dithering too long to take effective action to undertaking a botched up operation. However, the focal point of this week-long forces action was the Lal Masjid and the Jamia Hafsa Madrasah in Islamabad. This military action resulted in a total of 154 deaths, with many injured and 50 militants were captured alive. The religious right in Pakistan was, as expected, unanimous in its vociferous condemnation of this action and came out in open support of the Lal Masjid establishment. And this had its own fall out in the radicalized section of the Army; particularly at the lower levels including the officer cadre.

Also towards end of the year, General Musharraf shed his uniform and handed over command of the Army, after being its head for over nine years. General Ashfaq Parvez Kayani, also a former head of the ISI and reported to be a close confidant of Pervez Musharraf, was made the new COAS on November 29, 2007. He was to hold this post for the next six years. Handing over reins of the Army to another incumbent further diminished the already declining hold of Musharraf over the Pakistani establishment. With Benazir Bhutto returning home around the same time, the election fever fully gripped Pakistan. The last blow to Musharraf's prestige, authority and control came when Benazir Bhutto was assassinated in Liaqat Ali Park in Rawalpindi on December 27, 2007.

The peace process with India now truly lay in tatters. What started with Vajpayee's famous speech in Srinagar in April 2003 and peaked during the year 2005 was almost back to the starting point. The Indian government could only wait and watch for the elections to get completed in Pakistan and events to start unfolding after that. All the same cynics in India, which also included people in important circles in New Delhi, felt that notwithstanding the return of democracy in Pakistan the Army there would not let go of its privileged position of managing the country's defence and foreign policy; which certainly included relations with India.

The general elections in Pakistan which were proposed to be held on January 8, 2008 were rescheduled following the assassination of Benazir Bhutto. The PPP, one of the two main political parties of Pakistan, then headed by her was thrown into utter confusion, disarray and tizzy on her sudden departure from the scene. Her young son, not yet fully matured, was elected as the new chairman of the party and her widower, Asif Ali Zardari as the co-chairman of the party. It was Zardari who led PPP in the postponed elections that were held on February 18, 2008. With 44.01 % turn out these elections were seen as fairly credible exercise for the restoration of democracy in Pakistan. Out of a total of 342 seats in the National Assembly, the tally of PPP was 118 and that of PML (N) – headed by Nawaz Sharief – 89. The former formed a national government with the support of PML (N) in the beginning of March. After few months the PML (N) quit the alliance and the PPP still remained in power with the support of some left-oriented parties, as also tacit help from outside by the PML (N). The latter did not want to upset the apple cart with the twin objective of removal of its enemy number one – Pervez Musharraf – from the scene as also strengthen the roots of democracy in Pakistan. The new coalition government in Pakistan spearheaded by the PPP forced General Musharraf to resign and Asif Ali Zardari was elected as the new President on September 6, 2008.

In the meantime, there was some movement towards improvement in the Indo-Pak ties. Soon after the elections, Zardari made certain announcements relating to better bi-lateral relations. On the other end of the spectrum, some political analysts were not so optimistic. A typical write up in a local paper from Srinagar mentioned, "But empirical evidence points to a different direction. The Foreign Minister of Pakistan Shah Mehmood Qureshi, has said on record, in the National Assembly that 'Pakistan and India had held 83 meetings at various levels to attempt to resolve the issue of Kashmir.... 37 meetings were held at the level of head of state or head of government, 19 at the foreign minister level and 27 at the level of foreign secretary'. If all these meetings at various levels for all these years have not been able to break the logjam, what is the guarantee that the parleys in future will be able to produce any result?"[9].

All the same the two-day visit of Indian External Affairs Minister, Pranab Mukherjee, to Islamabad towards the second fortnight of May was deemed encouraging. He was able to engage fruitfully with the new government there, still feeling its way towards consolidation. Also, his Pakistani counterpart interestingly spoke about his government being "ready for grand reconciliation for the resolution of long-standing issues". Taken in the overall context of improving bilateral relations, Pranab Mukherjee visit was certainly a step forward in further firming up the confidence-building measures taken so far; including those aimed at promoting people-to-people contacts and improving trade, particularly across the divide in J&K. The increase in the frequency of Srinagar-Muzaffarabad and Poonch- Rawalakot bus services, as well as starting of trade between two parts of the state during later part of the year were certainly moves in the right direction.

Around almost the same time the internal situation in J&K took a nose dive. The whole sequence of events started on 25th May, with the state government allotting 39 hectares of land; near Baltal base camp in Ganderbal district of the Valley, to Shri Amarnath Shrine Board for developing pilgrim facilities. Objections to this step were raised by separatist outfits and some political elements in the Valley. Under this pressure, the said order was withdrawn on 1st July, which gave rise to a counter agitation in the Jammu belt. These developments resulted in the breakup of the Congress-PDP alliance government in J&K a week later and Governors Rule was imposed in the state. The new dispensation managed the deteriorating law and order situation adroitly, but with considerable difficulty over a period of two months. With the restoration of normalcy and bringing back the life and administration on tracks, a seven-phase election to the State Assembly was announced on October 15, 2008. These

9   Firdous Sayed in Greater Kashmir dated May 17, 2008.

elections were successfully conducted and concluded towards the end of December and the new National Conference-Congress alliance took over the reins of state government in the first week of January 2009.

In the intervening period, two significant developments having considerable bearing on the Indo-Pak relations took place; one each, during the months of October and November 2008.

A major CBM was started with the facility for travel across the borders for the separated families of J&K between Srinagar and Muzaffarabad on April 7, 2005. This step was further boosted next year with the initiation of a similar bus service on the Poonch- Rawalakot sector starting on June 20, 2006. As was expected, with some people moving across the divide, the demand for easier movement of goods and better trade facilities between the two sides picked up and the pressure kept on increasing on both central governments. After a series of discussions at various levels involving a host of departments and agencies; the trade was started from both sides, on the two routes, on October 21, 2008. This was done from the Indian side with least fanfare, as J&K was still under the Governor's rule. The laden vehicles from Uri side were flagged off by the Governor himself, whereas this ceremony was conducted in Poonch area by one of his Advisors. This certainly has been a major boost to the people to people interaction on both sides and another big leap by the two countries to make borders irrelevant in a situation where "LoC cannot become permanent border" and "boundaries cannot be re-drawn". This arrangement was also aimed at, what the Prime Minister Manmohan Singh had urged in Amritsar on March 29, 2006, to "...develop cross-border institutional mechanisms" and expressed a hope for "a cooperative future".

The starting of this truck trade practice has given rise, over the years, to similar demands of higher notches. These relate to allowing traffic for tourism and religious Shrines as well as functions; exchange of folk artists, theatre personalities and media professionals; allow availability of magazines and later newspapers; easy access to better medical facilities; enrollment of students in the higher/technical institution and the like. Over the intervening years though no new initiative has been added, it must be said on the credit side that, with situational hiccups, the two bus services and the truck trade has continued. Of course, there has been a consistent demand for increasing the frequency of bus journey as also making the journey easier and hassle-free. The improvement here is yet to materialize.

In the cross LoC trade, the following difficulties are being experienced by traders of both sides; which have not been sorted out;

> There is no agreed system in position to carry out currency based trading, leaving no choice with the traders but to resort to the barter system, which is obviously not a satisfactory arrangement.

> Lack of direct communication facilities between J&K and PoK.

> A persistent demand to increase the number of trade days in a week.

> The traders want the list of agreed items which can be traded to be expanded further.

> Consistent demand to open more border crossings, especially Jammu – Sialkot on the IB and Kargil – Skardu on the LoC.

But at the time of starting this facility in October 2008, and in fact couple months leading to this almost historic step, the cross-border bonhomie amongst the traders from both sides as also their representatives was worth watching. The willingness of the new Pakistani regime to further improve relations and sayings in this regard by Asif Ali Zardari were very re-assuring. Once again it appeared that the train of normalization was back on tracks. But then almost on a cue, that is exactly what it appeared like, little over a month later the terrorists from Pakistan struck in Mumbai in what is infamously known as the 26/11 episode.

The nightmare started on November 26, 2008; when a ten-member gang of Lashkar-e-Taiba, a terrorist organization based in Pakistan, managed to sneak into Mumbai from the seafront and carried out a series of coordinated bombings, shootings, siege crisis and hostage activities across the financial capital of India. This sickening carnage carried on for four days till the last terrorist was neutralized on 29th of November. The important locations that were targeted included Chhatrapati Shivaji Train Terminus, Cama Hospital, Nariman House, Leopold Café, Oberoi Trident and Taj Mahal Palace Hotel. It was the siege, damage and the causalities at the Taj Palace Hotel which lasted the longest and drew maximum international attention and condemnation. There has been a slight difference in arriving at the exact number of fatalities and injured, but it is generally agreed that over 170 persons were killed, including nine terrorists; and injured figure crossed the number of six hundred. One terrorist, Ajmal Kasab, was arrested from the Chhatrapati Shivaji Terminus. He gave very valuable and important inputs to his interrogators leaving no one in doubt about the origin and intentions of this sneaky and deplorable episode. Notwithstanding the public declaration of sympathy by the Pakistani government and an initial offer of Zardari to send his ISI chief to India for assisting investigations; a proposition he was later made to withdraw on pressure from the army, the indignation in India was very widespread and comprehensive. Those organizations and people in Pakistan who were not happy with the slow but steady improvement in relations with India, and it never had an insignificant number of such elements there, had ultimately managed to strangle and put an end to the peace process, at least for the next few years. The ferocity and brutality of the Mumbai attacks outraged the sensibilities of the Indian masses and their elected representatives to such a significant extent that none on the Indian side was prepared to bet on improved relations with Pakistan for years to come. The process of improving bilateral relations which was started by Atal Behari Vajpayee and Pervez Musharraf in 2003 and was later given momentum and boost by Manmohan Singh and the General; lay practically buried under the debris of Taj Palace Hotel Mumbai in November 2008. The short five year period of hope and sunshine had been effectively clouded. Taj Palace Hotel was repaired, renovated completely and opened for public exactly one year later; but peace process could not be effectively revived. The very next year, in 2009, general elections in India took place in which the UPA government headed by Manmohan Singh was returned to power. However, for the next five years, no major initiative was taken by either side. The thread was again picked up, so to say; by Prime Minister Narendra Modi heading the new BJP dominated NDA government in India in May 2014. The only remnants of the tattered peace initiatives between the two countries were the cross LoC bus services and truck trades at two points connecting with Srinagar and Poonch.

Could these be the starting point in the next round?

A very important internal dimension of the peace process has been the efforts to reach out to and engage the disaffected group of people in the state of J&K, particularly in the Valley, who have harbored actual and perceived grievances, which were taken advantage of for decades by external elements and players in Pakistan.

After the 2002 assembly elections, the PDP - Congress coalition government made concerted and serious efforts to address this issue; duly supported by the then NDA government in the centre. This momentum was later picked up by the UPA government in 2004. A very fine illustrative example of this endeavor is the speedy implementation of the Valley part of the Udhampur – Baramulla rail link. The accelerated process of land acquisition for this project, along with the timely release of adequate funds and deployment of requisite technical resources ensured its completion in record time. The 117 kilometers section between Qazigund and Baramulla, practically connecting South and North of the Valley was declared open in the month of October 2008. This remarkable success was achieved in the face of very heavy administrative, procedural and security-related odds. It is with the intention of using developmental plank as a policy tool that certain initiatives were set in motion by Prime Minister Manmohan Singh.

To reach out to the elements and organizations outside the political mainstream; the central government appointed different points-men, starting from K.C. Pant to Ram Jethmalani, followed by Arun Jaitley and lastly N.N. Vohra. These efforts also included interacting with important persons and groups, outside the mainstream, by both the NDA as well as UPA governments up to the highest levels. It is also a matter of record that the separatist elements did not reasonably respond to these initiatives. But none can blame the Centre for not having made sufficient and sustained efforts in this regard. In addition, particularly right from the beginning of this century; handsome infusion of funds has been made by the centre to accelerate the developmental activities in the state. The three Round Table Conferences, about which a reference has already been made, should be seen as a continuum and logical extension of this internal dimensional peace process.

When Prime Minister Manmohan Singh addressed the first RTC in New Delhi on February 25, 2006; it was an important initiative to have a comprehensive and composite dialogue across the political spectrum of J&K collectively. As expected it was an exploratory exercise. The Prime Minister was assisted by Home Minister Shivraj Patil, National Security Advisor M.K. Narayanan, Centre's interlocutor on J&K N.N. Vohra, Principal Secretary to the Prime Minister T.K.A. Nair and Home Secretary V.K. Duggal. The state was represented by 52 persons which included prominent leaders from political parties like Congress, National

Conference, PDP, BJP, Panthers Party, the CPI (M) as also some intellectuals and members of various organizations belonging to region-specific communities; including Kashmiri Pandits, Sikhs, Gujjars and Bakarwals etc. The APHC and other separatist outfits did not participate in spite of being invited. In a befitting sense it was truly an all-inclusive dialogue by people representing various shades of opinion in J&K with the Prime Minister of the country and his aides. At the seven hour-long session almost all things concerning the state were deliberated upon; including the issue of autonomy raised by National Conference and the self-rule proposal brought forth by PDP. In fact, the Prime Minister expressed confidence that a common understanding on autonomy and self-rule could be reached within the "vast flexibilities" of the Constitution. The Conference asserted that violence has no place in a civilized society and all concerned should uphold basic human rights. It was also decided that the second Round Table Conference would be held in Srinagar in the second half of May. During his opening remarks, the Prime Minister called for "real empowerment of the people" in the state. He went on to add, "Only when every man, woman and child from Ladakh to Lakhanpur and from Kargil to Kathua through Kashmir feels secure, in every sense of the word, can we truly say that the people have been empowered". In a significant way; this meeting underlined the forum and indicated the way forward for purposeful deliberations on the situation in the state and possible resolution of outstanding issues.

The second RTC was held at Srinagar on 24th and 25th May 2006; and the deliberations therein were more focused and fruitful. Even though major conditions of the APHC were met and the amalgam was invited, they still did not join the meetings. But, despite the call for *Bandh* by these elements, the deliberations of this RTC generated lot of excitement and hope amongst the people. This two-day meeting had 27 participants from the state including the Chief Minister, Deputy Chief Minister, Farooq Abdullah, Mufti Mohammed Sayeed, Omar Abdullah and Mehbooba Mufti. Also, there were important leaders from their parties; Congress, National Conference and PDP. Besides these, two members from National Panthers Party, one each from CPM and CPI and three Kashmiri Pandit leaders also attended.

In his opening remarks, the Prime Minister asserted that the very fact of holding this second session in Srinagar, only three months after the first round of discussions in New Delhi, underscored the reality that the welfare of all sections of J&K is the top priority of his government. While expressing the hope that the Hurriyat would also join and share their views at an "appropriate time", he also asserted that attempts by some elements in J&K to disrupt peace process would be firmly thwarted. An important thrust of his speech was that demilitarization had to be looked in the backdrop of terrorism. By all means, the misguided youth should be encouraged to return to their abandoned homes; simultaneously efforts also had to be made for improving the confidence of minorities. He also alluded to the fact that situation in the state had two dimensions; one was the relationship between New Delhi and Srinagar; whereas the other related to ties between India and Pakistan. Therefore, it was necessary to move independently but in a coordinated manner on both the tracks. For good measure, he also added that the series of Round Table Conferences was not only important for Jammu and Kashmir but for the whole of India.

A very significant achievement of this RTC was the constitution of five Working Groups; proposed by the Prime Minister, covering all-important political and development issues concerning the state. This, he said, would be the best way to move forward and ensure that the views of different segments are incorporated in the process. Briefly, these five Working Groups (W.G.) and their respective mandate could be summarized as:-

W.G.-I.   Confidence-building measures across segments of society in the state.

W.G.-II.   Strengthening relations across the Line of Control.

W.G.-III.   Economic Development.

W.G.-IV.   Ensuring Good Governance.

W.G.-V.   Strengthening relations between the State and the Centre.

It was an extraordinary two days deliberations held by the Prime Minister in Srinagar and the event generated considerable excitement, aspirations and expectations. Terming this process as offering real hope for the future; a leading national magazine opined, "Prime Minister Manmohan Singh's round-table process is without dispute historic in its scale. By enabling the elected representatives to negotiate collectively the future of the State with the Union of India, the Prime Minister has restored democratic praxis to the centre stage of its political life. Political parties, whose position has long derived from the exploitation of religious fundamentalism and dispensation of state patronage, will now have to discover a new meaning and purpose and set their minds to imagining what a transfigured Jammu and Kashmir might look like"[10].

All the Working Groups started a process of serious and expeditious discussions on their particular mandate and held a series of meetings with a view to complete their respective reports within the stipulated time of one year.

The third Round Table Conference was held in New Delhi on April 24, 2007, and like the earlier two, the broad profile of those who attended it remained unchanged. The excerpts of Prime Minister's opening remarks included, "We began this process slightly over a year ago. We have met twice before in this format, once in New Delhi and once in Srinagar. This series of conferences is part of our collective effort to find consensual solutions to the problems of Jammu and Kashmir through a process of dialogue. On both occasions, we affirmed that violence had no place in a civilized society.... We also realized that the process was not easy and would be a long one, requiring patience and fortitude... It is almost a year since we met in Srinagar. However, a lot of work has been done since then...I had said a year ago in Amritsar that the two parts of Jammu and Kashmir can, with the active encouragement of the governments of India and Pakistan, work out cooperative, consultative mechanisms so as to maximize the gains of cooperation in solving the problems of social and economic development of the region. I believe the work of the 2nd Working Group can take us forward in this direction... The entire nation wants the state to do well. We all wish that the people of the state live peaceful, secure lives looking forward hopefully to a future of prosperity and dignity..."

This RTC discussed the reports of four of the five Working Groups set up during the previous conference last May. The participants were told that the fifth WG, set up on Centre-State relations, had also commenced functioning and had held three meetings so far. Primarily, due to the absence of these recommendations, deliberations of the third RTC remained inconclusive. In fact report of this WG was finalized and presented to the

10 *Frontline*, June 16, 2006, p. 32.

State Chief Minister over two and half years later on December 23, 2009. By that time events had overtaken the RTC initiative.

Even at that time, and later with the advantage of the hindsight, a good number of political analysts felt that the RTCs had acquired their own momentum and also the government of India had seemed committed to achieve a breakthrough in making good progress towards effectively addressing the internal dimensions of the peace process. In the complex J&K situation; the internal issues were also of lot of significance and that is where the whole exercise was aimed to achieve tangible results. These elements also believed that, along with the other reports of the first four Working Groups, if the fifth one had also submitted its final report – which was possible given eleven months time for the purpose – then the fate of the otherwise failed RTCs would have morphed into something much more tangible and substantive. However, that did not happen due to the inordinate delay and long time taken by this group.

Any rational assessment of the mandate given to this WG would indicate that it was certainly not an easy task and involved addressing as also carefully considering difficult and tricky issues. Simply read this group was to work on and suggest ways to "Strengthening relations between the state and the centre". In this task they were expected to deliberate on the following important points:

➢ Matters relating to the special status of Jammu and Kashmir within the Indian Union.

➢ Methods of strengthening democracy, secularism and the rule of law in the state.

➢ Effective devolution of powers among different regions to meet regional, sub-regional and ethnic aspirations.

The plate, so to say, was almost full. Also, this group was headed by an eminent personality in the form of retired Justice Sageer Ahmed, who had served as a Judge of Supreme Court of India and Chief Justice of J&K and Andhra Pradesh High Courts. Any analysis of the final report or examination of its recommendations would be futile at this stage and will be at best an academic exercise. But if the report was submitted in time, which were a possibility, then the deliberations of the third RTC would have been much more conclusive and definitive. This is one of those 'ifs' and 'buts' of past events which return again and again to haunt the course of future events and actions.

Even at the cost of repetition, it would be worthwhile to recall that in the course of discussions between the two countries, during the heady period of 2005 to 2007, both India and Pakistan had agreed to the following: -

(a) No independence to J&K.

(b) No redrawing of borders.

(c) The LoC can be made irrelevant.

When these three formulations are combined with the demands of autonomy, demilitarization and self-rule by the mainstream regional parties of the state, viz, National Conference and the PDP, an interesting situation arises. The space for and maneuverability of the elements outside the mainstream evidently gets squeezed out and comprehensively restricted. All their possible major fall back planks were being hijacked by the NC and PDP etc. and these were further marginalized from the political scene of the Valley.

Some significant measures having a direct and positive impact on the internal peace process, and which still remain relevant, are: -

➤ People to people contact, which has now become a continuing process. With the opening of more entry points, this is likely to gain greater momentum. It would be interesting to note that the people of Jammu and Kargil are equally, if not more, keen on this matter.

➤ Increased pace of development, good governance, reaching out to people and redressal of grievances.

➤ Decentralization of governance.

➤ Effectively addressing the regional, sub-regional and ethnic aspirations.

➤ Mainstreaming of the population, particularly of the Valley, which has traditionally and historically remained insular.

It would be hugely useful to diligently work for the effective realization of these and similar goals; with a view to strengthening the internal dimensions of the J&K situation. For this, the nation and the state need not, and must not, wait for positive developments on the external front. The former should proceed ahead independently.

CHAPTER – IX

Impact of Relations with Important Countries

The United States

India was virtually unknown in the US till the last decade of the nineteenth century. In September 1893, Swami Vivekananda attended the World Parliament of Religions in Chicago and thereafter stayed in the country for a couple of years teaching and spreading the eternal wisdom and the concept of universal brotherhood, as contained in the ancient Indian scriptures, particularly in the *Vedas* and *Upanishads*. The popularity of this Indian monk and the message of *Advaita Vedanta* that he was preaching there did make a mark in the collective national consciousness of America. It was emphasized for the first time that India was not only a poor and impoverished country; but also had something substantive to give back to the world. This initial contact with India did result, in historical perspective, into a positive national attitude which was later witnessed in terms sympathy and moral support for the Indian independence movement during the first half of the next century.

But, for the next five decades, the US got entangled in the vortex of the two disastrous World Wars. Even though the American role in the First World War was not very prominent and decisive; it did substantially impact its economy and national psyche. But during the Second World War, the US involvement was total – particularly after the Japanese attack on Pearl Harbour on December 7, 1941; the day when America officially entered the fray. In the Pacific region, the US practically fought alone, its efforts spearheaded by renowned military leaders like General McArthur and Admiral Nimitz. In the European theater also the US became a leading ally with one of its five-star generals, Eisenhower, as supreme commander of the Allied forces in Europe. After this war, America certainly emerged as a leading world economic and military power. With its colonial empire in the process of breaking up and the economy left badly mauled after the war; the UK remained considerably behind. Even though it was slowly getting adjusted to playing a second fiddle to America, the UK still wielded considerable influence in the international arena, and the change of baton to America was a smooth, even if a painful process for the British. This whole picture of transition has been comprehensively captured by Lord Moran, in his biography of Sir Winston Churchill – the successful Prime Minister of UK during the Second World War. What is of crucial importance is to note that for over a decade after the Second World War, the American worldview essentially reflected the British diplomatic postures and frames of reference. It was during this period – August 1947 – that India became a free country and Pakistan was born. How deftly and masterfully the British handed over the case in the UN regarding India's complaint of Pakistani aggression in Kashmir, to the US, has been narrated in detail by two Indian authors; both of them former diplomats, belonging to the Indian Foreign Service.

The first book was published in 2002 by C. Dasgupta titled "The War and Diplomacy in Kashmir 1947-48". The second account has been authored by Narendra Singh Sarila under the caption, "The Shadow of the Great Game- The Untold Story of India's Partition", in 2005. Both these well-researched publications are based on the declassified documents in the UK and the USA archives; and give a graphic account of the high political and diplomatic games played by the two countries to secure their perceived strategic interests in this region. Excerpts from one of the books include, "....The archives are also engrossing because the Indian leaders' conversations with, and written communications to, the viceroys were meticulously recorded by the British and give details of their views and tactics, which do not fully emerge from the Indian records. The Indian nationalists' miscalculations, their upholding ideals divorced from realities and their inexperience in the field of international politics emerge in their own words in the records.... The successful use of religion by the British to fulfil political and strategic objectives in India was replicated by the Americans in building up the Islamic jihadis in Afghanistan for the same purpose, to keep the Soviets at bay.... Britain's pro-Pakistan policy on Kashmir was based on its desire to keep that part of its old Indian

Empire, which jutted into Central Asia and lay along Afghanistan, Soviet Russia and China, in the hands of the successor dominion that promised cooperation in matters of defence. In the open forum of the UN, Britain could not conceal its pro-Pakistani stand. The Americans, in their internal telegrams, have left a record of Britain's pro-Pakistani tilt on Kashmir..."[1]

With India charting an independent foreign policy course in a bi-polar world of the Cold War era; Pakistan with its inherent anti-India stance, valuable western support in the UN on Kashmir, as also promise of considerable economic and military assistance, became a firm ally of the American block. It joined the CENTO and SEATO as a member state. The US was also wary and suspicious of the Non-Aligned Movement spear-headed by Nehru of India, Tito of Yugoslavia, Nasser of Egypt and Sukarno of Indonesia. This closeness with Pakistan and distancing from India was much marked during the two terms of Eisenhower Presidency (1953- 61), who was probably still deeply influenced by the British strategic thought and diplomatic skills as he had seen during the war years. In the Great Game; Americans had replaced the British and were now directly involved in containing every southward move of the communist USSR. The famous shooting down of an American U-2 spy plane over Russian territory, during the early sixties typifies Pakistani involvement in this alliance; as this plane was reported to have taken off from a secret airfield inside that country. Also, the American largesse to the Pak army was so abundant that before the 1965 Indo-Pak war, many analysts believed it to be superior to the Indian fighting machine. This was so because on most of the parameters the Sabre jets in PAF were ahead of Indian Gnat aircrafts and similarly the Patton tanks in the Pak army were considered technically superior to their Indian counterpart, the outdated Centurion tanks. That India won in this confrontation is a different matter; but this fact in no way diminishes the value of American help to Pakistan and, to that extent, its efforts to put India down.

It was only during the few years of the Kennedy Presidency, in the early sixties that there was a pro-India stance in the US policies and an effort to contain, if not undo the damage. Unfortunately, with Kennedy's assassination much before the end of his first term; support to Pakistan at the cost of India, was firmly back in the American foreign policy regime.

1   Narendra Singh Sarila, *The Shadow of the Great Game: The Untold Story of India's Partition,* Harper Collins *Publishers* India, New Delhi, 2005, pp. 11 and 413.

This tilt towards Pakistan became pointedly anti-Indian in the Nixon-Kissinger era so much so that even during the Bangladesh crisis in 1971 the Americans were heavily leaning in favor of Pakistan. Notwithstanding the irrefutable and mounting evidence of Pak army atrocities in what was then East Pakistan, and now Bangladesh, as also the severe suppression of civil disobedience there, the American support continued. In the middle of the thirteen day Indo-Pak war in December 1971; the US President Nixon threatened India to either back off or be prepared to face the might of American Seventh Fleet. That India did not deter from the set course is a now a matter of history.

With the creation of Bangla Desh; the state of Pakistan was confined to the earlier West Pakistan and Z.A. Bhutto became the head of government of this region. He subsequently ruled as the Prime Minister of Pakistan, a position he was to hold for a little over the next five years. During his tenure, instead of a serious soul searching for the reasons of the breakup of the country and making resultant course correction; he continued with the anti-India stance and tirade, more so after the signing of Simla Agreement in July 1972. He also forged new and deep ties with Arab countries, in particular with Saudi Arabia and Libya. These alliances got Pakistan considerable economic benefits but had two important negative fallouts. Firstly, it annoyed the 'all weather friend' America – especially Pakistan's almost desperate and at times overt attempts to acquire nuclear weapons. It was during this period that Bhutto famously said, "We will eat grass but we will acquire an Islamic bomb". Islamic bomb was a euphemism for a nuclear device and also a ploy to get money for this project from cash rich Arab states. Secondly, what Pakistan got from merging its unique and rich identity with these countries was "infected aid and contaminated money". This was the beginning of fundamentalism entering the body politic of the nation; something that plagues Pakistan till today. After Bhutto was overthrown by the army in the middle of 1977, General Zia-ul-Haq took over the reins of Pakistan for the next eleven years. During this period he consolidated his position and grip of the army over Pakistan by making a compact with right wings parties and organizations. Resultantly, it was in this period that Pakistan saw a mushroom growth of the Madarssahs as well as the beginning of terrorist organizations taking roots there. Zia's religious zeal also adversely affected the rank and file of the army, particularly its officer cadre for the first time. Such expansion of fundamentalist influence would have generally produced a lot of dismay in the American mind but two developments in the immediate neighborhood of Pakistan came to the rescue of Zia regime. One was the Iranian revolution of February 1979 which resulted in the overthrow of the Shah of Iran and establishment of an Islamic State there; headed by a religious leader Ayatollah Khomeini. While the US was struggling to manage fallouts of this momentous change, the deposed Shah was a close American ally; it obviously did not want an unstable government in Pakistan next door.

The second significant event was the simmering Afghan crisis which resulted in the Soviet military intervention in December 1979. In fact, the Afghan political scene had been volatile for almost two decades but it took a dramatic turn in April 1978; bringing in its wake a communist type regime in Kabul headed by Nur Mohammad Taraki. This change of government, a sort of coup, was referred to as the Saur Revolution. Neither Pakistan, on its immediate border; nor the US, the leading power of the free and democratic world – a bulwark against the Soviet communism, reacted for over one and half years of fast deteriorating situation there till the arrival of Soviet troops in Kabul. It would be an interesting study for the students of History, Political Science and International Relations to compare how the British, then the greatest imperial power, dealt with a similar situation there almost fifty years ago, in the late twenties, when King Amanullah was getting close to the Russians. The British had got this ruler overthrown in an inspired uprising spearheaded by the clerics and followed it by effectively expanding their influence in the region.

Alarmed by the Russian physical intervention in Afghanistan the US made strenuous efforts to force it out of the country by collaborating with Pakistan which, under Zia-ul-Haq, was more than willing to act as a frontline state. The Russian army left Afghanistan ten years later in February 1989, but not before huge and long-term damage was done to the Pakistani society and state. This decade spawned a host of terrorist organizations of a transnational character, across the Durand Line; making the Af-Pak region a hot-bed and leading seminary of international terrorism. It is by now well known and well documented as to how the money, weapons, material and manpower poured into this region from the rich Arab regimes; with the active help of and under the benign American gaze. The entire sequence of events has been comprehensively covered by Steve Coll in his well researched and celebrated publication titled "Ghost Wars". This book, which won the Pulitzer prize in 2005, tantalizingly ends with the assassination of the Northern Alliance Commander Ahmad Shah Masood; two days before the World Trade Centre in New York was blown up by the terrorists on September 11, 2001.

After the Soviet retreat from Afghanistan; the US also quietly withdrew from the scene leaving Pakistan government, more particularly its army, to deal with the emerging scenario or collect the spoils. But it remained grateful to Pakistan for all the help that country provided to the Americans. The US, in turn, looked the other way on all transgressions of Pakistan; which included its being an epicenter of terrorism, creating huge problems of terrorism in India – first in Punjab and then in J&K; as also doggedly pursuing and succeeding in its dream of acquiring a nuclear nation status. The tale of its nuclear scientists, headed by A.Q. Khan, scouting different countries and even stealing designs, unauthorized and illegal nuclear proliferation, against all international norms –including dealings with North Korea- are already well known. But the Americans overlooked all transgressions and in fact mollycoddled Pakistan and also created no hurdles in stopping the country from its nuclear pursuits. Such permissiveness, as exhibited by America in relation to nuclear matters, cannot be construed as a purely bilateral issue. In the current world scenario and gaining momentum of terrorists' activities; this attitude can, in fact, endanger the entire world.

It is also a fact that in the wake of Russian withdrawal from Afghanistan and the US also pulling off from the scene; Pakistan was left free to play its game of creating problems for India. As the situation in Punjab was slowly but steadily being brought back to normalcy, the whole attention of Pak ISI and terrorists trained by it got concentrated on the state of Jammu and Kashmir. With the US fully backing Pakistan and in an almost adversarial relation with India, the latter was left alone to effectively deal with the menace of terrorism and its fallouts. In this backdrop, the decade of the 1990s was a difficult time for India. International human rights organizations like, Amnesty International, the Human Rights Watch, International Committee of Red Cross, to mention a few, were constantly at India's back asking a myriad of questions and constantly accusing the security forces of atrocities in J&K. This was, as is clear now, a well thought out strategy to keep India on the back foot and extract for Pakistan as many concessions from India as possible. This was not all. The Indian delegates and diplomats in Geneva were kept busy for years together to fashion responses and ward off mounting criticism and verbal attacks in the United Nations Commission on Human Rights (UNHCR) based there. A beleaguered India manfully faced all the assaults there for the first five years of this decade; after which the pressure eased a bit and many countries slowly started seeing through the Pakistani game and the merit in India's stand.

On the American relations with the two nations in the sub-continent it would be worthwhile to quote from the autobiography of Jaswant Singh, a former Indian Finance and also External Affairs Minister, " In 1993, a diplomatic crisis arose when the new American assistant secretary for South Asia, Robin Lynn Raphel, while replying to a question during a background briefing for journalists, noted that the United States did not recognize the 1947 document by which the late Maharaja had ceded Jammu and Kashmir to India, 'as meaning that Kashmir is forevermore an integral part of India'..... The first Clinton administration (1993 – 97) had made a virtue of seeing India through Pakistan-tinted glasses. In 1993, Robin Raphel had called the Simla Agreement signed between India and Pakistan in 1972, just after the Bangladesh War 'ineffectual'. She had further said that Pakistani complicity in the armed insurrection in Kashmir was 'no excuse for human right abuses in Kashmir Valley'. In January 1996, Clinton signed into law a congressional bill – the Brown Amendment – granting Pakistan a one-time waiver on the Pressler Amendment and allowing the sale of $ 370 million worth of military equipment, even though Pakistan had received M-11 missiles and 5,000 'ring magnets', used to refine bomb-grade uranium, from China. This was part of a continuing pattern".[2]

However, Robin Raphel continued her criticism of India *vis a vis* Pakistan. Her visit to Kashmir during 1995 was also full of vitriolic comments. It appeared that she developed a Pakistan bias during an earlier stay in Islamabad where her late husband was posted as the American Ambassador. It was only after her tenure as the American assistant secretary for South Asia finished in 1997; along with the first term of President Bill Clinton that she was mercifully off the scene. The installation of a popular government in J&K by late 1996 and a more effective grip on the security situation also helped matters. During the second term of Clinton presidency, the American administration was markedly less hostile towards India though there was no change in its pro-Pak leanings.

---

2   Jaswant Singh, *A Call to Honour*, Rupa & Co, New Delhi, 2006, pp. 279 and 283.

It would be no exaggeration to say that the coordinated terrorist attacks on targets in the US, on September 11, 2001, which destroyed the World Trade Centre in New York, shook entire America to the core. It retaliated, over the next month, with first air strikes in Afghanistan and then landing its army units there. Pakistan, under General Musharraf, became a willing ally in this American enterprise, and also an important actor in this new and emerging scenario. The scales in the sub-continent still remained tilted in Pakistan's favour; even though the United States government was increasingly becoming aware of the double game being played by Pakistan in matters related to terrorism. Also, when the peace process was rolled out between India and Pakistan in 2005 and 2006, the US was almost constantly urging India 'to do more' to accommodate its troublesome neighbour. According to a New York based report, published in India in mid September, 2005, "US Secretary of State Condoleezza Rice has urged Prime Minister Manmohan Singh to offer Pakistan's President Pervez Musharraf some concessions on Kashmir. Dr Rice's request came when she dropped in to see Dr. Manmohan Singh at his hotel".[3]

The leaning towards Pakistan remained a policy plank of the American administration also through the two terms of President Bush, till the end of 2008. There is enough evidence to support this premise; particularly the tone and tenor, as well as the material, of the statements issued by Richard Boucher – the US assistant secretary of state for South and Central Asia during the Bush administration. This, notwithstanding some straws in the wind indicating the new willingness in the ruling circles there to look at India in terms of its intrinsic strengths and merits; and not as part of a hyphenated entity with Pakistan. A significant beginning was made in the field of civil nuclear partnership. George Bush and Manmohan Singh set the process for the normalization of civil nuclear relations between the two countries in July 2005, and reaffirmed the way forward when the US President visited India the next March.

Terming the nuclear deal as a platform for a vibrant partnership, David Mulford then the US ambassador to India wrote in a national daily, "This transformed vision for US-India relations is widely embraced by our peoples and increasingly understood by our governments: a vigorous partnership between our two large democracies promises to help solve the difficult problems of our time, while fostering greater opportunities for

---

3   VIR Sanghvi in *Hindustan Times*, dated September 17, 2005.

prosperity and stability for citizens of both countries. Together we can also work to bring democratic values to the people of other countries who also seek to enjoy the freedoms and privileges of Indians and Americans."[4] A reference to Pakistan was too obvious to be missed in this statement. This inclining of the US towards India became more pronounced in the years to come.

Broad contours and the spectrum of US relations with India and Pakistan, as these developed over the decades and existed in 2010 – and have maintained the direction since then – are amply indicated in the four articles which appeared in the print media of the sub-continent during the first six months of the year. The excerpts are given in the sequence of their dateline.

Tayyab Siddiqui, a former Pakistani ambassador wrote in an article titled, 'Price of Partnership with the US', "There is a huge trust deficit acknowledged by both and hence, if this partnership has to prosper, the factors responsible for the credibility crisis need to be addressed by both sides.... For Pakistan, quite a few US initiatives soured the relationship. First and foremost has been the drone issue. The US unilaterally decided to employ drones..... President Obama knows too well that every partnership has a price. Pakistan has already paid more than its due share. The partnership can remain intact only if US performance and role matches Pakistan's. The US must positively respond to the issues critical for Pakistan's future.... The following provisions would be crucial in restoring the confidence and trust between the two allies: 1) US mediation on the Kashmir issue; 2) Offer to increase package for economic uplift; 3) Write- off the existing loans to provide Pakistan relief from the burden of foreign exchange and liabilities; 4) Adequate compensation for the families of civilian victims killed in drone attacks; 5) Urgent and positive consideration to nuclear cooperation along the Indian model".[5]

Chidanand Rajghatta wrote in *The Times of India* of January 17, 2010, "... The threat of jihadi take over is the ultimate American nightmare and the Pakistanis are adept at playing it, while camouflaging the fact that many jihadis are actually in uniform.... While there are several other smaller reasons for continued US patronage of Pakistan, one major immediate

4   David C Mulford in *The Times of India* dated July 30, 2007.
5   Tayyab Siddiqui in *DAWN* dated January 14, 2010.

reason is that Pakistan remains the most convenient logistical lifeline to US troops in Afghanistan. In effect, Pakistan has its foot on the American jugular in the region…. the fact is Pakistan is willing to play the game of brinkmanship better than others, certainly better than Washington. It is a brazen tactic that enables Islamabad to get away with continued support to the Taliban elements, even as the US fulminates helplessly…. Some things never change, and for now at least, despite its apparent irritation with its client state, Washington does not look like changing either".

The US secretary of defence Robert Gates arrived in India for a two-day visit on January 20, 2010. A part of the statement issued by him to the Indian media one day before read as, "Two months ago Dr. Manmohan Singh arrived in Washington for the first official state visit of the new US administration. In his welcoming remarks, Obama referred to the relationship between our countries as a defining partnership of the 21st century – a union between two of the world's great democracies. During my meetings with India's leaders this week, I look forward to solidifying these pillars – and strengthening a relationship indispensable to both our nations' future peace and prosperity".

The fourth citation relates to an article dated June 4, 2010 in the name of Hillary Clinton, the then US secretary of state. Parts of it read as, "India's rise is a defining storyline of early 21st century. And as President Barack Obama has said, India is an indispensable partner to the US. Given the complexity of the challenges we face and the values we share, the US – India partnership is critical to our mutual progress…. Apart from our cooperation on global and regional issues, the US also remains committed to a strong bilateral relationship with India, built on the ties that connect our governments, private sectors, civil societies, universities and citizens".[6]

The United Kingdom (UK)

It used to be said during the closing years of the nineteenth century and through the first half of the twentieth century that the sun never sets on the British Empire. Britain was indisputably the greatest imperial power in the world. The military strains and financial blow back of the First World War dimmed the sheen and glow of its vast possessions and resources base. Still, a much greater loss was yet to come a couple of decades later in the form of Second World War. By the time this six years long war

---

6   Hillary Clinton in *The Times of India* dated June 4, 2010.

finished in 1945; the UK economy was badly mauled, its human resources considerably diminished the colonial possessions in the process of getting disintegrated. Amongst the Allied Powers of the war, it was certainly reduced to the status of being behind the US in all respects; although the illusions and trappings of a great power continued for some more years. Over the next decade, the UK independently undertook two notable engagements on the international scene. The first one was the successful handling of the insurgency in Malaya by Templer, in the early fifties. The other related to the landing of Paratroops in Alexandria in response to the Egyptian move of nationalizing the Suez Canal. In fact, this led to the first Israel – Egypt war in 1956.

In the Indian sub-continent, the British appear to have very carefully planned their withdrawal strategy; given the long and peaceful struggle for independence. Their dealings with various entities in India, own domestic and foreign policies seem to have been based on two premises. One was to aim at keeping a foothold intact in this huge landmass for a host of geo-political reasons and the second concern was to remain an effective player in the Great Game – aimed at stopping southward expansion of the Russian empire. All this is duly reflected in its dealings with India and the newly created nation of Pakistan; as also before 1947, during the J&K Operations, in the UN debates and then through the cold war decades. In fact, the western policies for this region were basically fashioned by the UK and the US merely followed them; at least for a couple of decades up to the end of 1950s, after which the roles got reversed.

The British interests were clearly evident on their anti-India attitude and pro-Pak leanings during the Indo-Pak war in J&K which lasted from October 1947 to December 1948. Throughout this period, "The overall advice and encouragement by the British military establishment, both in Pakistan and in the UK, was unstinted. The Chief of Staff in London were convinced in the rather farfetched belief that India's long-term policy was to subjugate and incorporate Pakistan, which demanded every assistance to Pakistan Armed Forces. This was also the view of Field Marshal Montgomery, the then chief of the Imperial General Staff".[7] In the similar vein, Auchinleck wrote from New Delhi to his superiors in London on September 28, 1947, "I have no hesitation whatever in affirming that the

---

7   Lt.Gen Vijay Madan, "Jammu and Kashmir Operations, 1947-48: The Other Version", USI Journal July-September 1992, p. 318.

present Indian Cabinet are implacably determined to do all in their power to prevent the establishment of the Dominion of Pakistan on a firm basis. In this, I am supported by the unanimous opinion of my senior officers and indeed by all responsible British officers cognizant of the situation".[8]

In the overall analysis, it was not only the active role of British officers in Pakistan, which was detrimental to Indian interests. Their counterparts in India also contributed towards the same end by keeping the Indian political and military leadership on the desired course. This was achieved through a very effective mixture of advising, prodding, cajoling and cautioning. Britain had not yet come to terms with its diminishing status in the international power structure and in consonance with the geo-strategic perceptions; the Gilgit province continued to be of vital importance. If this area could not remain under British control after August 15, 1947, then it should be part of a more friendly and pliant State. For this, the ideal solution was for Jammu and Kashmir to become a part of Pakistan. If that was not possible; at least Gilgit should be under Pakistan's control with communications to the area secured. The UK complicity in the affairs of the Indian sub-continent achieved this objective successfully. Little wonder, Gilgit never became part of the so-called "Azad Kashmir"; but has always been administered as a Federal Territory by Pakistan.

After India went to the United Nations complaining against the Pakistani aggression in J&K, the course of debates there came as an eye-opening experience. The attitude of Western Powers - the UK and the US egged on by it - indicated by the stand taken by their representatives in the Security Council, created understandable consternation amongst the Indians. Reflecting this attitude, Alan Campbell-Jhonson the Press Attaché to Lord Mountbatten, recorded in his memoirs this entry on February 17, 1948, "Various suspicions are seeping in the minds of the Indian Government and the politically conscious public, which taken together, could well develop into a major unfriendly attack on Indo-British goodwill. In the first place there is bewilderment with the delay in the United Nations in accepting India's basic complaint that an aggression has taken place in Kashmir, hence grows the suspicion that the United Nations is being made the forum for the promotion of the international politics. As evidence of this the public attitude of the American and British delegates,

---

8   John Conell, "Auchinleck", London 1959, p. 920.

Warren Austin and Noel-Baker, are sighted. Both are wildly accused for being pro-Pakistan for a variety of un-edifying reasons."[9]

In the early nineties the records of the erstwhile India Office, London, were declassified. Some of these papers give an interesting indication of the manner in which important British officers were functioning. It appears that the senior British military commanders of the Indian forces and the British High Commissioner in India were operating together, more or less, as extensions of the same source. They were also working together to safeguard the UK, and by proxy the US, interests in the region. As the debates over Kashmir progressed in the United Nations Security Council and also the Cold War processes intensified; coupled with the Western perceptions of the Non Aligned Movement of which India was a founding and important member; the British very deftly and progressively handed over the dealings with India and Pakistan to the US and confined itself to a supportive role. It also remained a source of considerable satisfaction to Pakistan for the support and help provided, especially in the UN systems. There was hence no change in the broad policy contours followed by the British, in relation to the sub-continent, except for occasional advice to India to negotiate with Pakistan on Kashmir; which in fact meant a request for offering it ever more concessions. Even during the 1980s and 1990s when Pakistan had become an epicenter of terrorism in no uncertain terms and its state apparatus was exhibiting unmistakable fundamentalist tendencies; there was no discernible shift in the British policy. However, in consonance with its reputation of being a highly skilled trading nation, the economic ties with India did register improvement, particularly in commodities and military hardware.

It was only after the 9/11 terrorist attacks in the US, the resultant condemnation all over the civilized world and sharp reaction of the US, that the British started having a fresh look at Pakistan and calibrate its policy towards it accordingly. The next big change in this regard came in July 2005 when the London Metro was shaken by a series of blasts. This resulted in considerable loss of life and injuries and a huge public outcry. The UK visibly appeared to be reviewing policy and ties with Pakistan. The steady rise, over the years, of the Indian Diaspora in terms of economic and political clout may also have been a factor in this regard.

9   Alan Campbell Johnson, "Mission with Mountbatten", Robert Hale Ltd, London-1951, p.p. 286-87.

However, the most frank and candid statement on the Pakistani involvement in terrorist activities came from the British Prime Minister David Cameron when he publically accused Pakistan of running with the hare and hunting with the hounds in the war against terror. On his first visit to India on July 27, 2010, he addressed the IT audience at Infosys Technologies in Bangalore (now Bengaluru), where he spoke very forthrightly on the issue of terrorism. He insinuated Pakistan's involvement in the Mumbai 26/11 attacks, condemned its role in exporting terror and also said that Britain and India have both suffered from terrorism originating in Pakistan. Excerpts from this speech give an indication of the flow of his thoughts, "I am a new Prime Minister. I lead a new coalition government. And we are making a new start for Britain and its relationships around the world.... We cannot tolerate in any sense the idea that this country (Pakistan) is allowed to look both ways and is able, in any way, to promote the export of terror, whether to India or whether to Afghanistan or anywhere else in the world".[10]

That this direct and transparent speaking riled the Pakistani establishment is a different matter, but it certainly underlined a clear shift in the UK policy and an effort to distance itself from Pakistan. Over the past many years both US and UK are clearly reviewing their policies in respect of India and Pakistan, for better and worse respectively.

France is another country in the western world whose ties with the Indian sub-continent have been traditionally important. Historically speaking, after the recall of Dupleix (1697-1763), as the head of its Indian forces and possessions, in the middle of the eighteenth century, France really did not have a say in the Indian affairs. Also, its presence in colonial India had been reduced to a tiny pocket of Pondicherry (now Puducherry). Although it did not take sides in the first Indo-Pak confrontation in 1947-48; all the same as a permanent member of the UN Security Council, France voted with the other two western powers on Kashmir issue. Hence, her support for Pakistan and by implication, opposition to India can be construed. Beyond the UN; France tried to balance its relationship with both countries based on international situation, real politics and economic considerations. Occasionally it did make military sales to India, the Mirage 2000 aircrafts deal being an important item in this category. For over the last ten years its ties with India seem to have deepened and relations with

---

10   *The Times of India* dated July 31, 2010.

Pakistan somewhat dampened. The reasons for this are the increased economic clout of India, including strides in the fields of space, nuclear, science and technology. On the other hand, it has been seared by terrorist attacks in Paris and some other places in France; coupled with rising discontent and stridency amongst the Muslim population inhabiting the land, a large part of who are the residents of erstwhile colonies of France. In this perspective, it does consider Pakistan as a shielded sanctuary of terrorism and hence the tepidness in their current relationship. Thus, in the overall perspective of relations with India and Pakistan; as also the impact on developments in the sub-continent, the French factor does not have much impact.

On the other hand, the Russian shadow over this land mass has been looming large for almost two centuries now. As consolidation of the Indian possessions of the British moved into hinterland from the sea shores, by the nineteenth-century beginning; the Russian empire bordering the Northern highlands of India became a source of concern for the new Indian rulers. The first Anglo-Afghan war which lasted during 1839-42, proved disastrous for the British. This major setback further exacerbated their fear of the southward extension of influence and also expansion by the Russians. Activities of some neighboring Russian warlords and adventurers further fuelled these apprehensions. For over the next century the British remained much concerned about the prospects of the Russian southward expansion or extending their arc of influence this side. The actual or perceived Russian intentions and the counter moves by the British, in fact, forms core of the Great Game in this part of the world. The British policy has been succinctly reflected in two publications. One is a book named "Where Three Empires Meet", by F.E. Knight and the other is an official publication titled "Defence of India: Policy and Plans". In brief the British made it known that they would not tolerate any Russian occupation or influence south of Amu River in Afghanistan; as also in the northern possessions of the ruler of J&K, including far-flung principalities paying tributes to him. These were to be treated as a part of the British sphere of influence; including areas of Gilgit, Chitral, Hunza and even beyond. The British very zealously and effectively protected their interests in the entire region. This is evident from the way they reacted and responded with considerable speed to the threat to their small garrison located in far-flung Chitral, in 1895.

The ground situation saw no change till the Indian independence, and the Russians did not take sides during the Indo-Pak war in J&K in 1947-48. In the ensuing U.N. debates on Kashmir and with the western powers openly supporting Pakistani stand, it was the Russians (Soviet Union), which stood by India and also used its veto, in India's favour. Thus right from the beginning of independence, India found a dependable friend in the Russians. With Pakistan being firmly in the western camp and an active member of two of its alliances; her relations with Soviets were naturally at a low ebb. Also during this period, the Russian influence on India went much beyond taking sides in the U.N. Nehru was much impressed with the Soviet model of growth and desired to incorporate the basic ingredients of the Socialist pattern in India's development plans and growth strategy. This is markedly evident from the famous Industrial Policy Resolution of AICC in the mid-fifties, where it spoke of capturing the Commanding Heights of the economy. The Second Five Year Plan document and the direction it provided to the Indian economy were deeply influenced by the Soviet growth philosophy. The USSR also began effective aid programme to India in 1955. Also that year the two top Soviet leaders Khrushchev and Bulganin visited India on a well-advertised tour. During this trip, these eminent visitors along with Nehru famously spent some time in the Kashmir Valley. This was another token and pointer of the Russian support to Indian stand on Kashmir.

After the death of Nehru in 1964 and the change of guard in India, warmth between two countries reduced a bit. In the aftermath of 1965 Indo-Pak war; the Russian active interest leading to the Tashkent declaration next January effected peace between the two countries. The resultant vacation of hard won territories during the war was perceived in India to be against her interests and unduly favoring Pakistan; hence put a question mark over the Indo-Soviet relations. Thus, in the post Shastri period also ties with Russia were not very close till it came to reckoning again with Indira Gandhi firmly installed in New Delhi. It was during the developing crisis in the then East Pakistan, through the whole of 1971, that the relations between India and the Soviet Union scaled new heights. Faced with a very clear American support to Pakistan in this case, even in the face of mounting evidence of Pak atrocities in its Eastern wing; Indira Gandhi made a shrewd diplomatic move and executed an effective balancing act. The twenty-year Indo-Soviet Treaty of Peace, Friendship and Cooperation was signed in August 1971. This provided much-needed bulwark against the open US support to Pakistan; gave India considerable independence of action as also a reliable source of military hardware supplies. India's stunning victory in the December 1971 war with Pakistan resulting in the creation of Bangladesh further enhanced the contours of this relationship. The Soviet Union again emerged as a good friend in need for India.

Another important phase of Russian involvement in affairs of the sub-continent came following the Saur Revolution in Afghanistan in April 1978; which brought a communist backed regime in Kabul for the first time. To steady deteriorating conditions in the country; the Russian military intervened in December 1979 and stayed in Afghanistan for almost ten years till its final withdrawal in February 1989. During this period the Russians saw four rulers in Afghanistan; namely Nur Mohammad Taraki, Hafizullah Amin, Babrak Karmal and Najeebullah. But neither the local communist cadres nor the presence of military force could provide peace and proper governance in the country and the tribal, as well as ethnic connections, proved more powerful. These were further supplemented by the insurgency generated and fuelled by US-Pak joint efforts. After the Soviet troops left Afghanistan, the Americans also lost interest and pulled out of the country; leaving the field wide open to Pakistan.

The Soviet military's departure from Afghanistan was not an isolated occurrence, as the covert operations and resistance groups launched jointly by US and Pakistan were not solely responsible for this development; but it also signified a deeper malaise in the whole system of governance in the USSR. The inexorable march of events started in fact on March 11, 1985 when Mikhail Gorbachev was elected as General Secretary of the Politburo. He was eighth, and the last, leader of the Soviet Union. Soon the process of unraveling of the union began; culminating six years later in December 1991. The mighty Soviet Union or the USSR, with vast territories, massive military might and huge resources; disintegrated into fifteen separate countries. Also, thus ended almost five decades of cold war which had engulfed the two superpowers, and their allies, since the end of Second World War. This break up transformed the world political scenario leading to a reformulation of alliances and groupings all over the globe.

On December 25, 1991, Russia, undoubtedly premier amongst the 15 newly formed independent countries, came into being again; when the

Soviet flag was lowered from Kremlin, in Moscow, for the last time and replaced with the pre-revolutionary Russian flag. The new Russian state started the painful process of shoring up its economy, finding its feet in the comity of nations and building a new set of relations. It took almost a decade for it to stabilize. In the meantime the process of liberalization of Indian economy had started; spearheaded by Prime Minister Narasimha Rao and the Finance Minister Dr. Manmohan Singh. The new Russian state established effective and cordial relations with the resurgent Indian economy. It also made efforts to improve ties with Pakistan.

That is where the current direction of Russia's relations with India and Pakistan stands. It is mostly dealings on opportunity basis, and does not reflect any historical baggage. Russia, of course, has been quite concerned about the insurgency and separatism in Chechnya; which it has effectively tried to contain. Therefore to that extent it is wary of getting close to nations sponsoring terrorism; in which category Pakistan is certainly included.

India and China are undoubtedly two of the world's oldest civilizations. There is historical evidence of some famous travelers coming to India from China in the first millennium, in quest of learning and in search of Buddhist scriptures. But, this number remained very small and also it was a one-way traffic which did not develop into any meaningful exchange between the two cultures. Thereafter, even this little interaction dried up. As the empires, dynasties and feudal order developed in both regions; these followed different trajectories according to the local genius. The Chinese concepts of warfare were considerably influenced by the teachings of Sun-Tzu and her politico-administrative culture dominated by Confucius. Whereas in India; the war strategies and governance principles were greatly impacted by ancient scriptures and the concepts of Chanakya. In historical terms, all the three persons existed in the same time frame; and centuries before the beginning of Christian era. However, both countries were victims of British imperialism during the nineteenth and first half of twentieth century; with the Chinese also suffering under the Japanese occupation for ten years ending with the Second World War. With India becoming independent and Pakistan surfacing as a new country in the sub-continent in August 1947; and communists coming to power in China in 1949; the three nations emerged on the world scene almost simultaneously.

Right from the beginning of its independence India held a hand of friendship towards China; with the new state of Pakistan firmly an ally and also under the influence of western bloc. India also acquiesced, and many scholars of international relations believe wrongly, to the Chinese occupation of Tibet. The mid-fifties was a high period of good relations between these two countries. This was the time of singing high praises of the five principals of peaceful co-existence, the "Panchsheel". But, within few years the bonhomie gave rise to acrimony and mutual suspicion when India realized the extent of Chinese perfidy. Seventeen percent of the territory of the erstwhile princely state of J&K; which stood at 2.20 lakh square kilometers in 1947, had been surreptitiously and illegally occupied by China in the Aksai Chin area of Ladakh. Instead of vacating this land as demanded by India, China raised further claims and disputed many areas on the Indo-China border. This bitterness and estrangement led to a clash between the two armies almost all along the northern borders of India, from Ladakh to Arunachal Pradesh, during October- November 1962. For a host of reasons, the Indian army did not do well in this clash of arms, was overwhelmed and worsted by the Chinese counterparts. This was certainly the lowest point in the Indo-China relations and for over a quarter of a century next; there was practically no meaningful interaction between the two countries.

The situation in relation to Pakistan was entirely different. Working on the old maxim of the enemy's enemy is a friend; Pakistan was quick to grab this opportunity to upgrade relations with China and thus began a partnership which has only turned stronger over the decades. The first substantial and tangible achievement of this new found friendship materialized in the form of China-Pakistan agreement of March 2, 1963, demarcating the boundary between China's Sinkiang and "the contiguous areas the defence of which is under the actual control of Pakistan". This pact itself, by virtue of which two percent territory of old J&K under illegal occupation of Pakistan was unauthorizedly transferred to China for building the Karakoram highway linking the two countries; raises the question of eventual fate of the said land in case of India and Pakistan arriving at a final solution in relation to J&K. Herein both China and Pakistan agreed that "after the settlement of the Kashmir dispute between Pakistan and India, the sovereign authority concerned will reopen negotiations with the Government of China on the boundary so as to sign a formal treaty to replace the present agreement". The reference here to the ultimate "sovereign authority" is always pregnant with considerable implications. This agreement also opened a land route between the two countries.

The next important happening in the chronology of events was the Indo-Pak war of 1965; during which even though China did not materially help Pakistan but its posturing created an impression of being a reliable supporter. After that the ties between the two saw an upward swing in the early seventies when Pakistan became a conduit for establishing an American contact with China. The Pakistani channel, through General Yahya Khan and Bhutto, bore fruit when Henry Kissenger, the American National Security Advisor, made a secret trip to Beijing in mid 1971. This opening resulted in the Presidential visit by Richard Nixon to China in February 1972. During the 1971 crisis leading to the Indo-Pak war and creation of Bangladesh; the sub-continent seemed to be polarized around India-USSR axis and Pak-US-China grouping. Whereas Russian assistance to India and the American support to Pakistan were open and also quantifiable through this period; the Chinese very craftily made only the right noises and prudish posturing.

Over the next two decades, as Pakistan struggled first to meet its internal crisis situations and later got involved in the developing Afghanistan imbroglio, the Chinese were deeply immersed in tackling the post-Mao situation in the country and the resultantly fast-moving chain of events there. It was only in the beginning of the nineties that the Chinese communist leadership again became confident of itself and the future course of action in the political and economic fields. This time also saw China becoming an emerging economy to reckon with; as well as efforts to project its influence among the Afro-Asian countries. Pakistan, after the Russian military withdrawal and with the Americans also losing interest there; got heavily involved in the affairs of Afghanistan. This coupled with its ever-present hostility towards India and deep involvement in the J&K militancy; made it look more and more towards China – which by now had acquired the wherewithal to offer meaningful help. Thus in this decade, Pakistan was a grateful recipient of the Chinese largesse in the shape of considerable military hardware, advanced fighter aircrafts, missiles and nuclear technology. Towards the end of May 1999, in the middle of Kargil war, the world was astonished to find the then Pak Army Chief General Pervez Musharraf in Beijing. The technology transfer of sensitive nature was often carried out surreptitiously and through questionable channels-and also gratefully accepted. Notwithstanding the substantial American aid and financial grants; Pakistan's Defence and Foreign Policy establishment has done well for itself in getting such handsome support from the other side too. The Chinese obviously had medium and long-term interests in Pakistan; which also included balancing the rise of India.

In this connection, it would be notable to recall the views of two prominent Indian analysts expressed in 2007, which remain relevant even today. Commenting on the Chinese intentions in the sub-continent, the doyen of Indian strategic thinkers – K Subrahmanyam opined, "China has been assisting Pakistan in its nuclear weapons acquisition from 1976…. Understandably Chinese reaction to Indian nuclear test in 1998 was hostile. There are reports that Chinese personnel helped Pakistan to conduct its own test and were present at the Chagai test site…. China's strategy does not appear to be one of direct confrontation with India. By arming Pakistan with nuclear weapons, China is using Islamabad to counter India….. The Chinese strategy of dominating Asia, which all other major powers view with concern, needs India to be tied down perpetually by a nuclear-armed Pakistan".[11] Another identical opinion was expressed as, "China appears to be intent upon putting the Pakistan monkey on the shoulder of India to keep bothering us on long-term basis. That is the main reason why China is interested in keeping alive in Pakistan psyche the possibility of strategic weapons parity with India."[12]These two views very aptly sum up the Chinese intentions in so liberally assisting Pakistan, as the significant imperative of balancing India remains alive and prominent in Chinese strategic and military thinking perspectives.

Pakistan on its part takes the relationship with China very seriously; not so much in the beginning for a decade from 1951 when the two countries established diplomatic relations, but more particularly after the Indo-China border confrontations in 1962. The two came very close next year with the 1963 agreement resulting into the construction of the Karakoram highway by China. Since the 1965 war with India, in which China backed Pakistan, the latter has always shown complete faith in the Chinese friendship and treated it as an invaluable ally. So much so

---

11 K Subrahmanyam, in *The Times of India* dated August 28, 2007.

12 Ambassador S.K.Singh – Governor of Arunachal Pradesh – in a seminar in Jammu University on April 5, 2007.

that, going against its grain of spawning and supporting militancy in neighbouring countries; Pakistan went out of the way and placed many restrictions on the Uighur insurgents operating from its territory bordering Xinjiang province of China. President Hu Jintao of China visited Pakistan on November 23, 2006, and during his stay said the two countries have nurtured their relations through all manner of changes in the international arena to remain, "good neighbors, close friends, trusted partners and dear brothers.... An example of harmonious coexistence between countries of different civilizations".[13] Not much wonder that the two countries often describe their relationship as "higher than the mountains and deeper than the oceans". However, it was left to the successor of Hu to launch the biggest and most ambitious of the Chinese projects in Pakistan; the China-Pakistan Economic Corridor, generally referred to by its acronym CPEC. Given its geo-strategic importance, the sheer size of financial outlays and security implications for the India and Pakistan, the CPEC needs to be mentioned in some details.

Even though various components and different contours of the CPEC have been under mutual parleys and considerations for over ten years; current form of the project came up for detailed discussions amongst important functionaries in Pakistan during May 2013. Six months later the Chinese government clearly stated its intentions to finance these schemes. During the visit of President Xi Jinping to Pakistan, an agreement on CPEC was signed on April 20, 2015, signaling commencement of work on $ 46 billion worth clutch of plans. These include four major sectors of Port projects, Roadways infrastructure projects, Railways infrastructure projects and energy sector projects. These have horizontal and vertical linkages with other related sectors too.

The CPEC is also considered an extension of China's ambitious proposal of 21st Century Silk Road initiative and One Belt One Road (OBOR) plans; of which Pakistan is an enthusiastic supporter and partner. Thus CPEC becomes an important and integral component of the Chinese plan of international economic connectivity. Also, the plan is likely to have military dimensions as well and this would be a matter of considerable concern to India. The CPEC takes under its wings a number of important projects currently under construction at a total cost of, as already mentioned, $ 46 billion. The stated intention is to rapidly expand and

13 FRONTLINE, dated December 15, 2006.

upgrade infrastructure in Pakistan, as also deepen and broaden economic ties between the two countries. The extent of this massive infusion of capital can be gauged from the fact that in case all the planned projects are implemented; it is estimated that the total value of these schemes would be equal to all foreign direct investment in Pakistan since 1970.

Major planned infrastructural projects under the CPEC would cover the length and breadth of Pakistan. It would eventually link the port city of Gwadar in south-west Pakistan, with the north-western autonomous region of Xinjiang in China through a large network of highways and railways. A sum of $ 11 billion is earmarked for these schemes. In this package is included the proposed construction of eleven hundred kilometers long roads between the cities of Karachi and Lahore. In another significant road connectivity plan; it is proposed to completely overhaul and reconstruct the Karakoram highway connecting Rawalpindi and the Chinese border in the north. Important trunk roads connecting this corridor are also included for renovation and up gradation. Similarly, Karachi-Peshawar rail line is to be taken up for improvement and its phase-I proposed to be completed by 2019. There is also a proposal to extend the Pakistan railway network to connect with China's Southern Xinjiang Railway in Kashgar. The CPEC also includes a large network of pipelines to transport liquefied natural gas and oil as a part of the project. In short, this is intended to transform the face of infrastructural facilities in Pakistan.

While undoubtedly it will provide a huge stimulus for economic growth in Pakistan; the CPEC would also give China three important geo-strategic benefits. This would be the shortest route to the Indian Ocean available to China and in addition, it would give it the advantage of avoiding the straits of Malacca. The CPEC provides improved access to western China and neatly fits into its plans to upgrade infrastructure in this part of the country. In addition, China would get a new corridor and improved access to the Central Asian Republics (CAR). This also, however, raises important strategic issue with India. According to an Indian scholar, "Xi's refusal to delink the PoK (AJK) from the CPEC route-map is sufficient proof that he has now categorically reversed his predecessor's decision to treat the relevant Sino-Pakistani border agreement of 1963 as a 'temporary' settlement. In 1963, China had committed itself to renegotiating that border agreement – with India (not Pakistan) – if the Indians were to gain 'ownership' of the PoK under an Indo-Pakistani settlement in the future.... It is likely that the ongoing negotiations between China and India, with regard to the western sector of their disputed boundary, will now be hostage to Beijing's revised view that Islamabad has indisputable sovereign jurisdiction over the PoK (AJK). The CPEC route-map covers the adjacent 'Northern Areas' too; in Pakistan's discourse, these areas fall outside AJK (and therefore outside the PoK) which is of concern to India".[14]

An initiative as large as the CPEC naturally envisages involvement of a good number of Chinese private companies and other agencies; requiring deployment of considerable number of their personnel of different ranks and status to reside and work in Pakistan over extended periods. This inherently raises concerns for their safety and security, not only in the restive regions of Pakistan but also in most parts of that country. The overall security situation prevailing in Pakistan does not inspire confidence. This is currently being seen both as a challenge as well as an opportunity by the Pak army. The army has come forward with a larger role for itself in this regard and is also simultaneously eyeing a part of the big cake. It has already proposed positioning of a separate division to secure the Karakoram Highway and people working there; in the Gilgit-Baltistan area. The issue of security of the Chinese workers in Balochistan, right from the Gwadar port to the north also remains a matter of genuine worry.

With such enormous infusion of capital in the system, a substantial portion of which is set aside for infrastructure development – which in turn would mean the creation of a large number of new jobs, the Pakistan economy should get a big boost. The CPEC deal can almost be a game changer for the dynamics of the Pak economy. To derive maximum benefit from it, a concerted national effort is required with all institutions of the State working in tandem and in unison. That also makes it incumbent upon all provincial governments and all sections of the society to provide unstinted support to the projects and efforts undertaken under the banner of CPEC. This part relating to a collective national endeavor is not an easy thing to manage, as protests, dissenting voices and controversies are already becoming manifested in different parts and sections of Pakistan.

The foremost opposition emanates from the Baloch nationalists, who have not taken well to the whole idea of this project. Their main objection

---

14   P S Suryanarayana in BORDER AFFAIRS of October- December 2015, p. 8.

and worry is about the region not getting commensurate benefits from the federal investments and induction of resources. Hence the repeated allegations of Balochistan being exploited by Islamabad for its resources and commensurate investments not ploughing back into the province. It remains to be seen whether the federal response to this approach remains security based operations – as hereto before – or changes to finding a political solution for the outstanding issues. The latter course would be beneficial in the long run, but is certainly time-consuming. And there lies the rub. In the long run, success of the CPEC would also largely depend on how the Pakistani government is able to deal with the Baloch sentiments of the region; which certainly appear to be negative at this stage.

Some disgruntled voices are also heard from the Gilgit-Baltistan (G-B) region. This area lies in the northern end of the Pakistani controlled territory along the Karakoram highway, and to that extent is the beginning point of the CPEC from the Chinese end. Their grouse is somewhat similar in content to that of the Baloch nationalists; in that the people of the region want to be clearly told as to what advantages this region would get from various schemes under the CPEC. It appears that as at present there is not much transparency or sufficient availability of information on the subject. Unless Islamabad handles this region with sensitivity and compassion; the protests and the dissenting voices may grow stronger.

Also in the Provincial Assembly of Khyber Pakhtun Khwah (KPK) the members have leveled allegations that the alignment of the proposed multi-billion dollar highway under the CPEC is being changed to the disadvantage of the province. Even though the federal government has assured of no bias against this state, the matter is far from being resolved and the issue is still simmering. Controversies are also surfacing alleging that in respect of many major components of CPEC, particularly important infrastructural projects, the financial closures have not yet taken place. This means lurking doubts about the very credibility of such schemes and this can have a debilitating effect on other components. Some doubts are expressed regarding full funding of certain important undertakings and in such cases it is not clear as to where the balance of finances would come from; as these details have not been tied up so far. The basic problem at the root of all such criticism and negative fallout lies in the fact that the whole of CPEC project does not seem to have been fully worked out along with respective linkages; and put in the public domain.

An oft-repeated criticism generally encountered in Pakistan, relates to allegations emanating from other provinces and accusing Punjab of trying to garner maximum advantages from the CPEC. No doubt Punjab has dominated the armed forces, bureaucracy as well as public life since 1947 and such imputations are therefore not without a basis. Punjab has certainly garnered, over the decades, a major chunk of national resources much beyond its legitimate share based on accepted parameters. In addition, it has not done much to alleviate such apprehensions.

It is also true that in the national discourse of Pakistan these days, the CPEC is being projected as a sure cure for all the ills of Pakistan. No doubt that in its implementation these projects entail lot of good for the country and, if handled properly, it may even overhaul the Pak economy; but this cannot be a panacea for all the problems of Pakistan. It is in this background also that some influential voices in the country have started cautioning the policy makers of the nation not to put all eggs in one, the Chinese, basket; the consequences of which can be unpredictable and even dangerous in future. The grain of caution is very clear; do not snap off dealings and relations with other important countries irretrievably because of improved economic ties with China. In this milieu the most practicable option for Pakistan would be to carefully analyze all aspects of the CPEC before plunging headlong into it; as also to keep alternatives open and in focus.

India has been steadily engaging with China, particularly during the last two decades. There have been a series of interactions between the two countries at different levels, right up to the highest quarters. The trade ties, diplomatic discourses, educational exchanges and even military engagements have shown incremental improvements. The border talks too have been taking place at regular intervals. But the progress on all these counts does not appear to be substantive in nature and going beyond a point. There seems to be a non visible glass ceiling in the mutual relations, which has not been breached so far. The parameters and factors affecting India-China connections have been very prudently commented upon by learned and expert analysts in the two articles, excerpts from which are given hereinafter.

The comments of Teresita and Howard Schaffer, both former US ambassadors, on the contours of India- China relationship are very perceptive. In the course of a detailed analysis they made the following observations, "The India-China relationship is still asymmetrical. One Chinese observer commented that neither country was top priority for the other. The disparity in their trade relations tells the story: China is India's largest partner for merchandise trade; India is China's 10th partner. Despite this imbalance, Chinese thinkers, and apparently the Chinese government, take India far more seriously than they once did....Almost all argued that China's Comprehensive National Power (CNP) exceeded India's by a factor of three or four, and that the gap was widening....One observer noted that India treated China as an outsider in South Asia and the Indian Ocean; China did the same to India in East Asia. It was clear that China's India-watchers had noted India's 'look East' policy but did not particularly welcome it. They predictably dismissed India's fears of Chinese military bases on the Indian Ocean rim. The South China Sea was a major preoccupation, and our Chinese interlocutors pointedly dismissed any notion that India (or indeed the US) had legitimate interests there....For China, the easiest arena for India-China collaboration is global, both their interactions at the United Nations and on such issues as climate change. Bilateral issues are much more difficult, and regional cooperation almost non-existent....China has not yet accepted India's global role, and has kept India at arm's length when it comes to regional issues. Cooperation on multilateral global issues is valued both in Beijing and in Delhi, but does not seem to touch the core issues of India's role as a world power."[15]

Also, while delivering the 31st USI National Security Lecture on December 9, 2015, on the topic, "China's Growing Influence in India's Neighborhood and Implications for India", Kanwal Sibal, former Foreign Secretary of India, mentioned the following points which have impact on the two countries' mutual relationship, "India and China have an over 4,000 kilometers long unsettled border. China has not only occupied Indian territory but also lays claim to more of it....Some of India's neighbors are China's neighbors also. Pakistan, Nepal, Bhutan and Myanmar have contiguity with China. Therefore China could legitimately claim that developing relations with them was just a natural course and should not worry anyone. China has steadily expanded its influence in Nepal.... It is strongly entrenched in Bangladesh.... Sri Lanka has enjoyed close relations with China traditionally....Maldives is strengthening its relationship with China.... China has made deep inroads into Myanmar.... China is

---

15 Teresita and Howard Schaffer in article titled "Still Seriously Mismatched" in The Hindu dated June 7, 2012.

now seeking to extend its influence in Afghanistan....China would have interest in limiting the expansion of Indian influence eastwards to the extent it can by using neighbors to tie India down in the sub-continent.... China is today Pakistan's biggest defence partner. It panders to Pakistan's obsession with parity with India to the extent possible, at the core of which lies the transfer of nuclear and missile technologies to Pakistan....India is the only power in Asia that can stand up to it in the long run. India can pose a stronger challenge to China's assertion of its great power status in unilateral ways."[16]

Even after the lapse of few years; the two analyses appear refreshingly contemporary. On a different plane; the stability of India, in the coming decades, is ensured and based on the twin factors of deep-rooted democracy and an inclusive model of national growth. There is, on the other hand, inherent divergence of the Chinese growth model. The absence of democratic institutions is amplified by scant regard for the environment in matters related with national development. These could back-fire and recoil. All this, of course, is in the realm of future.

In its dealings with India; at times one does get an impression that China may be working on the celebrated maxim of Sun Tzu, the famous sixth century BC Chinese strategic thinker, which postulates, "Supreme excellence consists in breaking the enemy's resistance without fighting". Of course, there are always the ponderous possibilities in the future of the triangular relationship between India, Pakistan and China. As at present these appear to be on a divergent course.

16 USI Journal, October-December 2015, pp 441-448.

CHAPTER - X

The Peace Process - Internal Dimensions

The Rise of India (Economy, Military Power, Nuclear March over Pakistan)

The process of improving relations between India and Pakistan has constantly been engaging the attention of leaders of the two countries, may be more in India than in Pakistan, ever since Pakistan came into being on August 14, 1947. There were flashes of success in the bilateral engagements in the initial stages as is evident from the Nehru-Liaqat pact in early 1950, and the signing of Indus Water Treaty during the 1960.

The Tashkent Declaration of January 1966 and the Simla Agreement of July 1972 can also be taken as efforts of the two countries to forge a more cordial association; but except for the IWT, no measure in regard to mutual cooperation has stood the test of time. On the other hand, the two nations have fought four wars in 1947-48, 1965, 1971 and 1999. The grim and long shadow of these armed conflicts has further clouded the prospects of good neighborly connections. The scenario has been further muddled by the continuing militancy in J&K, sponsored and abetted by Pakistan since 1989; for almost three decades now. The widespread violence thus generated over this period, has left in its wake a gory trail of loss of lives, limbs and injuries as also considerable destruction of property and mental trauma to the people of the State. To curb this menace of cross-border infiltration and the scourge of militancy, some efforts – though not very successful – were made in the past; particularly in the latter half of 1990 onwards. Four of these do stand out to merit a mention.

In the backdrop of the then Prime Minister Narasimha Rao's remark that sky is the limit to tackle the issue of Kashmir, the first of these efforts took place. In 1996, the Hizbul Mujahideen commander Imran Rahi constituted the Forum for Permanent Resolution of Kashmir (FPRK), which consisted of three well known militant leaders like, Babar Badr, Bilal Lodhi and Master Aslam Dar. The leaders of this forum met the Union Home Minister once, and after a couple of weeks nothing much was heard of this initiative nor was the ground level impact of this good beginning much significant. Probably the 1996 Assembly elections overtook this event; and with Farooq Abdullah's National Conference getting a massive mandate in this electoral contest, New Delhi practically left the handling of the internal situation in J&K in the hands of the new Chief Minister. The second attempt at establishing peace was made in July 2000, when the Hizb commander Majid Dar came over ground in Srinagar and announced a ceasefire with the intention of meaningful negotiations leading to peace in the State. This group also held preliminary parleys with the Union Home Secretary and his officers, in the first week of August in Srinagar. But, before this bold move could fructify in the more tangible outcome, the ceasefire was called off from across the border by Hizb high-command; presumably under intense pressure from the ISI in Pakistan.

The third, and very potent, attempt to improve conditions in the State and give a push to the internal peace process was initiated with the installation of Mufti Mohammad Sayeed as Chief Minister of the State in November 2002; for a period of three years as per agreement with the coalition partner the Congress. Mufti's regime made a perceptible difference in relaxing the general atmosphere in the State and making the life of the common man more comfortable. There were unmistakable signs of a change for the better. Another useful effort in this direction was made towards the end on January 2004, when a group of Hurriyat leaders headed by its chairman, Moulvi Abbas Ansari, met the Deputy Prime Minister L.K. Advani and also called on the Prime Minister the next day. Another meeting of this group with Advani took place after two months. The third, and probably more fruitful, interaction in the series slated by the parties in the month of June could not take place as the then ruling NDA government at the centre lost the Parliamentary elections in May that year.

Beyond these not fully ripe measures, no useful attempts have been tried to positively impact and improve the internal dimensions of peace and tranquility in the State. This, notwithstanding two significant events aimed at helping the population on both sides of the LoC; in J&K and the PoK. Bus service and trade was started between these two regions of the erstwhile single State of J&K; crossing at Kaman Post near Uri, in the Valley in April 2005 and at Chakan Da Bagh, near Poonch in Jammu division, in October 2008. These steps could have considerably improved the atmospherics of the internal and external situations, if the other connected and intended measures were also put in place; which - for one reason or the other – did not happen. Therefore, the crossing points near Uri and Poonch have remained an end in themselves; at best a reasonably good foundation to build upon and enlarge the peace process at a more opportune moment.

A question which invariably comes up in any discussion related to generating a more conducive atmosphere in J&K, is how and why a growing and emerging power like India; with solid democratic foundations, a positive demographic profile, an expanding world-level economy and considerable military muscle has not succeeded in bringing peace to its northern most state of J&K. First a brief look at what this country has achieved in the last seventy years or so.

Indian Development Story

India is the seventh largest country in the world by area and with over 1.2 billion people; it is also the second most populated country. In addition, it is the most populous democracy in the world. These factors by themselves would catapult India into playing a big role in the world politics. Added to them are its geo-strategic location; a long coastline and sharing of land borders with Pakistan, China, Nepal, Bhutan, Myanmar and Bangladesh. The erstwhile princely state of Jammu and Kashmir also had common borders with Afghanistan before independence – the famous Wakhan corridor. India is also a proud inheritor of one of the oldest civilizations in the world. But, on the negative side; it has been under foreign dominations for almost a thousand years; the last being the British and from their colonial control India secured freedom in 1947. Since then it has embarked on an independent and neutral course to script its destiny in a democratic, inclusive and humane manner – taking along the multitude of religions, casts and creeds. A massive socio-political experiment is underway here for the uplifting and prosperity of such large and variegated population; which has rightly been termed as a pluralistic, multi-lingual and multiethnic society. Interestingly, this massive change is being attempted under the umbrella of a functioning, noisy and raucous democracy.

At the time of independence India was primarily an agrarian economy; having mostly missed the industrial revolution and its benefits because it had been under a colonial rule for almost two centuries. Therefore in its urge to accelerate the developmental process, it successfully leapfrogged over the industrial phase and is today recognized as one of the front-ranking nations in the field of Information Technology. During the first four decades as a free country, the Indian saga was largely influenced by the socialistic pattern and model of growth; and hence was also encumbered by those parameters. However, it opened up the economy in the beginning of 1990s; and since then the process of economic reforms has been almost continuous – moving the country towards a free market system with emphasis on foreign trade and also direct investment flows. Many Indian companies and business houses have already made their presence in the world market and more entities are joining their ranks. For over the last two decades, India's economic growth has been particularly impressive and today it is one of the fastest growing economies in the world; with significant business ties with major financial powers across the globe.

Since independence India has maintained cordial relations with most of the countries; the only exceptions being China and Pakistan with whom it has had border-related problems. Right from the beginning, it has been a champion of independence movements of the colonized nations across Asian and African continents. It also played a leading role in the formation of Non-Aligned Movement along with Indonesia, Egypt and Yugoslavia. Today it can boast of having strong ties with most of the important nations in the world; with active membership in a number of significant world and regional groupings. It is a nuclear power having the third largest standing army in the world and a high military spending nation - incurring one of the largest defence expenditure to service the acquisitions of modern military hardware. India has developed, over the years, wide-ranging defence relations with Russia, France, Israel and USA. Indian space technology is one of the most advanced amongst the front ranking nations. It is already a regional power; with the potential and ambitions of projecting itself on the larger world stage.

In spite of an impressive growth graph, the country is also struggling to ensure sufficient food security, health services and education facilities to its burgeoning population; in addition to the challenge of finding shelter for all – despite significant economic performance in the recent decades. Poverty is still an endemic affliction here, which must be tackled on a priority basis; so is the need to regulate a high population growth. In addition to facing these challenges head-on; India is also struggling with three major internal security issues of Naxalism in some states, insurgencies in its northeastern region and Pakistan inspired and aided militancy in J&K with its attendant collaterals still existing in the Valley. If India has to realize its full development potential and also meet the power aspirations; then it should quickly manage the poverty-related matters as also successfully handle the security challenges facing the country. The main issue in the latter category is related to Kashmir. Here, Pakistan has remained a factor right from the beginning in 1947. Seven decades and four wars later; the problems with Pakistan over J&K have not yet been resolved. During this period the internal conditions in Pakistan have steadily deteriorated instead of improving. On all parameters, there appears to be a downward slide. From democracy to development, education to environment, health to housing and security to sectarianism; the picture is dismal. That country is almost in the throes of a serious existentialist dilemma.

Pakistan Internal Situation

The condition of Pakistan is very much anomalous to that of a younger brother of an erstwhile undivided joint family; where he sets up a new home with his part of the family fortunes – but all the same is not satisfied with what comes to his share and aspires for more. Not only the simmering of discontent but also the howls of protests and demonstrable use of force to take possession of what he thinks should belong to him. In this case, the situation is more complex because the dis-satisfied party is not an individual but a whole nation-state; and that too with considerable internal difficulties, not able to firmly plant its feet on the ground and still struggling with its core identity even after seven decades. "That Pakistan today struggles still with a coherent national identity is widely acknowledged.... Pakistan's key problems: its failure to withstand military dictatorships; its uneven social and economic development; its severe ethnic divisions, and even the pursuit of questionable foreign policies. Yet these explanations are treated, for the most part, as *causes* of Pakistan's fragility as a nation-state rather than as *symptoms* of the underlying uncertainty about its identity – an uncertainty that stems from the lack of consensus over Islam....

Exploring the differences grounded in these competing conceptions of 'reformed' and 'corrupted' Islam might not only illuminate the multiple meanings attached to Islam in Pakistan, but also explain how Islam as a key component of Pakistan's national identity came to be a divisive rather than a unitary force.... Most of Pakistan's politicians, especially in the early years, lacked a political base in the regions and were unsure of democracy, thus leaving them open to the appeal of authoritarian rule. However, their doubts over the fundamental question of Pakistan's national identity and of the place of Islam in defining that identity were no more acute than those of their military counterparts."[1]

The difficulties of Pakistan were also compounded by the assertions and exclusivity of not only different ethnic identities but also 'class' interests – the latter exacerbated further by inability of various governments to implement meaningful land reforms as also improve agrarian relations. Urdu was practically imposed as the official and the link language over a population which consisted of Bengali, Punjabi, Sindhi, Balochi and Pashtun segments; each speaking its own different mother tongue and justifiably proud of their respective heritage. The distinct association of Urdu with the migratory Muslim population from U.P. and Bihar, in India, and the fact that they enjoyed greater political and administrative clout further complicated the situation. The whole confusing and often conflicting scenario has been competently described by Farzana Shaikh as, "Soon after independence conflicting discourses of Pakistan as both a point of destination for Indian Muslims and a consolidated centre of Muslim power accentuated tensions between Muslim migrants and indigenous groups, each armed with rival versions of 'the Pakistani'. On the one side were the moral claims of Muslim refugees from India, who sought to establish their pre-eminence as 'real' Pakistanis by comparing their migration to the archetypal Muslim exodus (*hijrat*) led by the Prophet Muhammad to establish the first Islamic community in seventh-century Arabia. On the other, there prevailed the political logic of so-called 'sons of the soil', who appealed to their demonstrable (if sometimes imagined) roots in the regions of Pakistan.... These communities faced not only the uncertainties of defining themselves as Pakistanis in a land to which they had hitherto belonged simply as Punjabis, Sindhis, Balochis or Pashtuns, but also the challenge of positioning themselves in relation to more than 7 million

---

1 Farzana Shaikh, *Making Sense of Pakistan,* Hurst & Company, London, 2009, pp. 9,10 and 12.

Muslim refugees from India who had arrived claiming an equal right to be Pakistani....wide-ranging implications were reflected in the civil war that led to the break-up of the country in 1971. They centered on the attempts by the Bengali majority to strengthen an ethnic definition of the Pakistani in opposition to others that favored an identity more closely tied to Islam.... Pakistan's altered contours after 1971 precipitated fresh uncertainties over Pakistani identity, which now assumed more complex forms.... where there emerged a strong shift in favor of more plural expressions of Pakistani identity.... The hardening of the state's Islamic identity in the 1980s intensified these concerns, but also sharpened sectarian differences that fostered the preference for a certain type of Sunni sectarian Islam as the defining feature of the 'universal' Pakistani.... Its consequences have contributed towards the dismantling of institutional protection for the country's non-Muslim minorities and fuelled doubts about their claim to qualify as 'real Pakistanis'."[2] It is in this background of consolidating Islamic solidarity with ethnic identity – more so in the times of General Zia-ul Haq when the question of the primacy of Islam was at the peak – that the political mobilization of Urdu speaking migrants from India should be seen. The formation of Mohajir Quomi Movement (MQM), its quick spread in the Sindh Province particularly around Karachi area, and political clout it acquired in the last two decades of the last century becomes far easier to understand when seen through this prism.

On the creation of Pakistan; the towering personality of Jinnah and also his proclivity for directly controlling the levers of power, were the two major and immediate reasons which prevented the laying of strong democratic foundations in the country. The matters got more complicated, in this respect, by the early dependence of the state on the military when Pakistan sent its tribal hordes followed by armed forces in Kashmir, during the later part of 1947. The death of Jinnah in September 1948 and the assassination of Prime Minister Liaqat Ali Khan, a couple of years thereafter, further loosened whatever little roots the democratic process had struck in there. In the resultant political vacuum the landowning groups, tribal entities and the nascent industrial bourgeoisie started competing for power; and in this struggle, the civil bureaucracy emerged on top as also a powerful stabilizing force in the country. It practically held sway over the levers of power and ruled the nation till late 1958 when, for the first time, Pakistan came under military control with the then army chief Ayub Khan

---

2   *Ibid*, pp. 46-47.

at the helm. Thus the Pakistani army pushed itself into direct governance by sidelining the weak political class and collapsing civil services' authority. Since then, the military has strengthened its position as a dominant player in power politics. Ayub was followed by Yahya Khan. The next military dictator was Zia-ul-Haq, who ousted Bhutto in 1977, and last in the line – so far – has been Pervez Musharraf. He ruled Pakistan for almost a decade after seizing power in a military *coup* ousting the elected Prime Minister Nawaz Sharief in October 1999. Thus, in the last seven decades, the army has experienced direct power four times and also acquired the expertise to be in the driving seat even when not directly in control of the government. As a result, the growth of political and civil society institutions in the country has remained stunted. Even now, during the last 3-4 years, the army chiefs have appeared to be weighing wings in the background for taking over controls of the regime.

It is generally believed that Pak economy showed good signs of growth during the Ayub decade; but things changed completely under the regime of Zia who, like everything else, wanted to usher an Islamic economic order in Pakistan. He was overtly enthusiastic to give a religious tinge to all institutions in the country and grabbed the opportunity provided by the Russian intervention in neighboring Afghanistan, a year after his assuming power, with both hands. The growth of fundamentalism, sectarianism and extremism there has been exponential since then. It all started with the educational institutions. "General Zia had played a vital role in the mushrooming of the *Madrasa* phenomenon during the 1980s as nurseries for the Afghan jihad, but the failure of successive Pakistani governments to invest in the public education system was another potent factor that led to increased student enrollment in these decadent religious seminaries. Free food, housing and clothing proved to be an effective incentive for the poor to avail these facilities, at times not knowing that their sons would be inculcated with a distorted version of Islam, and instead of learning to read and write they would be taught how to kill people. At the time of Pakistan's birth, it had only 136 *Madrasas*, but today it is home to around thirty thousand."[3] In addition to the mushrooming of *Madrasas*, Zia embarked on the more perilous course of clothing the army, which had so far retained its non-religious character based on the British training and ethos that it had inherited, with a distinct Muslim identity. In the difficult years following

---

3   Hassan Abbas, *Pakistanis Drift into Extremism*, Pentagon Press, New Delhi, 2005, pp. 203-204.

the break-up of Pakistan in 1971 and the creation of Bangladesh, the Pak army became an easy target of this makeover; following the national upsurge to link itself more closely with the Islamic orientation of the Middle-East and the Arabic countries. Zia hastened this process markedly with keen eyes on Afghanistan and J&K; where military adventures were to follow in succession. But, this process once set in motion was not easy to regulate or control; and in addition to the Islamization of the army and its intelligence apparatus, this scheme of things also gave legitimacy to the right-wing elements in Pakistan, primarily the religious parties. They steadily moved to the centre-stage of action, if not of the nation; and came to acquire muscle and lung power way more than their numerical strength. This process has been thoughtfully explained as, "For Islamists the alliance proved to be an unexpected boon. Co-operation with a key state institution not only averted the threat of political marginalization posed by the election results but also helped see off critics who had questioned the nationalist credentials of Islamic parties, which had expressed reservations about the idea of Pakistan before independence. It was the popular turn to Islam following the secession of East Pakistan that allowed the re-entry of Islamist parties into national politics and ensured that they lived to fight another day.... The army looked to Islam to strengthen Muslim communal discourse and prolong the conflict with India with the aim of buttressing its authority at home and lending momentum to its regional policies in Kashmir and Afghanistan. Islamist forces, however, invoked Islam not so much in opposition to India (though they are undeniably opposed to Indian secularism) but more clearly to seek to assert Pakistan's internal Islamic character."[4] This separate discourse and the struggle to establish supremacy continues.

Corruption in body politics of the nation, in high places of authority, amongst big land-owners and industrial magnates has been another bane of public life in Pakistan. This scourge received impetus, in no small degree, from the dabbling of the army in business and commercial interests right from the mid-fifties; and is constantly expanding since then in the three crucial segments of the national economy, *viz,* agriculture, manufacturing and service industry. In a seminal study of Pakistan military's business interests; and after analyzing its commercial entities like the Army Welfare Trust, the Fauji Foundation and Shaheen Foundation etc, Ayesha Siddiqa has come to the conclusion, "The most serious consequence of

---

4 n – 1, pp. 94 and 149-150.

the military's involvement in economic ventures relates to their sense of judgement regarding political control of the state. The financial autonomy of the armed forces, which is reflected through the burgeoning economic empire discussed in this book, establishes the officer cadre's interest in retaining political control of the state. Since political power nurtures greater financial benefits, the military fraternity sees it as beneficial to perpetuate it. In this respect, economic and political interests are linked in a cyclic process: political power guarantees economic benefits which, in turn, motivate the officer cadre to remain powerful and to play an influential role in governance.... In Pakistan, the military has been central in nourishing the religious right without necessarily realizing the strength of religious ideology as an alternative to itself. The military, in fact, also supported and built various militant organizations to serve its national security objectives. The religious parties, the militant groups and the armed forces are bound in a process of reinforcing each other's strength. The greatest beneficiary, however, is the religious right, which seems to have captured the imagination of the common people.... Although Pakistan's generals claim that they want to curb religious extremism and militancy, the published reports indicate otherwise."[5] These organizations continue to exist and carry on with their business enterprises and commercial activities involving huge monetary transactions.

Apart from the business activities being integral to the structure of armed forces in Pakistan, on the other end of the spectrum is the trouble its army has been creating for India, more specifically in Kashmir, since the late 1980s. The mischief-making capacity of the army and ISI enhanced considerably after their active involvement in Afghanistan; in the wake of Russian intervention there, consequently sucking the Americans also in the region. The ISI worked closely with the CIA and, in the bargain, honed up its skills in the art of covert warfare. The lessons it learnt in working together with CIA and groups of foreign jihadis belonging to many countries; it put to good use in its deep involvement in creating troubles across the western borders. It took the undeclared war into Kashmir and has been sustaining it, through various stratagems, for almost three decades. Many observers feel that from the expertise thus acquired; it translated into action by creating a number of militant organizations, making it difficult for the Indian establishment to negotiate with the trouble makers. Unlike Phizo in

---

5   Ayesha Siddiqa, *Military Inc. Inside Pakistan's Military Economy*, Pluto Press, London, 2007, pp. 248 and 251-252.

Nagaland or Laldenga in Mizoram, there was no single point of control in J&K; and the ISI could very well play favorites in increasing or decreasing its support to different militant outfits, depending upon its assessment of the recipients' level of commitment to the ISI cause and effectiveness on the ground. This strategy of creating multiple militant organizations, as also switching financial and material supports on a dynamic basis; did pay good dividends to the ISI and Pak army. But, also in the bargain, these armed groups tended to acquire a personality of their own and a capacity to bye-pass the benefactor. Of the monsters ISI helped evolve, some morphed into an identity with a capacity to turn around and prey on the creator itself. The terror incidents within Pakistan, and also in the restive eastern border regions, are pointed indicators of this phenomenon.

But, the Pak army and ISI have continued to foment trouble and mischief in J&K on a sustained basis. In the course of this single-minded pursuit, the GHQ in Rawalpindi – the Pakistan army headquarters – has also actively courted and collaborated with the Islamic right organizations. An alliance which is proving costly and is expected to extract even a higher price in the future; like riding a tiger and finding that it is difficult to get off. Hassan Abbas has very succinctly described this scenario as, "Barring a miracle, the influence of the rightist parties is bound to grow in Pakistan, or at the very least they will retain a solid following…. The Pakistan Army dare not confront them, knowing their strength and suspecting that they may have sympathizers, if not supporters, within its own ranks. It was therefore considered more feasible for the army to continue to direct its energies in the battle zone of Kashmir rather than to face the jihadis. … No one has a clear idea about their exact numbers, but their potential capability resides in the subconscious of those in authority, and this stays there because the reality is too hard to confront. Their funding will not dry up because thousands of Pakistanis and Arabs believe in them and contribute to them."[6] There is hardly any change in the situation as prevailing at present; if anything, the conditions have worsened.

Internal Situation in Kashmir

In the backdrop of the internal and emerging situations in the respective countries, both India and Pakistan have to somewhat dilute their respective 'core concerns', be prepared to meet half way; as their

---

6   n- 3, p.240.

respective maximalist positions have failed to reach any gainful and stable solution to the mutual bickering over the decades. An observation made by a political observer fifteen years ago, and still considerably relevant, says, "Besides being the bigger and more stable party to the issue, India would have to show additional patience, bordering on magnanimity, on another count – its relatively higher stakes. Unlike Pakistan, India has an expanding economy, to some extent an integrated civil society, stable institutions and people-centric governance, aiming at a place on the high table of global politerati."[7] From the Indian point of view, the situation would appear to be like the proverbial difficulty of trying to clap with one hand. The implication being that Pakistan is not refraining from carrying on its activities of aiding and abetting militancy and internal disturbances in J&K; particularly in the Kashmir valley.

Notwithstanding the traditional religious tolerance and pervasive *Sufi* influence in the Valley; there has always been a palpable right leaning fringe over the past one century. This segment became more vociferous after the birth of National Conference, under the leadership of Sheikh Abdullah; and acquired a tinge of being pro-Pak in its leanings in the post-1947 developments. For almost next four decades these elements did not pose a serious security threat to the state; its existence and influence being at the lowest level during the stewardship of G.M Sadiq, particularly from 1965 to 1972. Thereafter, it started re-asserting gradually and acquired a larger than life image; in consonance with events taking place at the national and international levels; particularly the rise of petro-dollar economy in the Middle-East. This was not many steps away from further growing into a credible challenge to the Farooq Abdullah government, in the later part of the 1980s and then transforming itself into militancy; liberally aided and abetted by ISI and the Pakistani state. During the six years of Governor's regime in J&K, from 1990 to 1996, security initiatives successfully blunted the mischief capacity of different armed groups and organizations and conducted the Assembly elections to install the elected government of National Conference headed by Dr. Abdullah. But, even his administration and the political organization did not strive sufficiently hard to wrest the political initiative from the separatist elements; both armed and otherwise. It was only after the 2002 Assembly elections that the popular coalition government of Congress and PDP, headed for the first three years by Mufti Sayeed, seriously confronted the political discourse of this group.

---

7   Asma Khan Lone, in *Indian Express*, dated May 15, 2003.

Mufti Sayeed addressed his first meeting of the Unified Headquarters - after he took over the reins of power in the State - on December 27, 2002, at Jammu. The Deputy Prime Minister Advani and the Defence Minister also took part in the deliberations; the former probably also wanted to size-up the new Chief Minister. In his opening remarks to the high-level gathering, he outlined the expectations of the public and priorities of his government. He first emphasized that general mandate of the people has been for good governance and the administration has to perform to the expected level; saying that people friendly policies will also help fight terrorism. In this context Mufti stressed on the requirement to keep all major roads in the State open for 24 hours. He rooted for no reduction in the level of security forces deployed in the state; further underlining that militancy needs to be dealt with firmly, with requisite determination and coordination; as well as accountability to the established hierarchy. Thus in this forum comprising top security professionals in the State; his views were well received for their operational relevance, soundness of content and clarity.

Mufti's comprehensive understanding of the overall situation and the general direction of the events and priorities is largely reflected in the interview he gave to the noted journalist, Praveen Swami; the excerpts of which read, "….we still have a long way to go. Perhaps we are over one hump, but there are still very many humps to be crossed….what has really changed is the energy and attitude of the people…. Today, there is a widespread consensus against violence. People are fed up with the endless death and destruction, and are determined that this must stop….. I think there is a widespread consensus that dialogue is necessary. Everyone has supported the Prime Minister's recent initiative…. But it is important to talk, even if it is only for the sake of talking. The very act of talking helps ease tension….there is no scaling back of operations against terrorists. I have repeatedly told our security force personnel that they must act vigorously against terrorists. What I do insist on, however, is that the human rights of ordinary citizens are respected and that innocent people do not face harassment and humiliation."[8]

He also had a very clear and erudite assessment of the hugely important internal dynamics of the problems facing the state and a practical understanding of the mischief-making capacity of major separatist

8   Praveen Swami in, *The Hindu*, dated July 13, 2003.

personalities. This knowledge he used with good effect to enhance the efficacy of his administration. A keen observer of J&K political scene described this trait as, "Mufti was someone who understood and cannily played on the Kashmiri psyche. He turned populism into politics.… For the common Kashmiri, it was the defining trait by which they judged Mufti's three years, saying these were the best they had had since 1996.…. About Geelani he said, 'I will not make a martyr out of him. Just let him be. It's better if he lets off steam. He is more harmless outside than he would be inside. We can deal with him politically.' And he was right."[9] As long as he remained in power, till beginning November 2005, Mufti managed to curb over ground separatists' activities and considerably reduce their influence. His practical advice to his ministers, legislators and officers was to concentrate their energies on accelerating developmental activities for the benefit of the general public; rather than spend efforts and time on exposing the acts of commissions and omissions of the predecessors. His logic was simple. By spending sufficient time and resources it was possible to dig out cases against the earlier regime, but the same efforts – he stressed – should be directed in a positive manner for the general betterment. The strategy was logical, useful and it worked on the ground. He was, in a way, able to take winds out of the sails of separatists. But, his successor government was not able to build upon the gains made by him. Mufti did an excellent job in assuaging the feelings of the Jammu and Ladakh regions; which have traditionally nursed complaints of neglect as compared to the Valley. As a matter of record; it may be recalled that he was one of the only three persons who contested elections from both Jammu and Kashmir divisions, since independence. He made good use of his knowledge of Jammu politics and important people of the area; being always approachable to address problems of the region. For Ladakh; he reached out to the elected Ladakh Autonomous Hill Development Council, of Leh district and amicably settled their pending demands. In addition, a separate Council was duly put in place for Kargil, the other district of Ladakh; thus taking on board the entire region. He had to hand over the Chief Ministership to the Congress, in accordance with the coalition agreement after three years at the beginning of November 2005, at a time when he was still attending to the problems of Kashmir region and his work there was not yet over. An important national newspaper like the

---

9   A.S. Dulat, *KASHMIR The Vajpayee Years*, HarperCollins *Publishers* India, 2015, pp. 243,248.

Times of India carried an editorial on October 19, 2005, under the title "Let Mufti Be" rooting for the continuation of his regime. In parts, the write-up said, "The Mufti government may not have ushered in normalcy in the state, but it has ensured that the peace process runs smooth. A regime change could upset the continuity of the past three years.... The symbolism of having a Valley politician as chief minister is enhanced in such times.... The hunger for power of the Congress's state leadership has played a major role in J&K's tragic history. This is the time for atonement; the best way to do that is to shelve power pangs for the time being". It was a serious mistake on the part of Congress, as subsequent events proved, which it has never publically acknowledged. In fact, there was practically a turnaround for worse in the next regime, after Mufti, and the first entity to assert itself was All Party Hurriyat Conference (APHC) – the Hurriyat; which has been in existence for almost twenty-five years now. Taking advantage of the developing situation, it practically re-invented itself and made strenuous efforts to be in the forefront of the Shri Amarnath Shrine Board land agitation in July 2008.

The All Party Hurriyat Conference (APHC)

To recapitulate; the APHC was born from the platform of Hazratbal Shrine on September 9, 1993; a result of years of strenuous efforts by the ISI which also played the traditional role of a 'midwife' in giving it a shape. This Pakistani intelligence agency wanted to create an umbrella kind of establishment or institution which could claim to speak on behalf of different secessionist elements in the state. Knowing the kind of groups it was dealing with, ISI no doubt must have realized the futility of expecting any unity amongst its proxies and dependents; but all the same such a step promised, at the least, a tempting publicity value and centre of attention for the electronic and print media. At its peak, the APHC claimed the support of 34 political, religious and underground organizations. Over the years it has acquired a presence on the political landscape of Kashmir and loosely come to represent the over ground separatist entities and sentiments in the Valley. Technically, it has a Chairman and eight-member Executive Committee, elected for a period of five years by the constituent groups; but for most period of its existence the working of APHC – as well as the receipt and utilization of funds received – have remained non-transparent and opaque. Also, notwithstanding the brief media attention and the limelight by its then Chairman, Moulvi Abbas Ansari, during the first few months of 2004 when he led a Hurriyat delegation to New Delhi to meet the Deputy Prime Minister Advani: the APHC has been practically led by the trio of Syed Ali Shah Geelani, Yasin Malik and Moulvi Umar Farooq. It would be useful to have a peek into the background of these three individuals.

Geelani was born in 1929 in a village near Sopore town, a famous apple growing area of Baramulla district in North Kashmir. A powerful orator in Urdu, he has a good knowledge of Arabic also. He worked as a government teacher for twelve years and joined the Jamait-i- Islami in 1950; becoming its prominent leader- and also chief for many years. When the Jamait took a decision to take a leap into politics - some analysts believe it did so on the promptings of the then Chief Minister and Congress Chief Mir Qasim - Geelani contested the Assembly elections and remained M.L.A. three times; winning from Sopore constituency in 1972, 1977 and 1987. Having remained a Legislator for such a long time; his anti-India stance is sometimes criticized by his opponents as an act of political opportunism. He has also come under scrutiny for amassing huge wealth, collecting a large amount of funds and on the charges of money laundering. The fact that his near relatives are doing well in business and government service; is also an issue of general talk against him. Geelani has been publically advocating the merger of Kashmir with Pakistan, as the only solution to the outstanding issue. He is known to have said, "….our fate and future are linked with Pakistan." Not much wonder that one Pakistani writer said about him, "Both friends and foes agree that Syed Ali Shah Geelani is more Pakistani than any Pakistani."[10]

Yasin Malik was born in a middle-class family of Srinagar in 1966. As a young student leader he founded the J&K Islamic Students League and took an active part in street-level protests and demonstrations; for which he was twice arrested. In the mid-eighties, he joined JKLF then headed by Amanullah Khan; and crossed over the LoC in 1986. After six weeks of arms training and indoctrination in Pakistan, he returned to the Valley along with a group of trained youth. He is reported to have been involved in the attack on the residence of the then DIG Police Ali Mohammad Watali in September 1988; in the kidnapping of Dr. Rubiya Sayeed in December 1989 and killing of four IAF personnel on January 25, 1990; amongst other incidents of such nature. As one of the prominent militant

---

10 Arif Jamal in an article in *NEWS* dated October 5, 2003.

commanders, he was arrested in Srinagar in August 1990 and spent the next four years in different jails in the state and other parts of the country. He, along with eleven others, was produced before the TADA designated court in Jammu on May 19, 1993, and charged on eleven counts including nine murders, one case of kidnapping and one incident of a bomb explosion. The cases are still pending and Malik is currently on bail on account of ill- health. In 1995 there was a rift in the JKLF; following differences with Pakistan based Amanullah Khan and Yasin Malik designated himself as the Chairman of his faction of the outfit named JKLF (M). Unlike Geelani, he believes that Pakistan has no claim or right to represent the Kashmiris and speaks for "the pre-partition status of entire Jammu and Kashmir State." After coming out the jail in 1994, he has mostly been engaged in non-violent protests and demonstrations and similar activities.

Youngest of the trio, Umar Farooq was born in Srinagar in 1974 and was proclaimed as Mirwaiz of Kashmir – almost a hereditary title – on the assassination of his father Moulvi Mohammad Farooq in May 1990 by a militant. He also slipped into his father's shoes as President of the Awami Action Committee, a political outfit, at that young age when he had not completed his academic pursuits or theological training. In spite of these handicaps; he has since then shouldered both responsibilities with a fair amount of competence. Umar has, over the period, finished his disrupted education and acquired the aspired degrees; also performing the requisite role at the pulpit with traditional competence and an inherited flair. His influence, almost a pocket borough of the family, is confined to a part of downtown Srinagar. In other towns of the Valley, as also in rural areas, the sway of his personality or the presence of his party is bare minimal. Being concentrated in a part of the big city – and also enjoying the traditional loyalty of followers for generations - he and his supporters have a prominent media presence and give an impression of much larger numbers than the actual. Umar Farooq notably became the first Chairman of the APHC in 1993; and is also believed to be close to both the ISI and IB. Politically and in respect of the Kashmir issue; he talks about "the right of self-determination by Kashmiris." In the separatists' camp his is a tragic-comic figure; in that knowing fully well that his father was brutally gunned down on the orders of the ISI, he has been on the right side of the same very elements. His supporters call this a survival tactics, but the excuse does not carry much conviction.

Thus, within the APHC, there are three distinct strands of separatist thoughts represented by "Kashmir for Pakistan" refrain of Geelani; restoration of the pre-1947 status of the state as demanded by Yasin Malik and the "right of self-determination" slogan of Umar Farooq. Apart from these apparently contradictory stands and resultant pulls exerted by the top three and their supporters; the beginning of this organization itself was not a successful one. In the general perception; the Hurriyat did not assert effectively during the Hazratbal crisis in October- November 1993 and later failed to secure the Shrine Complex, after the matter was duly resolved by the state government. The APHC almost proved a non-starter and these developments further exposed the inherent weakness of this hotchpotch combination. Also to start with, many militant groups were hesitant in lending their support. And yet for the underground, the Hurriyat seemed to be the only political hope; there being no other alternative on the horizon for them. Because of this, and also on the instructions from the ISI, many important militant outfits started work to secure support for the Hurriyat. This process was later well outlined as, "In General Musharraf's scheme of things the organization occupies a pivotal place.... This is not fortuitous, given that the Hurriyat was fabricated on the worktables of the ISI 15 years ago...."[11] The APHC has also been under sustained and constant criticism from the very beginning on two counts. It did not have any representation from Jammu and Ladakh regions and also no system was ever laid down about the method of collection and distribution of funds and the monitoring system thereof. Often questions have been raised about details of the funds received and their distribution and calls for making these public.

To keep itself afloat and also ostensibly on instructions from across the borders; APHC opposed and actively campaigned against all Parliamentary and Assembly elections in the state from 1996 onwards. A very apt assessment about its structure was made in 1999 as, "The new Army Commander for Jammu & Kashmir, Lt. Gen. H.M. Khanna, a few weeks after assuming Command and familiarization with the ground situation, addressing his first press conference in Jammu on February 3, 1999 said, 'APHC is, in fact, the parent organization of the militant and pro-Pakistan elements active in the State. Militants and the APHC are the two sides of the same coin and if one side, the militant side is washed out

---

11 Anand K Sahay in the *Times of India* dated December 7, 2004.

the coin is useless'."[12] However, in spite of considerable pressure and not very favourable developments, this group has managed to sustain itself. It hit the first major bump in the run-up to the 2002 Assembly elections; particularly after the assassination of Abdul Ghani Lone in May 2002. This tragic development further sharpened the ideological differences between different individual and groups; which came to the surface. As an organization, it was not able to tell the people, as it had done earlier, whether they should boycott these elections or not. This ambivalence proved costly, as "This ultimately created a deep conflict between the leaders of the conglomerate and they began to level serious charges against one another....The response to the election process proved a destabilizing factor for the APHC which got divided into two groups. One led by Moulvi Abbas Ansari is known as APHC (Ansari) and the other group led by Syed Ali Shah Geelani is known as APHC (Geelani)."[13]

This turn of events put the future of Geelani in jeopardy and he struggled for his political survival. A contemporary commentary on this matter reads as, "Today, after a life-long struggle to make the State of Jammu and Kashmir accede to Pakistan, Geelani stands alone in political wilderness. No significant political force stands behind him at a time when his party considers him 'retired'."[14] For the next few years the moderate Hurriyat, first lead by Moulvi Abbas Ansari and then by Umar Farooq; appeared to be on the move and made considerable gains. It first had two rounds of talks with Deputy P.M. Advani at the beginning of 2004; then also made a trip to Pakistan and PoK in June 2005. Their last round of talks was with the Prime Minister Manmohan Singh on May 3, 2006, in New Delhi, in the presence of Home Minister Shivraj Patil, National Security Advisor Narayanan and Centre's interlocutor for J&K, N.N. Vohra. This was their second interaction with the P.M; the earlier one had taken place in September 5, 2005. Thereafter, for inexplicable reasons the governments' efforts to reach out to Hurriyat and arrive at some workable understanding with them tapered off. One national daily report later claimed, though, that these talks were unilaterally scuttled by UPA regime due to internal strife in Pakistan. Whatever may have been the reasons; this change of attitude left the 'moderate' faction in a lurch. Geelani was quick in taking

12 Sati Sahni, *Kashmir Underground*, Har-Anand Publications, New Delhi, 1999, p. 105.
13 Fayaz Ahmad Mir, in monthly *Epilogue*, April 2008, p.39.
14 n- 10.

advantage of the changed circumstances and renewed his efforts to occupy centre-stage of the separatists' discourse. The Shri Amarnath Shrine Board (SASB) land agitation, in the middle of 2008, was almost a heaven-sent opportunity for him and he exploited the emerging situation to the hilt. Riding on the crest of a popular upsurge in the Valley against the state government headed by Ghulam Nabi Azad of Congress; he positioned himself at the head of this agitation and others just followed. According to Pushp Saraf, "This time, however, Mr. Geelani appears to have become desperate. He has shed all inhibitions.... In the present phase of protests in the Valley, he has been dictating terms from the beginning.... There is now unprecedented unity amongst the separatists. There is little difference between Mirwaiz Hurriyat and the Geelani Hurriyat at this point although both have been bitter opponents not long ago. Mr. Yaseen Malik too has jumped into the fray wholeheartedly."[15] The events in the Valley during this period once again proved, if any proof was needed, that the APHC had come to denote Pakistani interests in the State; in detriment to all other issues. It is a different matter that the state administration was able to deal effectively with the events relating to this agitation in the Valley as well as in Jammu division. The Assembly elections that took place in the months of November and December the same year; were conducted in a peaceful manner and people's participation, across all the three regions of the state, was impressive.

After installation of the popular government in the state in the beginning of 2009, the Hurriyat graph started declining once again. This loss of perch gave rise to rumblings within the combine and the discord between leaders spilled out in the open in 2012 when the supporters of Shabir Ahmad Shah and Prof. Abdul Ghani Bhat came to blows during a seminar in Hurriyat headquarters. Whereas the first split in APHC ranks, in 2003, occurred more due to ideological differences; the second split in 2014 was mainly due to personal issues between important personalities of APHC. On January 17, 2014, Shabir Shah announced the formal separation of his group Democratic Freedom Party from the combine. Along with Shah, others who moved away with their outfits also included Nayeem Khan and Azam Inquilabi. The Hurriyat has never looked its old self since then and has been lurching from one set of events to another; striving for

---

15 Pusp Saraf in *Border Affairs*, New Delhi, July – September 2008, pp. 3-4.

maximum media attention through staged events or resorting to the only other option it knows of calling for strikes. Its frequent resort to *Bandhs* and shut-downs has brought havoc to Kashmir economy; misery to the common man and virtually ruined the famed tourism sector.

To bring lasting peace in this State; which has undergone a series of convulsions right from 1947 onwards, managing equations with Pakistan externally is very important. But, of equal significance is to take care of the internal dimensions of this issue. This is where reaching out to Hurriyat becomes important. The huge media attention and notions of importance spread by Pakistan and by this organization itself; has created a general impression that the Hurriyat is the sole legitimate voice of the separatists in Kashmir. The central government presently has only two options; either to engage with it effectively or take recourse to stratagems in dismantling this edifice. As of now neither of the two is in sight and the *status quo* has always worked in favor of APHC. The internal situation in Kashmir is still waiting for the return of peace and complete normalcy.

Sadbhavna Efforts

In managing internal dimensions of the security situation in the State, goodwill earned by the army in border areas, over the decades, plays no small role. Each unit has been maintaining friendly relations with the local population around its locations ever since 1947 – now for seventy years. This process of consideration and cordiality started right at the beginning, and was subsequently consolidated when the militancy and the current state of disturbances were nowhere in sight. The mutual concern for welfare and dependence firmed up with one unit replacing another in a normal change-over cycle; with locations and attitudes remaining fixed. The army-civil cooperation in this State has been a historical fact; dating back to the troops landing at Srinagar airfield in the late October 1947. Each unit of the army was guided and helped by the National Conference volunteers; then under the leadership and guidance of Sheikh Abdullah and Bakshi Ghulam Mohammad. After the 1947-48 military operations were halted by the cease-fire and troops settled in respective locations; the local army units invariably maintained cordial relations with people around and respectable individuals of the area. Each new unit on relief was duly given a brief about how to further strengthen these ties. The troops generally helped locals with medical facilities, employment as pony-porters, occasional transport availability and the like. Senior commanders on visits also invariably invited and interacted with civilian elders of the area. The results of these contacts – though not formally recorded anywhere – were beneficial to both sides. It has been a cumulative asset which the Indian nation has neither taken due notice of nor tried to leverage on. This fund of goodwill around old army locations in the state, however, continues to grow.

After the militancy broke out; the army interactions came under greater media attention due to significant growth of the electronic media, as also induction of a good number of Rashtriya Rifle (R.R.) units near the urban centers. As the army was no more confined to the border areas; need was felt to institutionalize the help provided by individual units to the civilian population. Conceptual contours of these endeavors were consolidated by an enterprising Brigadier and his immediate superior – both posted in the Valley – in the late nineties. These efforts gave birth to the idea of 'Sadbhavna' that grouped various activities of the army under different heads, aimed at 'Winning Hearts and Minds' of the local population. The frame work of this notion has been outlined as "In view of the media invasion and the global economic development the aspirations of the present generation in the Valley have undergone a drastic change. The new generation has understood the fallacy of the armed struggle and is now looking forward towards the overall development of the region. The fundamentals of Sadbhavna are to help people to help themselves. The army is to act as a facilitator and catalyst for development projects identified in conjunction with the State Administration and local populace....Sadbhavna launched in 1998 started a culture of peace and harmony between men in uniform and locals. With its wide gamut of activities, the effort by the Army has restored a semblance of normalcy in the lives of The Common Man."[16]

The focus of activities under this scheme covers four sectors of Infrastructure development, Education, Healthcare and Women empowerment; all aimed at improving the quality of life of women and children, in particular, and ameliorate their sufferings since they have borne the brunt of terrorism. A set of skills in fruit preservation, computer training, vocational activities, and handicrafts is being imparted to the women and youth to make them more independent and self-reliant. Healthcare figures prominently in the Sadbhavna efforts; particularly in remote areas where

16 Maj. Gen. SA Hasnain (Ed), *Sadbhavna*, A Headquarters 15 Corps Publication, 2006.

state government's outreach is not sufficient – the presence of trained army personnel in these pockets and resources available provide considerable help and relief to the locals. These are further supplemented by holding health camps and educating people on child-immunization, hygiene and health awareness. Such measures have particularly helped the migratory population and their cattle a lot. However, in the fields of Infrastructure development, Education and Bharat Darshan; the army's contribution is particularly appreciative. Building of roads to connect leftover habitations and launching of bridges over fast flowing streams provide great relief to the concerned population. Launching of an additional Bailey- bridge on the busy Srinagar-Baramulla road; to ensure the free flow of traffic and construction of four similar bridges over fast-flowing streams in south Kashmir during 2003-04 were widely appreciated by the general public and civil administration.

In the field of education, efforts of the army have been focused on two areas of renovation and rebuilding of damaged schools; as also constructing and running of Army Goodwill Schools, to provide quality education to students enrolled there. The popularity of these institutions; practically one around every Brigade Headquarters, stand testimony to the standard of instructions imparted there. A special reference needs to be made of the two Army Goodwill Public Schools, with hostel facilities and fully paid for by the army; one being in Pahalgam in the Valley and the other located in Rajouri in Jammu division. Over the last ten years, these have become very popular and sought after schools by the locals.

Apart from the local excursions; the Bharat Darshan tours organized by the army under Sadbhavan initiatives have also attracted a lot of local attention and popularity over the years. The students, and sometimes village elders also, are taken on a conducted tour of various interesting and important locations in rest of the country. They see historical monuments, religious places, military installations, and bustling metros; and also meet with distinguished personalities of the nation. These visits help expand their horizons, look at a diverse and unified India, realize the military might of the nation and also appreciate the fact of being a part of such a large and magnificent country. This is also one area, where the concerned organizations of the Central and State Governments should pick up the lead and take the effort forward. The benefits may not be immediate and always quantifiable, but a favourable imprint on an impressionable mind is a sufficient compensation in itself. To be sure, the efforts and initiatives of the army under the Sadbhavna are not an end in them; but certainly, reflect a sincere wish to engage fruitfully with the local population. The idea and core philosophy should be picked up and replicated in an expanded manner to address the internal security dimensions of the State; as it underlines three important lessons of empathy with the people, making long-term investments and not expecting immediate results.

The Earth Quake Tragedy

A serious earthquake hit the sub-continent in the morning hours of October 8, 2005, with its epicenter in Muzaffarabad; causing extensive loss of life and property in that city and also major damages in Islamabad as well as some areas of the NWFP, in PoK and Pakistan. In this tragedy there, over seventy thousand, people were reportedly killed and about a lakh injured. The deadly tremors and aftershocks also badly affected Uri and Tangdhar sectors in the Valley resulting in loss of life in large numbers and wide spread destruction of private and government property. Poonch area in Jammu division also suffered considerable losses; including the destruction of historical and famous Moti Mahal palace, located on the outskirts of the town.

The Indian response was quick to this natural calamity of unprecedented intensity which resulted in widespread loss of life and property in both the divisions of Jammu and Kashmir; in Poonch and Uri-Tangdhar belt respectively. The army and air force swung into action to save human lives; provide sustenance to the affected population and restore damaged infrastructure. Working in tandem with effective measures quickly put in place by the state administration, these forces helped in saving hundreds of lives.

The Pakistan government's reaction to this tragedy of huge proportions was slow and tardy. The common man, in any case, was not expecting much from the civilian administration there, but had high hopes of the help coming from the army in these hours of crisis. But in this respect also massive disappointment was in store. Some quarters were also hoping for considerable relief efforts on behalf of the Americans. They too felt badly let down. An Islamabad based journalist lamented in his piece, "…. Thousands of hapless people under the wreckage of their homes could have been pulled out alive had the huge Pakistan Army come to their aid swiftly. Thousands of people would not have succumbed to their injuries had the big fleet of US choppers parked in the neighborhood (Afghanistan) flown promptly to transport them to hospitals. The Army and the US came into action too late – when all hope had died." The lack of timely action by army surprised and disappointed many people as also its ardent supporters; some observers termed this as callousness. A scathing criticism came from Irfan Siddiqui, a noted Urdu columnist who wrote in the October 27, 2005 number of the *Daily Nawa-i-Waqt*, "It is ironic that, with the first shocks of October 8, the 7th nuclear power of the world lost heart and started looking at others for help….the nation came to know that the Army it had been 'feeding' for the last 58 years did not have even a dozen helicopters to rescue a handful of its benefactors. The sun had not set on October 8 and each limb of our body had become a beggar…."

In sharp contrast to the slow and inadequate help from the army and the state structures; the right-wing and jihadi elements reacted with alacrity and urgency to the developing crisis and human misery, all over the affected areas in Pakistan and PoK. The military, to the surprise of some, appeared quite comfortable with initiatives of these groups. Apart from others, as many as seventeen organizations that had either been banned or put on the terrorism watch-list by Musharraf regime, were involved in the relief activities. At one point in time even the American Ambassador to Pakistan, Ryan Crocker, asked the Pakistan government to stop the jihadi groups from conducting relief operations. But, his protest and warning was brushed aside by the establishment. Taking advantage of the opportunity provided by the earthquake; the right wing and jihadi groups were able to once again occupy centre stage in the affairs of Pakistan. Following are some of the details scanned from media reports of the period regarding quick work done by these outfits;

> Jamat-ud Dawa, formerly LeT, was the first to reach the Margala Tower in Islamabad, a multi-storey building that had collapsed. Together with civilians, its workers used heavy hammers to work their way through the rubble and pulled out many trapped people. There were complaints that army did not help.

> The Hizbul Mujahideen personnel pulled out about 450 girls from the wreckage of Garhi Habibullah Secondary School in Hazara, NWFP. The local people while appreciating this work by HM,

lamented that there were hundreds of army soldiers around the location, but they did not extend any help.

> The Jaish-e-Mohammad and Al Badr, operating under different names, set up relief camps and provided succor to the local people in NWFP and PoK.

> The HM also picked up relief work in PoK and set up a big *langar* in Muzaffarabad.

These jihadi groups systematically stepped up efforts in areas where the state had failed; and were seen by people to rebuild schools, mosques and houses; as also adopt orphan children - actions which were lauded by the common man sorely in need of help from outside. A contemporary account recorded, "People in the affected areas are praising the jihadis to the skies and criticizing the army and the US vehemently." It was generally agreed by neutral observers that opportunities created by this human disaster of huge proportions were wasted by the Pakistani state and the jihadi elements seized these with speed and commitment. In the years to come, as would be borne out by the bloody events, the cost of this negligence by the government and the army there would be very heavy.

In the hindsight, it does appear odd that where the Pakistani regime was quite happy to cede ground and its role to the jihadis; it did not accept offers of help from India in this hour of crisis and difficult situation, when effectively dealing with the human tragedies should have been the priority. India had much shorter lines of communications to the PoK and also possessed the wherewithal to effectively step up the humanitarian work in the badly affected localities there. It is a sad commentary on how Pakistan lost a significant opportunity to build trust and further push the peace process with India. The four-point formula, which Musharraf proposed and pushed with India later; could have made a meaningful beginning with the tragedy unleashed by the earthquake.

On the Indian side the authorities, both civilians and in the armed forces, responded speedily and with sufficient dispatch to come to the help and rescue of the affected population. Even though these measures were quite well covered by all forms of media, these generally refrained from making a negative reference to the government's failure on the other side. Interestingly, there were calls in India to reach out and help those in distress on the other side; particularly the most badly affected areas across the LoC; specifically in and around Muzaffarabad. A local daily from Jammu reflected a common sentiment, when it commented in the editorial, as, "…. People on the other side are facing an unprecedented crisis much like our Uri and Poonch towns. It is a moral and human obligation on our part as a nation to assist in their rehabilitation. There are two more reasons why we should not be found wanting on this count. First, the sufferers in Muzaffarabad and in its vicinity belong to us and our region and secondly, they are in our immediate neighborhood."[17]

There was, however, a flip side to this tragedy. Over a hundred terrorists were reported to have infiltrated across the LoC, taking advantage of the unsettled conditions. This was adequately borne out by the sudden spurt in terror strikes by militants in Srinagar city itself; which registered seven militancy related incidents between October 18 and November 23, 2005. Such steep rise was rightly attributed to the phenomenon of the earthquake and its aftermath. The I.G. of Kashmir had gone on record, "I will say, more than a hundred militants have entered Srinagar city…. But after the earthquake, they seem to have taken advantage of the situation and are sneaking across".

India also failed to take advantage of the huge efforts it had made to successfully reach out to the people in distress. This was an opportunity that it could turn into its favor by skillful management of the media to highlight the measures it had undertaken for the benefit of the affected population; as also to underline the abject failure of Pakistan in dealing with the situation within its areas. There could possibly have been two reasons for this slip. One was the obvious reluctance of the Congress, then also in power in the Centre, to give credit to the state government headed by Mufti Sayeed, which was at the end of its three-year tenure. The other factor could possibly be that the affected population – in Uri and Tangdhar regions – was not of the Kashmiri stock but came under the generic term 'Paharis'. The fact remains that the earthquake and its aftermath did provide India with a chance to positively address internal dimensions of the Kashmir situation. The central and state administrations did a fairly good job in providing timely help and succor to the people in need in the affected areas; but all efforts to reach out to the population in distress across the LoC; in PoK, were thwarted by the Pakistani government.

17 *Daily Excelsior*, Jammu, dated November 10, 2005.

Round Table Conferences (RTCs) etc.

To reach out to the elements and organizations outside the political mainstream in Kashmir, the central government had appointed different points men- termed as the Interlocutors- starting from K.C. Pant, Ram Jethmalani, Arun Jaitley and lastly N.N. Vohra. These efforts also included reaching out to important persons and groups in the state; both by the NDA as well as UPA governments at the highest level. The process rolled out as the Round Table Conference (RTC) was, in fact, a continuum and logical extension of this endeavor to address some of the internal peace dimensions. When Prime Minister Manmohan Singh addressed the first RTC in New Delhi on February 25, 2006, it became an important attempt to have a comprehensive and composite dialogue across the political spectrum of J&K collectively. As expected it was an exploratory exercise. The second RTC at Srinagar on 24th and 25th May that year was more focused and fruitful. A mention about them has already been made.

The first four Working Groups, of the five, gave their reports within the prescribed time of less than a year; except for the last Working Group V, which took almost two years to prepare and finalize its recommendations. Though all the five groups sent their reports to the Prime Minister but neither the central government nor the state government made these public; making these deliberations points of wide-ranging speculations. In the meanwhile self-rule and demilitarization were made as major political planks by the PDP. This was in addition to the existing demand of autonomy by the National Conference. This was also the time when both India and Pakistan had agreed to the three-point structure for talks encompassing; a) No independence to J&K. b) No redrawing of borders. c) The LoC can be made irrelevant.

When these three formulations were combined with the demands of autonomy, demilitarization and self-rule by the two mainstream parties of the state; an interesting situation emerged. All major fall- back planks of elements outside the mainstream appeared as being hijacked by the NC and PDP. By including in this scenario the non participation of APHC; it becomes easier to understand as to why no fruitful impact became evident by the RTCs or the interlocutors; even though the intentions were good and parameters positive. Hence, these initiatives did not produce anything fruitful and trailed off, in time, as failed attempts.

Thereafter not much attention was paid to fruitfully address the internal aspects of the J&K situation as politically and administratively things appeared to have settled down in the state. But, like the proverbial lull before the storm; the situation nose dived in the middle of 2008. This happened in the context of Shri Amarnath Shrine Board land row; creating huge problems of public peace as also law and order issues in both the divisions of Jammu and Kashmir. These disturbances led to the imposition of Governor's rule in the state for almost six months in the latter half of the year. Following the holding of another credible Assembly elections; a newly elected government – a coalition of NC and Congress - headed by Omar Abdullah came to office at the beginning of January 2009. As usual New Delhi left the management of the internal situation entirely to the state government till the things literally went out of hands a year and a half down the line.

There were considerable civil disturbances in and around Srinagar during the summer of 2010 resulting in the death of over a hundred youth in clashes with the police and CRPF. Due to the resultant political commotion; an All-Party Parliamentary Delegation visited the state in September that year. Following its recommendations; the Government of India appointed another set of Interlocutors on October 13, 2010. This group of three was headed by Dileep Padgaonkar and the other two members included Radha Kumar and M.M. Ansari. The task of this team was not easy as later recollected by Radha Kumar, "In fact, the misgivings began even before our mission did.... We arrived in the state to be greeted by cynicism and worse. Indeed, our own hopes were low. There had been two decades of pain and suffering, and just as the state was beginning to glimpse peace, three summers of violence had polarized its communities and resulted in the trauma of summer 2010. We were lucky that this negativity changed within a month or two, and the people of the state came forward to talk to us."[18]

This body completed its work and produced a comprehensive document based on interaction with six thousand persons, including one thousand Sarpanches and Panches; meetings with more than seven hundred delegations and three round-table conferences; all across three regions of the state. The panel gave its report to the then Home Minister P. Chidambaram on October 12, 2011; almost exactly one year after it

18   *The Tribune*, dated August 9, 2012.

was constituted. This report was released in May 2012 and, as expected, generated lot of discussions and criticism in the media and amongst the civil society. By then the situation had much improved and calm prevailed; even though the stability appeared more on the surface as also precarious. There was no formal action initiated by the state or the central governments on this report – and in a way, it was also quietly forgotten; like the earlier similar exertions including the RTCs. In the hindsight all these measures appear to be something like fire-fighting in nature; whereas a perceptible process of internal peace and reconciliation could have been built around them. This lack of follow-up action, and failure to take effective timely measures, has all along and constantly been a negative point. M.Y. Tarigami, the lone CPI (M) MLA in the current Assembly, now in his fourth term, and an astute political observer has commented on this phenomenon as, "The real story goes back to 2010.... but again there was no follow-up action by the government. Interlocutors were appointed – not just at that time but also earlier, led by K.C. Pant, N.N. Vohra and the latest one by Dileep Padgaonkar. These recommendations were never reported to Parliament. At least the people of India had a right to know what the recommendations made by the interlocutors were. The average Kashmiri asks these questions – what happened to all these reports? The average Kashmiri feels that there is more and more reliance on force."[19]

In addition to the measures already mentioned, certain other steps taken in tandem would have had a direct and positive bearing on the internal peace process; and hence are necessary to be put in place expeditiously. Efforts to reduce the element of apprehensions in the local population should take a high precedence in this regard. Improvement in the overall security scenario would also have a favorable bearing on the peace process. The increased pace of development activities, good governance, reaching out to people and improved system of redressal of grievances should be quite high on this list. Effective decentralization of governance needs to be implemented on priority; meaning thereby organizing the Panchayat level bodies and making them strong as well as functional units of governance at the lowest levels. Side by side conduct of regular and fair elections to the Urban Local Bodies will give lot of satisfaction to the population. Inhabitants of the Valley, in particular, have traditionally and historically remained insular and therefore the need to mainstream them can hardly

---

19 *Frontline*, August 19, 2016, p.28.

be over-emphasized. Their sensitivities and aspirations require to be taken into account.

The Armed Forces Special Powers Act has been criticized ever since its promulgation, during 1990, in J&K by various human rights organizations and activists. Lately, this opposition has acquired political overtones also, demanding its repeal. The security forces, on the other hand, have expressed concern that without the legal cover provided by the provisions of this Act, their effectiveness in dealing with the militancy and terrorists acts would be dangerously eroded. The antagonists of this statute argue that Section 4 empowers security forces to search houses and make arrests without warrants; to destroy the hide-outs of suspected terrorists and to "shoot to kill". Likewise, the opposition of Section 7 is that it encourages unfettered use of force, due to the immunity granted therein, for any excesses committed. However, the fact is that militants are well trained in the use of handling of sophisticated arms, explosives and special equipment, and are highly motivated zealots. In spite of commendable turnaround, it is not always possible for the state police to deal with them and operations by security forces, independently or in support of the police, become necessary to effectively tackle such elements and the menace of terrorism that they spread. The problem has been confronted by the forces, on an ongoing basis for years together. For this role, there is no legal framework available except the AFSPA which was first enacted by the Parliament in 1958 to deal with insurgency situation in the North East. In its absence, the counterinsurgency structure would have collapsed many years ago and would be seriously undermined presently.

There is no mention of "shoot to kill" in Section 4 or any other section of the Act; and is therefore more of a figment of imagination of the critics. The expression, "even to the cause of death" is in the explanatory part of the text rather than a substantive segment of Section 4. It is a well known legal interpretation that the use of force is always construed to be only a reasonable level of force required to deal with a particular situation and nothing more than that. Indiscriminate use of force is not covered by any law including this Act. Similarly, Section 7 of the Act does not even remotely envisage any blanket immunity. The provision is there to prevent vexatious cases against the members of the forces. A provision whereby prosecution can be launched only after sanction of the government is, therefore, not only necessary but also justified, and creates no scope for any presumption on the part of the concerned forces that they are in any way above the law. The number of cases launched against and determination of convictions in respect of security forces personnel is a testimony to this fact. Public servants have such protection in the substantive law itself in the form of Section 197 Cr.P.C. There are similar provisions in the Army Act and BSF Act also.

However, a via media needs to be found out to substantially meet legitimate concerns against human rights violations and the genuine apprehensions of the security forces; more so in view of the improved security situation and increased responsibility being shouldered by the state police in J&K. It is, therefore, suggested to remove Section 5 of the Act, dealing with power to search etc as this is covered elsewhere in the statute. Also in the explanatory part of Section 4, the expression "even to the cause of death" could be considered for suitable replacement by a formulation which would exclude any allusion to death.

Between the armed militants and political elements, there is a spectrum of trouble makers headed by over ground workers (OGW's) of militant and separatist organizations as well as the stone throwing youth of certain pockets in the urban centers of the Valley. Inability to effectively deal with them has been one of the major failures of the state apparatus; for which both central and state governments should share the blame. It is a fallacy to presume that these groups and individuals can be checked effectively by detention under the Public Security Act. If that was so then by now this menace would have been tackled. The PSA detentions which started with substantial numbers in 1990, reached the peak at 2117 in 1994. The figure in 2009 was 374; around 150 out of this were confirmed militants. With the considerable reduction in the militancy and incremental return to normalcy; use of PSA would increasingly come under mounting criticism. There is no alternative but to deal with the mischief makers under the normal, substantives laws of the centre and the state.

Hardly any recourse has been taken to the preventive measures, during the militancy period, and the police, as well as magistracy, are not effectively making use of the provisions of Section 107 and 151, etc of the Criminal Procedure Code; which could be a lot of help in curbing the activities of the trouble creators. In the last few years, despite deteriorating law and order situation, not a single case of imprisonment or forfeiture of bond in respect of any of the Sections of the CrPC has been reported;

not a single case of prosecution for violating restrictions imposed under Section 144 of CrPC had been placed on record. Also, scarcely any case of conviction has come to notice involving offenses relating to assault on policemen, burning or looting of the government property. Going back to the preventive provisions of the law would be a major step forward in the maintenance of public order and effectively dealing with elements disturbing peace and tranquility. This would also be a positive step towards the restoration of normalcy.

Complete eradication of militancy and total stoppage of cross-border infiltration does not seem to be on anybody's time-bound agenda. The situation of flux is further complicated by the lack of consistent and effective policy formulation and substantive action against the overground workers of the separatist outfits and militant sympathizers. A widespread feeling has also gained ground that all the top leaders of various separatist parties and organization are beyond the reach of civil and criminal laws of the state and the nation. The separatist leaders do not consider themselves accountable to the state and the Indian legal system but, at the same time, are scared of Pakistani Establishment and the ISI. Even the jean-clad stone throwing city and urban youth consider themselves to be immune to normal legal action. At least that is a general perception. This impression is further bolstered by the unwillingness or inability of the law enforcing system to make the law-breakers face the consequences of transgressing provisions of the normal preventive and criminal laws.

For some inexplicable reasons; the Income Tax authorities do not seem willing to perform their normal duties in the Valley or even start making inquiries as to how in the last couple of decades certain people have acquired so much money. Similarly, the local branch of Enforcement Directorate has been almost non-functional for more than two decades; knowing full well that large-scale foreign exchange violations are taking place. If only the Income Tax Department, the Enforcement Directorate and the police effectively enforce the normal laws under their respective jurisdiction, a major source of ground-level support to the militants can be substantially reduced. This would also help in considerably improving the internal law and order situation in the state.

All insurgencies thrive on people's support. A militant without public support is like a fish out of water. Effective political mobilization of the population is the surest way to deny the essential life-saving ingredient to the militants. A credible public support to the state apparatus acts as a force multiplier to the counter-insurgency operations of the security forces. This also helps them to differentiate between those who are actively involved in militancy, the sympathizers and the people who are coerced into or provide help out of fear. It is important to make such differentiation and deal with each element on a selective basis as both overreaction and lack of action can lead to difficulties and are in fact detrimental to an effective anti-militancy strategy.

The aim of the administration and security forces should, therefore, be to identify and weed out the hardcore minority and inculcate an adequate sense of security and confidence in the general public. In the final analysis, combating terrorism by the armed forces is meant to blunt and destroy the capacity of the terrorists to wage an armed struggle against the state. Military strength can only bring about a decisive crushing of the armed capability of the terrorists; but this should be followed, and in fact, better accompanied, by neutralization of the active members of the terrorist groups as well as the pacification of the affected population. All organs of the State are required to function at their optimum level of efficiency individually and also as part of the larger apparatus. There cannot be compartmentalization in a successful fight against terrorism. The awesome coercive power of the state and its benevolent countenance should ideally be blended into an effective composite. A former commander of the Srinagar based Chinar Corps Headquarters has succinctly put this as, "But nothing can be achieved without domination of the public order domain. We cannot hope to carry forward the effect of our successful counter-terrorist operations without reaching out to the people directly and activating positive grass root politics. We come back to the age-old adage for such operations – the blending of hard and soft power operations. Repeating this message ad nauseum must remain a resolve."[20]

During the mid-eighties under intense pressure from the Russian leadership for his support to the Afghan "mujahidins" and when Russia had threatened direct action; General Zia-ul-Haq had advised his senior intelligence aides and force commanders to " keep the pot simmering but ensure that it doesn't boil over". The ISI and Pakistan GHQ have imbibed this lesson well, and would continue to keep the militancy alive in J&K unless forced by external and internal developments; including effective,

20   Lt Gen (Retd) Syed Ata Hasnain, *The Tribune*, dated August 2, 2017, p.18

sustained and coordinated policy formulations and actions by the Central and State governments, working in tandem. Neither the Union nor the State government on its own can decisively and irrevocably turn around the situation. Therefore, the vital need for a well thought out multi-pronged strategy encompassing the elements of security, politics, development, infrastructure and empowerment etc. In this context, the need to make civil administration more responsive and function with greater efficiency can hardly be over emphasized. The first step towards this should be to post handpicked officers at the district level – known for their honesty and integrity - and provide them with the necessary support in terms of resources, personnel as well as an institutional back-up.

The optimum utilization of the available resources itself would go a long way in remedying the situation. The revamped administration must ensure accelerated progress of ongoing schemes and projects and undertake such works and projects in hand which can be completed in a short time and benefit a larger number of people. Availability of essential commodities even in remote areas needs to be ensured. The infrastructure for this already exists and it is only a question of better management and administrative will to carry it out. That the process of development can be effectively used as a tool in the fight against the anti-national elements has been clearly demonstrated. Accelerating the pace of development, providing more funds in selected sectors and utilizing the money in a productive manner; results in enhanced satisfaction amongst the population. By stepping up the execution of work on projects which had been continuing for a long time and according priority to such activities which would benefit greater number of people; enthusiastic response from the local population was generated in the past and the strategy can be tried again successfully. Involvement of the people in the process of development, at various levels, enables directing and channelizing their energies in positive directions and towards beneficial activities.

Like rest of the country, this state also has a bulging youth demographic profile; youth that is becoming increasingly aspirational with better educational facilities. Any useful effort to address the internal critical dimensions should take into consideration the challenges of providing employment opportunities to the young men and women of J&K. A broad scan of the economic scene of the state would indicate some peculiar patterns. The state government has been, and is still being looked upon as, the biggest job provider. The number of government employees per thousand of population in J&K is amongst the highest in the country; maybe next only to the north-eastern states. There is a decided lack of interest, in the educated youth, to look for employment avenues outside the government. Add to this the pronounced proclivity of the job seekers to remain within the state. This lack of mobility may also have been partly due to centuries of isolated living for historical and geographical reasons. Also, the banks show a marked reluctance to invest in local ventures, the J&K Bank being the only exception. The process of micro-financing and support in organizing the Self Help Groups is still in its infancy in the state.

There is also a palpable hesitation on the part of Indian Corporate sector to invest in the Valley. This is due to a host of factors including the perception of continuing unsettled conditions; special laws in J&K regarding acquisition of land and property by non-state subjects and an impression that outsiders are generally not welcome in the state. This is truly a formidable list of dampeners. All the same, these issues have to be seriously addressed if the economic development of the state is to be put on sound footings. In order to flower and flourish, the native talent and resources need the outside capital, reach and expertise which is restricted and circumscribed by local conditions. To achieve the desired results the central government, the state government and captains of the local business establishments will have to work together to strive for a change of attitudes as well as investment and working environment. This is not going to happen overnight and will necessarily be a slow and extended endeavor. But, a beginning has to be made and earlier the better. The one model to be emulated, which readily comes to mind, is the relationship that has been forged between apple producers of the Valley and the outside traders, mostly from Delhi. As is well known, the apple trade did carry on almost uninterrupted during the last over three decades of disturbances in the Valley. There are important lessons in this phenomenon. Another noteworthy example is of the Houseboat operators of Srinagar and their exertions to attract the tourists back to the Valley during the late nineties onwards.

To make a beginning, the state in collaboration with the central government should play the role of catalysts and facilitators between the apex manufacturing and trade bodies at the national level and the local entrepreneurs. These trilateral or quadrilateral interactions should address and allay the real and perceived difficulties and inhibitions of all parties concerned. The governments will have to be imaginative, unorthodox and liberal in their approach. Recourse can be taken in this regard to various successful models, methods and approaches.

The efforts to assimilate people of the state in the national mainstream would further receive a boost if the employment opportunities are created for the local youth outside the state in the government sector, the Public Sector Undertakings as also in the private enterprises. This may appear to be a difficult prospect on the face of it but is certainly achievable with imagination and creative thinking. As it is the state's financial position is so weak that every job that is created by the state government is presently being paid for out of the grants received from the Centre. Therefore, the suggestion to provide outside employment opportunities for the youth of the state is not to make a plea for allocation of more resources from New Delhi; but is only a question of rearranging the priorities and thrust areas.

Media Management

The media can generally be divided into two broad categories of print and Electronic media. The Electronic media, in turn, comprises Radio and Television; notwithstanding the recent additions to this group in the form of Cyber media; like Internet, Face Book, Blogs and Twitter etc. The dissemination of information to the general public is broadly through the medium of radio and television. Even though the latter, being also a visual medium, is more popular and talked about; but the fact remains that the radio has still a far more extensive coverage and reach. In areas with no electricity or irregular power supply; a transistor with few cells is far more reliable. Anyone with a short wave radio receiver can access news and other programmes from all over the world without difficulty. This trend has received further fillip during the last decade or so with an ever increasing number of local FM radio stations growing in and around major urban centers.

While denying the Media information or waiting too long to structure a correct response might seem a safe thing to do from the Establishment's point of view; experience has shown that governments spend more time making up for the damage caused due to adverse press later on. Speed, though not at the cost of essential facts, is of essence to all sections of media which operate by the rules of the market in this 'consumer era'. The media is generally obsessed with its own goals, including the TRPs, and will go to any length to get news to the people – the consumers of information. The more sensational details and swifter it reaches audience, the better. In this endeavor; to maintain a healthy balance between promptness and correctness is forever a major challenge. The situation becomes even more difficult while reporting from a terrorism affected area – to maintain the requisite balance.

The terrorism-related news is aimed more at the people watching, rather than those at the receiving end. In this milieu the media persons are not the lone interested party; the militant groups are equally keen. Arresting footage and 'sound bytes' drive both the media and militant interests. The terrorists do have a strong vested stake in the projection of a distorted picture; and militant outfits generally tend to use some sections of local media as force-multipliers. This is where the biases of local stringers or local media do come into play at times; and official agencies – both civil and security forces – have to be ever watchful and quick on the uptake. The issue here is not of accusing the media of being in collusion with the terrorists; but rather that aggressive reporting in a highly charged situation, with the imperatives of competition between news agencies and channels as the major point of reference.

To be fair to the reporters, one should keep in mind that for covering difficult assignments, like in J&K or in Manipur, usually younger reporters are detailed by their papers/channels. While youth has its own charm, one sees little of it in these 'cub' reporters who come to difficult areas from the media. They are generally full of a sense of self-importance, sound brusque and brash; also at times appear to 'be demanding'. Still, they have a job to do; often a deadline to meet. They seldom get the necessary logistic support required for the kind of work being done and have to generally rough it out. All these media persons, reporting from the places of action, do have a considerable impact on their audiences. They help to focus attention on issues, subtly inject their own point of view and have an important role to play in forming or modifying public opinion. It is therefore of considerable significance to ensure that these people are provided with basic minimum facilities to make their life more comfortable and their jobs rewarding. On the other hand the situation has acquired difficult proportions with the mushroom growth of local print and electronic outlets. The job of public relation officials handling media persons is increasingly becoming more difficult and challenging.

The guidelines of General Padmanabhan, the erstwhile COAS of Indian Army, for the management of media – though meant primarily for the military officers – are equally valid for all such government agencies which have to frequently deal with media persons. It is a very sound advice which says,

"Some simple guidelines for military personnel interacting with the media have been drawn up, as a result of experiences of a number of military media managers. These are likely to prove useful to both the military personnel as well as the media persons. The major points of guidance are:

➤ Treat media persons as professional who have a difficult job to do. Treat them with courtesy and understanding. Do not be patronising or antagonistic.

➤ Listen to their questions carefully. Give out your replies crisply and clearly.

➤ Speak to them with well-chosen words; the fewer the better! Avoid bombast as well as jargon. Go bilingual from time to time if you find some of the media persons are not following your language or diction clearly.

➤ Use maps, sketches, photographs and exhibits to assist everyone to follow the talk.

➤ Give out facts and figures as a 'handout'.

➤ Whenever a media person asks you for any comment 'off the record', remember that you should say only that which you would not mind seeing published in print or telecast.

➤ Do not try to bluff if you do not have the answer to a question. A frank 'I do not know' will be the right thing to say.

➤ When a question calls for disclosure of classified material in reply, clearly tell the questioner that the matter is classified and you are not at liberty to speak about it.

> ➢ When questions call for your opinion on delicate matters on which you do not wish to speak, parry these with a terse 'No comment'.

> ➢ When dealing with unpleasant incidents on which media persons are asking you a barrage of questions, see that you have the facts of the case available to you. A clear statement giving the facts as the known and proposed action will clear the air first. Do not include in any form of 'cover-up'. Stick to facts.

> ➢ Rebut a wrong story immediately in clear and polite language.

> ➢ The media persons have deadlines to meet. Finish your meeting well in time and have them guided to a suitable place to file their story.

All these guidelines are quite straightforward and may appear to be 'basic'. Yet, how often have military men dealing with media in a field location 'come a cropper' because they violated something as 'basic' as what we have just listed! It may be better to follow these simple guidelines and by correct interactions with the media, win for the Armed Forces a useful friend and well-meaning critic."[21]

To this fairly comprehensive list, few more suggestions could be added. The easiest way, for instance, should be to influence the State-owned media like Door Darshan and radio network of the government; with persuasive initiatives from the official organs interested in this direction. This has to be a well-coordinated effort. It would also be quite useful to assess and analyze the reasons for a section of media supporting the militant cause; like monetary considerations, intimidation or fear; and try to neutralize these factors. Strong efforts should be directed towards educating the media in the whole gamut of activities of the concerned organizations. The emphasis should be more on 'influencing' the media rather than 'managing' it. One would do well to remember that credibility should be paramount at all times. It is also not permanent and has to be renewed periodically. One slip can prove costly in this gamut. There is also a case for ensuring that only specifically nominated and properly trained people interact with media representatives; particularly these days when one finds a marked proclivity amongst a lot of persons, irrespective

---

21 General (Retd) S. Padmanabhan, *A General Speaks*, Manas Publications, New Delhi, 2005, pp. 180-182.

of their position in the hierarchies, to read their names in the print or see their faces on the television screen.

With respect to the security scenario in Kashmir, four case studies of considerable importance, in the closing decade of the last century, provide ample evidence of the negative fallout of not handling the media promptly and carefully. In all these cases response of the official agencies to the media was generally sketchy, disjointed; often confusing and delayed. The first of these events related to the alleged mass rape of women during a cordon and search operation by the security forces in village Kunan Poshpora, in Kupwara district, during the night of February 23-24, 1991. A subsequent report by the Divisional Commissioner Kashmir found the villagers' claim riddled with contradictions. Later, an Inquiry Committee constituted by the Press Council of India, and headed by the veteran journalist B.G. Verghese, also expressed a similar opinion. Concluding parts of its findings include, "....It is riddled with contradictions of the most elementary kind.... In the absence of any credible evidence, it would appear to be an invention, a hurriedly contrived piece of dissimulation which finally broke down under the weight of its own contradictions". Notwithstanding these two credible and independent reports negating the allegations; the damage done by the initial wrong reporting in the media was not fully wiped out and some traces lingered on. This episode also reflected the degree to which the media can be manipulated by the interested parties; in this case the over ground groupings sympathetic to the terrorists. It was also a case of delayed reaction by the official media personnel.

On another occasion, in May 1995, when the Pakistani national Mast Gul escaped the tight army cordon, around the Charar-e-Sharief area; media handling by the state and security agencies was faulty and disjointed. The state government and the army chose to issue separate statements and brief the media without any coordination; which was not a sensible decision. Of course, both sides learnt their lessons but the wisdom came the hard way and after losing some valuable time. Similarly in the early phase of the Kargil war, during May- July 1999, not only the government and security forces were caught unaware, the Public Relations outfit of the Ministry of Defence was not able to handle the media competently; which led to misplaced and often contradictory reportage. This prompted the Army Headquarters to repair the damage by setting up, post-haste, an

Information and Public Relations Cell; headed and manned by competent and handpicked professionals. The media reporting on Kargil then improved hugely and also won all-round admiration. The whole episode left a trail of lessons to be learnt in media management. In this case, a remedial action was possible because the Kargil clash was extended over a period of two months. Had it been of a very short duration, the initial mistakes would have magnified many times over. The fourth incident happened on March 20, 2000 – the day President Bill Clinton arrived in New Delhi on an official visit. 35 Sikhs were killed by the militants at village Chattisinghpora in Kashmir. The gruesome act was of a magnitude to make heightened attention inevitable; which obviously was the intention of the perpetrators. But here again, the media response by the official agencies was delayed, sketchy and left much to be desired.

These four episodes underline the importance of professional handling of the media; timely dissemination of correct information and coordinated efforts where more than one agency is involved. Accuracy and speed are of essence. Not that things have not changed for the better over the years, but lot more needs to be done. Handling of media is serious enough a matter to be managed by trained manpower only. This should be done by competent and nominated official spokespersons only and no one else. Once the instructions prohibiting unauthorized individuals talking to the media are forcefully enforced; the process of effective media management would show considerable improvement.

For the media professionals, it is also a moot point to consider that a fine balance has to be maintained between the national and security considerations on one hand and the imperatives of freedom of information and reportage on the other.

Need for a National Policy on J&K

It is as clear as the daylight that apart from militancy there are law and order related issues in J&K and both have to be managed effectively. The internal sensitivities, in addition, need a nuanced and calibrated handling. Also in a democratic polity like India; changes at the helm are expected and indeed do take place in the centre as well as in the state periodically. One has noticed a tendency that, with the change in the composition of the government, there is a sad spectacle of the ruling party and the premier opposition outfit interchanging roles, policies and public statements. All this without even batting an eyelid and with ease that is very discomforting. Just as an example, after the BJP lost power at the national level in 2004, it began opposing the peace process almost at every turn. Similarly, the performance of the Congress has been equally dismal; as amply shown during the noisy exchanges prior to the implementation of GST in the country from July 1, 2017; easily forgetting that this measure was in fact initiated by the Congress-led regime in the centre and the policy was then opposed by the BJP. The position of the political party or parties heading the state administration in J&K is no different; and one can quote a number of examples to buttress this point. Such attitudes considerably dilute the efforts of the current government to deal with an emerging situation as also to handle the main issue at hand. It also provides enough material to the other side; in this case Pakistan and Pak-backed separatist outfits, to exploit the situation for its own ends. In absolute contrast, there is never a change in the policies and stands taken by Pakistan in relation to India or Kashmir. These matters are squarely controlled there by the army and are independent of the changes in the regime; whether democratic or dictatorship. Similarly, in mature democracies of the western world, the national stance on major policies does not undergo a substantive alteration with the change of guards at the apex level.

It is therefore high time that in India also important political parties should evolve and decide to follow a set of agreed parameters on significant national issues, affecting vital interests of the country. Security related geo-political matters would be high on any such agenda – including the Kashmir issue. A national consensus along the broadly agreed political contours would go a long way in dealing with various aspects of this issue in a much more effective manner. The adversaries of India have been having a comfortable sailing in this regard, right from 1947 onwards. Events of the past cannot be re-written or willed differently; but a national consensus on important matters, across the country's political spectrum, would certainly be the beginning of a new era in India and herald a positive change; for the better. It would also help the central and the state governments to manage more effectively various aspects of the J&K situation; especially dealing with the internal dimensions of the problem in all its manifestations – on a continuing and long term basis.

CHAPTER-XI

The Peace Process – External Dimensions

T he external dimensions of the peace process between India and Pakistan have always been J&K centric and largely revolved around the four factors of shifts in Pakistan's policies; internal problems of Pakistan; Pak designs in as also aspirations of PoK and Northern Areas; lastly the US and other countries' pressure on Pakistan in this regard. As has been well brought out by a number of scholars, based on the study of irrefutable archival material, the problem of Kashmir was, in fact, a brainchild of the British Imperialist structure and ambitions to maintain a toe-hold in the northern edge of the sub-continent. By the time India and Pakistan gained independence, in August 1947, Britain had almost become subservient to the economic and military powers of the US – in the aftermath of the Second World War - and practically handed over her strategic concerns, including the emerging Kashmir problem, to the reluctant American diplomats. Pakistan which had initiated the whole turn of events by sending first the tribal raiders and then the regular army into J&K; was delighted by the changed geo-political scenario and played the game merrily; first in the favorable climes of the United Nations and then by joining the western backed military alliances of SEATO and CENTO.

By the mid-fifties, Pakistan was feeling smug with the impression of having achieved arms parity with a much larger India. A couple of years later came the first military dictatorship of Ayub Khan and with that also a closer embrace with the US. By the early years of sixties, and following the humiliating performance of the Indian Army against the Chinese in 1962; Pakistan was having a sense of being better equipped militarily than India. This prompted it to start the 1965 war with unhappy consequences. The whole sequence of events did not take place in a vacuum but was the logical result of years of American military and diplomatic backing. Pakistani author, Tariq Ali, in his book titled *On the Flight Path of American Power* has mentioned that a US Senate report published on March 12, 1957 stated, "From a political viewpoint, U.S. military aid has strengthened Pakistan's armed services, the greatest single stabilizing force in the country, and has encouraged Pakistan to participate in collective defense arrangements."

As the head of Pakistan's government, Gen. Ayub was followed by Gen. Yahya Khan, Z.A. Bhutto and Gen. Zia-ul-Haq; with attendant cataclysmic events of 1971 war- leading to the creation of Bangladesh – and Soviet intervention in Afghanistan. These in varying degrees, coupled with the internal developments in J&K, were responsible for the militancy raising its ugly head in the state in 1989. The turmoil and mayhem in J&K has continued since then; now for almost three decades. It is a different matter that the character, contents, composition and support structure of this insurgency has undergone different phases. The deep involvement of Pakistan, its army and the ISI is a common knowledge and does not need to be proved any longer.

The first half of the 1990s was, in fact, a difficult period for India. The militancy in Punjab was finally tackled in the first two-three years of this decade, but in J&K the country was on its back foot. It had to face charges of alleged human rights violations in the state in a number of international forums; particularly in the Human Rights Commission based in Geneva. Pakistan used to be gleefully on the offensive – with the active American support. The first few years of the Clinton administration, with Robin Raphel calling the shots in the American State Department as Assistant Secretary of State, were especially trying. She was palpably pro- Pakistan and equally vehemently anti-India. The J&K state apparatus then under control of the Governor; was struggling to put in place effective security grid, rebuild intelligence structures, put administration back on feet and rebuild damaged infra-structure. With the successful holding of Parliamentary elections in May; Assembly elections four months later and restoration of the elected government in Srinagar, in October 1996; the officials in the state and centre could breathe easy. The pressure was slowly getting reduced. This change was duly reflected in a talk delivered by Ashraf Jehangir Qazi, High Commissioner of Pakistan to India, at the USI, New Delhi on January 28, 1998. He said, "For Pakistan, India is by far the most important country. It is the country with which the quality and state of relations determine our security and the economic environment as no other relationship does.... An ambiance has been generated at the highest level within which it is realistic to begin to think in terms of movement."[1]

The nuclear tests conducted by Pakistan, in almost quick response to the Indian action, further increased sable rattling between the two countries. The already difficult atmosphere was more vitiated by Pakistani ingressions in Kargil and the ensuing clashes there from May to July 1999. There was a change in the government in Pakistan during October that year; with Gen. Musharraf replacing the democratic dispensation headed by Nawaz Sharief. Pakistan once again came under the control of the military dictatorship. Although there was no variation in the Pakistani attitude towards India, with the change of guards in Islamabad; the next high-level contact took place at Agra Summit in July 2001; when the general travelled to India on the invitation of Prime Minister Vajpayee. This venture also ended in a failure with the anti-India rants of Musharraf at the much-publicized breakfast meeting with Indian editors. If Kargil war had represented the belligerence of the Pak military commanders; the Agra summit amply showed the impetuousness of its rulers. In fact Gen. Musharraf had clearly abused the traditional hospitality of the sub-continent as also transgressed the bounds of conduct expected of guests here.

It is quite possible that any change of attitudes in Pakistani establishment would have taken much longer but for the events of September 11, 2001 when the terrorist hit the very heartland of America by striking in Washington and New York. The West was now getting singed by the heat of terrorism and realized that this senseless violence knew no boundaries and respected no countries. The Americans, who had supported Pakistan so long, against India; also now woke up to the fact that Pakistan was one of the epicenters of this scourge. The response was quick and riposte effective. In addition to plugging loopholes in the internal security set up; the United States administration started actions against the known regimes supporting this kind of activities. Pakistan was marked to be one of such countries. In the famous telephone call from the American President Bush to General Musharraf; the former is reported to have threatened the military dictator to either join the American fight against terrorism or be prepared to see Pakistan going back to the Stone

---

1 *Journal of the United Service Institution of India*, April-June 1998, p. 200.

Age. Musharraf, practically under this severe threat, chose the former option and practically spent next year and a half securing Pakistani assets in Afghanistan and also showing sincerity of cooperation to the Americans by providing a number of ground-level operational facilities to them. Towards India, apart from occasional verbal platitudes mostly for the benefit of the western audience, there was no material change of attitude and the militancy in J&K state continued as usual.

However, this experience of the strong American reaction probably set in motion a process of slow change of heart and loosening of attitudes. This became evident for the first time when Pakistan Prime Minister Jamali responded positively to Vajpayee's offer of talks towards the end of April 2003. This was the beginning of thaw which led to the famous Vajpayee visit to Islamabad in January next year and a series of mutually beneficial steps by both countries over the coming few years. This was also the time when important voices in Pakistan media spoke in favor of a more balanced approach. Two examples of this genre of opinion are worth mentioning. Ayaz Amir, a well-known columnist in Pakistan, wrote in the internet edition of Dawn dated May 9, 2003, as, ".... Pakistan can't get on the negotiating table what it has failed to win on the battlefield. India can't pretend that Kashmir is like any other state of the Indian Union or that it faces no problems in Kashmir. As for the people of Kashmir, if they are for independence, as many of them appear to be, they won't get it because India and Pakistan both countenance the idea.... There is, alas, no going round the Line of Control which for as long as we can tell will remain the effective frontier dividing Kashmir.... By God how we have tried, from the first shots fired in 1947 right down to the Kargil adventure of 1999. We've only succeeded in making it more permanent. If ever a case can be made out for a farewell to arms it is here...."[2] The second write up is attributed to Mushahid Hussain, former Minister of Information Pakistan, who opined in the month of November as, ".... Pakistan's foreign policy has largely been on the defensive and somewhat reactive since 9/11. Its major success was to prevent an Indo-American gang-up against Pakistan which was in the offing, but thanks to the U-turn on Afghanistan, that was prevented....Pakistan's policy needs to be freed from its contradictions... ."[3]. However, on the Indian side doubts remained as to whether there was a real change of intentions on the part of Pakistan or if the whole thing

2   http://www.dawn.com/weekly/ayaz/20030509.htm

3   *GreaterKashmir*, dated November 21, 2003.

was merely posturing. In a handwritten note, dated October 10, 2003, the then Governor of J&K Lt. Gen. (Retd) S.K. Sinha expressed his doubts as, "Just as a leopard does not change its spots, Pakistan's line on Kashmir has remained constant. Jinnah's offer to withdraw the Pathan raiders from Kashmir if India withdrew her forces, sounds so much like Musharraf's recent offer to get the terrorists stop their depredations if India agreed to start talks on Kashmir with Pakistan."

Another fact that needs to be emphasized in this connection is the changed attitude of Pakistan as reflected in the statements of Gen. Musharraf, for little over two years, from December 2003.

➢ On December 25, 2003 came the first statement, in the course of an interview to Reuters, where he said that Pakistan had "left aside" the United Nations resolutions on plebiscite in Kashmir. This was a major shift in its policy towards J&K.

➢ October 25, 2004: Identify seven regions, demilitarize them and change their status. Some political analysts at that time felt that this 'seven- region' concept was a creation of Musharraf and it was a way to give some assurance to the people of 'Kashmir'.

➢ April 18, 2005; he said in New Delhi that the LoC cannot be made permanent but it can and should be made 'irrelevant'.

➢ May 20, 2005, "Self-government must be allowed to the people of J&K". No segmentation on the basis of religion.

➢ June 14, 2005. Complete independence is ruled out.

➢ October 21, 2005 – Open the LoC.

➢ January 8, 2006. In an interview with Karan Thapar he explained all his previous sayings in this regard and summed up these at a single place and in a more comprehensive manner. He was reported to have said, "Something between autonomy and independence…. I think self-governance fits in well. Let us work out self-governance and impose the rules in both parts…. Kashmiris will be involved…. Demilitarization and joint management concepts would need to be worked out carefully. There have to be subjects that are devolved; there have to be some subjects retained for the joint management.

India and Pakistan will be guaranteeing it and overseeing it, with each having a stake in guaranteeing the situation in the other half of Kashmir."

In short these formulations, put together at one place, later came to be known as the 'four-point formula' of Musharraf. While the public opinion and the political leadership in India generally welcomed the outlines of this initiative; the reaction to these ideas in Pakistan was not as positive. The general impression in that country was that these were the personal thoughts of Gen. Musharraf; maybe at best a thinking of top military leadership. The Pakistan establishment, which also includes their men in uniform, did not apparently have much say in the matter. Also, there were doubts expressed in different forums about the efficacy of this policy which had not taken on board different stakeholders nurtured by various wings of the government for years together. The Pakistani Parliament also did not discuss the matter during the course it ran for over two years. Different organizations, institutions and pressure groups perceived him as and may be Gen Musharraf preferred it that way, the sole architect and arbitrator of the India policy. All the same these ideas do form a workable frame around which peace process in the sub-continent could be built upon.

He realized that the circumstances, atmospherics as also the current leadership in both countries was conducive enough to take advantage of the historic opportunity. He said, "I personally feel it [grasping the fleeting moment] should be done within the tenures of Prime Minister Manmohan Singh and myself. There is harmony and understanding between the Indian Prime Minister and myself –this is a big difference between now and the past – therefore, I believe that this is a fleeting moment, which we must seize for the sake of the future of the two countries and South Asia. The fleeting moments in history are not available every time – they come and go – the governments and leaders, who grasp them, create history."[4] General Musharraf was right in that the two countries were unable to create history as both leaders failed to grasp the 'fleeting moments'; for whatever reasons and whoever is to be blamed for this lapse.

After 2006, things started changing for Musharraf in Pakistan; and the situation for peace with India was never the same again during the rest of his period as the President of Pakistan. With passing time he became

4   Quoted by B. Murlidhar Reddy in *The Hindu*, dated May 23, 2005.

less and less effective; with one crisis after another eroding his power and standing within the country and the army also. He had to manage the fall out of army action against the Lal Masjid complex near Islamabad in July 2007; take into consideration the situation developing in the Supreme Court of Pakistan leading to a country-wide agitation by lawyers; as also deal with *jihadi* groups and elements – in and out of uniform. All this, and some more resulted in him being increasingly sidelined and becoming more and more ineffective due to mounting domestic pressure. The militant threats to his personal safety, manifesting itself on a number of occasions, also must have been weighing on his mind. With these developments, the prospects of a change in the attitude of Pakistan and improved Indo-Pak relation practically came to a close.

The end of Musharraf's regime followed closely the assassination of Benazir Bhutto, in December 2007 in a militant strike. The ensuing elections in February 2008 brought Pakistan Peoples Party to power in Islamabad; with Asif Ali Zardari, husband of Benazir Bhutto, taking over as the President of Pakistan. The next signs of change in the country's stance towards the problems in Kashmir came in the form of admission by Zardari of Pak involvement in the creation and sustaining of terrorist outfits. He said words to this effect in the beginning of July 2009 by asserting, "Let us be truthful to ourselves and make a candid admission of realities. The terrorists of today were the heroes of yesteryears until 9/11 occurred and they began to haunt us as well." By then the Pak army was actively engaged in a campaign against the militant elements in the northwestern Swat valley and was gearing up to undertake such operations in the South Waziristan tribal region also. The *Times of India*, in an editorial dated July 9, 2009, highlighted Zardari statement as, "….This is unprecedented. No Pakistani head of state has ever gone on record to acknowledge the country's culpability as Zardari has done. And whatever may come of it, it signals a fundamental shift in the security discourse between India and its neighbor…. New Delhi would be keen to see Zardari's new view of militancy institutionalized on the ground. Militants who affect Pakistan are not clearly separable from militants who affect its neighbors. A dual policy in terms of fighting one while nurturing the other is bound to fail." After this small window of admission and a positive development from the Indian point of view; there were no more such statements coming from either Zardari or any other official sources in Pakistan. That was the last of a hint of change in the Pakistani stance on terrorism; notwithstanding the fact that its army was getting increasingly involved in the anti-militancy operations on the western borders and also within some pockets in the country. Zardari himself or no other Pakistani leader since then has spoken against militants' and in favor of improving ties with India. The "deep state" within Pakistan seemed to have again taken over and be in effective control from that point of time onwards.

It was also during the period of the efforts of Musharraf regime to improve ties with India – roughly a span of three years from the middle of 2003 – that the Pakistani and Indian chapters of the South Asian Free Media Association (SAFMA) became quite active. Their exertions were also facilitated by the Indian government's assurances to Pakistani and media persons of other SAARC countries of free access and travel in the country. Thus SAFMA too became a factor influencing the external dimensions of the peace process between India and Pakistan. The two countries' delegations made much-publicized visits to the other side towards the end of 2004. The rationale and benefits of such opportunities has been comprehensively described by one Indian journalist, who was also a part of this exchange, as "….my visit to Pakistan and "Azad" Kashmir was made possible this time as the member of a larger delegation of India Chapter of the SAFMA which believes that there should be no no-go areas for journalists in the Indian sub-continent as elsewhere. The SAFMA has a laudable concept and should be encouraged. By reporting on the situation as we see in the media world can help in projecting a correct and objective picture. Truth is a great cementing force. Any apprehension that journalists may be constrained in their functioning by their personal likes and dislikes are misplaced. For, the credibility of journalists depends upon how objectively they report: if they were biased they would never enjoy the respect in the area, be it India or Pakistan. Sometimes it is argued that journalists also have national interests. This is true. But who says that national interests are better served by distortion of facts."[5]

The first such visit to J&K was a five day trip by a sixteen member delegation of Pakistani journalists from 3rd to 8th October 2004. This team comprised of media persons representing major newspapers and TV channels of Pakistan and included Imtiyaz Alam, Secretary General of SAFMA. On the day one, the group travelled by road through the Wagah border and reached Press Club of Jammu late in the evening for their

---

5   Pushp Saraf, *Border Affairs*, Jan – March, 2005, p. 6.

first and formal welcome in the state. The next day these people spent in Jammu meeting and interacting with important persons and representatives of various political parties. On 5th October the party left for Srinagar by road reaching there by evening – thus having almost three clear days for visiting local places of interest and meeting with individuals and groups of their interest.

During their stay in Srinagar, the visitors met with leaders and representatives of all important political parties; separatists like S.A.S Geelani, Mirwaiz Umar Farooq, Yasin Malik, Shabir Shah and the like. They also interacted with groups with known and unconcealed anti-India stance as the APHC, J&K High Court Bar Association Srinagar, some faculty members and students of Kashmir University, as well as few well-known members of the civil society. The visiting delegation had dinners at the residence of the Chief Minister and Deputy Chief Minister of the state. From various local media reports and dispatches sent home an assessment could be made of their collective and general feeling about the overall situation prevailing in J&K. One could feel that they got sufficient idea about complexity of the problem and many nuances of the issues involved as also the difficulty to find a common denominator which could lead out of the impasse. They also made use of every opportunity to project that the primary aim of this visit was to have a feel of the ground situation and give a fillip to the peace process by increasing and encouraging more people to people contact between India and Pakistan. The group was impressed by the relaxed atmosphere and overall sense of warm hospitality by the officials as also common citizens. According to a local political analyst; the delegates went back with an impression that Geelani would not allow peace process to proceed ahead. They found Yasin Malik and the Kashmir Bar Association to be the most confused of the individuals and groups that they met.

A few of the members could ill conceal their surprise and shared their amazement with local acquaintances that, contrary to what has been told to the public back home, the Muslim population in J&K faced absolutely no form of restriction in following their religious customs and practices; with most of the mosques filled with people at the appointed time and days. Yet, in an otherwise environment of welcome there were few discordant notes also; one such sample being the statement of Asiya Andrabi, president of Dukhtran-e-Millat, dated October 4, 2004, asking the people of Kashmir not to welcome visiting Pakistani journalists as they were mere tools in the hands of Pakistan government which wanted a sell out on Kashmir. Notwithstanding such aberrations, this round of the state by these visitors left a very positive impression about central and state authorities. They left for New Delhi by air on 8th October.

It would be interesting to go through the extracts of one of the dispatches sent back by a member of the delegation, which mentioned, ".... After many months of hard pursuing, activists of SAFMA could convince India that its archrival, Pakistan, also have a community of regular journalists and they need some access to their side of Kashmir for an objective comprehension of the ground realities there.... Sitting in Islamabad, one had some idea of the intensity of demand for resumption of Srinagar-Muzaffarabad road links. Only after spending a day in Jammu, one discovered that even in that city, emotions for a quick restoration of the commercial and transport links with Sialkot are equally strong and tremendously popular.... So far, this visit is letting a large number of civil society representatives and political activists to forcefully expend the accumulated bitterness of decades. Perhaps only after unloading their hearts with explosive catharsis, they can address the questions, journalists and diplomats ask for their professional compulsions."[6]

A group of Indian journalists, including some from J&K, undertook a return visit under the auspices of SAFMA almost two months later. In addition to stay in Pakistan; the trip also took them to PoK as well as to Gilgit and Northern Areas. The journalists were not allowed to meet the Jehad Council or the HM commander Syed Salah-ud-din, in spite of an earlier understanding to this effect; but they were able to interact with a number of politically important persons, opinion makers and groups in these areas. Also, to the dislike of Pakistani authorities, the visiting media persons came across substantial voices of 'independence' in PoK. Especially the people in Mirpur town and the students of "Azad Kashmir" University, Muzzafarabad were more vocal than others. There was ample evidence of overwhelming support for cross-border movement amongst the people and intellectuals. A veteran Indian journalist wrote about his impressions of this visit as, "....However, one gets more than one signal that the Pakistan establishment is not much too happy with the reports spread by its own media that it has started losing ground in the Valley, huge

---

6   *The News*, Lahore, dated October 7, 2004.

inputs of money and ammunition notwithstanding. This has rather come as a shock. Looked from another angle, Pakistan's lack of information is surprising.... Be that as it may, it is clear that Pakistan establishment is not quite comfortable with the feeling that it has virtually lost out in comparison with the pro-liberation sentiments.....I could not resist the impression during these absolutely free and frank conversations that the Pakistani journalists' on-the-spot reports from Srinagar might have played their own part to convince President Musharraf that the people in the Valley do not consider Pakistan as a clear choice in any ultimate solution of the problem there."[7]

These were the two well-publicized visits of the media persons, under the aegis of SAFMA, thereafter this laudable measure took a downturn mainly due to the hurdles created by different layers of decision-making system in Pakistan. This also becomes quite evident from a dispatch made by an Indian scribe from Islamabad; according to which, "Access to Indian and South Asian journalists to freely travel within Pakistan is a case in point. In response to a similar unilateral gesture by India, Gen. Musharraf announced a reciprocal measure at a conference in Lahore in November 2004. Till date, there is no movement on the announcement. At the latest SAFMA conference here when the organizers reminded Gen. Musharraf of his November promise, he looked at Foreign Minister Khurshid Mehmud Kasuri present on the same dais. 'We are all for it. The Ministry of Interior needs to be instructed', he told the Pakistan President amidst peals of laughter from the audience."[8]

The initiative as long as it lasted, by both countries to facilitate the visits of media persons to each other's territories was indeed an admirable one. Considerable good came out of this step as was evident from the general tenor and stance of the writings and dispatches made by them. The interaction by these people with different persons and sections of society and attendant reportages created a general feeling of positivity; which process should have been taken forward instead of being smothered. Ease of access and transparency does pay its own dividends in the long run; and this point should be understood by policymakers across the divide. The slow strangulation of this measure was certainly a blow to the peace process between the two countries.

---

7   n – 5, p.5.

8   n-4.

Another measure which positively impacted on the relations between India and Pakistan, and to a considerable extent improved them, relates to the exertions of well-meaning individuals and groups - working independently and also sometimes in tandem - with a view to foster closer ties between the two neighbors. Behind the scene efforts and contacts between the concerned parties, beyond the media glare, has been an accepted form of interaction in a number of hot-spots in the world. A famous example of this is the almost regular contact between the Americans and North Vietnamese representatives in Paris during the late sixties and seventies of the 20th century. Such initiatives have also been taking place in the sub-continent over the last two decades; and have a considerable bright future. These Track-II efforts, particularly during the first decade of 2000, played an important role in improving the general environment between the two countries.

It seems pertinent to mention here that groups engaged in Track II diplomacy are formed in two ways: first, as an initiative of a local individual or an institution that results in the formation of such a group; second, the efforts of outsiders to create such a process with an emphasis on the avoidance of external interference on the subjects to be discussed. The participants on these occasions themselves agree upon the rules of discussion; including the element of confidentiality of views expressed and freedom of speech. In some cases the participants agree to have a chairperson from outside who is known for his/her expertise on a specific subject; impartial treatment of the issues and also that such person has earned the respect of both parties. The primary objectives of any Track II diplomacy are threefold: to make attempts to resolve ongoing disputes; to discourage and prevent the emergence of new disputes; and to make efforts to bring the two estranged countries and societies closer by introducing Confidence Building Measures (CBMs). Perhaps the most difficult task is to resolve an ongoing dispute that has outlived resolution efforts for many years - like the Kashmir problem. Indeed, the recent developments both inside and outside the territory of Kashmir clearly highlight the fact that relations between India and Pakistan will never be normal until this issue is negotiated to the satisfaction of both parties. However, while taking into consideration the intensity and adverse impact of the J&K situation on Indo-Pak relations; the usefulness of CBMs for improvement in this regard cannot be denied. The introduction of CBMs can ease the tension and may even help in securing better comprehension of each other's perceptions; can facilitate the enhanced communication network and also help in maintaining some kind of contact useful to both parties. In theory as also in practice, Track II diplomacy is expected to provide positively orientated alternatives facilitating and enabling the governments to arrest a drift towards adversarial relations; if anything of this kind is happening or is likely to take place.

Ever since the peace process started in the sub-continent; Track II meetings also increased correspondingly and in many ways – particularly during the 2003 to 2007 period. These can generally be divided into two categories: open and secret confabulations. The open meetings have been organized in the forms of seminars, conferences, symposiums; the other one consisting of regular and irregular meetings between small groups –generally comprising well-known professionals from both sides. While the open meetings are often reported in the media and, in some cases, books based on conference/seminar proceedings are published; the meetings of small groups – normally with a purpose or specific agenda - rarely make their deliberations public. The tendency there is to work out an agreed text or crystallize the issues and then transmit these to the concerned authorities. Such meetings, of both kinds, have considerably contributed towards further improvement of relationships. For instance, when the Indian and Pakistani governments were unable to agree upon a working arrangement for the bus service from Srinagar to Muzaffarabad; it was Track II diplomacy - namely the Neemrana Initiative - that is understood to have suggested a way out. Similarly, the meetings, seminars and conferences not only attract a wider participation but also facilitate the generation of ideas meant for a larger chunk of the public. In many ways, the success of people-to-people contact has been considerably influenced by the contributions of Track II meetings. The three major outcomes of Track II meetings have been the development of increased understanding of each other's perceptions and operative limitations; the provision of feasible alternatives and suggestions regarding CBMs. The agreed formulae and proposals for CBMs are communicated to the respective governments, which in turn take their own time and thoroughly deliberate upon the suggestions. It needs to be mentioned that India-Pakistan have also been discussing, though behind the scenes, complex issues and disputes at these levels. Admittedly, these dialogues are generally not open to public debate as sometimes the complex nature of issues requires confidentiality. The contributions of Track II and back-channel diplomacy can never be relegated to the realms of insignificance. It is not too far-fetched to assume that in the context of India-Pakistan relations, Track II and back-channel diplomacy have turned out to be quite appropriate and useful tools. These would continue to be of benefit in future also.

In an interview with the *Frontline* in December 2008, Khurshid Mahmud Kasuri, who had been the Foreign Minister of Pakistan for over five years since 2002, said that he preferred the back channel talks for more focused discussions on outstanding issues. As such parleys are beyond the glare of media-persons; the participants are under no obligation to say things that could later on be twisted to convey different meaning. In his assessment the instant publicity which formal talks attract could be more harmful, in totality, as it also 'enables those who are opposed to the peace process, on both sides of the international border, to put their own spin and scuttle the process.' He further went on to say, "I have always believed that there will never be peace between Pakistan and India if you confine the talks to the two Establishments. They are too frozen in their attitudes. We need to involve a lot of people outside the official umbrella. I do admit that some of them have frozen ideas; as frozen as those of the Establishment. But when retired soldiers, admirals, bureaucrats and diplomats, academics and public figures meet, it creates the right idea for a resolution."[9] For a person who had witnessed the whole peace process from a close proximity; his views very strongly favor the Track-II diplomacy and professional level parleys; both open as well as closed-door discussions.

The first serious effort in this direction was made when Vajpayee was the Prime Minister of India and Nawaz Sharief his Pakistani counterpart. The two points-men of their respective governments were R.K. Mishra – a private person and confidant of Vajpayee – and Niaz Naik – a former Foreign Secretary of Pakistan. This group was put in place at Lahore during early 1999; but because of Kargil war a few months later and other adverse developments, the two were not able to achieve much. Later, Brijesh Mishra the Principal Secretary to the Indian Prime Minister became the Indian counterpart; and according to some political analysts considerable behind the scene good work was done by this team. These exertions resulted in the breaking of ice between the two countries and led to the famous visit of Vajpayee to Islamabad in January 2004; which was to become the beginning of a serious peace process.

---

9   *Frontline*, dated December 5, 2008, p. 63.

But before this initiative could mature into something substantive; the coalition headed by Vajpayee led B.J.P. lost the national elections in the month of May and the new U.P.A. regime headed by Congress assumed power in New Delhi, with Dr. Manmohan Singh as the new Prime Minister. The Track II and back-channel efforts were then headed by S.K. Lambah, as Dr. Singh's envoy and his Pakistani counterpart being Tariq Aziz. Both were seasoned diplomats and had the full support of their respective principals; who themselves were keen to give a decisive push to the peace process. The two began serious work during the entire 2005 and good part of 2006 and arrived at a broad framework of five mutually agreed parameters. These included, a) no redrawing of LoC, minor adjustments could be considered as mutually agreed later on, b) there would be greater political autonomy on both sides of J&K, c) India would move troops from the state as the activities of Pakistani backed *jihadi* groups scaled down, d) manage some mutually valuable resources like water-sheds, forests and glaciers in a cooperative manner, e) open the LoC for travel and trade. These ingredients were later to form the basis of the four-point formula of Gen. Musharraf. Before India and Pakistan could jointly work on these lines; considerable groundwork was required in both countries. Time and circumstances, however, did not appear favorable for the peace process thus evolved to become irreversible. Soon after, Musharraf found himself in the middle of political storms which swept him out of power. Any unbiased assessment of his period in power would indicate that towards the later years of his regime; he had certainly played a big role in bringing the Kashmir problem to the door-steps of a solution. Notwithstanding some efforts by his successor, President Zardari, and expressed positive signals by Manmohan Singh, the stalled peace initiatives did not really pick up. Due to these off the record and back-channel efforts, both countries had almost agreed on the broad outline of a solution to the Kashmir issue but the conclusions had to be spelt out precisely and in a mutually acceptable format. After that, one development or the other prevented reaching a formal agreement and wrapping up of the matter. The train blasts in Mumbai in July 2006, the crisis in Pakistan's judiciary in March 2007 and the terrorists attack in Mumbai on November 26, 2008. That position has continued for over a decade now. In the meanwhile, a lot has happened on both sides.

Apart from the official level back-channel endeavours; certain groups and organizations – foreign as well as indigenous – supplemented with their own exertions spread over the years to strengthen and bring in focus efforts of the Track-II diplomacy. A reference to the contributions of the Neemrana initiative has already been made. In a similar mould could be described the efforts of the German Friedrich Ebert Stiftung and Italy based NGO Pugwash International. The former organized a series of India-Pakistan Peace Process conferences at venues outside the sub-continent. Its fifth round of the IPPP, held at Singapore in the beginning of September 2007, was regarded as particularly successful in view of the meaningful deliberations by a good number of opinion makers from India and Pakistan. This group optimistically noted, "....The gains from the first ever four-year long border ceasefire have permeated to various levels of society and constituted the most striking feature of a tension-free discourse, though the trust deficit has not gone away altogether.... That while 'small successes' did not constitute a 'breakthrough', there was no 'breakdown' either...."[10] In much a similar vein were the two efforts of the Pugwash, which organized its first meeting in Islamabad in March 2006; in the backdrop of Gen Musharraf's peace efforts and a general atmosphere of positivity then prevailing. One of the participants from J&K, Mohammed Yusuf Tarigami – the CPI-M leader and MLA from Kulgam in the Valley – had gone on record to assert that the just concluded Pugwash conference was a very successful event and it would help in further improving the situation in the sub-continent. But, because of a series of events in the region nothing much tangible came out at that time. Pugwash revived its efforts to pick up the thread again by convening another Track-II meeting in Islamabad in August 2013. This was done in the backdrop of some favourable comments of the new Prime Minister Nawaz Sharief; and in an effort to find a middle ground for the peace efforts to move forward. The absence of tangible results do not reflect adversely on the exertions of the organization or the quality of inputs made by a number of leading security experts from both sides of the divide. The very fact that a large number of former defence officers, civil servants, diplomats and intellectuals, from both countries, had gathered at one place to exchange meaningful ideas focused on the task of improving atmospherics and ties; was itself a substantive move forward. This one single facet itself was a considerable movement in the right direction. This, in fact, has always been the core strength of the Track-II diplomacy and back-channel efforts.

---

10 *Kashmir Images*, dated September 10, 2007.

Apart from some foreign-based NGOs and organizations; few Indian and Pakistani 'think tanks' and forums also contributed handsomely to the process of developing closer interaction between various sections of the two people and respective security experts. A leading name in this context emerges to be the New Delhi based Institute for Peace and Conflict Studies (IPCS). It held a number of conferences aimed at arriving at mutually agreed common grounds between India and Pakistan. For this purpose, it invited a host of eminent persons from both sides of the divide at neutral places in the neighborhood like Colombo, Bangkok etc and held a series of discussions focused on improving the peace prospects. This activity, a good example of Track-II efforts, peaked during hey-days of the peace process; but has also continued thereafter over the years. One of its more prominent efforts culminated in a Panel presentation held in New Delhi on April 30, 2004. A team of the IPCS, including amongst others P.R. Chari, Maj Gen. Dipankar Bannerji (Retd) and C. Raja Mohan had visited Pakistan earlier during the month. The group had a wide range of discussions and exchange of ideas with a large number of knowledgeable people in Pakistan; which included well-known names like General Karamat, Shireen Mazari, Brig. Naseem Salik and the like. After a formal presentation by the group and an open-house discussion; the following interesting conclusions surfaced:-

➢ India should try and penetrate different constituencies in Pakistan, as the people there were its best bet. New Delhi should encourage Pakistanis to visit India as they would go back as its unofficial ambassadors.

➢ The people of PoK were averse to jihad and fundamentalism.

➢ The hopes for an early solution to the Kashmir question were misplaced. There were many contradictions and several things happening in Pakistan that were weakening its democratic forces.

➢ It was important for India to start working on its available options on Kashmir without losing the present momentum. We should also first try and put our own house in order in Kashmir. The dialogue between New Delhi and Kashmir was significant and necessary.

➢ Without the active participation of the Pakistan Army, it was difficult to settle any outstanding issues between the two countries.

It was doubtful whether the army would ever allow a genuine peace constituency in Pakistan to flourish.

➤ It was not realistic to look for solutions to Kashmir at this juncture. They would only emerge in due course.

A broad overview of this whole gamut of activities underlines the efficacy and importance of Track-II efforts and back-channel diplomacy as potent means of creating a conducive environment as well as building of a common ground for the resolution of tricky and thorny issues. Both processes operating in the public domain as also in secrecy; essentially aim at achieving the same purpose even though progress is generally slow and results take time in becoming visible. India and Pakistan would do well to continue exertions in this direction; there are enough people and organizations of goodwill in both countries to bridge the existing gaps and work for the day when the two will live like normal and good neighbours.

The Problems of Pakistan, including Afghanistan and Balochistan

The significant problems in Pakistan manifestly started with the death of its creator Jinnah in September 1948; but the beginning was made even earlier as the Qaid, as Jinnah is generally referred to in Pakistan, was largely a stranger to the Provinces of Pakistan and had not been able to build a strong and lasting party structure in the newly created country. He resorted to a short-cut method and confirmed the feudal elements and landlords; then holding offices and stations of power in Provinces, as the senior functionaries of his party. This step did manage to create the semblance of a party structure; but in the long run proved a bane to the development of Pakistan on modern lines. The ruling elite were never able to create a political party capable of mass appeal and mass mobilization; which in turn negatively affected building of essential public institutions. The feudal mentality and a lop-sided agrarian relationship; two negative outcomes directly attributable to this process have stunted the growth of entire nation over the last seven decades. Of many problems and challenges that this country has faced; two of them relating to Pathans and Balochs have spilled over from being purely internal issues and have had a bearing on neighbours also. Balochistan, NWFP (now Khyber Pakhtunkhwa) and Afghanistan developments are closely interlinked with Pakistan - India relations and also thereby with the Kashmir situation.

The use of religious fervor by Pakistan army; first in Afghanistan and then in Kashmir, as an instrument of state and foreign policy, has profoundly impacted the civil society in that country. This damaged the very roots, the sub-continental ethos, of the people there in a way that one wonders whether Zia and his cohorts could have intended or imagined. The unleashing of a narrow and focused brand of religious extremism – including the multi-national perspective of this cult – eminently suited the short-term goals of America to corner and then force the Russian exit from Afghanistan. But they had let the *Genie*; so to say, out of the bottle and have struggled unsuccessfully since then to control it or extinguish the fires they started. The heat was, in time, felt at the very shores of USA itself and only with considerable efforts, cost and negative global publicity America has been able to consolidate its internal security. Also the unsettled conditions in Afghanistan since the late seventies have had adverse and deleterious effect on the Indo-Pak relations. In the historical perspective, Indian and Afghanistan relations date back to the pre-Christian era with this land mass and the famous Khyber Pass providing defensive bulwark against inimical forces. In fact some historians do believe that the decline in the fortunes of the Mughal Empire did not begin during the reign of Aurangzeb; but were triggered earlier in the regime of his father Shahjahan when he finally lost control of Kandahar fort, in southern Afghanistan, in 1648. In the modern times the borders between the British Indian territories and the Afghan state was determined with the 2430 kilometers long Durand Line, by a bilateral agreement dated November 12, 1893. This delineation was slightly modified by the Anglo-Afghan treaty of 1919 and was inherited by Pakistan in 1947 when it came into existence as an independent country. The Durand Line cuts through the Pathan tribal areas and further south through the Balochistan region; politically dividing ethnic Pathan and Baloch groups who live on either side of the Durand Line. It is also a hard fact that no Afghan government has recognized this as the border ever since 1947. Even in the early nineties, during his worst period, the then ruler of Afghanistan – Najeebullah – refused to accept Durand Line as the border with Pakistan. It is in this context that the Indian support to Afghanistan is taken as a negative step by Pakistan; and India has its own geo-political and geo-strategic reasons to offer assistance to Afghanistan. In a similar manner Pakistan sees the Indian hand in the internal problems that country faces in Balochistan. Even though the trouble started brewing in Balochistan from the very day Pakistan came into existence.

The Khan of Kalat, which ruled over most of the present day Balochistan, was even treated as a separate entity and not an Indian princely state. The Anglo-Baloch treaty of 1876 records, "the territories did not pass so as to become part of British India but remain part of Kalat state". After the announcement of British withdrawal from India the Khan of Kalat emphasized that the areas leased to the Crown would revert to his state. On August 11, 1947; Kalat declared independence from 15th August. The British conveniently reneged on their promises to this princely entity and its imperial interests supported the Balochistan becoming a part of Pakistan. Subsequent events took place in this groove. The Pakistani troops moved into the region in March 1948 and the Pakistani government chose to settle the issue by dispatching two newly acquired combat jets to strafe the Khan's palace. On March 28, 1948 the region became a part of Pakistan. "Balochistan is presently in the throes of a fifth uprising since 1948. Last year, Narendra Modi added fuel to the fire with a reference to it in his Independence-Day speech....His jab at Pakistan lends the latter ammunition to accuse India of meddling...."[11]

The regional rulers and opinion makers, including traditionally influential tribal chiefs, have always been at odds with the central government in Pakistan asking for greater autonomy to run the provincial affairs and control its assets; with the latter showing palpable reluctance. With the opposite efforts by both parties, matters came to a head in 1973 when Bhutto was ruling in Pakistan. He dismissed the provincial Balochistan government headed by Sardar Attaullah Mengal and sent in army and air force to quell the serious uprising there. The then Iranian Monarch, for his own reasons, helped the Pak army by providing tanks and helicopter gunships. The skirmishes in Balochistan carried on for years till Bhutto was overthrown by Zia in 1977. Over the decades pipe-lines have carried natural gas from Sui there to major urban centers of Pakistan and a major port has been developed at Gwadar, now with Chinese involvement. Pakistan's perceptions of Indian interests in this region have, over the decades, soured relations between the two nations; notwithstanding the fact that the Pak establishment has failed to make effective political engagement with stakeholders there.

Arguably, the most serious crisis to hit this region took place on August 26, 2006; when Pakistan army killed the 79 year old Baloch leader,

---

11 Ashis Ray in *The Tribune*, dated 28 February 2017.

Nawab Akbar Khan Bugti; who was also the head of a political outfit Jamhoori Watan Party (JWP). He was, along with two other prominent tribal chiefs – Attaullah Mengal and Khair Baksh Marri, leading the Baloch struggle against the rulers of Pakistan. According to a perceptive observer, "….there can be no denying that Baloch nationalism is real and not just the creation of the tribal triumvirate for their own vested interests….Indeed from now on, attitudes against Islamabad may harden….The political demand of the majority of the Baloch people is still provincial autonomy, not secession. In any case, with a population of less than six million, the Baloch lack the capacity and resources to build the critical mass required for such a struggle."[12]

It was only after the 9/11 terrorist attacks in America in September 2001, followed by the commitment of Pakistan to side with the USA in its fight against global terrorism - at least officially – that heralded the beginning of internal security related problems in the country. Pakistan which had been smugly training and exporting militancy from its soil for over two decades got caught up in the whirlpool of its own making and resultant armed violence, of all kinds – fundamentalist, ethnic, regional and tribal; has badly scorched the nation since then. The insurrection, clashes and encounters have been steadily rising and spiraling out of state control. In the resulting crisis and mayhem of violence first the para-military forces and then the army also got sucked in the terror-related vortex of outrages. Just picking up one month, in the middle since then at random; the situation during February 2009 is graphically described as, "As many as 233 terrorist and insurgent attacks killed 213 people and injured another 490 across Pakistan….Five incidents of clashes between security forces and militants/insurgents (4 in NWFP and 1 in Balochistan) killed 33 people and injured 48 others. Security forces launched 32 operational attacks…. that killed 319 people and injured another 284. Meanwhile, 4 cross-border attacks were reported inside Pakistani tribal areas and 1 border clash was reported from Pak-Afghan border in Balochistan. Inter-tribal infightings in tribal and frontier areas, and incidents of ethno-political and criminal violence in Karachi were another addition to the security scenario of militancy and violence-hit Pakistan. In total 679 people were killed and 915 injured during February in these all kinds of attacks, operations, clashes and incidents of violence across Pakistan…."[13]

---

12 Nirupama Subramanian in *Frontline*, September 22, 2006. Pp. 116-117.

13 *Border Affairs*, Jan – Mar 2009, p. 27.

PoK Perceptions/Aspirations

Statistically speaking, the PoK region comprises an area of over thirteen thousand square kilometers, generally having sub-tropical climate over most of the place and a population of around thirty-five lakhs. The average growth rate hovers around three percent, with a population density of 252 persons per square kilometer and a literacy rate around 60 %. It has two divisions, namely Muzaffarabad and Mirpur; which together manage eight districts of Muzzafarabad, Neelum, Poonch, Bagh, Sudhnoti, Mirpur, Bhimber and Kotli.

Muzaffarabad, the largest town of the PoK, is a fairly developed urban centre as also the seat of the 'Azad' Kashmir government. It has the trappings of the headquarters of a small province and also boasts of a university named as 'Azad' Kashmir University. A visitor could find there the headquarters or the local nerve centre of militant organizations like Lashkar-e-Taiba, Jaish-e-Mohhamad, Harkat-ul-Mujahiden, Hizbul Mujahideen, Al-Barq and several others. This place is practically the base camp of all militant activities in J&K. It is reported that way back in 2001also, one could find a sizeable group of Kashmiri youth there; almost around twenty thousand according to one rough estimate – a mix of militants and refugees – although the locals perceive all Kashmiris as militants. Interestingly, and contrary to general belief, the relations between locals and militants have not been warm right from the beginning. These tensions have not been reflected in the media, for obvious reasons.

Mirpur is the second biggest urban centre of PoK. A strong presence of Mirpuris in UK has been a well-known matter for many decades; in fact these people have been functioning there as a rich and powerful pro-Pakistan 'Kashmir lobby'. There are estimated to be over four lakh Mirpuri voters in the Parliamentary constituencies of UK. The effect of their collective prosperity and remittances is reflected in the buildings and structures of new Mirpur; the old town having been drowned in the lake formed by the Mangla dam. For a variety of reasons, Pakistan keeps a close tab on the developments in this region and the entry of foreigners is practically prohibited.

In 2004 the Human Rights Commission of Pakistan, a highly respected organization of international repute, expressed concern over the interference of intelligence agencies in the local politics and treatment of locals by the security forces. In a similar vein, the delegates from PoK also complained to the Geneva based UN Commission for Human Rights about violations of human rights by the security forces and intelligence agencies of Pakistan; simultaneously accusing these of harassing the political workers. There have been wide spread reports of lack of basic education and health facilities in the region leading to palpable illiteracy, ignorance and backwardness.

One also comes across many mentions of 'pro-Azadi' demonstrations by the students of the 'Azad' Kashmir University in Muzzafarabad. Equally strident are the voices in the region which profess pro-Pakistani tilt and hence the overall situation in the PoK appears to be rather a mixed one; with pro-independence constituency being more prominent in and around Mirpur town. There is also an underlying current of unease in Muzzafarabad about the presence of foreign, Kashmiri and local militants in considerable numbers; as their existence in the local milieu has created some social tensions in the region. Some instances have also been reported of adverse societal relations between Kashmir migrants and original inhabitants because of a few unsuccessful marriages amongst the outsiders and local girls.

Hashim Qureshi, a Kashmir based separatist and who was for quite some time hailed as a hero by Pakistani establishment, has critically examined conditions in the region and then reached to the conclusion that what Pakistan calls as 'Azad' Kashmir (AK); is actually not free (Azad) in any sense of the word as the people there do not exercise their right to self-determination, self-rule and sovereignty; it should be referred to as Pakistani 'Occupied Kashmir'. In a signed article commenting on the conditions existing there, he wrote, "....From my freedom in 1980 till my exile in 1986, I was active in AK and Pakistan politics. Eight times I was banned to enter the district (Muzaffarabad) and four times I was arrested....AK has no medical college or engineering college or a polytechnic institute or agricultural college or a forestry college.... On the other hand, in IHK whom so ever you meet is either a doctor, engineer, professor, technocrat or scientist etc....AK youth working hard in foreign countries remit enormous foreign exchange to Pakistan....AK does not get a royalty of Mangla Dam or its share of foreign exchange earnings nor the share towards tax realization and sales tax....High ranking officers like Chief Secretary, Finance Secretary, I.G.P. etc for AK come from Islamabad....Governments are made or broken in AK/POK at the behest of rulers in Islamabad....All sincere nationalists call AK as Pakistan occupied Kashmir...."[14] In a nutshell one could say, without any fear of contradiction, that Pakistan has not only maintained an iron clad control over the PoK but has also been milking the area by taking benefit of resources available there.

Gilgit – Baltistan

The British have been taking considerable interest in the Gilgit region - right through the colonial period because of its strategic importance - particularly in the context of perceived Russian southward expansionist plans. With a population of around 15 lakhs and the territory extending over seventy thousand square kilometers this landmass, bordering China and Afghanistan does command a strategic location. The British, for their own imperial designs, constructed two rudimentary land routes; one was called the Gilgit Road – connecting the town of Gilgit with Srinagar – and the other was named Indus Road linking this region with North West Frontier and Punjab. The region was directly controlled by the British administration in India practically since 1877 till August 1, 1947; when this area technically reverted back to the ruler of J&K state. However, a British inspired revolt there towards ending October that year ensured that this region never practically came under the ruler's possession. Pakistani takeover of the entire belt was engineered and facilitated then by the imperialistic designs and motives. In the pre-1947 era, the whole state of Jammu and Kashmir consisted of four provinces of Jammu, Kashmir, Ladakh and Gilgit plus Frontier Ilaqas of Hunza, Chitral, Nagar, Punial, Yasin etc. The last unit, of Gilgit and others, was re-designated as 'Northern Areas' by Pakistan on illegally taking possession of the same during the disturbed conditions of 1947-48. The Northern Areas were further rechristened as Gigit-Baltistan by an executive order of the Pakistan government on September 9, 2009.

In a landmark judgment on March 8, 1993, delivered by Justice Abdul Majeed Mallick the then Chief Justice of the 'Azad' Kashmir High Court; the Pakistan government was directed to "provide an adequate assistance and facility to the 'Azad' Kashmir government in immediately assuming the administrative control of the Northern Areas." Those directions have

---

14 *Greater Kashmir*, Srinagar, dated July 29, 2011.

been ignored by the Pak government in spite of the fact that this judgment was confirmed, on appeal, by the Supreme Court of Azad Kashmir. Thus the judicial verdict which was aimed at providing civil liberties and basic human rights to the people of Gilgit-Baltistan has remained unimplemented. But, it appears that strategic considerations of Pakistan, which do not favor this region becoming a part of 'Azad' Kashmir, have prevailed over the above mentioned judicial pronouncement.

Sectarian violence between original Shia population and the settled Sunni inhabitants is a recurring phenomenon in the region, earlier known for peaceful relations between communities. This is in contrast to the feeling of brotherhood and understanding which existed till the seventies. Presently even a minor provocation is sufficient to trigger Shia-Sunni tensions in the region right up to Skardu. The roots of this trouble are traced to the Zia regime - in the late seventies - when he tried to change the demographic profile of the region by encouraging Sunni settlers there and also giving preference to them in matters of employment; further widening the rift amongst the communities. The Shias of the area have also shown resentment in the past over what they perceive as attempts by the official agencies to impose Sunni inspired curriculum in the school syllabus. These steps have added fuel to the already existing suspicions in the local minds about the designs of rulers in Islamabad; and successive governments have done pretty little to win the confidence of the locals. Around 2015, when the Chinese CPEC was aggressively sold in this belt, the main theme revolved around the promise that this project will result in the creation of a large number of jobs for the locals. That promise has not yet materialized; and to make matters worse bulk of the limited number of jobs under this scheme have fallen in the laps of the migrant people. The rift between the indigenous population and the new settlers has been widening, with adverse consequences for the entire area.

Even seven decades after this region was taken over by Pakistan; hardly any rights of governance have been given to the local people, notwithstanding repeated pleas and even remonstrations by the inhabitants. Even today the elected Assembly is only for the name and hardly any legislative and administrative powers are delegated to it. Affairs of the region, at the apex level, are managed by the Gilgit-Baltistan Council headed by the Prime Minister of Pakistan which is also clothed with major legislative powers. The composition of this Council is so ordained that the majority in that would always be of the official and nominated members. The Federal Minister for Kashmir Affairs and the Northern Areas effectively controls the region. Hence for all practical purposes, Pakistan government rules this territory; the administration is run by the federally appointed senior civil and police officers. The army and intelligence agencies also occupy large spaces of influence in the region. The judiciary structure there is hardly worth the name. Successive governments over the past seven decades have followed a policy which left its inhabitants with no political identity, civil rights or even constitutional status.

The barter trade with China is particularly robust, with Chinese goods freely available in the local markets. In fact, Pakistan has collaborated with China in a significant manner in this region. Pakistan also ceded 5180 square kilometers of area to China on March 2, 1963, from this region illegally. The old Indus Road connecting this landmass with rest of Pakistan was widened and upgraded with considerable technical and financial assistance from China. The practically new link was commissioned in 1978 and named as the Karakoram Highway. Apart from opening up the region, this road also improved the economic conditions in the area – particularly enhancing the border trade with China.

There are strong under-currents of independence from Islamabad in the whole Gilgit-Baltistan region. The seething discontentment does occasionally blow up into anti-establishment demonstrations and slogan shouting by groups which feel marginalized and left out; and are legitimately aggrieved on that count. In totality, the people are deprived of their basic rights and have a very weak voice in the political process of the region.

The comments of a foreign national, Belgian, aptly describes the conditions in this area. He observes, "The Human Rights Commission of Pakistan calls the situation as volatile and is of the opinion that the Federal Government is directly responsible for this sorry state of affairs. Pakistani policymakers have kept the constitutional status of the area in a limbo… The region lacks fundamental rights…. Economically the region is the most backward area. It doesn't have basic infrastructures like roads, power supply and health care. It has no university, no professional college; no post-graduate facilities….Demographic shifts are being engineered….by encouraging influx of Punjabis, Pathans and other Sunni people from the rest of Pakistan...."[15] The situation has not improved in the last decade; if anything the matters are even worse now.

In addition to the efforts of Pakistani administration, consistently from the 1970s onwards, to change the demographic profile of this region and reduce the Shia population to a minority; it has allowed outsiders to purchase large tracts of land in violation of the State Subject rules enforced by the ruler of J&K much before 1947. Also, in spite of a long history of protests and strikes, Gilgit-Baltistan remains a poor and backward area; indeed a 'neglected centre of inequity'. The plight of people in this area has been very appropriately described by an intellectual of the region as, "We are a part of Pakistan when they want to rule us and our land, but not a part of Pakistan when we want the rights that other Pakistanis have."Sporadic efforts by Islamabad to address development and reforms issues have not created meaningful avenues of political participation and neither addressed the burning problem of economic stagnation of the area.

It is in this background of neglect and deliberate suppression of the local aspirations; a view should be taken of the fact that while road network linking major cities of Pakistan is excellent; it is in a poor condition within the PoK and G-B area. For instance, if a person has to go to Muzzafarabad from Mirpur, one is advised to go via Islamabad to reach quickly. Similar is the case with Gilgit, where the Karakoram Highway does provide a good and dependable link with rest of Pakistan; but the internal road network is in a very poor state. It seems to be a well thought out strategy of the Pakistan government to deny the focal points of the region a good road network; and therefore dependable internal means of communication. On all parameters of development; an absolute contrast can be noticed in the conditions existing, across the divide, in the state of Jammu and Kashmir.

These two regions of the erstwhile J&K state – the PoK and the Gilgit-Baltistan areas – now under the control of Pakistan government, have been suffering badly ever since 1947. The Pak establishment, including army and intelligence agencies, has only shown interest in consolidating hold of the state authorities there; without bothering about the welfare of the general people. It is very clear that Islamabad has failed to create meaningful avenues of political participation by the locals; as well as not addressed the issues of their economic neglect. Another moot point to

---

15 Paul Beersmans in *Epilogue*, Jammu, March 2008, pp. 52-53.

consider is that not a single type but different kinds of people are living there; whose language, culture and ethnicity differ from each other. Every community needs sensitive and careful handling for optimally harnessing its potential.

The long history of discord and friction between India and Pakistan has had a detrimental impact on the people of these regions; who have remained deprived of economic benefits and even basic rights due to them. The conflict in J&K continues to shape political discourse and economic development of this landmass. Thus, logically the process of peace between India and Pakistan would also, most likely, be a harbinger of better days for these people. On the other hand without waiting for this to happen; it just may be useful to address the internal problems of the regions; as that may also have a positive impact on the external situation; in turn improving prospects of the peace process. The continued militancy and conflict situation in Kashmir has shaped the bleak economic scenario in PoK; as also its relations with Pakistan. The connection between internal dimensions and the Indo-Pak peace process cannot be overemphasized. This line of action may be worth a try, but the contours of this policy frame work have to be properly understood and appreciated by rulers in Pakistan – both *de facto* and *de jure*.

The US and World Pressure

The cataclysmic events of September 11, 2001; also in the almost immediate aftermath of the failed India – Pakistan summit at Agra in July that year, proved a turning point in the fortunes of Pakistan. It was unable to garner any international support on the jihadi activities inside J&K; which was now being seen as an off-shoot of the larger international terror apparatus. For tactical reasons, Pakistan agreed to review its state policy in this regard only after getting singed in the blowback effects of the tragic events and international condemnation in one voice. This change in stance, which appears to have been well thought out by the military leadership there, also helped the Pak regime to shore up its falling economy by way of the lifting of US economic sanctions. Thus it was able to get financial assistance from the US, the EU and international financial institutions. This gave much-needed assistance to Pakistan to tide over the imminent crisis in its economy and literally brought the country back from the brink. But the long-term damage to its stature in the comity of nations and international standing was substantial and enduring.

This was also the beginning of the US putting pressure on Pakistan to work for the former's security interests in Afghanistan as also try to improve relations with India by visibly scaling down cross-border militant activity. But all this edging and prodding was discreet and behind the scene persuasions; which hardly worked in either case. However, the US did move decisively to get the two jihadi groups of Lashkar-e-Taiba and Jaish-e-Mohammed declared as international terrorist organizations. This was followed, in July 2005, by the Indo-US civil nuclear deal which helped India to virtually see the end of international nuclear sanctions. India could also access the US technology with greater ease henceforth. Obviously this did not go well with Pakistan as the US – or any other country for that matter – did not offer any matching facility to Pakistan. Any observer could see the de-hyphenation of the two countries by the US; probably for the first time. More was to follow.

The visit of US President Bush to India and Pakistan during the early part of March 2006 made his country's intentions even more clear in this regard. Apart from prodding General Musharraf to effectively rein in the jihadis; Bush not only not offered any nuclear sops to Pakistan, but said, "I told him that Pakistan and India are different countries with different needs and different histories". The message was clear that henceforth America will look at the two nations on respective merits and not see them together anymore. The implicit lesson in this also was that the two should move positively to improve relations and upgrade the process of normalization. This meeting of 4th March between Bush and Musharraf was certainly a watershed in defining relations amongst the three countries. The US administration continued to lean on Pakistan to put an end to the ongoing militancy in J&K. It's Under Secretary of State Nicholas Burns said on September 27, 2006, "….Pakistan also needs to work with India to reduce the threat from Kashmiri separatist groups". Less than a month later, on 12th October, he reiterated "….We wish to see no more terrorism emanating from Kashmiri terrorist groups and we have told the Pakistani government that we would hope that Pakistan would use its influence with these groups to curb and stop any attacks on India". The trend has continued unabated in all the US administrations following that of President Bush, that is, two terms of Barrack Obama and now Donald Trump.

The progressively building up of American pressure was not the only thing Pakistan was faced with; a European Union report released in March

2007 also impressed upon Pakistan to disarm militants and shut down terror training camps operating from its territory. This EU report was prepared by one of the MPs, Baroness Emma Nicholson and passed by 60 votes to one by the Foreign Affairs Committee. In this she pointedly berated Pakistan for supporting terrorism against India; saying "….Pakistan has provided Kashmiri militants with training, weapons, funding and sanctuary and has failed to hold militants accountable for atrocities they have committed on the Indian-administered side". There was another reason for Pakistan to feel uncomfortable about this EU report; which for its own reasons it tried to block as well as denigrate without success. There had not been any other such reports in the past which focused so much on the poor conditions prevailing in the PoK. This shift from J&K to the PoK; in an international forum of repute also rankled the Pak establishment a lot. Quite surprisingly, India did not make enough efforts to use this report to put Pakistan in the dock in the eyes of international community. Was this a callous neglect or a deliberate omission in the interest of furthering peace process between the two countries?

Even though Pakistan professed enduring fidelity to and has remained an American ally since the second half of the previous century; mutual relations of the two countries have passed through three apparent phases. The two came together for the first time in the mid 1950s when the US was looking for anti-Soviet allies and Pakistan fitted the bill on more than one counts. The relations became frosty a decade later when President Johnson blocked the arms supply to Pakistan during the 1965 Indo-Pak war. The high point in the second upswing in ties came at the time of Soviet occupation of Afghanistan in 1979; when Pakistan was declared as a frontline ally by an alarmed President Jimmy Carter. Eleven years later, this phase also tapered off in the face of mounting and verifiable evidence regarding Pakistan's nuclear weapons programme and Pressler Amendment in the American Senate. The third cycle happened when Al Qaeda destroyed the World Trade Centre and also targeted other places in America on September 11, 2001 and Pakistan once again became a close US ally. But this time General Musharraf, the then military ruler of Pakistan, was practically coerced into this partnership and joined America rather half-heartedly. As by then a considerable part of Pakistan was influenced by the jihadi culture and a part of its army had also been radicalized. So, the companionship was uncomfortable and – at times – rocky. The Pakistanis wanted 1980s type of relationship when it received from America virtually unlimited military and economic assistance without any accounting or accountability; something which the US under President Bush or his successors was not prepared to offer. The world had changed; but the Pak establishment – more particularly its army - failed to recognize the tell-tale signs and accept that the American aims were more global in nature than being confined to the happenings in Afghanistan.

The Pak-US relations have over the decades become probably the most important external factor in the ties between India and Pakistan. The overall assessment of affinity in the former grouping is quite perplexing, but some of the contours are discernible. It is quite clear that Al-Qaeda and Taliban are the original fountainheads of terrorism and, because of international dimensions as also ramifications, the US cannot afford to give up on Afghanistan as the Soviet Union did. In this context, it is interesting to see as to how long the Pakistanis can afford to continue with the game of running with the jihadi hares and hunting with the US hounds. Also, at the same time, Pakistan does need the American assistance badly to shore up its tottering economy. One thing is quite certain that without liberal US help; Pakistan would run the risk of becoming almost a failed state. It is also doubtful if after antagonizing America, the Pakistan establishment can hope for a liberal flow of aid from Saudi Arabia. The Chinese benevolence towards Pakistan in monetary terms is yet to be tested; and the past record of China's assistance to the dependent states is not encouraging. Equally relevant is the fact that Pakistan is very sensitive to the enhancing Indo-US affinity, and in that context also, it would not gamble on giving up all its influence over the US and pushing their mutual ties to a breaking point.

The American calculations, on the other hand, would also be reaching a similar set of conclusions; though may be for different reasons. Observing from that end, it becomes quite evident that political entities cannot deliver much in Pakistan and have been effectively kept out of the key areas of defence, foreign affairs, nuclear weapons and internal security by the army-ISI combine. The US also has to cater for the fact that notwithstanding the closeness at the official levels; there is a considerable level of anti-American sentiment amongst the general public in Pakistan. This reality has become even more palpable during the last two decades. In addition there appears to be an inconsistency between short-term and long-term American objectives in Pakistan; as also between these and the wider American aims in the region - like keeping the war on terror in

Afghanistan going as well as pursuing policies relating to countries like Russia, China and Iran. On one hand, Pakistan is important to the US for regional security equations and on the other, it is also seen as a source of the problem in Afghanistan rather than a part of the solution. There could be other dichotomies as well. All these factors add up to make the Pak-US closeness a troubled relationship – particularly of late.

India came into this calculus quite late; but with sure footings. For the second half of the last century, the Indo-Pak peace process could not get the desired traction partly because of latter's closeness to the Americans and the level of intransigence this must have generated therein. Now, when for geo-political and geo-strategic reasons Indian ties with America are on the upswing; Pakistan does seem to be taking this development as a negative factor in improving its relations with India. In fact, all through the last seven decades, India has remained the corner stone of Pak strategic thinking; both of its military as well as amongst the policymakers. Without underestimating the significance of the various factors mentioned here-in-before – some of which may appear contradictory - the possibilities of closer and better ties amongst the two neighbors remain a vision and hope worth pursuing.

CHAPTER – XII

The Crystal Gazing

Analysis of the Current situation

Right from the very beginning, Pakistan has positioned itself in an antagonistic position against India and all along the latter has been its central obsession. During the Cold War era, the main aim of the Pak establishment's decision to join the western bloc was to use the liberal aid thus received in keeping a much larger India off balance. Having well-endowed friends on the right side gave that country almost an immunity to create problems for India, and unmindful of the consequences including long-term internal implications, it went ahead to foment huge problems for India first in Punjab and then in J&K. For more than five decades that country had almost a free run with its new found weapons and instruments of jihad and terrorism. It was only after the West, particularly America, got badly singed with international terror network – after 9/11 – that Pakistan was at least asked uncomfortable questions and confronted with facts and data which virtually showed it the mirror. Even at that critical period, it tried to wriggle out by claiming to take on the Islamic terrorism and almost convincing the West of its sincerity of purpose, while actually being a base and sanctuary to groups like Haqqani network in Afghanistan or to insurgent groups in Kashmir. Having had its way for so long, and feeling smug about it, the country is now engaged in playing its China card. While it is for America and China to carefully read the real intentions of Pakistan; it is overdue for rest of the world, particularly for India, to call the bluff of Islamabad and get it to end support to terror and mayhem which destabilizes the region and the world. Right from the day this country was born on August 14, 1947, to the very recent happenings, Pakistan has been lurching from one crisis to another. The economy is in ruins; health and educational institutions in shambles; developmental indices paint a grim picture and right-wing extremism has virtually enveloped the whole country. What does the future hold for Pakistan?

An unemotional, thought-provoking and very real assessment of the task of nation-building by Pakistan has been made by a perceptively practical analyst as, "Thus the new governments of Independent India and Pakistan not only stepped into the shoes of the departing colonial power without much difficulty and transfer of power went off smoothly and painlessly, they were also able to handle the genocidal post-partition riots and the rehabilitation of a massive refugee population with a fair measure of success. India was able to deal with the immediate post-partition problems and their long-term fall-out somewhat more effectively because first, it inherited intact a fully functional central secretariat at Delhi while Pakistan had to set up a wholly new establishment at Karachi. And secondly, Indian political leaders had over two years of experience of governance from 1937 to 1939 when they had held ministerial positions in the government constituted under the scheme of the 1935 Government of India Act in many provinces. Pakistan ministers, on the other hand, were by and large new to their jobs. The early death of Jinnah and the assassination of Liaquat Ali Khan made a bad situation worse and the vacuum created thereby at the top could not be filled for a long time to come. The pre-partition generation of politically oriented leaders in the Punjab, Sind, North-West Frontier Province and Baluchistan who had opposed the concept of Pakistan almost till the end and who could readily replace the departing ruling class, were not acceptable to the founders of Pakistan, primarily belonging to provinces which did not now form part of Pakistan. The vacuum was filled up initially by civil servants and then by army generals who remained in power for major part of Pakistan's history. Lack of a mature and experienced political leadership in the initial formative years of its existence, could not but cast its malignant shadow on the growth and evolution of political institutions in Pakistan, as also the development of a neutral civil service and an independent judiciary. The army collectively came to acquire a dominant voice in its body-politic and continued to wield considerable clout in the corridors of power even after the restoration of democracy. Both the Civil Service and the police were content to play a subservient role. It was not till the late 1980's that the army generals noticeably and willingly appeared to have assumed a non-political stance though the country's nuclear programme and a considerable component of its subversive intelligence activity continued to be dictated by the army top-brass, possibly independent of political direction. Also, the army chief continued to commend a great deal of influence in governance as an important member of the all-powerful triumvirate together with the President and the Prime Minister."[1] This analysis largely remains true even to date.

Pakistan has been oscillating between a seemingly democratic dispensation and military dictatorship, but for the common man, the state has mostly been run on an authoritarian pattern. This has been primarily so due to the fact that from the beginning itself the foreign policy and security-related issues have been dictated by the military which never ceded any ground in this respect to the genuine and concerned branches of the government. The country has literally stumbled from one crisis to another till the present time; and the situation is nowhere near any improvement as the shadow of the big brother – army – always looms large over the managers of affairs of the state even when a democratic dispensation is in power. In this situation, a number of political analysts do believe that perpetuation of enmity with India over Kashmir – or any other matter for that purpose – is necessary for Pakistan army, Pakistan clergy and various terrorist groups to sustain themselves as well as their importance on the national scene.

In a way, the lackluster Indian response to the decades of the problem created by Pakistan has also been responsible for the current impasse. The Indian establishment has always been obliging enough to accommodate Pakistani interests right from 1947 and over these many decades. At the time of accession, India had inherited a loyal and friendly population in Kashmir, deeply committed to the basic tenets and foundations of the Constitution and the Republic. It is a historic reality that at a great cost to lives and property; the people of this state fought the Pakistani raiders and the hostiles. Equally true is the hard fact that a section of the population in the Valley had felt alienated by the time militancy gained a foothold in the state, especially in the Valley. Notwithstanding the deep involvement of Pakistan in creating problems in the state; a palpable failure of policies and systems had also taken place. An overall assessment would indicate that Indian handling of economic, defence and political policies has been

---

1 K.S. Dhillon, *Defenders of the Establishment*, The Indian Institute of Advance Study, Shimla, 1998, pp. 149-150.

less than successful. It failed to take advantage of superior armed strength as well as an extremely favorable military situation – almost poised for victory - in 1947-48 conflict with Pakistan. This inability to wrest an optimum advantage, having gained dominance in an armed conflict, was again repeated in 1965 when India agreed to vacate, in addition to other conquered territory, the strategic Haji Pir Pass connecting Poonch with Uri and thus providing an alternative land route to Kashmir Valley. Similar military restrain and diplomatic control was on display during the Kargil operations in 1999. In addition to the continuing military status quo from 1948 onwards, the two countries have got involved in a low-intensity conflict in the icy bleaks of Siachen; gaining the dubious distinction of operationally deploying armies in the highest altitude ever. The Indian state has been more than fair; in fact, it has been generous, in dealing with Pakistan. Coupled with this fact of accommodation; there is also the lack of a clear-cut and well defined national policy with respect to Pakistan; transcending narrow political interests.

Looking at Pakistan, one finds that after the early departure of Jinnah and Liaqat Ali Khan from the political scene; the only period when the country came close to a democratic consolidation was during the period of Z.A. Bhutto. This was also ironical in a way that it happened immediately after Pakistan lost its Eastern wing in December 1971 and the same man was responsible for it in a significant manner. At least most of the Pakistanis thought at that time that a new era of democracy and prosperity had dawned in their country. Bhutto came to power on December 20, 1971; was ousted by a military coup on July 5, 1977 and was executed - on the charges of complicity in a political murder - on April 5, 1979. He, in fact, was catapulted to power on the twin planks of the political popularity, of his own and the Pakistan People's Party (PPP) that he headed; and the huge discredit that the army there had suffered during the December 1971 war with India.

No other political party in Pakistan has caught the imagination of its people, as the PPP did in the late 1960s. The Muslim League ably led by Jinnah did establish Pakistan, but the party was more of the elites and did not evolve from grass root levels in Pakistan. PPP and Zulfikar Ali Bhutto were not only synonymous but also part of a sort of revolution for almost a decade at the time of coming to power; as the party had emerged from below, with a popular imagination. The party started with a socialist ideology and a powerful slogan of *Roti, Kapara, Makan (food, clothing and shelter)*. Bhutto had managed to create a party of the masses. An incident pertaining to that period underlines this point well. During a PPP conference in Karachi in the year 1973, a number of peasant delegates criticized Bhutto for not delivering on his promises. He listened patiently as the speakers attacked the regime and contrasted the promises made with what had been achieved on the ground. At the end, Bhutto stood up and replied, "Many of the points you have made are correct. We have proceeded slowly. But, let me ask you one question. Who gave you the courage to stand up and confront the Prime Minister of this country as you have done? Who gave you that voice?...." Bhutto had in fact given a voice to the large and silent majority of people, for the first time in the short history of Pakistan.

The PPP had also come to occupy an important position in Pakistan's federal politics. With Jinnah's sudden demise, the subsequent decline of the Muslim League and its factionalization, the country did not have a party cutting across all the provinces. Besides the decline of the Muslim League, the initial decades also witnessed the ascendancy of the military Establishment at the cost of politics and political parties across the provinces. The rise of Bhutto and the PPP thus filled an important void in the federal politics of Pakistan. Even though it did not wield enough influence to cover both parts of Pakistan then; Bhutto was perhaps the only leader to rise above the regional politics and have a national standing in his time. However, on the political front, he did commit two significant mistakes. A major one pertained to his inability to affect any noteworthy and meaningful land reforms to finish the old agrarian structure once for all. The agrarian relationship and the regimes' agricultural policies had always been in favor of large land owners and detrimental to the interests of small farmers, tenants and agricultural laborers. Once Bhutto had decided to indulge on in cosmetic reforms, there was little hope of any real social change. However, his biggest failure was his own inability to emerge as a democrat and institute inner-party democratic systems in the PPP which could have built the political structure on a more firm and lasting basis. He also committed a huge mistake by using army to suppress the uprising in Balochistan as also for his political ends there. This enabled a discredited and enfeebled high command of army to recoup its prestige and standing; which it had lost after the 1971 war with India. The revived military structure hit back and army seized power on July 5, 1977 with the army chief Gen. Zia-ul-Haq appointing himself as the Chief Martial Law Administrator. "The populist tide in Pakistani politics had come to an end".[2]

Bhutto also had certain positive contributions to his credit and his greatest gift to Pakistan was the 1973 Constitution. For the first time a definite political structure was given to the country's polity and the concept of executive accountability to the elected Parliament was accepted. Though it has now been deformed almost beyond recognition; nonetheless its concept does remain a rallying point for parties and groups struggling to usher in the real democracy in Pakistan. Constitutional oversight is a crucial cornerstone of any democratic polity.

Since then, from the departure of Bhutto from political power in 1977, Pakistan has been ruled by two military dictators – Zia-ul-Haq and Parvez Musharraf – and the civilian governments at the centre headed at various times by Nawaz Sharif, Benazir Bhutto and Asif Zardari. But even at the times elected government was in power, the shadow of army loomed large; in fact assuming palpably threatening postures at times. The almost constant US support during this period, and the largesse by implication has also been greatly responsible for keeping the Pakistani state afloat and its army generally happy. The Americans have been literally eating out of the hands of their client state; particularly during the last two decades of the twentieth century. The very sound financial health of the ISI of Pakistan is very much due to the large-hearted backing of the Uncle Sam. Even after the 9/11 attacks on the World Trade Centre in New York in 2001, Pakistan has well maneuvered itself in a position of receiving considerable American generosity. There has been a costly price tag for an outwardly Pak backing of the American and coalition operations in Afghanistan; all the while Pakistan retained an unhindered capacity to follow its own state policy of supporting armed groups of various hues and categories. Even after Osama-bin-Laden was targeted and neutralized by the Americans in the Pakistani town of Abbottabad, in May 2011, there has hardly been any curtailment in the mischief-making capacity of Pakistan on its eastern or Western border or the liberal US financial support. Of course, since the last couple of years, China is emerging as the new economic ally of Pakistan with its CPEC projects exceeding investments of over 50 billion dollars; but the contours of this big buck game are yet not fully delineated. Would

2   Tariq Ali, *Can Pakistan Survive*, Penguin Books, London, 1983, p- 131.

Pakistan be able to manage both Americans and the Chinese simultaneously or get much closer to one at the cost of other; is something yet to be seen. The future prosperity of the country is crucially dependent on this aspect; as also equally on the Pak capacity to effectively tackle the problems created by armed bands of various types, ideologies and organizations covered under the generic term "Taliban". These people are turned out in big numbers by the indoctrination of young and impressionable boys lodged and educated in a large number of religious seminaries – called *Madarsas* - located almost all over Pakistan. These Talibans, who have over the years created problems in Kashmir and Afghanistan, are now also causing destruction and mayhem within Pakistan itself and this particular group is loosely called TTP (*Tehrik-e-Taliban Pakistan*).

Security

The TTP is particularly active in the two provinces of Punjab and Khyber-Pakhtunkhwa; and has caused large-scale damage in this region in the last few years. While Pakistani security forces are engaged in fighting these elements within the country, its state policy of supporting the similar armed groups operating in Afghanistan and Kashmir continues unabated. This policy of dividing the Taliban into 'good' group, those who operate in Afghanistan and Kashmir, and a 'bad' sort - who create problems within Pakistan - has been flawed from the beginning itself. This became sufficiently evident because of the linkages the two categories developed when Islamabad tried peace talks with the 'bad' TTP. Legitimizing the TTP has, in fact, increased the sense of insecurity not only among the minority sects, but is also of concern to the majority Sunni Muslims who collectively believe in a more tolerant form of Islam. Any deal with the TTP on its terms is likely to plunge that country into turmoil as also destroy its social fabric.

But, the Indian response to and dealing with the armed intruders has also been less than effective. It has been limited to eliminating the terrorists, in which there have been successes of varying degrees over the years, but the problem still continues even after three decades. It is practically a low-cost proxy war being executed by Pakistan; spearheaded by the army and the ISI. The latter has also established sleeper cells in major cities and towns across India; and some of these keep getting exposed with sickening frequency. The challenge that this poses to the internal security and social mosaic of the country, has not received proper and due attention here.

That the Indian polity is a democratic set up should not be an excuse for being termed as a 'soft state' that this country is sometimes described as. A democracy like America, for example, has been successful in preventing a major terrorist attack since September 2001. No doubt the border fencing along the International Border and LoC by India has been an effective measure in tackling the issue of cross-border armed infiltration; but it also reflects a defensive attitude – a singular inability to put across a strong message to Pakistan to stop this mischief. A point in this respect was very forcefully – though innocently – made around 2003 by a resident of a border village near Poonch town to an officer supervising the erection of border fence in that area; who was also trying to persuade the villagers not to raise objections for the completion of this important project. The villager posed a very relevant question to the officer. India, he said, is admittedly a greater military power than Pakistan; then why India was erecting the fence and not Pakistan as such defensive measures are usually taken by the weaker party and not the stronger one. This simple logic very effectively underlines the different national attitudes to the same festering problem; the reactive and defensive Indian mindset as compared to the aggressive Pakistani postures. The policy makers in New Delhi would do well to remember that even a confirmed believer in non-violence like the Mauryan Emperor Ashok, in his 12th Rock Edict warned the forest tribes against terror acts and to be wary of his "power even in his remorse". Also, whether one likes it or not, the fact is that India is placed next door to a country which has been many times described by economists and geo-strategic observers as the most dangerous place in the world; and therefore the Indian line of conduct, goals and responses should be tailored accordingly.

Across the borders; all security-related matters as also major policies issues pertaining to important countries and neighbors, including India, are the exclusive preserve of the army there. It has been so right from the beginning. On a number of occasions; even when an elected Prime Minister of Pakistan said something out of line with the army thinking, he or she was quickly made to back-track and literally eat own words. There are many such examples. The "deep state" - as the army-ISI combine is generally referred to - has been graphically described by an astute Pakistani scholar as 'an unbridled horse, without the reins of constitutional oversight'. Even after the great tragedy of December 2014, when 141 people lost their lives – including 132 schoolchildren – in the terrorist attack at the Army Public

School Peshawar; the Pakistan army high command literally bulldozed the government and the National Assembly into granting more powers to the army, including some judicial functions, under the National Action Plan (NAP) for fighting terrorism. While the forces there are now locked up in a struggle with various hues of armed extremists in almost all parts of Pakistan – the so called 'bad Talibans' - the army top brass still thinks that trouble makers in Afghanistan and Kashmir are the 'good Talibans' and treats them as its strategic assets. With Taliban sanctuaries located on both sides of the Durand Line and constant flow of militants across the LoC, for almost three decades now, this sort of categorization and differential treatment beats all logic. But the Pak army continues with the premise and pursues with vigor the anti-India policy; ever unmindful of the international criticism, domestic difficulties and also mounting casualties in its own ranks. The only possible explanation for this irrational approach can be traced back to the element of fundamentalism introduced by Gen. Zia-ul-Haq in the army during his rule. It had then affected the lower rank officer cadre of the army, but over a period it has now travelled right up to the top. It is quite usual now to find and trace the Taliban sympathizers in the army at all levels.

Pakistan's friends and allies are naturally worried over this phenomenon. Whereas the Chinese and other Pak friends in the OIC have refrained from publically mentioning this issue - the Chinese reluctance may be understandable as it is unlikely to abandon its existing nexus with Pakistan for a variety of reasons - but, the Americans have warned Pakistan, on record, that it faces the danger of losing a part of territory to the Talibans. The US has also been expressing its anxiety over the safe keeping of Pakistan's nuclear assets and the probability of an extremist group getting access to or taking control of a part of it. Pak assurances to the contrary do not assuage the American feelings as they had once felt equally smug about Shah's regime in Iran until it was too late. They would certainly not like to take many chances again. It surely is a frightening scenario, not only for Pakistan – which does not seem worried about it – but also for many other entities, not the least India. Therefore, both hardware and software are issues of concern; as also the safety of Pak atomic stockpile and the creeping extremism mentality in the rank and file of the country's armed forces. These matters require careful evaluation and analyses.

The Pakistan army, and of course the ISI, have at different times been accused, often publically, of sheltering and supporting extremist elements and in particular with regard to groups like Haqqani network and Quetta Shura. But these allegations have been flatly denied, in spite of mounting evidence to the contrary. The Pak army is a rule unto itself as no one in that country can either question or criticize it; including the Prime Minister, the National Assembly and the judiciary. It has also been pointed out by perceptive observers in Pakistan that when the Prime Minister or high civilian dignitaries meet with their foreign counterparts, the army chief or his representative is generally present; but when the army chief holds parleys with visiting VIPs, no civilian is ever present in these meetings. This is contrary to the accepted practice in other countries, especially democratic systems.

Ever since the democratic government was re-established in Pakistan, at the beginning of 2008, with Asif Zardari heading the civilian dispensation; the ominous shadow of the army and the threat of a military take-over have been ever present, if not looming large over the polity. At different times, during the period, there has been intense media speculation in this regard and if the successive governments have survived the credit for this has been quite openly given to the respective army chiefs- right from Kayani to Bajwa. The attitude of COAS towards his civilian counterpart can, at best, be described as mild toleration and amused benevolence. Whenever the Prime Minister or his followers appear to be going off the script or against the interests and wishes of army; a rap is delivered on the knuckles or the requisite message is put across in a very perceivable manner.

The Army Chief speaks himself on rare occasions and his mind is generally conveyed through the press briefings of the Directorate of Inter Services Public Relations (ISPR); which is seen – and also functions - as a mouth piece of the Pakistan army. A very interesting overview of the interplay between the political set up and the army appeared in an editorial of the daily Dawn on October 7, 2017. This in parts said, "It was a political tour de force, a performance worthy of an information minister in a democratic regime. Maj Gen Asif Ghafoor's news conference at the ISPR headquarters on Thursday (October 5, 2017) was remarkable for the ground that was covered – and, crucially, for what was left unsaid....; his remarks were carefully prepared and his answers hewed to a carefully prepared script.... There may be a temptation to view the intrusion into the civilian domain merely in the context of the current political crisis in the country. But a historical perspective would suggest that the intrusion is nothing new and indeed goes back to the very earliest years of the republic…. There is also the unfortunate reality that the civilians have at times willingly ceded space – willing to trade constitutional prerogatives for a bit of political longevity. Undoubtedly, the pressure at the very top is intense, but a true democratic leadership would fight harder for principle than self-interest…. Indeed the perceived significance of the news conference was precisely the intensive military deliberations at a time when Pakistan is facing great uncertainty in its relations with the US and the country has a political government that has effectively stalled…." This was almost like showing a thumb to the existing political regime.

After the November 2008 terrorists attack in Mumbai, Zardari, the then Pakistani President, offered to be cooperative by proposing to send the ISI chief to India to assist investigations. The army high command stoutly opposed this and the move backfired. There was no more talk of Pakistani collaboration in getting to the roots of this mayhem. This was another formidable example of the domination of army over the civilian handling of foreign affairs. In connection with the same episode and in the backdrop of a meeting between the Prime Ministers of India and Pakistan in Ufa on July 10, 2015; the views of a high ranking civilian official of Pakistan – Tariq Khosa former Director General of Federal Investigating Agency (DG of FIA) – became public. It was practically a call for the nation to look into the mirror. After mentioning seven 'pertinent facts' pointing towards an irrefutable involvement of Pakistan in the Mumbai tragedy; Tariq goes on to say, "…. The duality and distinction between good and bad Taliban, including all militants and terrorists, should stand removed from Miramshah to Muridke, from Karachi to Quetta…. Let both India and Pakistan admit their mistakes and follies and learn to co-exist while trying to find solutions to their thorny issues through peaceful means…. The Mumbai case is quite unique: one incident with two jurisdictions and two trials…. Therefore, the legal experts from both sides need to sit together rather than sulk and point fingers…. Are we as a nation prepared to muster the courage to face uncomfortable truths and combat the demons of militancy that haunt our land? That is the question!"[3]

---

3   Daily Excelsior, Jammu, August 5, 2015 (Courtesy: Dawn)

In this connection it is also important to recall that in May 2011, the Americans located and killed Osama bin Laden in Abbottabad and Pakistan army was left red-faced. The event had an international significance and was certainly a major success of the civilized world's fight against the dark forces of terrorism and extremism. Much has been written about the graphic account and details pertaining to this operation and there may not be a need to repeat the narrative. The army high command and the political executive in Pakistan tried their best to cover up the fall out of this momentous event and these efforts did achieve considerable success; notwithstanding an extremely difficult situation for the establishment. The only major, and also official, casualty of this occurrence turned out to be the professional and personal loss to the then Ambassador in Washington, Husain Haqqani. Former American President Obama, who was incumbent in the White House then, was in India on a private visit in the beginning of December 2017 and in one of his interviews, practically gave a clean chit to the Pakistani establishment. This statement; coupled with the absolute lack of timely response by the Pak army and the ease with which Osama bin Laden was killed, points to a significant aspect of an important element of the army being either a silent supporter or in active collaboration with the American efforts. The premise, which is not altogether unfounded, also raises the probability of an American plan being in place to thwart the possibilities of rouge elements laying hands on the Pakistani nuclear assets. This scenario raises its own plethora of eventualities.

The Pakistan army's mindset of treating the right-wing elements in the country as its allies in the machinations against India, for at least four decades now, has not only helped the rise of extremism in that country but also emboldened these elements beyond measure. The terrorist groups there have now graduated into full-fledged 'armies' capable of challenging the military itself; which they have done credibly in a number of places and the process continues. Their arsenals are well-stocked — AK47s, grenades, rocket launchers, surface-to-air missiles and a most terrible weapon — the suicide bomber. The armed and indoctrinated cadres of Pakistan's terrorist organizations are cold-blooded murderers who bomb schools, mosques and shrines without a qualm. According to one estimate, the number of the dead in the country since 2007 has stood over 50,000. These elements also thrive in their respective zones of comfort and Pakistani extremist parties have no dearth of doles from religious entities; some of them masquerading as charities. The terror groups get intellectual backing too — sometimes subtle, sometimes quite openly — from sections of the academia, religious elements and the media. But, all the same, they flourish and operate under the overarching umbrella of the army. A small and contrary view does exist in the country – reflecting a longing for divine intervention or maybe the concept of inevitability – reflected in an article by a Pakistani journalist as, "….An overwhelming majority believes that the military will keep its jihadi option intact by differentiating between good and bad Taliban and other extremist groups. A very tiny minority, including myself, optimistically believes that the military has no choice but to take out all kinds of jihadis. The military may wish otherwise and may not be fully cognizant of its limited choices but circumstances will force it to clean up the mess it created…."[4]

One of the recent condemnations of army's role in the governance structure has come from a Karachi based political economist; who has written, "Around three thousand unarmed men, of a recently formed group, the Tehreek-i-Labaik Ya Rasool Allah (TLY), have been able to close down key parts of Pakistan's main cities, which included Rawalpindi, Islamabad, Lahore and Karachi…. has created such a major crisis for a government which is trying to stabilize itself under a new Prime Minister shows how a miniscule political entity can have such major consequences…. Before social media went off the air, there was a strong reaction to the numerous remarks made by military spokesmen as well as the Chief of the Army Staff, General Qamar Javed Bajwa. Before the action against the protestors started, Gen. Bajwa said that violence should be avoided 'by both sides', meaning the protestors and the government, which got a strong reaction from many on social media, pointing out that it was the protestors who were being violent, not the government. When the civilian government asked for the military's help in removing the protestors, he said that since the people 'loved the Army', the Army could not become part of any such action…."[5] In no other democracy could a forces chief use such expressions. It also clearly indicates how close the army and extreme right-wing elements in Pakistan are.

Pakistan has had to face a number of critical situations during the first seventeen years of this century. These include the decisions made in the wake of 9/11 and the US-led war in Afghanistan; the events leading

---

4   Dr. Manzur Ejaz, *Daily Times*, dated January 5, 2016.

5   S. Akbar Zaidi, *The Hindu*, dated November 28, 2017.

up to the Lal Masjid operation and its aftermath; the death of Benazir Bhutto; the military operation in Swat; the killing of Osama bin Laden; Operations Zarb-i-Azab and Radd-ul-Fasaad in which over four thousand people are estimated to have died; the Army Public School terrorist attack in Peshawar; and several others. The country has been lurching from one crisis to another; barely able to keep its head above water. The National Action Plan crafted in the aftermath of a national outrage in the wake of APS Peshawar tragedy has mostly remained on paper and not implemented in a way which can be deemed satisfactory. An overview of the last few decades would indicate that Pakistan's military establishment seems able to twist the tap of terrorist violence in response to international pressure upon it to de-escalate; but has seen no compelling need to actually turn off the flow. The state of stalemate, in the favor of army, thus continues. In spite of two timely elections in 2008 and 2013 – and the third one in 2018 around the corner – political executive has not been able to assert itself sufficiently. The main fault lies in the fact that there has not been credible institution building in general and political efficacy and maturity in particular.

Political

There are three main political parties which matter in the affairs of Pakistan, the oldest being the Pakistan People's Party (PPP), followed by Pakistan Muslim League (Nawaz) commonly called PML (N) and the youngest being Pakistan Tehreek-e-Insaf (PTI) established by the famous cricketer Imran Khan in April 1996 in Lahore. The first two have been in power in Pakistan for more than two stints each and the third one is yet to be tried by the electorate in governance matters at the national level. The PPP was first headed by Bhutto, then by his daughter Benazir and now by her son Bilal. The PML (N), as the name suggests, continues to be dominated by Nawaz Sharif who has been at the helm of affairs of the party for almost three decades now. The PTI is mainly dependent upon its founder Imran Khan. Therefore all the three entities are dynasty and personality driven and bereft of any real intra-party democracy. Seen from a different perspective, each of these three were started by a strong and energetic personality. Even though the parties do have cadre and respective organizational units at different levels; the leadership is not thrown up or elected by the primary members up the line. The whole organizational process is not a case of being bottoms up structure – as it should be in any democratic system

– but a top-down scenario; most of the office bearers of the party being the choice of the apex leader or his nominee(s). This also shows a lack of effective voices and institutions amongst the toiling masses.

The peasants and workers - normally the bulwark of any democratic setup and who form the bulk of population at the lowest rung - have remained woefully disorganized. There has been no serious effort, in the short history of Pakistan, to change the agrarian relationship or execute a meaningful policy of land reforms. The feudal land management arrangement as inherited at the time Pakistan came into being, has not been much disturbed and large land holdings in the countryside exist and thrive as a rule. Thus the peasant-peasant and peasant-landlord relationships are still based on the traditional customs and bear no connection with the modern concepts, patterns and technologies. Resultantly, per acre production figures from the irrigated and un-irrigated lands are lower than similar statistics in the developed world. Lack of efficient use of water resources and increasing salinity in the lands is also largely attributable to this static agrarian relationship. Such a situation, in turn, has a debilitating and negative bearing on the emergence of public institutions with positive and lasting impact on the national psyche and its development on modern lines.

Similarly, conditions of the labor class as also the state of the labor movement in the country have not been healthy. Back in 1947, when Pakistan came into being it did not have many industries; but inherited the strong and working railway and port unions; as a legacy from an effective workers organizational structure evolved in undivided India. In the sixties the strength of railway workers was nearly one hundred thousand; and that of Karachi docks and ports exceeded twenty thousand. This not insignificant nucleus failed to spark a larger and more effective workers programme and efforts for collective bargaining. One of the important reasons for this lack of active labor assertion, despite notable industrialization in the 1960s, was because the role of unions and their federations remained dormant due to martial law. In the decade of seventies, industrial labor scene witnessed some positive changes and upheavals resulting in the growing number of registered trade unions and also throwing up some powerful leaders having support from workers across the country. This also coincided with the rise of PPP on the national political scene and its growing affiliations with the left wing elements in the country. The important entities included names like; Pakistan Mazdoor Federation, Pakistan National Federation of Trade Unions, United Labour Federation and Pakistan Trade Union Federation. However, over the decades these workers and labors bodies have failed to make their presence felt and also not succeeded in persuading the federal and provincial governments to enact favorable workers' welfare labor laws.

The distressing and pitiable conditions of peasants and workers do reflect a similar state of affairs in fortunes of the over-arching left-wing movement or organizations in Pakistan. As the sub-continent was approaching the era of independence from British rule; the region experienced tumultuous developments and revolts, in the early and mid-forties. These largely benefitted Congress and the Muslim League and did not prove beneficial to the fortunes of CPI; then the sole representative of left ideology in India. After the partition, a separate communist party was formed called Communist Party of Pakistan (CPP), which inherited the cadres as well as the ideology of CPI in the new country. Its association with the Muslim League, dominated by the Muslim feudalists, created doctrinal confusion in the ranks; and the extreme elements in the party briefly flirted with the idea of a short cut- the coup. This resulted in the famous Rawalpindi Conspiracy Case, also involving General Akbar Khan; but the plot was unearthed before execution in 1951. The affair dealt a further blow to the fledgling left movement in Pakistan. The next phase came in 1958, in the wake of a deteriorating economic situation, giving rise to a working-class movement in which the peasants also joined. Before this agitation could gain momentum; the then army chief General Ayub Khan seized power and declared martial law towards end of October. This literally crushed the new effort in its infancy. However, a seed for social change was probably planted in the collective subconscious of the weaker and lower middle class of the population; and that presumably explains the quick and credible popularity of the PPP in the decade of late sixties and early seventies. It was not without reason that PPP became a mass party and when it came to power in 1972; many left-leaning persons joined the government. But this party could not bring radical reforms and was not organized as a true socialist entity – as a section had anticipated. The left could not change the PPP which was structured more as a capitalist outfit with only a socialist veneer; Bhutto himself was a feudal lord from Sindh. With increasing disillusionment with the party and Bhutto; the workers took to the streets in increasing numbers. The agitation, more prominent in Karachi, was dealt with a heavy hand by the government; which further alienated the leader from the peasants and working class which abandoned him when the crunch came. Another faulty alliance, this time with some right-wing elements also, to overthrow the ruling party only resulted in another military dictatorship led by General Zia-ul-Haq. The left suffered most in this turn of events; in fact it could never really recover from it.

The early nineties were a period of counter-revolutionary consciousness in Pakistan; giving birth to the rise of fundamentalism and extremism. In this process, the events in Afghanistan and the American support and help also contributed. At the present time, none of the left parties has a mass base. The left as a whole is hardly recognized as a force in the political landscape of the country. The future events and developments, which hint at downsizing and privatization, may lead to increasing loss of jobs. This, in turn, is likely to instigate the work force to take to streets. Whereas the scenario may give left some chance to get organized; these elements have to contest with better established fundamentalists who certainly have greater resources and muscle power coupled with effective street presence. The right is more organized and stronger; it has seeped deep into layers of the Pakistani poor and lower middle-class society; the two segments which traditionally are the main base of the left. The struggle, in the years to come, would be between these two ideologies and the doctrine which dominates the psyche of the people would also in large measure determine the future course of Pakistan. The economic situation in the country, over the coming years, will have an impact on the developing situation.

Pakistan's economy has not been doing well enough for the country to feel comfortable. It has generally been kept afloat because of liberal assistance and loans from developed and oil rich countries as well as international lending agencies; U.S.A. and Saudi Arabia being prominent amongst them in the former category whereas International Monetary Fund, World Bank and Asian Development Bank come in the latter grouping. The remittances of Pakistanis living abroad have traditionally played an important role in shoring up the economy and pushing up the foreign exchange reserves. For example, it is estimated that the nine million strong Pakistani Diaspora, mostly living in the Middle East and Western countries, contributed 19.3 billion dollars to the national economy in the financial year 2016-17. On the downward side; a major problem facing the economy is a low tax base as well as a low tax/GDP ratio. Tax evasion is wide spread; fewer than two percent pay income tax, resultantly Pakistan's revenue from taxes is among the lowest in the world. A fast-growing population too adds to the economic woes of the country; its total fertility rate is the highest in South Asia and among the highest in the world. The problem of increasing external debts also exists, which means an accompanying growth of external debt-service payments. Another worrisome aspect for the economic planners of the country is that occasional positive indicators as also the shoring up of the reserves is accomplished through borrowed money. In a nutshell, the economy of Pakistan can be summed up as a product of low savings, low investments and a huge expansion in population.

The two important drags on Pakistan's economy are the extra ordinary expenditure the nation has to bear for the maintenance and upkeep of its defence forces – way outside its capacity and size – and a pathological hostility towards India. In a way, these factors are also two faces of the same coin. Some analysts do believe that Pakistani ambition to become a hub of economic activity would be difficult to achieve without the opening of trade as well as transit routes to India. A well-known Pakistani author has opined, "Pakistan has suffered economic damage pursuing the unchanging 'principled' policy of revisionist challenge to India but this may not have hurt it enough to make it repent. In his latest comment, ex-World Bank Pakistani economist Shahid Javed Burki says, 'The past process was 'India- centric' in the sense that Pakistan tried, sometimes with desperation, to balance India's growing military might. That approach proved costly. In a 2007 report, I wrote I estimated the cost to Pakistan of the running dispute with India over Kashmir and other issues. I estimated that the Kashmir dispute alone had cost Pakistan 2.5 per cent to 3.2 per cent a year of growth loss in GDP terms. Compounded over a period of six decades, this suggests the magnitude of the colossal damage Pakistan has done to its economy by following this particular quarrel with India. This study used purely economic factors; it did not take into account the undeniable fact that some of the cost of this approach towards India contributed to the rise of Islamic extremism in the country. That, too, has resulted in serious economic losses'."[6] In a similar assessment, a perceptive scholar has pointed out, "At a time when tomatoes were selling for Rs 300 a kilo in Lahore they were available at Indian Rs 40 a kilo in Amritsar a mere 30

6   Khaled Ahmed, *Sleepwalking To Surrender- Dealing With Terrorism In Pakistan*, Penguin Random House, India, 2016, p. 127.

miles away. But a visceral Indo-phobia, shared by many of our influentials, stood in the way of consumers benefiting from the lower priced supply…. The point to note is that this India-centric anti-trade hysteria is shared by many who have no compunctions consuming products imported from all other countries and whose income brackets are such that commodities like tomatoes and onions are a miniscule proportion of their budgets….. The ultimate irony is that such callous and shallow prejudice does virtually nothing to hurt India. On the contrary, the gap between the two countries continues to widen…"[7]

The US aid and assistance to Pakistan has been declining in the recent years; with occasional threats of lowering it further. It reflects the American exasperation with Pakistan in the way latter has handled terrorism and various groups and individuals connected with it. Pakistan, at least outwardly, does not seem much bothered about the change in American attitude. The main reason for this appears to be the windfall benefits it perceives to be coming from China, in the form of China Pakistan Economic Corridor (CPEC) – estimated at the cost of over 50 billion dollars – which it hopes, will more than compensate the loss of reduced American assistance. But, apart from the fact that not many details of this ambitious scheme have been put in the public domain by the federal government; some of the provinces too have questioned its overall usefulness. India has also raised objections about one of the major infrastructural projects under this scheme; the up gradation of existing Karakoram highway into a four-lane all-weather road, linking Gwadar port with Xinxiang province in China, as a part of this passes through the Gilgit region currently under illegal occupation of Pakistan. China has done it without even recognizing the disputed nature of this territory; contrary to the way China had adopted when the Karakoram highway was first constructed in the early nineteen sixties.

As per media reports, Pakistan is already facing problems in implementing some of the important infrastructural projects mentioned, with fanfare, under the CPEC. One of the main reasons for this is the reluctance of the Pakistanis to agree to the new financial terms spelled out by the Chinese. To complicate matters further the experts in Pakistan are realizing that apart from the fact that there is very little transfer of technology; the local involvement in the Chinese construction projects is

---

7   Anjum Altaf in *Dawn*, dated October 27, 2017.

also very low – as the Chinese would prefer to use their surplus labor and machinery in implementing these schemes. Some financial experts and shrewd businessmen in Pakistan are also raising questions about the resources, or the lack of these, to repay the over $50 billion debt that comes with the CPEC projects. As the money under this project is not "aid' but in the shape of "loans"; which has to be paid back along with interest. There is also a strong possibility of the Gwadar Port becoming a Chinese military base, managed entirely by the Chinese manpower; and Pakistanis practically losing the sovereignty over it.

This scenario may not be as farfetched as it appears at first. Some quarters want Pakistan to learn from the Sri Lankan experience in this respect. Apart from the significant debt liability of the Colombo Port City Project, Chinese investments and projects in and around the Hambantota port have imposed a crushing debt burden on Sri Lanka. There, unable to pay the debts to China, Sri Lanka has been forced to convert Chinese investment into equity; thus giving the Chinese partial ownership of the port. This is the lesson that Pakistan, and also other nations wanting to receive the Chinese assistance should understand about the real nature and sequence of Chinese "aid" and "goodwill". In this model, much of Chinese investment is actually a loan that the host nation has to repay. Also, bulk of the Chinese money does not go to locals but is transferred from a state-owned Chinese bank or credit institution to the Chinese company that executes the project using Chinese workers.

The critics also allege that many of the CPEC projects are financially unviable. The power plants, for example, it is building will require power tariffs – to become sustainable – that are not acceptable to most Pakistani consumers. According to media reports in Pakistan, some negative aspects of the whole scheme are slowly emerging. The business community there has noticed that Chinese entities prefer dealing with the government rather than investing efforts in private-sector partnerships. Also, the perception is that the Chinese do not negotiate very much; they lay down their terms and expect them to be fully met. Over there, profits come first and sentiments second; the premises, projections and parameters are cold and calculated. In short, the CPEC has raised many uncomfortable questions and answered very few; for both the government as well as individual businessmen. A pertinent point made in one of the media reports state, "Answers to questions like what sort of dispute-resolution mechanism will govern the partnerships envisioned under CPEC, and what investments are being prepared for which areas, will help dispel the growing anxieties". In short, the public debate is polarized on this issue. Besides the domestic differences, Pakistan also has to face some tough demands from China, for example, acceptance of the Chinese Yuan as a legal tender. As the CPEC focus and budget expands, there are likely to be more demands of different nature from Beijing. Islamabad may soon realize that Chinese are not easy to handle like Americans. Still the fact remains that notwithstanding the efficacy or otherwise of the various infrastructural projects; Pakistan's political and military elite has willingly signed on this Chinese scheme of things. This firmly turns Pakistan's back to South Asia and puts it in the Chinese strategic orbit. What the cost of this change is going to be is still not fully clear. Both countries look at it from their perspective; Chinese consider it a strategic project of considerable significance whereas Pakistanis expectations are that the CPEC is a sure cure for lot of its economic woes. As the Dawn had very aptly put it; this is only the opening of the door; what comes out of the door is difficult to predict.

A major challenge for Pakistan is also that the provinces are divided over the operationalization of CPEC schemes and routes; Balochistan and Gilgit-Baltistan, along with Sindh and KP are worried about Punjab getting a larger share of the CPEC. Main reason for this suspicion is the Federal government's refusal, or inability, to share all details of the project with various stake holders and also bring these in the public domain. The fact remains that no other external project has raised as much interest and suspicion inside Pakistan as this; giving further impetus to the centrifugal forces already present and active to varying degrees in different areas.

Right from the beginning Pakistan opted for a heavily centralized administration, polity and structure; which could not meet the legitimate demands of its ethnically diverse population. In the early period Punjabis and the migrants from India dominated the military and bureaucracy. These two organizations did provide the requisite stability in the initial years, but Jinnah's single-minded ideological quest crucially missed the social realities of Pakistan and the fact that the country was a home to many cultures and languages within its frontiers. Adoption of Urdu as the state language, not spoken in any of the provinces, was also the result of this mindset. Pakistan's political elite thought that an over-arching Islamic ideology would subsume the ethnic identities and discourage regional or linguistic groupings. But that did not happen and the people of different provinces with separate languages and cultures have been trying to assert their specific distinctiveness. In the initial years, the personality of Jinnah coupled with the euphoria of a new nation dominated over all other feelings. A decade or so later, the dictatorial military rule kept the lid tightly shut. But after the loss of its eastern wing and creation of Bangladesh in 1971, the provincial and regional identities once again started coming to the fore. The first crisis for Pakistan – in this regard – came in 1973 with large-scale disturbances in Balochistan and the second significant development was the creation of Mohajir Quami Movement (MQM), in 1984 in Karachi-Sindh. Manifestations of the demands of Pakhtuns and Seraiki speaking people of Punjab have been equally strong.

Sub-nationalism is almost a perennial problem Pakistan has to contend with. This has become even more strident lately; and the intensity of regional emotions is directly proportional to the efficacy and solvency of the state. Except Punjab, practically all other provinces are dissatisfied with the federal government. One of the major reasons is also the inequality in the distribution of water resources and hence the uncertainty in the irrigation sector. Pakistan is water-stressed; the drinking water demands are not fully met and irrigation is faltering because the country cannot store enough water – while the groundwater levels are sinking. Its barrages, including the oldest Sukkur Barrage commissioned in 1932, are silting. The country does not have enough resources to rejuvenate the ailing canal net-work. To make matters worse, Pakistan's lower riparian complaints against India are in fact similar and reflected in the concerns and fears of Sindh about Punjab. Loss of irrigation is one of the major alarms expressed by Sindhis against upper-riparian Punjab. That is why the proposed construction of Kalabagh Dam attracts such strong emotions and objections from this region; as it is perceived that it could further reduce the availability of water there. The three main cities of Sindh – Karachi, Hyderabad and Sukkur - are dominated by the Mohajirs and the fertile tracts of its northern region are mainly under the control of Punjabis, which includes many serving and retired military men. The seeds of ethnic conflict in Karachi and other urban parts of Sindh lie in the concentration of Mohajirs there and thread of a common religion has proved too weak to bind locals with the migrants. After the problems in Afghanistan and the restive frontier region erupted, in the eighties, the steady Pakhtun migration to Karachi started changing the population mix and the nature of problems in that large city. Today

Karachi is the biggest Pakhtun city in the world. This community is now jostling with the Mohajirs for domination; and creating tensions which further aggravate an already tense and complex law and order situation in this metropolis. The Sindhis have been resenting their marginalization in this province by other communities and this feeling gave rise to a strong assertion by the ethnic population in the form of Jeay Sindh movement in the past; advocating Sindh for the Sindhis. But, due to various factors, this stir failed to achieve enough traction as also the requisite critical mass and consequently petered off. All the same a feeling of separate and specific identity remains very strong amongst the Sindhis. The MQM - seen in Pakistan as the combined face of Mohajirs – has evolved into a political mutant entity, but mainstreaming the Jeay Sindh elements would be a joint trial of the country's political class in times to come.

Many political analysts believe that the Baloch nationalism endangers Pakistan state the most and holds primacy in the various ethnic movements that threaten this nation. The Baloch people have risen in revolt a number of times demanding greater autonomy and even complete independence. The ultimate dream of this segment of population is stated to be to unite the Baloch in Pakistan, Iran and Afghanistan under one flag. The entire region has remained restive, in varying degrees, right from the days of independence itself; dominated by a strong perception of persecution and domination by the Pakistani state. In fact the Balochis quote past events to emphasize that this region joined Pakistan quite reluctantly, and also under the threat of use of force, in the first place. Over the decades, a sense of political isolation as also economic deprivation has further accentuated this feeling of exploitation of the region. Punjabi domination coupled with exploitation of the natural resources of Balochistan for the benefit of other regions of Pakistan has further accentuated this feeling. The development of Gwadar Port and increasing Chinese interest in the CPEC are also factors which adversely affect stability in this region. There is a strong feeling of being marginalized in their own province; further heightened by unexplained disappearance of many individuals and an almost complete grip over the region by the security forces and intelligence agencies. The challenge of Balochi nationalists to the Pakistani state still remains palpable and feudal nature of the society may further add to this problem. It is a restive province of Pakistan where peace and stability would be at a great premium in the years to come. In fact the very success of CPEC plans in the country – and by implications the economic development of

Pakistan itself – largely depends upon orderly execution of its various plans in the region. Response of the Pakistani state to the issues and problems of Balochistan has largely been security centric; depending mostly upon the military and intelligence agencies to deal with crisis situations. But, this approach of throwing water over the fire has achieved only that much; and failed to comprehensively address the main issue of disaffection and disenchantment of a sulking population. Regular disappearances, deaths in encounters and continued exploitation of the area's natural resources have further aggravated the problem. People there have not forgotten the death of Nawab Akbar Bugti in an encounter with security forces in August 2006. A future secessionist movement in Balochistan could revolve around the memory of someone like Nawab Bugti or the person of the present Khan of Kalat – scion of the hereditary rulers of the region – currently staying in London.

The Khyber Pakhtunkhwa, earlier known as NWFP – North-West Frontier Province – is predominantly inhabited by Pathans. The population here, especially on the East of Durand Line, has been restive since long. The societal and tribal nature here exhibits a very strong streak of independence and historically speaking these people foiled all attempts by the British to subjugate them. The Durand line, marked by the British almost 125 years ago, was a manifestation of this failure and they were able to maintain an uneasy peace by minimum governance in the region. Things have not changed much for Pakistan since 1947. In fact, the country's polity also did not exert much in this direction. Things have remained volatile on both sides of the Durand Line, which incidentally the Pathans never accepted – particularly those living on the West of it. The Afghan dislike of the Durand line can be very well gauged from the fact that no Afghan government, in recent memory, has recognized this as the border. Najeebullah, as the last communist ruler of Afghanistan and also during the worst period of the early 1990s, also repudiated this. Even when Talibans were in power in Afghanistan they refused to recognize the existence of this as the *defacto* border between the two countries. Former Afghan President Hamid Karzai was reported to have said that his country would never recognize the Durand Line. The conditions in this province are expected to remain unstable during the coming years. The Pakhtun nationalism; embracing the Pathan population living on both sides of the Pak-Afghan border, as defined by the Durand Line, is alive and kicking; posing a palpable threat to either of the nations.

The feelings of a distinct Pakhtun identity have been quite strong in the entire belt much before the Independence; and certainly from the times of Khan Abdul Ghaffar Khan. If the tendency did not create problems for Pakistan then there have been two important reasons for this. One is the large-scale presence of Pakhtuns in the armed forces of the country. On the one hand it had a sobering influence on any kind of split feelings and on the other, the Pakhtuns derived a disproportionately higher share of benefits from a military-dominated state; which Pakistan has been, directly or indirectly throughout its history. Secondly, this area received huge financial support from the US and Saudi Arabia during the communist rule in Afghanistan; as a large section of Mujahideen fighters were trained in this region and also belonged to the soil. However, if affairs of this province are not handled with sensitivity and political sagacity the Pakhtun situation has the potential of getting out of hand.

Punjab is generally recognized as a symbol of stability in Pakistan. It has the largest population amongst the provinces and also sends maximum number of elected members to the National Assembly. Apart from these figures, and also more importantly, it has the highest share of officers and men enlisted in the Pakistan army; the pillar of reliability and respect in the country. It is generally an accepted premise that whoever controls Punjab holds a grip on the federal government. From such a description it would appear that the province of Punjab would be an example of balance and soundness in the entire country. But, in reality, this is not fully true. The militant groups, particularly the TTP (Tehrik-e-Taliban Pakistan), are demonstrably active in the province creating considerable violence. These actions result in loss of lives and properties; as also adversely affect the performance and primacy of Punjab at the national level. In addition, in southern Punjab the Seraiki population is quite restive and has been demanding a separate province; which would in effect mean a division of existing Punjab into two units – with all attendant ramifications. The fault-lines in Punjab are becoming sharper with the passage of time and have the potential of developing into a crisis situation.

The Seraiki dialect is spoken by a large population in the south of Punjab and this segment considers itself a separate ethno-linguistic group with ambitious expectations. Like other major ethnic groups in Pakistan, the Seraikis also argue that their culture is being dominated and the economic resources exploited by Punjab. To buttress the argument it is often mentioned that even though this belt produces substantial proportion of two of Pakistan's main crops of wheat and cotton; but hardly any industry has been set up in the region. There is a surfeit of similar arguments in favor of the demand for a separate province. However, at the political level the opinion for this seems to be divided. While the Punjabi politicians do not favour a positive consideration of the Seraiki demand, for obvious reasons; the other regional players – all belonging to the smaller provinces – do not hesitate to promote the idea. The division of Punjab, by far the much bigger entity than others today, would be any day welcomed by the other three provinces. Seen from this angle, if the political equations in Pakistan were to change in a particular fashion – in any foreseeable future – then the creation of a separate Seraiki province out of present Punjab would not be such a far-fetched idea.

In all the three smaller provinces of Pakistan the separatist proclivities are marked; a desire to break away from the federal structure. In the fourth province, Punjab, Seraiki speaking population is not striving for another country for itself, but merely struggling to be recognized as a distinct entity. Thus taken as a whole, the political structure of Pakistan does not appear to be in a truly sound state. The regime of military dictatorships, in power in Pakistan for varying periods and at different times, only succeeded in putting the lid over these issues; without making any effort to solve the basic causes of the problems. In fact, these only postponed the inevitable to be handled by the democratic dispensations that were to follow. The fact that the population of Punjabis and Mohajirs is growing at a slower rate as compared to the Sindhis, Pakhtuns and Baloch would also be a relevant element in due course. With the passage of time it is logical to surmise that the demand of different ethnic identities for a suitable place in the federal scheme of things is going to grow in Pakistan. The experience of functioning democracies in the world indicates that it is more appropriate to accommodate genuine ethnic aspirations rather than to feel threatened by them. In the case of Pakistan, such a course of action would involve considerable mental adjustment by the Punjabi dominated federal leadership structure. This is all the more inevitable as the experience of last many decades has amply demonstrated that the pull of religion, contrary to the expectations of the founding fathers of Pakistan, has not been a great unifying factor. As is well known, Pakistan was created as a separate homeland for the ostensible security of the Muslims of the sub-continent. But, that was not to happen for more than one reasons and this aspect remains a contentious issue till date giving rise to comments from various people. An extremely interesting, and representative, analysis has been made by Farzana Shaikh as "It would appear that history, politics and geostrategic compulsions have all conspired to hasten the decline of Pakistan and deepen its uncertainty as a nation....it is the country's problematic and contested relationship with Islam that has most decisively frustrated its quest for a coherent national identity and for stability as a nation-state capable of absorbing the challenges of its rich and diverse society."[8]

However, in the face of these and some other problematic issues confronted by the country, Pakistan has not altered its policy of continued hostility and unconcealed belligerence towards India; notwithstanding the peace process efforts. This course is likely to continue; and in fact Pakistan appears to be feeling emboldened by the realization that in spite of major changes in the international scenario as well as on the domestic front; the policy of sustaining the militancy in J&K has continued over the last three decades. The level of infiltration and presence of local militants on the scene have been varying from year to year, but, the fact remains that this approach has made India deploy a considerable portion of security forces in the state. These forces have never really relaxed the vigil – both external and internal – as also not lowered their guards. Pakistan has kept the pot boiling and has never let the things cool down to a level from where it would be difficult to revive the scheme of things again. Notwithstanding the four intervening wars, there seems to be no change in the Pak policy. One possible way for India to break this impasse would be to raise the costs for Pakistan. In the military sphere, this course of action does not appear easy to follow. The Indian army demonstrably lacks the conventional capability to effectively take this route and nuclear option is not possible for more than one reasons. Hence, Pakistan is not under much pressure to change its current stance of making things uncomfortable for India in J&K; and if possible in the rest of the country. For its long-term planning, it would be useful for India to accept this premise and try to fashion security and diplomatic responses accordingly. Bringing international pressure on Pakistan, as an alternative measure has also not produced requisite results as has been evident in the recent past. Thus, the challenge for policy makers in India continues.

---

8   Farzana Shaikh, *Making Sense of Pakistan*, Hurst & Company, London, 2009, p. 209.

The overall situation and developments around the sub-continent indicate the continuance of the *status quo* and neither country, at least on the face of it, seems keen to change this position. Both appear to be quite used to absorbing the current level of tensions and conflicts that afflict their bi-lateral relations. The negativity in the mutual relationships has been contained and not allowed to spiral out of control or escalate to any dangerous point. The military adventure on both sides has been confined along the LoC and escalations on the international borders have remained under control for quite some time. But change, and not the *status quo*, is also a primal law of the nature. Since hard borders and hard policies have failed to yield positive results beneficial to both countries; many people believe that in the near future following a pragmatic mix of soft borders and soft policies may produce encouraging results. Various signals emanating from Pakistan during the past few years indicate that the people there may be ready to try this way. Youth of that country, with no connection with the past – Kashmir or 1947 – is probably aspiring to put the animosity with India behind and pursue the path which would lead to peace, job creation and prosperity. All the better if these can be achieved in ways which ensure that the issues of territory and use of resources are resolved for the benefit of people of both countries. This formulation is a possibility if the policy makers of both sides discuss matters with the intent to break the impasse. Perceptive analysts in either country have outlined a number of matters on which good progress can be achieved. These include adequate cooperation and increased linkages in the fields of trade, tourism, educational institutions, disaster management, natural resources management, financial linkages, as also opening of new routes etc. It is in this endeavor, that the state of Jammu and Kashmir which has been a source of friction and sour relations between India and Pakistan can have the potential of being a bridge and fulcrum of new relationship of friendship and cooperation between the two countries.

Another possible scenario in this respect relates to freezing the current ground situation; providing maximum autonomy to both parts of J&K, on either side of the LoC, by India and Pakistan and let them manage their local affairs. These broad policy outlines which came to be seriously discussed at the highest levels in the past, during 2004 – 2007, were also then commonly called the Musharraf Formula. This was also an effort to arrive at a compromise between "joint management" as proposed by President Musharraf and the Indian Prime Minister Manmohan Singh's offer of "Institutional arrangements". Many political analysts believe that this is a formulation which is most likely to succeed as well as acceptable to both sides; as it is almost a recipe of a win: win situation for India and Pakistan. In short the proposals involve accepting the factum of disputed nature of the erstwhile J&K territory; freeze the current situation for next two decades or for a period mutually agreed upon. Which means; do not attempt to resolve the tangled issue, which has remained tied in knots for so many decades and leave the problem of finding an acceptable solution to the next generation; or maybe beyond that. In this interim period both federal governments should make efforts to secure the best of deal to the state governments and the people of J&K living on both sides of the LoC. The process of this scheme of things was reportedly set in motion in January 2004 when Vajpayee, as the Prime Minister of India, visited Islamabad to attend the SAARC meeting. On the sidelines, he and President Musharraf spent some time together, in a well publicized bilateral exchange; and that is where both discussed contours of the plan.

After few months there was a change in the government of India, in the wake of a general election, and a UPA regime headed by Dr. Manmohan Singh was installed in New Delhi. Musharraf pushed ahead with his plan and series of meetings were held at official, political and summit level. These generated considerable hope and goodwill on both sides. Some people felt that Musharraf – a Mohajir from India – and Manmohan Singh – a refugee from Pakistan – were best suited to hammer out a workable blue print.

In short this formula is outlined in Musharraf's own words as, "I have myself spent hours on many a day pondering a possible "outside the box" solution. The idea that I have evolved – which ought to satisfy Pakistan, India and the Kashmiris – involves a partial stepping back by all. The idea has four elements and can be summarized as follows: First, identify the geographic regions of Kashmir that need resolution.... Second, demilitarize the identified region or the regions and curb all militant aspects.... Third, introduce self-governance or self-rule in the identified region or regions.... Fourth, and most important, have a joint management mechanism with a membership consisting of Pakistanis, Indians and Kashmiris overseeing self-governance and dealing with residual subjects common to all identified regions and those subjects that are beyond the scope of self-governance....This idea is purely personal and would need refinement. It would also need to be sold to the public by all involved parties for acceptance"[9]. Musharraf further elaborated the concept in an interview to Karan Thapar, a well-known TV anchor of India, on January 8, 2007. He said there, ".... Autonomy within the Indian Constitution is not acceptable.... We are working for something between autonomy and independence and I think self-governance fits in well..."

Once in operation, it was expected that the functioning of governmental structures from the state level down to the grass roots would receive a fillip and help in building as well as consolidating the institutions at all these levels. It was also assumed that in addition to the two existing routes of Srinagar-Muzzafrabad and Poonch-Rawalakot; at least two more axes would be considered for operationalization. Jammu-Sialkot and Kargil-Skardu appeared to be the preferred destinations by both sides. These measures, including the new links, it was hoped would result in greater people to people contacts and also give greater fillip to the trade between the two sides of the divided J&K; thus giving rise to organic development of relations amongst the people. The ease of travel restrictions envisaged much simpler travel procedures aimed at greater interaction and reduction of tensions thereby considerably reducing the hostilities; leading to steady enhancement of confidence and trust in each other. The commonality of languages and culture, on both sides, was considered as a great source on which the foundations of a bright future could be laid.

Also as side benefits of this plan, the outstanding Sir Creek issues in the Kutch sector of Gujarat State and the festering Siachen dispute on those icy heights – which have bedeviled the relations between two countries for decades – could too be resolved to mutual satisfaction. As a matter of record, it should be mentioned that these two issues almost came close to a resolution more than once in the past; but the outstanding matters and differing national perceptions on Kashmir came as an obstruction in the way. In this manner – it was argued – both sides would have substantial take-aways from the table; without anyone losing face.

But that was not to be.

The problem was not with India where a broad political consensus on these matters could safely be presumed. The process of dialogue revolving around them was started during the Vajpayee regime of NDA and was taken

---

9   Pervez Musharraf, *In The Line Of Fire*, Free Press, New York, 2006, pp. 302-303.

forward by the UPA government of Manmohan Singh, for the first three years at least. As per reports in the media, both he and Musharraf "almost reached an agreement". However, during 2007 Musharraf got badly bogged down in domestic problems and was unable to pursue this matter any further due to fast-changing political scene and lack of adequate clout at home. Then, Benazir Bhutto was killed in an assassination bid towards the end of December 2007; and by next February a civilian government was in place in Pakistan headed by Zardari. None of the three mainstream political parties there – PPP, PML(N) and PTI – publicly supported this plan; which was perceived to be a brain-child of Musharraf, and he was out of power and reckoning. This lack of support there at the political level was further compounded by the stoic refusal of the army – the powerful gathering of Corps Commanders and other senior officers of the High Command at Rawalpindi – to back it with their patronage.

In fact some observers had started realizing the inherent difficulties about the overall legitimacy of the plan. A representative sample by the noted Pakistani defence analyst Ayesha Siddiqa outlines, "… Musharraf needs time to understand and sell his idea to his main constituency: the Pakistan Army…. The fact is that the peace process is intrinsically tied to the internal politics of the two countries. From Pakistan's standpoint, the peace process has increasingly begun to look like an orphan and the question is: would the political parties eventually be willing to adopt a child fathered by a military general? The issue here is no longer that of India-Pakistan relations but the internal political dynamics of the country…"[10]

After the Mumbai terrorist carnage of November 26, 2008, President Zardari offered a hand of cooperation in the shape of joint investigation; he went so far as showing his preparedness to depute the ISI chief for this purpose. The way he was quickly made to literally eat his words, clearly indicated the collective mind of the army top brass there.

This plan, and the connected scheme of things, may be dormant right now but the idea is certainly not dead; and its contours do carry the possibilities of success and seeds of potential. It is decidedly a recipe worth trying for dealing comprehensively with the Kashmir issue and carries in its womb the chances of improved relations between India and Pakistan – a formula for bettering the prospects of the peace process.

---

10 Ayesha Siddiqa, quoted in *Kashmir Images*, Srinagar, dated 24 March 2006.

Of the various viable considerations, the one having potential of furthering this cause is to transform the LoC into International Border. This possibility was reportedly discussed way back in 1972 between Indira Gandhi and Bhutto during the Simla Agreement talks.

The feasibility of converting the LoC into IB has been on the table for quite some time; at least from the Indian side till the eighties. This line of thinking also recognizes the need for partial adjustments in the current position – some kind of give and take to make the new boundary more logical and follow well defined geographical features. Obviously, the LoC must be redrawn as part of a settlement. It is particularly cruel to Jammu where some villages are divided. India finds the existing line too close for comfort in Kargil. Pakistan feels the same in the Neelam Valley. In the process, it is probable that the Siachen issue can also be resolved. However, the approach pre-supposes considerable goodwill between India and Pakistan and a desire to live as good neighbors. This is something which does not appear plausible to some people in the current scenario and the main reason for this is the pathological hostility of Pakistan army towards India right from the very beginning. There is also the unanimous resolution passed by the Indian Parliament in 1994, which calls upon the government of India to get all the territories under illegal occupation of Pakistan vacated. That means getting the entire PoK and Gilgit – Baltistan area back from Pakistan. Taking a realistic view of the overall situation the whole matter appears to be an improbable proposition; unless a cataclysmic change takes place in the region. On the other hand, supporters of this line of action argue that it is not only a very practical solution to this vexed and long pending issue, but would also be welcomed by the people on both sides of the divide. This presumption is based on two premises. One is that the people of the entire state are sick and tired of the violence and a sense of uncertainty which has gripped the region for many decades now; and would like to come out of this messy situation. General Musharraf, while explaining his four-point formula on Kashmir has also alluded to this phenomenon as. "....This will give comfort to the Kashmiris, who are fed up with the fighting and killing on both sides..."[11] The second reasoning in favor of this line of thinking is that settlement of the problem by permanently accepting the current ground situation would lead to the preservation of the existing political configuration and balance on both sides.

11   n -9, p.303.

It is a well-known fact that a very insignificant portion of the population in PoK speaks Kashmiri language and that linguistically and culturally the people of that area are closer to the Jammu region. Therefore, if hypothetically it is presumed that both parts of the State join together, as it was before independence, then the Jammu region would gain predominance over Kashmir, thereby upsetting the existing political equation in J&K. The current ruling elite in the PoK region also will most likely be faced with political upheavals of unpredictable nature. Therefore, the only way to maintain the current *status quo*, and in fact to perpetuate it, is to somehow get both India and Pakistan agree to conversion of the current LoC to the permanent International Border. And for that, a desire for peaceful co-existence is a pre-requisite. Therefore, on the balance, this turns out to be a catch 22 situation.

Many times the fact of India's pre-dominance in the area of soft power has come under discussions. It has been suggested by some people that India should more effectively use its soft power in dealing with Pakistan. That means programs and events related to arts, culture, music, languages and films etc. should be leveraged in this direction. No doubt India has considerable advantage in each of these areas, but as the past experience shows this approach yields limited advantage only – at least perceptibly – and then Pakistani regulatory mechanisms clamp down heavily on the creeping Indian influence. This has happened in the past with Hindi films, Indian TV serials, classical music, dance and the like. As long as the streak of fundamentalism remains strong in the Pak psyche, the soft power ascendency of India is not likely to be of much advantage. Pakistan is still struggling to come to grips with the elements of mindless savagery in the national life. Under the circumstances, the advantage of Indian soft power can only be employed and used in unperceptive and indirect manner. It can make an impression only over a long period and that impact can hardly ever be quantified.

The Pakistani society is currently afflicted by three maladies of terrorism, extremism and sectarianism. The terrorist groups and their over ground sympathizers have seriously disrupted the normal life; almost striking at will in the entire country. Their targets range from devotees in the Sufi Shrines to followers of other sects – both Islamic and non Islamic – and innocent children, like dastardly attack on the Army Public School in Peshawar in December 2014. The Madarasa culture, so prevalent in

Pakistan, is also eating into the vitals of the society. In fact, these religious seminaries have become *defacto* breeding grounds for producing recruits for various terror outfits. Uncontrolled population growth and lack of sufficient employment opportunities have further aggravated these serious problems.

Along with growing cult of terrorism and increasing influence of Madarasas; another of Pakistani problem is the undiluted influence of the army over all structures of governance in the country – in fact over the entire social fabric of the nation. Its vice-like grip and the long shadow have always been felt by various political heavy weights there. This phenomenon has become more pronounced from February 2008, ever since the democratic government was installed in Pakistan. The army has never allowed the civilian rulers to forget who holds the real authority there; be in the shape of sit-ins by protesters in and around Islamabad as also other major cities or cases of corruption in various forums against important political personalities. It is not a secret that the army holds complete sway in matters related to security, foreign policy, nuclear issues and Jammu and Kashmir. In these areas, the political class comes a poor second. In fact, the terror structure and Madarasa culture in Pakistan are, in a way, spin-offs to the stronghold of the army over levers of power. The linkages between these three entities are close and obvious. In the desire to perpetuate its primary position, the army has managed to ensure that civilian institutions do not grow in the country. Also by painting itself as the main guardian of the country's security the military have always taken a lion's share of the scarce resources further blunting the economic progress of the nation. The army has also built up a strong network of business interests in diverse fields all over the country running into tens of billions. Although a precise estimate of this business empire is not possible; quite a courageous effort was made in the form of an original study by a Pakistani scholar of repute, who has this to say about the army business interests in Pakistan, "The military is one of the vital organs of the state. However, in some countries the military becomes deeply involved in the politics of the state, and dominates all other institutions....the military's economic predatoriness, especially inside its national boundaries, is both a cause and effect of a feudal authoritarian, and non-democratic, political system....The majority of military personnel talk about the exceptional efficiency of military-controlled commercial ventures.... This notion, as demonstrated in this chapter, is questionable at best, and arguably only a myth....The most serious consequence of the military's involvement in economic ventures relates to their sense of judgement regarding political control of the state."[12]

Influence of the army can be restricted and its interests circumscribed only if the democratic polity in the country asserts itself to claim its legitimate rights as per the constitutional scheme of things. Alternatively also the same end result is possible if the armed forces spread themselves too thin on the ground and undertake multiple tasks beyond their means – in that case the whole structure may come under tremendous strain. Both these scenarios may be difficult to perceive as at present but are certainly within the realm of possibilities. A glance at the spread of Pakistan army's involvement brings in focus its active deployment on the Western and Eastern borders; as well as its propensities to create problems for both neighboring countries. This by itself is more than sufficient to keep it fully occupied. But, it also undertakes the additional tasks of shepherding the 'good' terrorists and using them as 'strategic assets' as also fighting the 'bad' ones – like the TTP plus also taking care of, both ways, their respective right-wing supporting elements. The institutional involvement in parts of Waziristan and FATA is already well known and a considerable section of troops is actively deployed there. The deteriorating law and order situation within the country will also place increasing demands on the forces. According to some estimates, about twenty percent of its combat capacity is employed in the 'anti-terror' effort. The international pressure on the country to put its house in order by controlling armed groups is increasing – as is evident from the American attitude lately. Add to this the responsibility that the army high command has undertaken to secure the Chinese personnel and Chinese business interests in various parts of Pakistan for the CPEC projects; which would be progressively increasing. The list is formidable and certainly gives the impression that the Pakistan army may have bit more than it can chew or digest.

The existing armed forces structure would not be able to undertake all these tasks, and may be a bit more in times to come, without increasing its size and structure as also consuming much more national resources than at present; which is already very high. The economic base of the country is already under strain and it cannot sustain open-ended expenditure on the armed forces. Unless, of course, the Chinese step in to support Pakistan

12 Ayesha Siddiqa, *Military Inc*, Pluto Press, London, pp.1, 3,241 and 248.

in a big way by way of outright grants and untied aid in money, arms and equipment. The Chinese responses in this field are yet to be tested in Pakistan; notwithstanding their record in other parts of the world. Soon a time may come for the Pakistan army to make hard choices. The precise scenario (s) or timing for this may be difficult to predict as also the responses of different organs.

The one fact which also needs to be kept in mind is that in all likelihood Pakistan will have the third general elections in 2018. That would be a straight run of ten years under a civilian government in the country. As the democratic polity stabilizes and its institutions strike deeper roots it does appear within the realm of possibility that a future Prime Minister may like to bring the armed forces under the ambit of constitutional oversight. That would be the beginning of extending civilian control over the army, like in any other functioning democracy. Well-wishers of Pakistan would fervently hope for the establishment of a genuine democracy there in which power is securely concentrated in the hands of the people and by implication in the representatives elected by them. So far both sides in Pakistan, more particularly the army, have been hesitating to take this step; the civilian control over the armed forces. If this kind of scenario does take place, it would mean an unprecedented development happening there. But, other extraordinary situations can also arise in Pakistan about which many people may not be prepared. Two of the oft-repeated conditions – the pictures painted of the likely happenings – refer to the possibilities of some of the country's nuclear assets falling in unauthorized hands – rogue elements – and a set of internal and external developments leading to the balkanization of Pakistan.

The likelihood of the first scenario being played out is not such impossibility as it might appear at first sight. The Pakistan government has often in the past assured the international community that there is no chance of its nuclear weapons falling in jihadi hands as these are completely secure and stand very well protected by the armed forces. Without contradicting or doubting the veracity of such statements; it must be well kept in mind that Gen Zia-ul- Haq injected the virus of fundamentalism in the Pakistani society towards the end of the 1970s. He also deliberately chose to bring the armed forces into the ambit of this policy and thus destroyed the secular ethos which it had inherited from the British. Not only the lower ranks but also the officer cadres, particularly the younger lot, were infected by the newly found religious zeal. Over the years, as was natural, this malady also spread upwards reaching up to the highest echelons. Some of the views expressed publically by few ISI chiefs in the past and also some of the Corps Commanders – all officers of the rank of Lt. Generals in the army – bear a strong testimony to this phenomenon. Pakistan's nuclear weapons may be safely stored in the silos, tunnels and underground shelters and also adequately protected by the security forces; but what about the minds of the men and officers charged with this responsibility? The element of radicalization has penetrated so deep within the society and also in the army that it may not be presently possible for any system there to completely vouch for the 'sterile' functioning of any unit or sub-unit of the forces. Under such circumstances, the chances of a small part of these weapons, or even a single or couple of units, coming under the control of dark forces cannot be completely ruled out. And what happens in case such a thing takes place?

It is almost certain that countries directly affected or concerned about such a development would have catered for this eventuality and planned for appropriate responses. India, America and Israel would certainly be foremost among such nations. Whereas India and Israel – irrespective of their resources and capabilities - are an anathema to the present Pakistan society and any precipitative action by them, would more than anything else, unite the people there behind the army; the same may not be true in case of America. The US, it can be prudently premised, does maintain reasonably effective contacts at different levels of the 'deep state' in Pakistan. The successful action of the Americans in eliminating Osama bin Laden, inside Pakistan, is one such indication. In the case of Pak nuclear assets falling in wrong hands, the American's influence in the Pakistan command structure will certainly lean strongly on the army elements there to isolate and militarily contain the aberrant sections. Failing this; another alternative would be a swift aerial strike by the US alone or jointly by a coalition of nations. In any such case, India should best not get involved, for obvious reasons, unless there is actual use of such devices or the threat of its use. An eventuality of this kind, whether involving India or not, would bring a great upheaval in its wake in Pakistan and that country would never be the same again.

Geographically Pakistan is placed in a very strategic location; with a see ward access through two good ports and physical closeness to the

Central Asian region and China. No wonder CPEC is such an important part of China's One Belt One Road initiative. It is also a fact that in spite of this locational advantage; the country's political development and regional imbalances during the last seven decades have given rise to very potent centrifugal forces and the specter of balkanization does haunt Pakistan. In a common scenario Punjab's dominant role in the national assertions comes in direct confrontation with the country's Pakhtun, Baloch and Sindhi minorities. This clash of interests or the separatist tendencies of the smaller provinces gaining a critical mass or sufficient traction; may one day give rise to the balkanization of this country into smaller units. This break up may also be driven by a permutation and combination of international developments of which there is considerable probability in such a fast changing world.

It is generally believed that the breakup of Pakistan, if and when it takes place, is likely to throw up more than one alternative combination. The Pakhtuns mostly concentrated in the north-western tribal areas as also in the province of Khyber-Pakhtunkhwa, are likely to connect with ethnic brethren across the Durand Line – generally in the south-west of Afghanistan - to form an independent Pakhtunistan; a unit of about forty million people. Incidentally, this arrangement may have the silent blessings of the US. The Sindhis and Balochis can unite and form a separate confederation touching Afghanistan, Iran and India; with two important openings into the Arabian Sea at Karachi and Gwadar. Present Pakistan would then be confined to a land-locked and nuclear-armed Punjab. An interesting commentary about this contingency has been made by Selig Harrison as, "….In historical context, such a break-up would not be surprising. There had never been a national entity encompassing the areas now constituting Pakistan, an ethnic mélange thrown together hastily by the British for strategic reasons when they partitioned the sub-continent in 1947. For those of Pakhtun, Sindhi and Baloch ethnicity, independence from colonial rule created a bitter paradox. After resisting Punjabi domination for centuries, they found themselves subjected to Punjabi-dominated military regimes that have appropriated many of the natural resources in the minority provinces…."[13] In another such presumption, the Pakistani breakup results in separate Baloch and Sindh units; rest of the parameters remaining same as the first premise. In either case, the regions of PoK and Gilgit-Baltistan presently under the illegal occupation of Pakistan would likely be under the controlling

13 Selig S Harrison in *The Times of India* dated February 2, 2008.

influence of Punjab and army. It is therefore in the interest of Pakistan that instead of feeling threatened; it should celebrate the cultural diversities and ethnic multiplicities of the nation and make efforts to coalesce these into a strong and democratic federal polity. Whether this happens or not; would crucially impact the future course of events in Pakistan – and by implications the very future of the country – in the years to come.

Fundamentalism, army and the three constituent provinces' apprehensions about the Centre and Punjab are the three main challenges stacked against the Pakistani state. It is also a fact that the foundations of the malady were laid almost at the beginning. Just six months after the death of Jinnah; the Objective Resolution was passed which practically negated the elegant and oft-quoted speech of the departed leader in the Constituent Assembly, on August 11, 1947, where he said, "…. You may belong to any religion or caste or creed – that has nothing to do with the business of the state." Bhutto's second amendment to the 1973 Constitution – drafted in his own regime – gave another blow to the secular framework of the national polity and was a step towards further bigotry and intolerance. The religious right and the cleric fraternity started tightening their grip with the passing years thereafter. This process received a formidable boost during the rule of Gen. Zia-ul-Haq who further radicalized the country with the motive to gain the support of the Islamic extremists within and outside. He created an infrastructure to produce the jihadis to fight in India and Afghanistan; which also suited the Americans then. Also, few Middle East countries rich with petro-dollars pumped money that increased Wahabi influence in Pakistan giving rise to increased animosity between Shias and Sunnis. The consequent bitter sectarian struggle is still continuing in the country. Over the years this conflict has also taken some international colors. The Islamic State, which is a Sunni terrorist entity, is recruiting young Sunni Pakistanis to kill the Shias and also carry out terror activities. Iran, on the other hand, is also reported to enroll some Pakistani Shia youths to assist President Assad's troops in Syria. This battle-hardened and radicalized youth would in all probability create problems once they return to Pakistan. In addition, there is the demonstrated propensity of the current ruler to repudiate the earlier agreements with India. In this category are examples of Zia making efforts to renounce the Simla Agreement and equally strenuous efforts by Musharraf to repudiate the Lahore declaration duly signed by the two Prime Ministers. Little wonder then; that the peace process between India and Pakistan which, after a reasonably bright start, was practically put on hold in 2007 by Musharraf has remained in limbo since then; notwithstanding sporadic efforts to take it forward. In the current situation prevailing in Pakistan and the general mood of the Establishment there; it is difficult to visualize considerable forward movement on this front.

Where does one go from here?

Both nations must appreciate the basic facts of the strategic indivisibility of the sub-continent which also bolsters the premise that it is imperative for India to see the continuance of Pakistan as a stable nation-state. A friendly Pakistan would make it central to India's strategic interests. Pakistan must also realize that India can guarantee its stabilization by trying to contain its centrifugal forces. It is a fact that the divergence of perceptions and issues of discord are many whereas areas of convergence of views and cooperation are few. Hence the framework of bilateralism is fragile and ever- threatened by the disruptive forces. There is a lot which both countries can give to each other. These are some of the basic facts which need to be realized on either side of the divide and also by the important stakeholders. Only then some forward movement in the genuine peace process is possible. Need of the time therefore is to build an infrastructure of hope and mutual interests which enables the people to look forward to a peaceful future which guarantees the accelerated development of both countries. The stakes for Pakistan may be higher in this process as peace with India would firmly put it on the path of transformation to a modern and forward-looking society. For this, the accumulated webs of suspicion and hostility have to be removed.

For any new beginning; the Track Two diplomacy abandoned years ago could form the basis and in this respect, the items under discussions in the Lambah-Aziz talks may be a practical starting point.

The Indian experience has also shown that unilateral concessions do not ensure peace and stability; for that conscious efforts have to be made on both sides. The alternative is terrorism, violence and mayhem; enough of which has been seen in the state of J&K. This culture can only sap the vitals of a civil society and take it back in historical context; a phenomenon that is best avoided for the benefit of future generations.

A perceptive Pakistani scholar has this observation about the country, "If Pakistan is to be saved from its likely future, it must invest in its envisioned future, and start doing so now. It must start by coming to a sincere accommodation with India over Kashmir.... And all this is impossible to achieve in the absence of strong democratic institutions. Democracy is not alien to Pakistan. It had come into being as a democracy, though autocratic tendencies of the Pakistani elite and military dictators changed its direction. Still, the people of Pakistan yearn for true democracy. For this dream to become a reality, Pakistan's military establishment has to take a back seat..."[14] The comments remain as true even today, after more than a decade.

A comprehensive analysis of India's increasing strength and enhanced clout in the international affairs, as also continued Pakistani efforts to stoke the militancy in J&K; underlines the need to evolve a more effective policy mix. Almost like medically improving the immune system in a body; it is imperative that the internal situation in India is more suitably managed. A strong India coupled with well-managed security and developmental aspects of J&K – in short working in tandem with the aspirations and dreams of the people of the state – would be a sure recipe in inducing and motivating Pakistan to strive for a more productive peace process. The powers that be in Pakistan should also realize that even after four wars with India over J&K and a proxy war waged now for thirty years has not made an inch of difference: literally. The cup of patience of locals and government of India, on the other hand, is fully filled now; and might soon spill over with consequences that would certainly be adverse to Pakistani interests.

A process of peace between India and Pakistan taken to its logical conclusion appears a most reasonable and fruitful course of action.

In the overall context Peace Process is the best option available.

---

14 Hassan Abbas, *Pakistanis Drift into Extremism,* Pentagon Press, New Delhi, 2005, p. 241.

Index

About The Author

Dr. Sudhir S. Bloeria, lAS (J&K- 1968) is an ex- Army Officer having served in the Infantry, The Jammu And Kashmir Rifles, from 1966 to 1972. He took part in the 1971 war with Pakistan, in the Fazilka sector.

An alumnus of the Scindia School Gwalior, he is a science graduate, also holds a Masters Degree in History, and acquired the Ph.D Degree for his thesis on "The Battles of Zojila-1948". A graduate of the National Defence College, New Delhi, he takes keen interest in military history and national security matters.

Important assignments held by him include, Deputy Commissioner, Jammu, Development Commissioner, Ladakh, Divisional Commissioner, Jammu, Principal Secretary to Governor, Secretary to the Government of Jammu and Kashmir in the departments of Food, Civil Supplies, Transport, Forest, Public Works, Health and Medical Education.

Dr. Bloeria was posted as Special Commissioner, Rajouri and Poonch districts during 1990-1992, with the specific responsibility to keep that region free from militancy during that critical period. He remained Home Secretary to the State Government in 1995 and 1996 when Parliament and Assembly elections were conducted in the State after a gap of almost ten years. His last assignment was Chief Secretary J&K Government from November 2002 till his superannuation in September 2005.

In July 2008, when Governor's rule was imposed in J&K, Dr. Bloeria was appointed as Advisor to the Governor. He was instrumental in successfully handling the Shri Amarnath Shrine Board land agitation and, later, conducting the Assembly Elections.

In August 2011, he became the founder Vice Chancellor of the Central University of Jammu, for a period of three years, and relinquished that post in August 2014.

He has authored four books, "The Battles of Zojila-1948", "Pakistan's Insurgency and India's Security", "The Dying Terrorism" and "The Men Who Served J&K".